25/-

ST OMERS TO STONYHURST

Stonyhurst College: aerial view

ST OMERS TO STONYHURST

A History of two Centuries

ST OMERS, 1593
BRUGES, 1762
LIEGE, 1773
STONYHURST, 1794

by
HUBERT CHADWICK, S.J.

LONDON
BURNS & OATES

De Licentia Superiorum Ordinis:
JOHN COVENTRY, S.J.
Praep. Prov. Angliae.

Nihil obstat:
Rev. CHARLES EGAN
Censor deputatus.

Imprimatur:
✠ GEORGIUS ANDREAS
Episcopus Salfordiensis.

Wardley Hall
die 11 Decembris 1961

MADE AND PRINTED IN GREAT BRITAIN BY
THE DITCHLING PRESS LTD, DITCHLING SUSSEX, FOR
BURNS AND OATES LIMITED,
25 ASHLEY PLACE, LONDON, S.W.1

CONTENTS

Chapter		*Page*
	PREFACE	vii
	ABBREVIATIONS	x
	PROLOGUE	1
1.	BEGINNINGS	10
2.	"SWADDLING-CLOUTS"	23
3.	FR GILES SCHONDONCH	43
4.	INSTITUTIONS AND CUSTOMS	68
5.	THE FIRST ENGLISH RECTOR	98
6.	THEATRE AND PRINTING PRESS	125
7.	WARS WITHOUT AND TROUBLES WITHIN	147
8.	ST OMERS VERSUS OATES	172
9.	FR WARNER AND THE FIRE OF 1684	211
10.	A SECOND FIRE: THE PREP. SCHOOL	249
11.	EXPULSION FROM ST OMERS	281
12.	THE SETTLEMENT AT BRUGES	312
13.	SUPPRESSION OF THE BRUGES COLLEGES	334
14.	THE LIEGE ACADEMY	360
15.	MIGRATION TO STONYHURST	384
	APPENDIX: List of Provincials and Rectors	403
	INDEX	406

ILLUSTRATIONS

Stonyhurst College: aerial view   *Frontispiece*

1 Fr Robert Persons, S.J., Founder of St Omers

Facing page 118

2 Modern Street Map of Saint-Omer   119

3 Notation for a song in Fr Simons' *Zeno*, Act II, Sc. 1   150

4 Engraving by Montbard of St Omers College as it
  was in 1689
                                                     151

5 Bl. Thomas Whitbread, S.J., Provincial. Martyred
  at Tyburn, June 1679
                                                     214

6 Bruges: The House of the Seven Towers   215

7 Liège: The English Jesuit Seminary   215

8 The English Noviciate at Watten   246

9 St Omers College today. Front view   246

10 Ground plan for proposed Great College, Bruges   247

PREFACE

THE chief merit of a Preface, so one reads, is its brevity. This Preface shall be as brief as may be; but some explanatory remarks seem called for.

Fr John Gerard wrote a history of Stonyhurst and published it in 1894 as a *Centenary Record*. Seven years later a smaller and less expensive book, *Stonyhurst College*, by Frs Gruggen and Keating, did little more than condense the work of Fr Gerard. Yet Stonyhurst in 1894 had completed, not merely 100, but roughly 300 years of existence as a school: the first 200 years were spent perforce on the Continent, and could be dealt with by Fr Gerard only in a few preliminary pages. This book therefore is designed to supply the deficiency. For St Omers, Bruges, Liege, Stonyhurst are in reality but one College under different names. There is a clear continuity, as will be seen, between all four, the difference being no more than a difference of locality. Stonyhurst College, in short, was founded, not in 1794, but in 1593.

For these first 200 years (or 201, to be quite accurate) the available documents are, if not scanty, at least insufficient. When the Society of Jesus was temporarily suppressed in 1773, all documents and papers were confiscated by those who carried out the local suppressions—school registers, books of accounts, journals and everything else. At Bruges even some of the Jesuits were "confiscated" for a while. Some documents have been recovered, others copied, or more recently microfilmed, where they could be found in many archives abroad and in England. There are valuable documents in England which still are not available to research; and doubtless there are others that are at present unknown. The history of these 200 years is to that extent incomplete.

Problems of nomenclature arise. During the long period of

Catholic persecution both priests and schoolboys on the Continent were apt to adopt a false name, or *alias*, for very obvious reasons. The problem arises: should a Jesuit, for instance—there are many who come into this history—be referred to by his real name (if known) or by his *alias*? The course here taken has been to use the name, real or adopted, by which the person is now best known. There is the obvious example of the writer Fr Edward Knott, whose real name was Matthew Wilson. All his priestly life he was known as Fr Knott, he called himself Father (or Mr) Knott, and we shall meet him as Fr Knott. Fr Henry Silisdon or Silesdon (Bedingfeld) and Fr Michael Alford (Griffith) and several others are in the same case. Others there are, such as Fr John Gerard, Fr Henry More, Fr Baldwin, who had more than one *alias*—Fr Gerard had at least ten—who nevertheless are now best known by their real names. In several other cases discretion has been used, even at the cost of consistency.

In the pages that follow the anglicized form "St Omers" is used to designate the English Jesuit College, and "Saint-Omer" the town. So too the English Jesuit Seminary and Academy have in either case been written "Liege"—a word which the residents pronounced as one syllable as if it rhymed with "siege". Where the city is meant, it is written Liège with the grave accent which is now *de rigueur* by decision of the local City Fathers.

Until comparatively recent times secular priests and members of Religious Orders were alike referred to in England as *Mr* X. Abroad, the more informative distinction has been made between M. l'*abbé* X and *Père* X. In this book a secular priest retains his old and honourable title of "Mr", unless he is better known otherwise, as for instance Dr Howard or the Abbé Strickland. Religious priests—they are mainly Jesuits—are differentiated by the more modern title of "Father".

It is necessary to add that "the Society" is a common and well-known economy of words, a shortened form of "the Society of Jesus". But in case some reader is suspicious of

Jesuit presumption, be it said that the first of the two words is unemphatic!

Some of the later chapters borrow freely—but with considerable alterations and additions and subtractions—from a series of articles written at intervals by the present writer for the *Stonyhurst Magazine* (1950-1952). Acknowledgement of help received from others has, it is hoped, been recorded in each case in the notes to various chapters. If any such kind help has inadvertently been passed over, an apology is called for and most sincerely rendered.

Stonyhurst, July 1961.

ABBREVIATIONS

Manuscripts:
E. P. Arch.: English Province Archives S. J.
  (1): Correspondence relating to St Omers and to North Wales.
  (2): Colleges in Belgium, 1762–1879.
  (3): English Province Correspondence, 1746–1854.
Rom. Arch.: Roman Archives S. J.
S. Arch.: Stonyhurst Archives.
Westm. Arch.: Westminster Archives.
  (1): Vol. 48 (Douai College: St Omers College).
  (2): C. 16 (Paris Seminary Collection, Vol. I).
Custom Book: Custom Book of St Omers College.
Ep. Gen.: Epistolae Generalium; Anglia.
Hist. Mem.: Historical Memorials for f. Rector of St Omers.
Litt. Ann.: Litterae Annuae Soc. Jesu.
Plowden: C. Plowden, Account of the Destruction of the English Colleges at Bruges, 1773.
Reeve: Jos. Reeve, Plain and Succinct Narration of facts, 1762–63.

Printed Sources:
Bled: O. Bled, *Les Jésuites Anglais à Saint-Omer.*
C.R.S.: Catholic Record Society.
C. S. P. Dom.: Calendar of State Papers, Domestic.
Foley: H. Foley, *Records of the English Province S. J.*
L. Hicks: *Foundation of the College of St Omers.*
Mon. Hist. S.J.: *Monumenta Historica Soc. Jesu.*
H. More: *Historia Provinciae Anglicanae S. J.*
Poncelet: *Histoire de la Compagnie de Jésus dans les anciens Pays-Bas.*
Wadsworth: J. Wadsworth, *The English Spanish Pilgrime.*

PROLOGUE

IT is in the later years of the reign of Queen Elizabeth I that this history must begin. The "alteration of religion" from old to new had become statute law in 1559, within her first regnal year: the effective execution of the statute was the active business of her long reign, and extended far beyond it; for the religion of a nation, the heritage of a thousand years, was not of course to be changed by mere Act of Parliament. Toleration of other forms of worship and belief, or even the more or less peaceful methods of persuasion, were not in fashion in this century, and certainly beyond the purview of a Tudor sovereign and no less against the interests of her advisers. Refusal to comply with the requirements of Government was punished by sanctions, severe from the first, which grew progressively severer and more cruel as the reign advanced and the underground resistance became stronger and better organized. The organization of this counteraction stands to the everlasting credit of Dr Allen, ably supported, amongst others, by his Jesuit friend, Fr Robert Persons. From the seminary established by Allen in 1569 at Douay there soon began to pour into England a succession of secular priests—well over four hundred of them in the course of the reign. A fresh enthusiasm amongst Catholics, a distinct quickening of pulses, followed in 1580 and 1581 from the "brilliant offensive" and new technique of two Jesuits, Fathers Persons and Campion, two Oxford converts ordained but two years previously. There followed, too, from now onwards, a yet fiercer effort on the part of Government to eradicate Catholicism from the land.

The details however of the Elizabethan persecution are here concerned only in so far as they bear upon the education of Catholic youth. The Act of 1581 (23 Eliz. cap. 1), which made it high treason to reconcile or be reconciled to the Catholic faith, included also the penalty of a year's imprisonment for any schoolmaster who should absent himself from a Protestant church on Sundays or holydays. Catholic schools, such as we understand them, existed no longer, of course, in Elizabethan England. But there was many a Catholic household where a schoolmaster or, let us say, a private tutor was engaged, under the guise of a servant, to teach his master's children and perhaps a few other children of the neighbourhood. Whosoever kept such a tutor was to be fined £10 a month (£100 or more in modern value): and informers were encouraged by a third share of the booty. Four years later, by the famous Act of 27 Eliz. cap. 2 (1585), an English student in a seminary abroad became guilty of treason unless he returned to England within six months and within two days of his landing took the oath of supremacy. To contribute to the support of such seminaries was to be subject to the penalties of praemunire, involving forfeiture of all lands and goods.

Dr Bridgewater's detailed story[1] of the four Worthington boys arrested in February 1584, near Warrington, aptly illustrates the pains taken by the authorities in obstructing (to use a gentle word) the work of the Catholic seminaries or schools abroad—for by this date Douay was both seminary and school. These four brothers, Thomas, Robert, Richard and John—we shall meet some of their younger brothers presently—were worthy sons of Richard Worthington of Blainscough Hall, who himself endured much and ended his life in 1590 as a prisoner for his faith. It appears that they were preparing to set out for Douay in the care of their uncle, Thomas Worthington, a priest who became in later years the third President of that College. Bridgewater's account of the rough, cruel treatment they received in an endeavour to make them betray their faith is far too long to repeat here: let one incident be a sample of the rest.

All four had been subjected to a preliminary examination.

---

[1] *Concertatio Ecclesiae Catholicae in Anglia* (Trèves, 1594), ff. [213ᵛ-222ᵛ]. It is translated with some omissions and inaccuracies by Foley: II, pp. 116-132.

Were they not intending to go to some seminary abroad? Where was their father or their uncle? Had they been present at a Mass? To all such questions the boys had resolutely refused to answer. A few days later they were brought before a royal Commission, headed by the Earl of Derby and Chaderton, Bishop of Chester, appointed to search for local recusants. In a crowded court John, aged eleven, the youngest of the four, was the first to be interrogated, for a reason that jumps to the mind. John, however, as plucky and self-possessed as his brothers, was doubtless feeling like a martyr in embryo, and fully determined not to "blab". He at once complained to Lord Derby: it was now six o'clock in the evening, and he had been given nothing to eat all day: but a little while ago the attendants had given him some wine and forced him to take more than he wanted. "I think", said he, "they were trying to make me drunk; but, thank God, they didn't succeed. It's not my brain but my belly that's ill. I'm not fit to appear before your Lordships." Their Lordships of course thought otherwise, for the nasty plan was presumably of their contrivance. They proceeded with their questions, and John continued, ever more urgently, to plead his stomach-ache. The inevitable finally occurred, as might have been foreseen. The small boy, *vi naturae*, vomited violently in presence of their Lordships, and was hastily removed. All four brothers through many weeks of ill usage stultified the efforts made to induce them to conform to the new religion. Eventually they all escaped, one way or another, and three of them after several adventures reached Douay—or rather Rheims, whither the English College had temporarily migrated in 1578.

This case of the Worthington boys, though it may have seemed a digression, is not at all beside our subject. As in modern times, so in the days of Elizabeth and Burghley the technique of repression was soon seen to be incomplete and inconclusive until the education of the rising generation had been tackled. The attempt to hinder the Worthingtons from travelling to a "foreign" seminary failed, although for a while they were forced to attend a Protestant school. To attend a Catholic school in Flanders was not at that date a matter of treason, and in any case the boys were legally "infants". In any case, too, the Act of 27 Elizabeth passed in the following year did not achieve its full purpose, for Douay continued to increase and grow fat, even though financially its means were stretched to the uttermost. There are many stories of the capture of boys and youths in subsequent years,[2] often when, having finished school, they were on their way by sea from Flanders to one of the English seminaries in Spain. But the very succession of such arrests, with their attendant bullying and hardships, provides clear evidence of the continued vitality and activity of the seminaries abroad.

Fr Robert Persons, whose brain was at least as quick as that of Lord Burghley, had also realized that on the rising generation rested the answer to the urgent question, can England even yet be saved for Catholicism. The two English seminaries in Flanders and Rome were doing active work in providing missionaries—and martyrs. Persons himself and Campion, in their hurricane mission through the English counties, had taken their full share in the work. And when, after Campion's arrest in July 1581, Fr Persons crossed over to the Continent to continue his activities from abroad, one of his main preoccupations was concerned with the provision of further opportunities for both lay and clerical education. Of the seminaries which he established in Spain for the formation of missionary priests, Valladolid (1589) and Seville (1592) are the best known. But more to the present purpose is the little school founded in 1582 in Normandy in the small town of Eu, midway between Dieppe and the mouth of the Somme. It is needful to speak in some detail of this "College" of Eu; for it has been often maintained that the Jesuit College of St Omers[3] began its life

[2] Some of these stories have been pleasantly re-told by Dom Bede Camm, O.S.B., in *In the Brave Days of Old* (London, 1899).
[3] "St Omers" is the anglicized form used then—and still in use—in reference to the English Jesuit College. In these pages, "Saint-Omer" will refer to the town, "St Omers" to the College.

at Eu, whence by force of circumstances some ten years later the boys migrated to Saint-Omer without loss of continuity. It may safely be said that this is not at all the case.

It was in 1581 that the French Jesuits, at the invitation of Henry Duke of Guise, a cousin of Mary Queen of Scots, established themselves temporarily in the ancient Hôpital Normand in Eu whilst a new college in the vicinity was a-building. Seizing his opportunity, Fr Persons obtained next year the Duke's consent to start an English school in a part of the Hôpital Normand already vacated by the French Fathers. An annual pension of the contemporary value of £100, together with various other gifts collected, was sufficient to maintain a small school of some thirty boys. It was in fact a small *pensionnat* or hostel which housed the boys and from which they attended each day the classes in the neighbouring French College. To take charge of this school Fr Persons managed to find a "grave ancient man named M. Chambers"[4] —evidently a secular priest. But with the assassination of the Duke in December 1588 the pension ceased; and though the school lingered on for a few years more, one hears no more of it in the *Second Douay Diary* after the beginning of February 1592. It is the *Douay Diaries* that should provide the evidence in chief; for it is clear that between Douay College (then at Rheims) and the school at Eu—"aedicula *nostra*", says the *Douay Diary*—there was a fairly constant flow of pupils both to and fro until the summer of 1589 when a gradual evacuation of Eu becomes apparent. In fact it is safe to conclude, without going here into every detail,[5] that the little school at Eu, although founded by a Jesuit, was never a Jesuit school nor in charge of Jesuits, but was rather a preparatory school to

4 *Persons: A Briefe Apologie* (1601), f. 185; cf. C.R.S. iv, 36, 37; ii, 31. Foley (VII, 127) would identify this priest with Fr Sabine Chambers, who became a Jesuit in 1587. Apart from the fact that in 1581 Sabine Chambers was still a Protestant and a tutor in Oxford, he was in 1582 a man of 22 or 23 years of age, whom Fr Persons could never have described as a "grave ancient man".

5 Further details may be found in an article by L. Hicks, s.j. See pp. 146-156.

Douay College, designed by Fr Persons to relieve as far as possible the congestion that was harassing the authorities at Rheims. Indeed it was the need for the establishment of some such school that in 1581 had weighed with Persons in his decision to cross over to France.

Divers Catholickes in England [he tells us] percyving the difficultyes of the tyme . . . had treated with the father to provide them some succour or place of education beyond the Seas for their yonger children that were not yet fit for their yeares or learning to be of the Seminaries of Rhemes or Rome, which he could not hope to do but by his presence beyond the Seas.[6]

Nevertheless in 1592 the President of the College of Rheims, having closed the school at Eu, decided to re-establish it, or at least to start a similar school, at Saint-Omer, a locality more remote at that time from the ravages of civil war which had endangered the school in Normandy. From the municipal records of Saint-Omer[7] one learns that the President, Dr Barrett, entered into negotiations with the authorities of the town for leave to establish such a school. By 18 September 1592, he had bought a small house, and on that day the municipal authorities gave their consent. Conditions laid down were that the school was to be limited to fifteen boys, who were to attend the classes at the Walloon College, and that no "strangers" should be admitted without the previous consent of the magistracy. The school, according to a previous petition of Dr Barrett, was to be placed in charge of "quelques prêtres vénérables"—presumably secular priests as before. It seems clear that these negotiations of Dr Barrett, conducted with the full knowledge and approval of Allen, now Cardinal in Rome, had likewise the backing of Fr Persons in Spain and of his Jesuit colleague, Fr Holt, in Brussels.

And here we come to a sudden stop. Before the close of

[6] *Persons: A Briefe Apologie*, f. 184.
[7] Table des délibérations du Magistrat. M., f. 116 (Archives de Saint-Omer).

1592 the English Seminary had begun the process of migrating back to Douay from Rheims: and after the last entry in the *Second Diary*, made at Rheims in early August 1593, there is a gap of four or five years. The last twelve months of the *Second Diary* are singularly uninformative. No mention is made of Dr Barrett's purchase nor of the formal sanction of that purchase. Possibly the diarist was unaware of the facts. But what is of interest is that from October 1592 to the end of the *Diary* batches of boys, seventeen in all, were sent from Rheims to attend the classes of the Jesuits ("a patribus Societatis erudiendi"), not to Saint-Omer but to Douay, where also was a flourishing College of the Society of Jesus. Saint-Omer, indeed, is not even mentioned in this *Diary*. Why were none of these boys sent to Dr Barrett's house in Saint-Omer? An obvious answer is that Dr Barrett had bought the house in too great a hurry: that in view of the decision to return from Rheims to Douay the need for a preparatory or auxiliary school at Saint-Omer no longer existed. If such a school should be still required—it does not seem to have been—Douay, not Saint-Omer, would be the more suitable choice and less expensive. That, as we shall see presently, was the opinion of Cardinal Allen as well as of Dr Barrett when in the following spring or summer the rumour spread that the Jesuits were preparing to establish a new school in Saint-Omer. Dr Barrett for his part made it very plain that, whatever may have happened to his house in Saint-Omer, he had abandoned it as a school and wanted no other school there to take its place.

Two conclusions therefore, even at the risk of being tedious, must be noted here, as a preliminary to the history of the Jesuit College of St Omers. In the first place, the little English school founded by Fr Persons at Eu was not continued at Saint-Omer but died a natural death at its birthplace in Haute Normandie. It was not founded as a Jesuit school nor was it under Jesuit control. Its purpose was to help Dr Allen by relieving some at least of the overcrowding and consequent expense experienced in his seminary at Rheims. It was a friendly and generous

B

adventure on the part of Fr Persons in the cause of the English mission.

Yet more needful is it to draw the second conclusion, which does not of necessity follow from the first. Although undoubtedly Dr Barrett planned to start a similar school at Saint-Omer, and in 1592 had even purchased a house for that purpose, yet he proceeded no further. He abandoned that idea in favour of the larger plan of moving his seminary back to Douay, which was accomplished by stages in 1592 and 1593. At Rheims there had been no College of the Society. But there at Douay was the Jesuit College of Anchin, ever at Dr Barrett's service, and far more convenient than the distant College of the Walloons at Saint-Omer. During Dr Allen's presidency Anchin College had always been ready to house in its capacious dormitories any overflow of pupils from the English Seminary. No doubt the seminary had increased in numbers during its fifteen years at Rheims: but there is no reason to suppose the Jesuit Fathers were less accommodating now. As a matter of fact it is on record that in October 1592—a month after buying the Saint-Omer house—Dr Barrett rented a large house in Douay at some distance from the original house and garden rented by Dr Allen in 1568. The friendly help of the College of Anchin was thus perhaps not needed. Three years later both premises were given up and the College was moved to its permanent site near the Church of Saint-Jacques.[8]

It is Dr Barrett's unfortunate house-hunting at Saint-Omer in the September of 1592 or a little earlier that has confused so many writers of various nationalities, Jesuit as well as others. It is needless to enumerate them here. Until quite recent years this petition of Dr Barrett, supported by the Jesuit Rector of the Walloon College, has misled such writers to join together what should have been kept asunder, to amalgamate the

[8] From information kindly supplied by M. Frédéric Fabre. For the relations of Douay College with the College of Anchin, cf. a long note in an article by M. Fabre: *The English Benedictines at Douai*, in *The Downside Review*, Vol. 52 (1934), p. 99.

negotiations of Dr Barrett in 1592 with those of Father Flack in 1593, and thus to reach the false conclusion that it was in 1592 that the Jesuit College of St Omers was founded. It was very probably this same false interpretation of the facts that accounts for the inscription placed about the middle of the nineteenth century over the main entrance of the old College, now converted into a Lycée: "Fondé par les Jésuites en 1592...". Some decades later the error found its way to Stonyhurst College, the lineal descendant of St Omers. The older and true tradition seems to have died out gradually after the suppression of the Society in 1773: a new and false tradition arose based on that ill-starred inscription.[9] Dr Barrett's purchase is ultimately to blame.

---

[9] Cf. *Stonyhurst Magazine*, Vol. xxxi (October 1954), pp. 426-7, where examples are cited to prove the older tradition.

I

BEGINNINGS

LET us now return for a moment to England and the storm of persecution which grew ever more violent as the long reign advanced. The policy of exploiting the youth of the nation, of drawing them by one means or another into the Protestant fold, had not of course been forgotten. The local schoolmasters and family tutors had been dealt with by the statute of 1581, and in 1585 the foreign seminaries likewise. A student who did not return to England within six months and apostatize was to be declared a traitor. But evidently, if he chose to remain abroad, he remained beyond the reach of the law, although an occasional chance of kidnapping was not to be overlooked. Nor did the flow of youths from England to Rheims or Rome or the Spanish seminaries notably decrease. It became however a common practice to adopt another surname, an *alias*, as a protection both for themselves and for their parents. On the whole, the statute of 1585 was not as effective as its framers meant it to be. Nor in many places was there much enthusiasm shown in the enforcement of the penal laws. For instance, a report to the Council, probably in 1591, on the condition of Lancashire and Cheshire, where admittedly the number of recusants was growing, laments the apathy and slack- of the local authorities. Churches are empty, sometimes only the curate and clerk being present; the proclamations for the arrest of priests are not executed by the Justices; no attention is paid to the statute concerning schools and schoolmasters; and so on.[1] Clearly there was need of fresh vigour and even sterner statutes if Catholicism was to be "liquidated" within any reasonable time.

Hence it was that, following upon a Proclamation of October 1591, renewed efforts were made throughout the

[1] C.S.P. Domestic, 1591-1594, p. 158.

country to render the Government's policy effective. Throughout 1592 the storm was increasing to the strength of a gale; and early in the following year new and more rigorous penalties and restraints were imposed by Parliament. By a statute of this Parliament (35 Eliz. cap. 2), for instance, all Catholics over sixteen years of age convicted of recusancy were confined to a radius of five miles from their homes, under threat of forfeiture of all goods, lands and annuities during life. The consequences of this and other statutes of the Parliament of 1593, superimposed upon the many penal laws already enacted, were disastrous, even if not as yet irremediable. The position would have become devastatingly worse, had another proposed clause not been withdrawn before its submission to the final vote of Parliament.

It was this clause that led to the establishment of the English College of St Omers. The proposal was that the children of Catholic parents should be removed after the age of seven from their parents' care and placed, at their parents' expense, in the homes of approved Protestants, to be brought up in the Queen's religion. How the clause came to be excluded from the Bill, which had its first reading in the Lower House on 26 February (1593), is uncertain. It may perhaps have been withdrawn during the course of debate, as being too extreme or as creating more difficulties than it solved. At all events a report of the proposed law reached Fr Persons in Spain some while before the opening of Parliament on 19 February: for it is clear that he had heard of it and had broached the subject of a school at Saint-Omer to the Jesuit General, Fr Aquaviva, in a letter either of the 16 or 27 February[2]—that is to say 6 or 17 February according to the "old style" in use in England. Among Fr Persons' correspondents, as is well known, there were Catholics or sympathizers at the English Court who on occasion supplied him with "stop-press" news derived from

2 Cf. L. Hicks, pp. 158-161, where this subject is discussed more fully. This Chapter is indebted at various points to his article. And cf. C.R.S. Vol. 52, p. 123 and Notes.

some friendly or venal official. That such was the source of his information is a good guess to account for the facts. Certain it is that before Parliament had ended its session on 10 April, Fr Persons' plans were completed and Fr William Flack had already sailed from San Lucar for Flanders to put the plan into execution.

The reader will have observed that Fr Persons did not wait to form his plans until he had assurance that Parliament had accepted the Bill and this obnoxious clause. The very news that it was contemplated was sufficient to stir him to action; and the speed of his decision may perhaps suggest that the foundation of a Jesuit school somewhere in the Netherlands was not for him a new idea. Be that as it may, he at once sought an audience with King Philip II, knowing from experience his sympathy with the sad plight of the English Catholics and his generosity in their regard. The happy result was a royal letter dated 13 March 1593, granting a yearly sum of 1,920 crowns for the proposed school or seminary (in its origin it was to be both). The number of boys was set at sixteen for a start, the estimate for a boy's yearly maintenance being thus 120 crowns or about £27 in English Elizabethan value. The choice of Saint-Omer, included at that period in the Spanish Netherlands, was quite in accord with the views of Fr Persons, for of the Spanish Dominions "no part thereof liked him better than the low countrys in regard of their neereness to England, & ayr most like onto the ayr of our English climate: especially France being in garboiles & the jarres between these two Crowns being like frequently to hinder theire passing out of one Kings Dominions in to the other."[3]

[3] Hist. Mem., p. 2. This MS. recently discovered (the credit goes to Rev. D. Brigstocke, s.j.), written on twenty-one small pages in a 17th-century hand, is unsigned and undated, but from internal evidence appears to have been composed about 1635. Marginal notes—e.g. "from F. Flack"—make evident the main source of information. Fr Flack died in 1637.
France was in "garboiles", i.e. in turmoil, on account of the religious struggle between Catholics and Huguenots. Spain was at war with both France and England until France made peace in 1598. England continued the war until 1604.

Next perhaps to Louvain, Saint-Omer and Douay were the towns most frequented by the numerous Catholic exiles. As has been said, Dr Richard Barrett had in 1592 decided to found a small school at Saint-Omer, but had changed his plans. And when late in 1592 he began to move his College back from Rheims to Douay, both Allen and Barrett agreed that if another school was needed at all, Douay and not Saint-Omer was the obvious place for it. Both towns were within the dominions of the King of Spain. So the question naturally arises: why in 1593 did Fr Persons decide, not to establish another auxiliary school at Douay as previously he had done at Eu, but to found an entirely new kind of school—probably, as shall be explained later, the first of its kind in Jesuit history—in the town of Saint-Omer already abandoned by Dr Barrett? One might answer, but very dubiously, that such was the pleasure of His Majesty the King. That indeed was the official and sufficient answer to the magistracy of Saint-Omer when they raised objections. But what was Fr Persons' reason? Although he seems nowhere to have given an explanation, one answer at least appears to be clear enough: but one needs to tread delicately while suggesting it.

In a Memorial to Cardinal Caetano, the Cardinal Protector of England, sent a couple of years later by two Douay Doctors of Theology, Dr Worthington the Vice-President and Dr William Percy, there is much criticism of their own College under its present presidentship. Various reasons and remedies are suggested for the "stirrs" that had broken out against the Jesuits in the English College at Rome: one such reason, they assert, was the state of their own College, whence Rome was partly recruited. Since Dr Allen's departure in 1585, lack of discipline, a spirit of insubordination and hostility to the English Jesuits had grown apace.

Whereas in the early years of the seminary there were sent to England men of high ideals, of proved integrity, sufficiently grounded to meet the arguments advanced by the heretics, nowadays it is far otherwise. Very few men of that calibre find their way to England, and many of them are of a poor standard in learning, to say nothing of their morals.

Such at all events was the opinion of these two priests: and for a remedy they beg the Cardinal Protector to insist that "some college discipline and definite regulations be established in the English College of Douay", and enforced.

It is by such means that their high purpose can be preserved, and that by the curbing of excessive freedom they may presently bear with less impatience the college way of life. This undoubtedly was the main reason why the Fathers in charge of our seminaries in Spain acquired a new seminary for English boys at Saint-Omer here in Flanders, namely, that from it they might receive students who were more innocent and better adapted to the requisite discipline than those they could obtain from the other seminary at Douay.[4]

Dr Worthington speaks with assurance of the views of Fr Persons and his fellow Jesuits in Spain. His friendship with the former was of some twenty years' standing. And Fr Persons certainly established his new school in the expectation—an expectation abundantly fulfilled—that some at least of the students would aspire to the priesthood and in due course proceed to the Spanish seminaries for their higher studies. If only for this reason he had decided to train his recruits from as early an age as was possible, and to entrust that training to his fellow Jesuits over whom he had, even at that date, some considerable authority. The fact that St Omers was also established as a boarding school—not for church students only—coincided conveniently with this project of his.

Lest it may seem that too much credence is being given to Dr Worthington, an unpopular figure in the eyes of some Catholic writers, it may be well to add a passage from a Jesuit document already quoted,[5] which tells much the same story of deficient training amongst those more recently admitted to the Spanish seminaries:

[4] The quotations are from Knox, *First & Second Douay Diaries*, pp. 372 and 373.   [5] Hist. Mem., p. 1.

From England it was hard to get fitt subjects immediatly in to Spaine in those days of warre, especially such as were sufficiently advanced in theire Lower studyes & were sure in the grounds of Religion & virtue . . . and now late examples had taught that grown men newly converted are soon posted through theire studyes without time enough to roote out ill habits & inclinations, returning soon again from the Seminaries in to theire former occasions fell easily from God & were no small disparagement to the cause.

Fr William Flack had set sail from San Lucar for Belgium on 8 April 1593. A Cambridge man, aged about thirty-two, he had entered the Jesuit noviciate in Rome in 1585—he was a fellow novice of St Aloysius Gonzaga—and had spent the last three years in Spain, where after ordination he had been appointed Minister of the new English seminary at Valladolid. Very competent and energetic he seems to have been, fully justifying Fr Persons' choice: somewhat obstinate, perhaps, and unadaptable. From all accounts he suffered much from his future Rector, as did no less his Rector from him: a sound, solid Englishman from Suffolk, but of a temperament that did not blend well with a foreign environment.

It was Fr Flack who, under the authority of Fr Persons in Spain, was responsible for the actual spade-work. A difficult task it proved to be: opposition arose from almost every quarter. Letters from the King, dated 13 March 1593, had been dispatched to the aged Count Mansfeld, the acting Governor of the Low Countries since the recent death of the Duke of Parma, as well as to the young Count de Fuentes commanding the Spanish troops and most other matters as well. Both were notified of the royal pension of 1,920 crowns and of its occasion: arrangements were to be made locally for the payment of this annual grant. Meanwhile Fr Persons collected alms from his Spanish friends and acquaintances, with which Fr Flack was able to carry on until the Spanish pension took visible shape—which was not until the close of the year.

Opposition to the scheme was widespread. The finance

department in Brussels raised the familiar objections to expenditure of money. The magistracy of Saint-Omer resented the intrusion into their town of nationals of the country with which they were at war. Some of the English Jesuits, such as Fr Holt, then resident in Brussels, either considered the idea impracticable or at least objected to the choice of locality, maintaining that Saint-Omer was "too unholsome an ayr for that purpose". Nor were the Walloon Jesuits much impressed. "Fr Christian [Dalmerius] the Rector of the Waloone Colledge in St Omers Laught at it as a thing unlikely, but Fr Flack ... did still assure him that it would take, & that it being then May before the end of July he should see allmost a score of English Schollars come dayly to their Schooles."[6]

One of Fr Flack's early interviews was with the Belgian Provincial, Fr Oliver Manare, in whose Province the proposed school was to be established. Fr Manare was at the time presiding over one of the customary triennial Provincial Congregations, assembled at Tournai. Thither went Fr Flack in full confidence, well aware that the General, Aquaviva, had already written favourably to the Provincial on the subject. But for reasons of his own Fr Manare chose to gather some dozen of the assembled Rectors to discuss the matter. Asked their opinions, most of them disapproved of Saint-Omer as a fit town for starting the school. The Provincial turned to Fr Flack. What had he to say against so many? He had, it appears, plenty to say. The King and Fr Persons had already agreed upon Saint-Omer: His Majesty's letters had been delivered, and it was too late to change without causing much trouble and annoyance to those concerned and much affliction and sorrow to Fr Persons. If, after trial, experience should prove the selected town to be for any reason unsuitable, then would be the time to petition His Majesty to bestow his grant elsewhere.

F. Oliverius made no other reply, but presently upon ye answer, not to contristate good Fr Persons, as he sayd, gave

[6] *Ibid.*, p. 3.

Fr Flack order to goe forward in ye business: and happily he knew that Father Generall had given order that none should hinder Fr Flack in his negotiation; who knew very well upon what grounds he went.[7]

That important matter having been settled in Fr Oliver's subtle fashion, Fr Flack proceeded to Douay to break the news to Dr Barrett—whether good news or bad remained to be seen. Unwelcome news it turned out to be: this design, said the President fretfully, "would not be to help his Colledge, but to undoe it rather, and to intercept such as would otherwise come to it". Fr Flack endeavoured to reassure him, maintaining that there was ample room for two colleges. Indeed, said he, if Douay should receive more applications than it could support, St Omers would, after a while, be willing to accept them for the new school. Dr Barrett, however, according to Fr Flack, rejected the offer by reason of Cardinal Allen's disapproval of the plan, and produced "a very crabbyed letter" from the Cardinal as proof. All this was duly reported to Fr Persons, who promised to satisfy the Cardinal's "mislike". It was fortunately but a temporary misunderstanding which Fr Persons was able to rectify as soon as postal communication between Spain and Rome, disorganized for a while, had again resumed its normal course. Hitherto the General, whilst giving his conditional consent to the establishment of a new "seminary", had delayed his definite sanction in deference to Cardinal Allen's view. That obstacle being now removed, Aquaviva sent Persons his formal sanction by letter of 31 August.[8]

The obstacles raised, one after another, by the Finance Department in particular and the *échevinage* of Saint-Omer, presently forced Fr Persons again to have recourse to King Philip II. Undeterred by a first failure, he made use of a second intermediary, Fr Henry Walpole, the future martyr, whom he was sending into England and who therefore by custom was due to take leave of the King before his departure. Here he met

---

[7] *Ibid.*, pp. 4–5. Much that follows is from the same source, the ultimate authority being usually Fr Flack himself.   [8] L. Hicks, p. 163.

with success. Royal letters, dated 29 or 30 July, were written
to Mansfeld and Fuentes, as also to Secretary de Ibarra, urging
them to take steps that would overcome all opposition to the
King's will. Having thanked His Majesty for his kindness and
for "all his former liberalityes", Fr Walpole returned to
Valladolid and thence set off for Flanders, reaching Saint-Omer
in early September.[9] On the 10th of that month it was,
according to Fr Flack, that the Comte de Mansfeld wrote to
the magistrates of Saint-Omer, enjoining them to render
prompt aid, "assistant de tout vostre pouvoir ceulx de la
Société de Jésus pour trouver commoditié de quelque logis,
le plus proche que faire se pourra de leur collège, les favourisans
de tous bénéfices et immunités qui sont dues en oeuvre sy
bonne et sy saincte". To finish with this chronicle of dates, it
should be added that Fr Flack and Fr Walpole set off on 21
September for Brussels on business connected with the project
in hand; whence it would appear that the school—at all events
as a separate entity—was not yet in being.[10] At Brussels they
had the support of Fr Holt, well acquainted with the officials
of the Court, who was acting as an informal representative in
Flanders of Fr Persons in the affairs of the Jesuit mission in
England.

When then did St Omers College definitely begin its long
life? It would be pleasant to be able to give a definite answer.
But one cannot of course expect much precision in the case of a
school founded on foreign soil, and recruited with much
difficulty and danger from Elizabethan England. St Omers did
not really "begin" on any precise date: it quietly and gradually
began to begin. Fr Flack's recollection, forty years later, of
what happened is reported as follows, after his account of his
interview with Dr Barrett and of the departure for Rome of

[9] Hist. Mem., p. 16: C.R.S., V, 254, 248 (Walpole's confessions).
[10] "1593, Sep. 27: . . . ad negotia seminarii Anglicani in hac urbe con-
stituendi promovenda"—Diarium Collegii Audomarensis, i.e. the Diary of the
Walloon College in Saint-Omer, a MS. preserved in the Jesuit house of
studies formerly at Enghien, now moved to Chantilly, near Paris.

two or three Belgian Fathers to attend the fifth General Congregation, the first session of which was held on 3 November.

In ye mean time Fr Flack went to St Omers, and with 500 crowns which he took up by virtue of a bill of exchainge which he brought from Spain to Fr Holt, he maintayned four of ye Worthingtons, whom ye Doctor theyr Unckle presently called thether from Doway; and 3 of ye Ruckwoods who lay sick of ye small poxe in an inne, & for whom he was to receive 30 £, wheras ye rest brought nothing at all having lodged them in Inns for a while with others, who came out of England according to orders sent from Fr Persons. After a while he hired Mr George Persons corner house from about autumne til Candlemas following for some 14 flor: whither he got Mr Persons himself (Brother to Fr Persons) to come from Doway for a time to be their caterer, and soon after himself and Fr Nicholas Smith went to live amongst them in the same house one as Procurator & Minister, ye other as Confessarius over some 18 schollers.[11]

The only sure date amidst these indefinite indications of time is 23 November, which the Walloon Diary records as the day on which Fr Flack, the temporary Superior, moved with Fr Smith into the new school. Fr Smith had hitherto been Subminister at the Jesuit house in Brussels, and had arrived on 3 October at the Walloon College where Fr Flack had made his headquarters since the preceding May.

It would seem therefore that one must take account of both an informal and a formal opening of the school. If we interpret Fr Flack aright—both the grammar and the punctuation of his reporter are difficult—the first boys to assemble at Saint-Omer were lodged in various inns of the town until, "about autumne", they, or some of them, were gathered together in a "corner house", rented from Fr Robert Persons' brother George. Fr Flack, it may be remembered, had replied to the scepticism of the Walloon Rector by assuring him that "allmost a score of English Schollars" would have assembled

11 Hist. Mem., p. 8.

before July was over. Some at least may have assembled in July and the following month or two, and may even have joined the classes of the Walloon College—for as yet, and indeed for several years to come, no provision was made in the new school for class-masters or classes. September however was mainly a month of vacation: the new school year would begin as usual on 1 October, feast of Saint-Remi. It was on that day that a *Procès Verbal* was discussed by the vigilant town council, which had learnt with some annoyance that the maximum of sixteen students provided for by the Spanish pension had been exceeded and that nineteen boys were in the seminary".[12] The "seminary", one must presume, was Mr George Persons' corner house, whither that gentleman had come from Douay to be "caterer" or provisional caretaker (in the widest sense of both words). It is noteworthy that of the two English Jesuits as yet assigned to the school, the temporary Rector or Superior, Fr Flack, was away in Brussels on this date, and Fr Nicholas Smith had not yet arrived at Saint-Omer. Not yet, surely, have we reached the formal opening day of St Omers.

Of these eighteen or nineteen boys the majority can be identified with a considerable degree of certainty. Fr Flack himself tells us of seven, presumably the first seven to arrive. Of the three Rookwoods, Ambrose certainly was one, heir of Coldham in Suffolk and destined to become almost un-wittingly an associate of Catesby and the other conspirators of the Gunpowder Plot. His two brothers no doubt were Christopher, who joined the Franciscans, and Robert, a future Jesuit. The other four were Worthingtons, younger brothers of the four whose adventures in 1584 were mentioned earlier in this story. Their father having died in prison for his faith, they were now in the care of their uncle, Dr Thomas Worthing-ton, at this date Vice-President of the English College, Douay. Remembering Dr Worthington's views, previously quoted, of the state of Douay College under Dr Barrett, one is not

[12] Municipal Archives of Saint-Omer, liasse 241, No. 4.

surprised to learn of the transference of his nephews to St Omers. The two eldest of these four, William and Lawrence, became Jesuits.

Not all of these earliest St Omers boys, of course, went on to study for the priesthood. But of those who went to the seminary at Valladolid—a first batch of four arrived there in May 1594—one can pick out some half dozen who, if their answers in the *Liber Primi Examinis* are accurate, must have entered St Omers in the course of the autumn of 1593. Of these the most illustrious in after-life was Fr Andrew White, s.j., still remembered and revered as the "Apostle of Maryland." He had come to St Omers, as had some others, from Douay, and had reached Valladolid in mid-October 1595 in company with Walter Hildesley. Four members of this old Berkshire family of Hildesley, according to one of Fr Henry Walpole's confessions, were at St Omers before he left for England at the beginning of December 1593. Walter, at all events, apparently had arrived in the August or September of that year, where he had spent two years under the *alias* of Mallet.[13]

Fr Henry More, s.j., in his account of the beginnings of St Omers College, tells us somewhat laconically: "A small house was rented and some boys were placed in it—seven at first, eighteen later".[14] This then is what in Fr Flack's account appears as "Mr George Persons corner house". The house in question, so one gathers from the very knowledgeable Abbé Bled,[15] was known as the Maison de Berghes. Situated on the corner of the Place de l'Etat and the present Rue Gambetta, it was distant from the Walloon College by the mere width of the street. According to the Abbé Bled, this was the house acquired by Dr Barrett: yet it seems fairly certain that it was

13 C.R.S., XXX, pp. 34, 35; cf. *ibid.*, V, p. 262.
14 H. More, p. 162.
15 O. Bled, *Les Jesuites Anglais a Saint-Omer* . . . (Saint-Omer, 1890). Although at times he is clearly at fault in his facts and his chronology, this learned antiquarian is considered a very reliable authority in matters of topography.

the corner house rented by Fr Flack. There remains however
the possibility that it was both.

Here then in the Maison de Berghes the first boys slept and
studied and took their meals, under the care of George Persons,
until on Tuesday, 23 November,[16] Fr Flack and Fr Smith
finally moved across and took up residence in the "royal
seminary"—as the Walloon Diary sometimes terms it: "and
Fr Foucart a Walloon, who had been Minister of Tournay, a
man about 40 years of age their designed Rector lived in the
French College and was only once with them at dinner in that
house whilst they were in these straits".[17] What now became of
Mr Persons is unrecorded. But the Maison de Berghes is now
definitely a Jesuit house, not in charge of a "caterer" but under
the immediate supervision of Jesuits. The informal period is
past. 23 November 1593, if we mistake not, is the date of the
formal opening of St Omers College.

[16] (October 1593) "Tertio huius, Bruxellis huc cum studiosis Anglis habita-
turus venit P. Nicolaus Smitheus, qui hinc cum P. flacco ad seminarium
exiit vigesimo tertio sequentis mensis" (Walloon Coll. Diary, p. 114).
[17] Hist. Mem., p. 8. The French or "Walloon" College was a large handsome building facing the old Rue du Vieil Brusle (Rue Gambetta), which
had opened some twenty-five years previously at the request and by the
munificence of Gérard d'Hamericourt, first Bishop of Saint-Omer. The
course comprised five classes of humanities and a school of moral theology.
Like other Colleges S.J. it catered only for extern students.

2

"SWADDLING-CLOUTS"

KING PHILIP had laid it down as a condition, possibly to appease the local authorities, that the Rector of the new school should be a native of the country. The Belgian Provincial selected Père Jean Foucart for the post; but as yet he had not been officially installed, and Fr Flack, although calling himself "Procurator and Minister", was in reality the acting Superior. When he asserts, a little sharply, that Fr Foucart came only once to dine at the Maison de Berghes, he forgets that his future Rector arrived at the Walloon College from Tournai only on 8 January of the following year.[1] Before that date the rented corner house had been abandoned as too small.

It would seem to have been whilst the school was still in the Maison de Berghes that an untoward incident occurred. Fr Flack was already looking out for more spacious quarters when quite unexpectedly there appeared on his doorstep some dozen boys from Douay. He had offered Dr Barrett in a previous ungracious interview, it may be recalled, to receive some of his boys "after a while", if Dr Barrett should have too many on his hands. He had, however, met with a curt refusal. Well, here they were: they had been sent after a while! The President had softened, one may suppose, and changed his mind. But, if Fr Flack's memory may be trusted, there had been no previous announcement of their coming: and certainly there was no possible room for them in the Maison de Berghes. What could Fr Flack do? He entertained them in the diminutive refectory—gave them "a meales meat", as the Memoir puts it —and sent them back to Douay. A letter of explanation followed, of course. "Yet did not ye Doctor take their sending

[1] Diary of Walloon College, p. 122.

back in good part."[2] Thus early did friction arise between two rival schools.

Fr Flack continued his search for a larger house and soon heard of one to let, "a good large house and not unfitt", belonging to the Sieur de Croix, a friend of the Walloon Rector. On 9 December, therefore, Fr Flack hired two horses and rode out with the Rector, Fr Dalmerius, to the owner's mansion a few miles out of town. Whilst Fr Dalmerius and his friend confabulated apart, Fr Flack was counting his chickens. . . . A rent of £10 seemed to him eminently suitable. And no doubt the Rector in his charity was trying his best, whatever may have been his personal views on an English school at Saint-Omer. "After a long discourse" the Rector "returned to F. Flack and told him that ye house doubtless was not to his purpose", that the owner flatly refused to let the house for less than £25 p.a. on a three years' lease. Left with no room for manoeuvre, Fr Flack accepted the offer.[3] The contract was signed on the 17th, the lease to date from the following Candlemas.

At Candlemas therefore, or rather on the next day, 3 February 1594, after a High Mass celebrated by Fr Foucart and attended by the "young British exiles", the new Rector entered into office and made his formal entrance into the house rented from the Sieur de Croix. With him went Fr Henry Bray, "lent" by the Walloon College, a man in his fifties although not more than ten years in the Society of Jesus. He was to be Prefect of the boys. The Rector had thus a staff of three Jesuits with which to run the school, the household being completed by the presence of a novice laybrother and a servant. This second house was situated in the Tenne Rue (now Rue de Dunkerque) opposite the present Rue Simon Ogier.[4] It was

[2] Hist. Mem., p. 9.

[3] Ibid., p. 11. Contract signed on 17 December (Diary of Walloon College, p. 116).

[4] Bled, p. 2. He says they occupied "*une partie* de l'ancien hôtel du grand bâtard de Bourgogne en la Tenne rue"; and identifies the house from a passage in H. More's History (p. 162) which refers to it as the house "which

thus at a considerable distance from the Walloon College, which had its main entrance on the Rue Gambetta, a parallel street several blocks away. And here the school remained for some twelve months, about thirty boys trudging daily through the streets to their classes, come wind, come weather.

Meanwhile opposition to the school still continued on the part of the town authorities and the officials of the Finance Department at Brussels. They were pessimists, considered the establishment of the school a "beggarly business", as Fr Flack tells us, and that money spent on it, at the expense of their country's revenue, would be wasted. In point of fact, of the Spanish pension of 1,920 ducats nothing at all was paid until November 1593 when, as it would seem, half the payment for a quarter of a year, amounting to 700 florins (£70), became available. For this state of affairs, however, the Netherlands Government was not entirely to blame. Even the friendly Secretary Ibarra was of opinion that the particular source of revenue designated by King Philip for payment of the pension was scarcely capable of bearing the burden. The burden for the time being was mainly borne by Fr Persons, who by dint of begging or borrowing from his Spanish friends managed to keep Fr Flack supplied with at least a bare sufficiency to meet his current expenses.[5]

As to the town *échevins*—the "city fathers"—they were still harping on what they considered the illicit increase of numbers in the English school. If they could not go against the expressed will of the King of Spain and disband the pupils altogether, they were determined at least to keep the school as small as was possible. One must not blame them for their attitude, fortunately but a temporary one. The Spaniards were far from popular in the Southern Provinces of the Netherlands—the Northern Provinces were already in revolt—and orders

now the Capuchins inhabit". The Capuchins, he says, are known to have occupied the house from 1594. The Walloon Diary uses almost the same words—"quam iam occupant Capuchini"—in an entry of December 1593, but perhaps the diary was "written up" some months later.
[5] Cf. L. Hicks, pp. 167-168.

emanating from the remote Escorial, never welcome, were impatiently endured. In any case the English school constituted an enemy colony in their midst—a Catholic exile colony, it is true, which evoked sympathy, but was nevertheless potentially hostile and, as they forecast, not even a financial benefit to the town. But Fr Flack, it appears, was furious at the opposition he encountered. Witness a letter from Fr Henry Walpole to Fr Persons written from "St Omers" (he was living at the Walloon College) just three weeks before he set out for England and martyrdom.[6] Speaking of Fr Flack as the "Rector" of the boys gathered in George Persons' corner house, he writes:

> After I had written thus far, F. Rector cometh here and he showeth himself altogether resolved to sett forward this work what he can, and for the number he saith "On Gods name when there be means let them come an hundreth". And whereas some of the Magistrates have seemed backward, he will reprehend them to their faces and tell them their duty to the King, and how they should be ashamed to be more rude and uncivil or rather uncharitable then they in Doway, France, Spain and Rome. And if that will not serve, will cry out upon them in the pulpit in behalf of God. Some there be which had need be cried at the fier of . . . (*MS. torn*).

The torn manuscript leaves room for quite a probable guess at what is missing. Incidentally Fr Walpole goes on to recommend that when the "new Rector" enters upon his office, Fr Flack and the others should receive from Fr Persons himself their several posts, "which they will better take from you then from any other, as I perceyve, and perhaps otherwise not be so at their contentment". Fr Walpole, one observes, was a man of some perception!

Such opposition as came from the Walloon Jesuits seems to have been more of the nature of discouragement, of cold water thrown upon the whole scheme. Opposition of this nature there certainly was: *humanum est*. Especially did it come from Fr Oranus, Vice-Provincial of Belgium during the absence of

[6] November 13 1593. (C.R.S., V, 225.)

Fr Oliver Manare in Rome. "He has shown himself", wrote
Fr Persons to the General, "colder about this business than
anyone I have ever seen in my life."[7] Fr Persons, however, was
taking active measures against the difficulties and objections
that were hindering the progress of the little school, not yet out
of the cradle. The result proved very satisfactory. A letter of
4 March 1594, from the King to the Archduke Ernest—he had
succeeded as Governor of the Netherlands a month or two
earlier—after informing him of the arrangements already made,
charged him to increase the pension to 2,000 golden crowns,
to be paid without fail from "the Licences and Pastports at
Graveling or if those be hindered out of the more sure Licences
in the Country". The arrears of payment, as from 13 March
1593, were to be an additional charge on these custom duties.
By the same courier went letters to the Bishop and to the
mayor and town council of Saint-Omer. To the Bishop, Jean
de Vernois, King Philip urgently recommended to his favour
and assistance the English school. The Fathers of the Society
were to have the government of it, under a Rector who should
be a native of the Low Countries.

Finally, Letters Patent of the King, dated 6 May 1594,
confirmed his previous commands. "Where it may be noted",
as Fr Flack recalls, "that the writing was dispatch'd after all
the aforesaid letters, and the chief of all, his Majesty declaring
his whole intention therein, neither appoints any determinate
number of Schollars, but admits as many as the Fathers can
bring, nor names any determinate Nation that the Rector should
be of, and counting the Revenue by Crowns he explicates that
he meanes the yearly summe of 6200 fl.".[8] As to the nationality

---

[7] Quoted by L. Hicks, p. 169.
[8] Hist. Mem., p. 17. A copy of the royal Letters Patent of 6 May, followed
by an acknowledgment of its receipt by the Treasury at Brussels dated 29
May 1594, is printed, with a facsimile of the original, in the *Stonyhurst
Magazine*, xii, 348 seqq. (December 1911). A note (p. 355) by the learned
Dr Boardman gives the equivalent of 2,000 golden crowns as £600 of
Elizabethan money. Twenty times that sum would perhaps be of less value
today in purchasing power.

of the Rector, this had already been mentioned in the royal letter to the Bishop of Saint-Omer. Indeed the condition must have been made from the very beginning of the negotiations, since it is mentioned, or at least assumed by Fr Persons as early as March 1593.[9] The silence, however, of these latest Letters Patent on the point was not without its value in after years when there arose the question of an English Rector for the College.

Let us complete the financial statement before proceeding further. On 24 April 1596, Philip II wrote to the Cardinal Archduke Andrew of Austria at Brussels, telling him he had been petitioned to double his former pension in view of a great increase in numbers, and asking for further information and advice. A few weeks later the Bishop of Saint-Omer, Jean de Vernois, wrote similarly in support of the application:

> And in 1600, 1 Martii, Philip the 3rd by a writing settled 2000 (golden crowns) graunted by Philip the 2d (behold the first almes doubled) upon the Jures of Madrid, taking it from the silks of Granada, saying that being Prince he was made Protectour of this seminary & by meanes of so pious a work God was pleased to give him good success in his Monarchy & that the same seminary went on profiting notoriously & doing much good.[10]

This doubling of the pension or alms seems to have been procured by the Cardinal Archduke at the instance of Fr William Baldwin, now residing in Brussels as successor to Fr Holt and "very intimate" with the Cardinal. The grant of a Spanish pension, unfortunately, and the payment of it seldom coincided. The new grant was a gracious and generous gesture on the part of the pious Philip III. But little seems to have come of it. An investigation made in 1714 (to be referred to later) into the history of the pension shows that from the very

[9] Persons to Aquaviva, 22 March 1593 (Rom. Arch., Hisp. 135, f. 147), a letter summarized by L. Hicks, pp. 161-162.
[10] Hist. Mem., pp. 17-18; cf. L. Hicks, p. 177.

beginning of St Omers the "Spanish Pension", more often than not, remained unpaid.

Fr Foucart, as has been said, entered into office in February 1594 as Rector in the house in the Tenne Rue, where the school remained for about a year. It was assuming now the more formal shape of a Jesuit school, with a Rector, Minister, Procurator (or Bursar) and Prefect. The number of boys was increasing: but it was an obvious inconvenience that they should be so distant from the Walloon College. Not only every school-day had they to walk to their classes, like modern day-boys, in all conditions of weather, but on Sundays too they attended Mass at the College Church and were there again for evening Vespers. Whereto hangs a tale of Fr Flack's which is worth recording: for incidentally it tells us of a revolt or "strike" of St Omers boys—not, be it added, against the authority of their own countrymen, but against that of their Walloon masters.

Ambrose Rookwood, the eldest of the three brothers already referred to, and a future victim of the Powder Plot, "at the news of this seminary was come from Lisle (Lille) where he study'd and being enter'd there was the 1st in Syntax, and famous for having acted Constantine most admirably a little before". One Sunday at Vespers, lacking a book of words, he asked his next neighbour for a "Primmer".

He was observed and noted therefore by ye Syndicus.[11] The next morning his name was given up to the Master and tho' the Syndicus acknowledged that the fault was no greater than has been say'd, yet wou'd the Master have whipp'd him for it, had it not rung from Schooles whilst ye matter was in debateing, saying that he had done against orders.

[11] A "Syndicus", in Fr Flack's use of the term, apparently meant an un-pleasing and, one hopes, obsolete type of boy-prefect, more usually known as "Censor" or "Decurio maximus", whose duty it was, not to keep order in his class, but to observe and report disorder or irregularities to the master. The Jesuit *Ratio Studiorum* prescribes this practice "pro regionum consue-tudine". One knows of no evidence that this particular custom ever existed at St Omers.

But the school bell merely postponed the trouble. The English boys—"it disgusted them much"—refused to attend further classes until the matter was settled satisfactorily in Ambrose's favour. The Censor was a fool (one can almost hear them say) to report so harmless an incident, and the Master no less for paying any attention to the report. Both Fr Foucart and Fr Flack sided with the boys: it must have been one of the few occasions on which they saw eye to eye. Together they went to the College and represented the matter to the Rector, pointing out "the inconveniences that might ensue" if he did not take quick action. But Fr Christian, as he was called, was not greatly interested. The sequel must be given verbatim:

His answer was in a scornful kind of answer that we English were proud and ought to be humbled, he understood the matter well enough &c. Notwithstanding F. Foucart urg'd him to consider well of it with his Consultors, and then give his answer whether he judged that to be a fault worthy of so great a correction: adding moreover that if he did not resolve upon the freeing the youth from that undeserving punishment he wou'd let Superiours understand how he had proceeded in this matter. F. Christian therefore call'd his Consultors and afterwards promis'd nothing shou'd be done to the youth. Wherewith the Fathers return'd home and ye schollars appeas'd and content to go to ye school.[12]

Fr Flack related the story to the Provincial on his return from Rome that June. Fr Manare, however, side-tracked the issue for the moment by enquiring how it came about that the English boys attended Mass and Vespers at the Walloon College when they had so convenient a chapel at home. Hence a series of Regulations, drawn up in the form of question and answer, and dated from Antwerp, 19 June 1594.[13] It was thereby settled that in future the boys, if the Rector so wished, might make use of their own domestic chapel for Mass, Communion, Vespers and other public services. The reason

[12] Hist. Mem., p. 15.
[13] Primae determinationes R. P. Oliverii Manarii pro seminario Audomarensi (Rom. Arch. Germ. 177, f. 313).

is tactfully given as the need to avoid distraction of mind and waste of time whilst crossing the town to the Walloon Church. For the same reasons leave was granted for Catechism—or Religious Doctrine, as we would now call it—to be taught at home rather than at the College.

Two major questions were also answered to the satisfaction of the English school. Firstly there was the question of the status of the Rector. Was he, like the Primarius or Principal of a Jesuit *pensionnat*, subordinate to the Rector of the College, or was he a Rector in his own right? The answer was clear enough, although its practical application remained for many years a source of friction. Fr Foucart and his successors were to be in no way subordinate to the Walloon Rector but, like other Rectors, directly subordinate to the Provincial of the Province. The second matter concerned the question of punishments, so recently brought to the fore by the outrageous case of Ambrose Rookwood. Here again Fr Manare was for putting the "seminary"—for him it could be nothing else—on the same footing as the other seminaries governed by Jesuits in Rome and Spain. Except in the case of scandalous faults, he decided, let such punishments as might be necessary be administered after schools when the boys had returned home.

Is there need to remark that the English Government was interested in this new Jesuit Establishment? Spies soon began to appear, like the first wasps of the season. About November 1593 one hears, for instance, of a certain Simon Knowles at Saint-Omer who in the following February or March was chosen by Fr Bray as a safe guide to conduct to Brussels a small party of Englishmen, lately come out of England. On his return journey to Saint-Omer he carried letters from Fr Holt to Fathers Bray and Nicholas Smith, and of course read them on the way. Pretending to be returning to Brussels in a few days, he was entrusted with the replies to Fr Holt's letters: but he carried them, not to Brussels, but, more fruitfully, to the Government in London.[14]

[14] C.S.P. Dom Eliz. 1591-1594, p. 474. Foley, IV, 577.

A few weeks later Thomas Jefferies, merchant of Calais and spy combined, sent a sheaf of information to Sir Robert Cecil. He tells him, besides other items of news, how the students, or at least some of them, manage to reach St Omers. They get out of England, he writes, under the guise of soldiers, or else in Flemish ships, travel by way of Flushing or Dieppe, "and thence to St Omer, and study under the Jesuits". He gives the number of scholars as fifty: and there is an arrangement with a certain merchant of Antwerp for the payment of their fees.[15] As to numbers, a better authority than Jefferies informs us that in 1594 the scholars had increased to thirty-three, and next year to nearly fifty. The growth is ascribed largely to the unimpeachable courage of a batch of youths who set out for Spain in the January of 1595 but were intercepted at sea by an English cruiser. Lodged at the residence of the Archbishop of Canterbury—whence two of them presently escaped—they shared his table, being careful, we are told, to make an especially large Sign of the Cross at their Grace before and after meals. At intervals they managed secretly to converse with Catholics: and it was their enthusiastic accounts of the English school at Saint-Omer that is said to have inspired other Catholic parents to seek admission for their sons.[16]

It may be of interest to note that on their frustrated sea-journey to Spain the boys were accompanied by an Italian merchant, utterly ignorant of English, who went by the name of Ottavio Fuscinelli, though actually he was Fr Baldwin, whom we have already met and shall meet later as the first

[15] Thomas Jefferies to Sir Robert Cecil, Calais, 8 April 1594 (Hist. MSS. Commission: MSS. of Marquis of Salisbury, IV, 506).

[16] Litt. Ann. 1594 and 1595 (Naples, 1604), pp. 302-3. It should be noted that a reference to these Annual Letters may be to (a) an annual report from each "College" or "District" sent to the Provincial of the Province, or (b) an abstract of these reports sent by each Province to the Jesuit head-quarters in Rome, or (c) a further abstract of (b) included in a combined printed Litterae Annuae of the whole Society. Evidently (a) is the most detailed of the three accounts of any College: but not all of these have survived. Only (c) was printed—from 1581 to 1614, and from 1660 for a few years. Future references will be to (a) unless otherwise stated.

English Rector of St Omers. Under suspicion as a priest and Jesuit, he too was arrested and spent a month or two in the Bridewell prison. But he was too clever for his captors. Try as they would—sometimes, for example, waking him up with a sudden warning cry, "Look out, Baldwin"—they could never catch him out; and he was soon released for sheer lack of evidence.[17]

To return to the English school in Tenne Rue. Although the house they were renting from the Sieur de Croix was considerably larger than their first house, yet it too was becoming too small for its inhabitants: in any case it was not their own property. For many months the procurator, Fr Flack, had had an eye on a large and lordly mansion in the Rue St Bertin, known as the Hôtel de Licques, or du Comte de Fressin, a former residence of the Comtesse de Roeux, widow of Eustache de Croy who had once held the post of *grand bailli* in the town.[18] It was objected by the authorities that the English Jesuits were growing too ambitious: they should be content with houses less pretentious than "les maisons de seigneurs". Nevertheless Fr Oliver Manare approved of the project, and Fr Persons "having understood of it liked it very well & bid him buy it, tho' it were ye fairest in ye town". The property consisted of a house and garden, together with a farm which alone, so Fr Flack was assured, was worth 12,000 florins. He had begun to negotiate with an offer of 22,000 fl. when he learnt that the property had been sold "underhand" to Canon Louis de Bersacques, Dean of the Chapter, for 15,000 florins. Subsequently the farm was bought back by the kindred

[17] "Baldwin, bearing himself as one borne in Italie, was by meanes of money gotten out of their hands and is with Garnet." Worthington, one of the five boys, "the most resolute of all, hathe made an escape oute of the Bishop his house and cannot be heard of".—Verstegan to Persons, Antwerp, 30 March 1595 (S. Arch: Anglia II, No. 3, f. 23; printed in C.R.S. 52, p. 228). Cf. Foley, III, 502 seqq., who however thinks "Bawden" is the real name of Fr Baldwin, whereas it is but a phonetic *alias*.

[18] Bled, p. 3: Justin de Pas: *A travers le Vieux Saint-Omer* (Saint-Omer, 1914), p. 118.

of the late Comte de Fressin. The house and garden, however, Fr Flack was able to secure from the Dean at what seems the reasonable price of 7,500 fl. (£750), adding another 300 fl. "to build up ye wall before ye Infirmary".

> This is the house and ground which the Seminary now enjoys, containing then the hall and Refectory, ye kitchin and Roomes over it, the backhouse Infirmary as it was antiently, and part of the bake-house with the garden: which bargain caus'd much muttering, when it came to be divulg'd . . . and the town did their endeavour to charge the house with as many burdens as they could.

It was only the pressure of the Spanish Court and the advocacy of the Dominican Bishop of Saint-Omer, Jean de Vernois, that induced the *échevinage* to sanction the sale. To dispose of the house in the Tenne Rue, rented on a three-year contract, the alternatives were either to sub-let the house for the remaining two years, if a suitable tenant could be found, or else to induce Monsieur de Croix to forgo his rights. Fortunately M. de Croix was complaisant: he agreed to terminate the lease at Candlemas 1595 on receipt of the 250 fl. due for a year's tenancy. Seizin of the new property was somewhat grudgingly allowed by the authorities on 24 October: and by the following February 1595 the school had moved into its new quarters.[19]

Here then, after a year and more of cramped existence in rented buildings, the school in its third attempt emerges permanently into the full light of day. It has become a prominent feature of the town, a spacious College which, at least architecturally, might dare to rival its neighbour the Walloon College. So at least one may suppose, for it was a *Mansion de seigneurs*: but as the College suffered from two disastrous fires in the course of its Jesuit occupation and yet a third fire in 1826, its original dimensions and architectural beauties can be no more than a guess. At all events it was "fairer and larger by far" than the house they had left. Situated on the south side of

---

[19] Hist. Mem., pp. 12, 13. Archives de St-Omer: Table des délibérations du Magistrat. M. ff. 158, 159.

the Rue Saint-Bertin, about half-way between the Church of
Notre Dame—the Cathedral as long as there were Bishops of
Saint-Omer—and the great Abbey of St Bertin, now a
melancholy ruin, it ran back together with its garden some
250 yards to the parallel Rue de Vieil Brusle (Rue de Gambetta). Along its eastern side ran the Rue des Cordeliers (Rue
Notre-Dame de Patience), whilst to the west it was only a
narrow strip of property that separated its garden from the
grounds of the Walloon College. By a door or gate opening
on to the Rue Gambetta the daily journeys to class were
reduced to but a minute or two. Fr Flack could scarcely have
found a better or more convenient site.

It will be remembered that all this while, war was being
waged by both France and England against Spain. Even as the
move was in progress from the Tenne Rue to the Rue St
Bertin, an attack on the town was launched by the French
Governor of Picardy, the Duc de Longueville. With five or
six thousand troops he attempted a surprise attack in the early
morning of 24 November. The defenders, however, had had
previous warning and the assault was repulsed by the garrison
without the loss, it is said, of a single soldier.[20] An annual
procession (the townsfolk appear to have loved processions)
was instituted by the Bishop to commemorate the event: and
we may be sure St Omers, anxious to demonstrate its civic
loyalty, took part in it, as indeed it did in many another
public procession. In the years that followed war was never far
away from Artois: and Saint-Omer, defending the entrance
to that province, needed continually to be vigilant. Calais and
its neighbourhood saw much incidental fighting, Calais itself
changing hands more than once. The new Governor, Archduke
Albert, captured it from the French in April 1596, some two
months after assuming office in the Netherlands. But when the
war with France ended at the Treaty of Vervins (2 May 1598),
Calais was handed back rather ignominiously to the French.
Just four months earlier Fr Henry Bray, the Prefect at St

20 J. Derheims, *Histoire de la Ville de Saint-Omer* (Saint-Omer, 1843), p. 329.

Omers, who for some reason had ventured into this dangerous area, was captured by a French patrol and taken to Boulogne. "It's an ill wind that blows nobody any good", so his boys may have agreed. However, he had some influential friends and with their help he was released a few days later.[21]

Earlier, in the late summer of 1596, a plague or pestilence swept over the district and took its heavy toll of human lives. It lasted all through the winter; and Fr Foucart decided—not, one gathers, with the full approbation of Fr Flack—to send away most of the boys to a safer locality near Courtrai. Some remained at Saint-Omer, for reasons unexplained. Next spring they were recalled from their winter quarters, as the pestilence seemed to be dying away. But it grew worse again after their return, although providentially they all escaped contagion. Each Sunday and greater feast-day the boys were marshalled after Mass for a procession in the College grounds, where they chanted the litany and prayed for preservation from "pestilence, famine and war".[22]

As has been noted, the official relation of Fr Foucart to the Rector of the Walloon College was settled by Fr Manare (at least on paper) in 1594. The Rector of the English College was in no way to be subordinate to the Walloon Rector. Unfortunately this ordinance did not settle the matter: the arrangement was surely unworkable, from either point of view. Here were two Rectors within a hundred yards of each other, equally independent of the other's authority, yet with the pupils of both Colleges subject in scholastic matters to the Prefect of Studies and to the Rector of one of them. In the few *pensionnats* as yet established in the Society, the Superior was not a Rector but a "Primarius", a subordinate official, subject to the Rector of the College of which the *pensionnat* formed an integral part. But this English College was not a *pensionnat*, even though for the present it shared many of its characteristics. It was an English "seminary", subject indeed to the Provincial of the

---

[21] Diary of Walloon College, p. 205.
[22] Jean Foucart to Aquaviva, 26 July 1597 (Rom. Arch., Germ. 177, f. 205).

Belgian Province, but subject also, by a kind of "gentleman's agreement", to Fr Persons who was unofficially—and in 1598 became officially—the Prefect of the English Mission. The real solution of this embarrassing problem only came in 1614 when, as we shall see, the two establishments became entirely separate from one another.

In the interim Fr Manare, acting as Vice-Provincial now in the absence of the Provincial at Rome, was called upon in 1597 to decide further difficulties of organization proposed to him by Fr Foucart.[23] His answers turned out to be less favourable than they had been on the previous occasion in 1594. For instance, may the Rector of St Omers free his boys from school on some special occasion without having actually to ask leave from the Prefect of Studies? By no means, was the answer. Or may he not in case of need exempt a sick boy from attending class? Well, only for very solid reasons which must be explained without delay to the Prefect of Studies. Of course there was reason for Fr Manare's decisions. The direction and conduct of scholastic matters must, as he said, be one and undivided—a direction extending to both Colleges. The poor Rector was being harried on both sides. Fr Holt in Brussels was assuring him that when Rector of the English College in Rome he had experienced no opposition if on occasion he gave his students a holiday: that by Fr Manare's own decision in 1594 St Omers was to be governed after the manner of the other English seminaries in Rome and Spain.

The question of punishments was still a source of friction from time to time. An unfortunate incident, when three or four boys were given corporal punishment of some unmentioned, possibly unmentionable, kind in presence of the assembled school for what seems to have been a mere youthful prank, provoked the ire of some of Fr Foucart's community and an angry letter from Fr Holt when he came to hear of it. Fr Flack continued to be a thorn in his side. He evidently

[23] Posteriores determinationes P. Oliverii, 16 Junii 1597 (Rom. Arch., Germ. 177, f. 314).

considered that his Rector needed advice from one who understood English boys and English character. Fr Foucart, a pious man with a certain sense of humour, shouldered his burden as best he could. We find him writing in 1597 to a fellow Jesuit, Fr Oranus, now on business in Rome—he had been Vice-Provincial when Fr Foucart began his rectorate: "I have not always had, and I have not now, the same ideas or the same opinions as Fr Flack. But we both agree on one point: his judgment and desire is that the Rector of this seminary be changed." He adds that when Fr Oranus sent him to be Rector, he had said, "Compatior Reverentiae Vestrae": so please show the same "compassion" again and ask Fr General to appoint another Rector here.[24] But his petition did not succeed: he had yet to wait another three or four years before he was relieved from his office. *Tantae molis erat . . . condere gentem.*

By this date the community numbered nine, including three "Praefecti Cubiculorum"—one of them a Belgian—not yet ordained, on whom devolved the administration of corporal punishment for the less serious faults, previously the duty of the Minister. Discipline, it is reported, was the better for the change. One is left uncertain as to the precise meaning of a "cubiculum" in this context. If we mistake not, it was some sort of study-hall, and possibly at this early period a dormitory as well. At all events, the boys were divided, perhaps according to age, into three sets, with a Prefect in charge of each. In 1597 the number of boys had increased to about fifty: at the close of Fr Foucart's rectorate in 1601 the total had mounted to a hundred or more. Thus in eight years St Omers had outstripped in numbers the English College of Douay or indeed any of the English or Scottish seminaries on the Continent.

According to the Jesuit nomenclature of this period St Omers College ranked as a seminary, even though by no means every student was an ecclesiastical student. In the eyes

[24] Cf. J. Foucart to J. Oranus (d'Heur), 6 December 1597 (*ibid.*, Germ. 177, f. 306).

too of the Roman authorities St Omers was evidently a seminary and nothing but a seminary. In 1599 Pope Clement VIII commissioned two Cardinals, Caetano and Borghese, the Cardinals Protector and Vice-Protector of England, for the purpose of organizing and co-ordinating the constitutions of the several English seminaries. Accordingly Visitors were appointed to inspect each seminary—and St Omers was included—and consult with the authorities of each as to what was needed or proper to be revised. Two priests, Dr Richard Hall and John Wright, Dean of Courtrai, visited Douay in August of that year, and after a week Dr Hall, and probably his colleague as well, set out for Saint-Omer.[25] Although the records of St Omers are missing, it seems very likely that their more precise destination was St Omers College. Considerable delay followed the death in December of Cardinal Caetano, since his successor, Cardinal Farnese, brother of the Duke of Parma, wished to form his own judgment on the matter in hand. The *Constitutiones Collegii Anglorum Audomarensis*, like those of Valladolid, were finally signed on 20 April 1600, and no doubt received at St Omers not many weeks later.

In September two Jesuit Fathers were commissioned by Cardinal Farnese to make a visitation of St Omers and see to the introduction there of the new regulations, as had been done in the case of the seminaries in Spain. As a matter of fact the General, Aquaviva, two years earlier had expressed his wish that Fr Holt, together with Fr Baldwin who was coming from Rome to succeed him, should visit the College and settle the vexed question of punishments and other kindred matters that were still causing some tension between the two neighbouring Colleges. For some reason or other the visit had been deferred. But on the occasion of the change of Rectors in 1601 directions

[25] *Third Douay Diary* (C.R.S. 10, p. 8). The full text of the revised Constitutions of the English College, Valladolid, signed by the two Cardinals on 20 April 1600, is printed in Appendix II of the Register (C.R.S. 30). A copy of the Constitutions of St Omers, likewise signed on 20 April, is in S. Arch., Anglia II, No. 67.

D

were again sent to the Provincial to ensure that the two Jesuits, Fr Thomas Conyers (nephew of Cardinal Allen) and Fr Baldwin, should make the visitation and put into execution the orders of the Cardinal Protector.

A comparison made between the Constitutions imposed upon St Omers and upon Valladolid shows the former to be not much more than a shorter version of the Valladolid Constitution. This latter is divided into seven chapters, followed by a form of College oath to be taken by all seminarians. No oath is prescribed for St Omers: but its four chapters with some omissions and additions follow closely, and usually even word for word, the corresponding chapters of the longer version. Much emphasis is laid on the need for careful selection of entrants, their character, qualities, health and attainments. They must be English, from greater Britain, or if born abroad both parents must be English and Catholic. But whereas at Valladolid the age for admission is placed at about eighteen, a St Omers boy on arrival should be "not less as a rule than fourteen, so that he can more quickly be sent on from there to other Seminaries in accordance with the established purpose of the College". At least an elementary knowledge of Latin is a prerequisite. Indeed Latin is prescribed as the common mode of communication: "in all places they must speak as a rule in Latin, except on occasion in time of recreation according as the Superior shall decide" (cap. 3, no. 2).

In their spiritual training they share the regulations laid down for the older seminarians at Valladolid. A quarter of an hour's meditation is to be made each morning before Mass: and before going to bed another quarter of an hour is to be spent in examination of conscience and litany, after which the prefect or vice-prefect of each living-room (cubiculum) shall read aloud the points of the morrow's meditation, and next morning repeat the points once more. But allowance is made for those who find even this short meditation beyond their powers: with the confessor's approval they may substitute the Rosary or the Office of Our Lady. One regular confessor is to be appointed for the boys, but from time to time one or two other "extraordinary" confessors may be added. Confession and Communion, at least once a month and on the greater feasts, are enjoined, subject always in particular cases to the confessor's discretion. Spiritual books and Lives of the Saints are to be provided, and definite times, especially on holy days, must be allotted for the reading of them. Other regulations, which are mainly concerned with studies and domestic discipline, are either too obvious or too vague to be in need of comment.

To what extent these ordinances modified the existing practice at St Omers it is now impossible to say. Taken in their historical background they would seem to have been salutary and perhaps necessary. It would nevertheless have been interesting to have had some English Father's—preferably Fr Flack's—opinion on the subject. For those many who at this period went on from St Omer's to one or other of the English seminaries to prepare for the priesthood, such an introduction to seminary life must have been a distinct advantage. Indeed it may well have been a help to some in their choice of a state of life. But as a matter of fact, during the six or seven years preceding this new regime, a very high percentage of St Omers boys had already made choice of the ecclesiastical state. Exact numbers are of course not available: but at Valladolid one can count at least forty-five boys recorded in the Register as having entered from St Omers—in other words, at the average rate of six or seven a year. From 1594 to 1601 or 1602 the number of boys at the College increased from 33 to "nearly 120". The "Annual Letters" for 1601 record that this year— surely a most exceptional year—as many as nineteen were sent from St Omers—three to Rome and sixteen to Spain. Of these sixteen all but two were captured at sea and imprisoned in the Bridewell. Their further adventures are not described, but some at least seem to have escaped and managed to trickle back to the College, thus hindering the admission of new boys. Evidently the College was full to capacity.

In this same report a curious incident is related of one of the boys, Henry More, a great-grandson of the martyr Sir Thomas More and in later life a Provincial of the English Province and twice Rector of St Omers as well as its historian. Whilst on a visit to the town the Countess of "Zueda", a lady of the Court of the Infanta Isabella at Brussels, asked to see the College. All the boys were assembled to greet her: whereupon she picked out this Henry More, "a gracious youth", "embraced him with motherly affection" (a rather trying ordeal) "and adopted him as her son"—so the Annual Letters express it—at least in the sense that she promised to pay henceforth for his education. His parents are not likely to have objected. Next morning she returned to the College for Mass, was welcomed with Latin and Greek verses, and young Master Henry was able to show his gratitude and that of the College by presenting her with a crucifix—a gift which apparently delighted her.[26]

One cannot say whether this small incident occurred whilst Fr Foucart was still Rector, since he was relieved of his burdensome post in the July of this year, 1601. He had deserved well of the College. He had nursed the infant school with success through the difficult years of its babyhood, had borne patiently the burden and heat of many tiresome days, and was able to hand over to his successor a thriving school. His rectorate, however, has been overshadowed by that of Fr Giles Schondonch, who was formally installed as Rector on 22 July by the Walloon Rector in presence of the boys of both Colleges. This new Rector most certainly deserves a new chapter.

[26] Litt. Ann. 1601 (printed Antwerp, 1618).

3

FR GILES SCHONDONCH

ST OMERS COLLEGE evidently rejoiced in more than one founder. Fr Robert Persons ranks and has every right to rank as the principal founder: his was the original idea, his the driving force, the stubborn determination and resourcefulness that turned a Spanish blueprint into a practical and thriving reality. After three and a half centuries and several migrations from place to place he is still held in due veneration at Stonyhurst as the Founder. But in the early days of which we are treating it was King Philip II of Spain who ranked as the founder. The Custom Book of St Omers—more shall be heard of it in the sequel—does not so much as mention Fr Persons' name. Yet on 13 September, anniversary of King Philip's awesome death, "a Requiem Mass is celebrated by all priests for the late Philip II, King of the Spanish Dominions, founder of the Seminary: and there is one sung Mass". Without the favour and munificence of the King the foundation of the College would have been well-nigh impossible.

If one should look for yet another "founder", Fr Giles Schondonch is the obvious choice. In the course of a long and benign rectorate, with tact and skill and push and faculty of organization he did more than bring the College to full maturity. Under his direction and with his energetic help and encouragement, St Omers reached a standard of spiritual fervour, of keenness in studies, of classical attainment such as was never surpassed in later years and which gained for the school a wide reputation quite out of proportion to its age and numbers.

Fr Schondonch, a Fleming born in Bruges, was a priest of considerably wider experience than was his predecessor. Having entered the Society in 1576 at the age of twenty, he had taught classics for several years to Poetry and Rhetoric classes. Later he had been a Prefect of Studies for seven years, and then Rector of the College at Courtrai for another eight. He brought with him to St Omers an *élan vital*, a zest for humanistic scholarship and a love—an expert's love—for schoolmastering which evidently aroused a responsive enthusiasm in both teachers and taught. Of course there were set-backs, many of them. There must, as always, have been unresponsive boys, and probably undiscerning and inefficient masters. But the memory of them is lost amid the quite astonishing chorus of praise which the records have preserved. Sir Tobie Mathew, for instance, after visiting St Omers on his return from Rome to England in 1607, wrote to Fr Persons in language extravagant indeed but substantially not at variance with other calmer tributes voiced by his contemporaries.

> Returning from Italy I have seen many splendid cities on my way: but nothing have I admired so much as the Seminary of St Omers—a spot which, of all I have ever seen, is most like to what I hope to see in heaven. Such great devotion, such regularity, such eagerness did I find; and such a Rector, and such scholars![1]

He is in doubt, he adds rhetorically, which to admire more—the diligence of the scholars and their warm affection for the Rector, or the Rector's wise and fatherly government of the scholars. It was a saying of Fr Schondonch that whosoever was Rector of St Omers should think of himself as a thorough Englishman. This he tried to put into practice and with considerable success. The writer of the "Annual Letter" for 1613 was certainly of that opinion and went out of his way to say so. "An excellent man", he calls him, "a great lover of the English Mission, being himself thoroughly anglicized (*ipse totus Anglus*). He is pre-eminent in piety, in learning, in zeal for souls: the best and greatest Rector this College has ever known." It is true that the College had had but one previous Rector; but one

---

[1] Tobie Mathew to Persons, Calais, 19 June 1607 (Rom. Arch., Anglia 38 (1), f. 270.

can gather his meaning. More interesting it may be to note that St Omers is termed a College rather than a Seminary; possibly a slip of the pen, yet instructive as to the manner in which the English Fathers regarded it.

One of Fr Schondonch's early problems was the material one of providing sufficient accommodation. There were now nearly 120 boys in the College, and the staff and servants accounted for another twenty. Applications from parents were frequent, often persistent. As the years passed and St Omers became more and more widely known, the problem grew increasingly urgent.

If there had been sufficient room, and had we been willing to accept all applicants, we should, I think, have admitted a hundred, such is the reputation that has spread of our manner of education and of the discipline in this College. We are daily worried with letters and petitions asking admissions not only for English boys but for others too who have never even seen England and know not a single word of English.[2]

For some years Fr Schondonch was content to relieve the situation by renting or purchasing various neighbouring houses —their exact localities are not mentioned.[3] A further problem, however, presently confronted him. The hope that with the death of Queen Elizabeth the bitter persecution of Catholics— not to mention the Puritans—would cease or at least diminish was not fulfilled. Under James I persecution soon raged as fiercely, if not more fiercely, than before. The effect was felt at Saint-Omer by the increase of voluntary English exiles in search of safety and comparative peace. After the conclusion of peace in 1604 between England and Spain, the inflow grew in volume: soldiers, both officers and men, were constant visitors to the town, and would often come, or be brought by their Catholic friends, to the College for spiritual aid. But

[2] Litt. Ann., 1605 (Royal Archives, Brussels: Fonds Jésuitiques—Province Gallo-Belge. Copy in S. Arch., A. IV. 13 (3), p. 393).
[3] Bled, p. 6.

hitherto there had been no chapel open to the public. In 1597 the suggestion had been made of building one, but Fr Manare had strictly forbidden any such idea. Let them be content, he had replied, with their inner domestic chapel. However, by 1604 this severe prohibition had presumably been relaxed, for there is mention that year of a chapel, dedicated to St Thomas of Canterbury and accessible from the street.[4] Nevertheless it was not a separate structure; more probably just some large room near the main entrance, which had been converted into a temporary chapel. And already by 1607 it was considered too small for the English residents and visitors who frequented it. The beauty and precision of the ceremonies carried out under the watchful eye of Fr Schondonch, combined with the singing of the well-trained boys' choir, complete with orchestral accompaniment, provided a constant attraction.

In the following year the Rector saw his opportunity. Next door to the College on the west side and facing Rue St Bertin was a large house of some pretensions, known as the Hôtel de Regnauville. This property came into the market in 1608. Fr Schondonch had had his eye on it for several years and now, though only after long and difficult negotiation, he succeeded in buying it, only to find that the municipal authorities refused to grant him seizin. Here, said they, is another *maison de seigneur*: they had given in on the previous occasion and were determined this time to stand firm against the grandiose ambitions of "*les anglois*". They reckoned without Fr Schondonch. Equally determined to have the property and build a church on its site, he appealed to the Archdukes, the town authorities following his example. This first round went to Fr Schondonch; for by letter of 26 January 1609, the Archdukes admitted him to the seizin, with certain customary "charges" attached, such as "*guet et garde*"—three watchmen,

---

[4] Jean Hendricq, *Receuil Historique des Choses Memorables de S. Omer*, I, p. 629 (Archives de S. Omer, MS. 808). Cf. Litt. Ann., 1607 (A. IV. 13 [3], p. 382).

that is, to be provided or the equivalent in money, namely eight florins and ten sols.[5]

Realizing the need for caution when dealing with a frustrated opponent, Fr Schondonch proceeded with native cunning. He had some support from his friend, Bishop Blaise, who recognized at least the need for a larger church. The site however was of his own choosing. His method was to begin building unostentatiously at the rear of the Hôtel de Regnauville, gradually demolishing the mansion as the work proceeded. He must have realized that sooner or later the ruse would be discovered, and of course it was. The building was begun in August 1609, and for some three months all went well. In mid-October the Nuncio, Cardinal Bentivoglio, on a visit to the College seems to have expressed his approval of the site, although it is unlikely that his host told him the whole story. Two or three weeks later the local authorities got wind of the Rector's proceedings and with the authority of the Archdukes ordered all work to cease. By this time the building—or the back portion of it—was almost up to the roof: but the workmen had to be dismissed and the work left to the caprice of wind and weather. The magistracy had taken the matter to the Court: very well, Fr Schondonch would of course do the same: indeed he went this time in person to Brussels to obtain a reversal of the order. Against the objection of the authorities that the Hôtel de Regnauville was too fine a mansion and too useful to the town to be thus ruthlessly pulled down he pleaded that the house was old and unsafe for human habitation, even apart from the fact that it was now too late for the town to intervene. How he managed it one does not know; but once again he obtained a decision in his favour. The new church was opened with much ceremony on 8 September 1610, feast of Our Lady's Nativity, and dedicated to "Notre Dame des Anges"[6]—perhaps a delicate, if optimistic, compliment to the pupils under Our Lady's care, but more probably to their busy Angel Guardians.

[5] Bled, pp. 6-7.　　[6] Hendricq, *op. cit.*, II, p. 195.

Jean Hendricq, a rather discursive chronicler, has noted some of the features of this English church. Besides the high altar, described as "*tres bien acomodé*" (the spelling is his own), there was on the right or epistle side a side-chapel, dedicated to St Thomas of Canterbury (Patron of St Omers), and two other altars, one of them in the choir-loft at the back of the church, a gallery containing an organ, and of a size large enough to accommodate all the College boys. He mentions too the pulpit, which seems to have been built into the wall. The whole church in fact was well arranged and extremely devotional. Henceforth it was much frequented by both Belgians and English, especially on Sunday evenings when at 8 o'clock the Litany of Our Lady was sung. Often on these occasions the church was packed to the door, and even overflowing into the Rue St Bertin.[7]

It was likewise in 1608, or possibly even earlier, that the house and property adjoining the old Hôtel de Regnauville was acquired, at first apparently on a long lease. This was a narrow house belonging to a physician, M. Joly, the grounds of which extended back to the modern Rue Gambetta and had thus separated the garden of the English Jesuits from the Walloon College. By these two additions the property of the English Jesuits was squared up, and the garden of St Omers was now divided by no more than a high wall from that of their Walloon neighbours. The house, with its frontage on the Rue St Bertin, was converted into a printing establishment which began to function in 1608. Of this important activity connected with the College more shall be said later. It may be remarked here that on the occasion of the Bishop's visit in the course of 1608, after a very special High Mass accompanied by choir and full orchestra, his Lordship confirmed some forty boys, blessed a bell for the church at Watten, dined with the community and boys and was then shown round the College. He approved of all he saw, including the proposed site for the

[7] *Ibid.*, II, pp. 258-59.

new church. But what most caught his fancy was "a little house, equipped with a printing press and all the accessories of printing, which we have lately fitted up and very handsomely too".[8] Evidently the Bishop's admiration for the new "print" was shared by those showing him around.

The reference to a bell blessed by Bishop Blaise for the church at Watten—a rite closely watched by the boys, who never before had seen this ceremony—introduces us to the beginnings of the English noviciate at Watten. Although the subject concerns St Omers College but indirectly, yet Fr Schondonch played an important part in the affair, and the Watten noviciate will be mentioned so often in subsequent pages that its foundation seems to demand some space in this history.

The ruins of the old abbey still crown the hill which rises sharply behind Watten—or Waten, as once it was spelt—a little town or village bordering the river Aa, five miles or so to the north of Saint-Omer. It was an abbey founded by a Count of Flanders in the eleventh century for Canons Regular of St Augustine.[9] After the destruction of Thérouanne by the Emperor Charles V, the bishopric of Thérouanne was suppressed in 1559, and three new bishoprics, namely of Boulogne, Ypres and Saint-Omer, were created in its place, the Prévoté of Watten coming under the jurisdiction of the Bishop of Saint-Omer. But for many years the abbey, once so flourishing, had been in decline: and when in 1577 the abbey was sacked by French troops and set on fire, there were but seven old, decrepit and unedifying Canons to flee from the wrath to come

---

[8] Litt. Ann., 1608 (A. IV. 13 [3], p. 380).
[9] What follows concerning Watten is derived from (i) *Rerum Memorabilium Praepositurae vulgo Abbatiae Watenensis Compendiosa Narratio*, an unfinished MS. of the eighteenth century in Rom. Arch; (ii) *Mémoire à consulter, et Consultations pour M. l'Evêque de Saint-Omer* (Paris, 1774) one of the last of many *Mémoires* printed during the dispute for possession of the (former) Watten noviciate between the Bishop of Saint-Omer and the secular priests who in 1762 had succeeded to the English Jesuits at Saint-Omer; (iii) H. More, pp. 293 seqq.

and escape to their "refuge" in Saint-Omer—a house in the Rue St Bertin, not far from the English College. A year or two later one of these Canons apostatized and departed to the Protestant North, adding nimbly to his baggage such church plate and silver as had escaped the notice of the marauding soldiers. By the time the remnant had dwindled in number to two or three, the Bishop had reached the decision that this Prêvoté must be suppressed and the Founder's intentions fulfilled by some other means. It lay upon the conscience of the worthy Bishop Blaise (1600-1618) that too little had been done since 1577 either to restore the abbey's fabric or the spiritual services for the sake of which the abbey had been built and endowed. His Dominican predecessor, Jean de Vernois, had offered the abbey to members of his Order. Bishop Blaise, a Franciscan, offered it to the Franciscans. Both Bishops had met with a refusal. How then was the problem to be solved?

Fr Schondonch was able to supply the answer. Recently a large sum of money had been offered by a pious and noble Spanish lady, Luisa de Carvajal, for the founding of an English Jesuit noviciate. Fr Persons, disliking Fr Cresswell's suggestion that Bilbao would be a fit place for its establishment, had written to Fr Schondonch from Rome in the hope that he might find a better locality in the Low Countries; for Bilbao, he said, was too far from England and its climate unsuited to an Englishman. At his next visit to the Bishop—his Lordship frequently sought his advice—the Rector produced Fr Person's letter and enquired whether the Bishop knew of any such place. Bishop Blaise jumped at the idea that came to him: hand over Watten to the English Jesuits and all his difficulties would be solved. Fr Persons was quite enthusiastic on learning of the Bishop's offer. "God Bless his Lordship's pious thought," he replied at once: "this seems indeed a matter of the greatest importance for the future conversion of England, if only the plan succeeds."[10]

[10] Persons (Rome) to Schondonch, 5 October 1603; copy in S. Arch., A. IV. 13 (3), p. 209.

It would be out of place to follow here in detail the difficult and protracted negotiations that ensued. The Spanish King, Philip III, interested himself in the affair and in June 1604 wrote to the Archduke Albert in favour of the Jesuits. Everything and everybody seemed in favour of the idea until the English Ambassador at Brussels, Sir Thomas Edmondes, got wind of what was happening. His insistent intervention induced the Archduke to refuse his Placet unless all reference to England and English Jesuits was omitted. Pope Paul V, annoyed at this *contretemps*, consented nevertheless to alter the wording (though not the intention) of his Bull, and another one was issued, dated 28 June 1608, whereby was sanctioned the dissolution of the "Monastery or Prêvoté of Watten" and the gift by Bishop Blaise to the "Fathers of the Society of Jesus" of the half-ruined church and monastery, to become a Jesuit noviciate. The Bishop, however, never wavered in his determination that the noviciate must be an English noviciate. A little before his death he made yet again a solemn Declaration that such was his firm intention. Although on account of the "iniquitas temporum", as he expressed it, and the opposition of the English Ambassador Pope Paul V had issued a second Bull suppressing all mention of England, yet the Pope well understood his mind, as did likewise the Jesuit General Aquaviva and his successor Mutius Vitelleschi. Five years previously, on 17 January 1611, Archduke Albert had issued his "Lettres de Placet" to the Bull of 1608—he would seem to have been somewhat dilatory in the matter—and on 8 August 1611, all formalities being now completed, Fr Schondonch took formal possession of the Watten property in the name of the Society of Jesus. Whether it was by design or by accident, the choice of Fr Schondonch was well suited to the circumstances—a non-English Jesuit, but Rector of an English College. So for some years Watten became a Residence of the Belgian Jesuits. The Archduke's reluctance to resist the demands of the English Ambassador lasted until the former's death in July 1621. Nevertheless we find Fr Cresswell appointed Superior of that Residence in the autumn of 1620;[11] and next year the Belgian Fathers had disappeared from the scene.

What then of Doña Luisa de Carvajal's generous gift? Since Watten was not as yet available, Fr Persons used the money to purchase in 1606 a property in Louvain, and in spite of the English Ambassador[12] to convert it into a temporary noviciate. The first batch of novices, seven in number (six of them priests), arrived there on 1 February 1607. After some years the Louvain house began to be occupied by older Jesuit students of philosophy and theology: the novices, lesser lights, were in 1614 pushed out into the garden, where a smaller building had to suffice for the present.

For this reason, no doubt, namely to provide a more suitable home for the novices, as well as to avoid as far as possible the attentions of the English Ambassador and of the English spies who were swarming in Louvain, Fr John Gerard managed with the aid of generous friends to acquire a property in Liège, beyond the confines of the friendly but timid Archduke's jurisdiction. By the summer of 1615 all the novices had migrated thither, under Fr Gerard (then known as Father "John Tomson") as Rector and Master of Novices. After the Archduke's death negotiations were again undertaken for permission to carry out the intentions of the late Bishop Blaise. The Archduchess Isabella, now sole Governor of the Spanish Netherlands, graciously acceded to the request. In view of the project of a Spanish marriage for Prince Charles which was a-brewing, she had less reason than had her late husband to fear intervention on the part of England. The old King, James I, was more or less on his best behaviour. So it was that in the course of 1623 the English novices, numbering about thirty, moved to Watten:[13] and there the noviceship remained until

[11] General S.J. to Richard Blount (Vice-Provincial), 17 October 1620 (Ep. Gen. I, f. 127).
[12] Sir T. Edmondes to Lord Salisbury, 10 October 1606 (Hatfield Calendar, xviii, 320).
[13] "Durabat haec . . . delatio ab anno 1611 . . . ad annum usque 1623, non

in 1765 it migrated perforce to Ghent, well out of reach of French jurisdiction.

There still survives a register of those who entered the Louvain noviciate in 1607 and 1608.[14] The first two on the register were "Old Boys" of St Omers—Fr Thomas Garnet and Fr Andrew White, both of them held in honour to this day, one as an Apostle of Maryland, the other as a martyr. They would have known one another at St Omers and again at Valladolid. Fr White, founder of the Maryland mission, has already been mentioned. Of Fr Thomas Garnet, nephew of the more famous Fr Henry Garnet who was executed at Tyburn in the preceding May, something must here be said, for he is venerated as the proto-martyr of St Omers College.

Thomas Garnet had entered St Omers in 1594 or perhaps late in 1593, whence, like so many others, he had gone to Spain to study for the priesthood at Valladolid.[15] Six years and more of missionary work in England were followed by some six months in the Gatehouse and the Tower of London on a charge of complicity in the Powder Plot, not to mention his relationship to Fr Henry Garnet. It became clear, however, that he knew nothing whatever about the plot: and it could scarcely be called a treasonable offence to have an uncle, even a Jesuit uncle. So he was included in a large batch of Catholics, mostly priests, who were banished and shipped off to the Continent in the July of 1606. Two years before this he had been admitted into the Society by his uncle, Fr Henry, at that time Superior in England. After a brief noviceship of five months at Louvain—doubtless his imprisonment counted for

vero vigesimum quintum, ut habet Pater Morus" (Watten MS. as above, f. 54v). Cf. Ep. Gen., f. 188: Gen. to Silisdon (Watten), 30 December 1623.

[14] S. Arch, Anglia III, No. 98.

[15] Fr Henry Walpole, who had left Saint-Omer for England on 4 December 1593, confessed in June 1594 that "one Garnet . . alyed to f. Garnett" (i.e. Fr Henry Garnet) was "nowe" a student at St Omers College. (C.R.S. v, 259). On the other hand Fr Thomas Garnet when under examination denied that he went abroad in "1594 or thereabouts" (Foley, II. 486). At all events he presumably left St Omers for Spain about January 1596 (C.R.S. xxx, 40).

the rest—he returned to England in September 1607. Before
the end of October he was back again in the Gatehouse prison,
betrayed by an apostate priest, probably Anthony Rouse. The
new-fangled Oath of Allegiance was presented to him. Would
he take it? He refused point-blank, even though the Arch-
priest Blackwell had taken it—and by Papal Brief of 1 February
1608 had been removed from office as a result. On 19 June he
was tried for his life. Of the four points of his indictment for
treason none was proved except the fourth—his refusal to take
the oath—which was not as yet a matter of treason. There
followed the customary sequence of events: the savage sentence
of condemnation and his confinement in "Limbo", the condemned cell, whence on the 23rd he passed, through many
tribulations, to Tyburn and to heaven. In 1929 he was beatified
by Pope Pius XI.

We return to Fr Schondonch and the more material activities
for which he was responsible. As recorded already, by 1608 he
had made shift to house his growing establishment by the
purchase or lease of neighbouring tenements, and had started
a most serviceable "secret" press for the production of pious
and controversial works to be imported surreptitiously into
England. In 1610 he had completed and opened a church large
enough to accommodate the College boys as well as most, or
at least many, of the English exiles in Saint-Omer. His building
programme however was not yet complete, for the College
continued to grow. In 1610, so the Annual Letter informs us,
about twenty students had left to pursue their studies for the
priesthood in Rome and Spain. Forty-eight new boys, however, had arrived, bringing the number up to 135. With
twenty-one Jesuits (including ten laybrothers) and more than
as many inside and outside servants, the grand total was over
180.

In these difficult times our Government takes particular
pains that as few as possible—indeed, that none at all—
cross over from England to this College, or that at all events
they do not reach their destination. And yet nothing is more

frequent or common. . . . At the risk of their lives parents send abroad their sons, youths of gentle birth and excellent promise. It happens every year, every month: it would happen every day without intermission, were there not lacking, not indeed the opportunity, for eagerness would easily overcome that obstacle, but sufficient accommodation.[16]

Before the end of 1610 a new building had been constructed —perhaps an addition to the original house—which the College could ill afford. In 1613 (the two intervening years are silent as to St Omers) the Annual Letter records yet another structure containing eight rooms, with the prospect of more to come. In a long and rather obscure description of this latest venture of the Rector, "the greatest and best Rector the College has known", the new building is said to be "at first sight quad-rangular, but by a skilful device it is really of five sides". There survives a formal bond of this same year, signed by Fr Schondonch and his four "Consultors" or advisers, for repay-ment of a debt of 20,000 florins (£2,000), a large sum in contemporary values, borrowed from the Jesuit "English Mission" at 6¼ per cent interest, by permission of the Vice-Prefect of the Mission, Fr Anthony Hoskins. This is to pay off "only the more urgent debts of the said College".[17]

Certainly the financial state was by this time alarming— indeed, deplorable, as the General insisted more than once. Fr Aquaviva had been growing progressively more forceful on the subject for some years, and his successor, Fr Vitelleschi (1615-1645), was, if anything, even more decisive. There must henceforth, he wrote, be no more building, unless with the General's express permission. No new boys are to be admitted whilst the College remains in debt, except the sons of parents who are capable and willing to make prompt and full payment of the fees. In short, every feasible economy must be at once enforced, in the number of the teaching staff and the servants, in the entertainment of guests, and so forth. Even dramatic

[16] Litt. Ann., 1610 (A. IV. 13 [1], p. 252).
[17] S. Arch., Anglia III, No. 125. The date is 19 March 1613.

E

performances (produced, it would seem, frequently and at considerable expense) are to be either abolished entirely or at least severely curtailed in number and in cost.[18] Early in 1616 one finds Fr Cresswell at St Omers. After many years in Spain he had left in 1614 and, being well experienced in money matters, he was to spend the next few years in promoting the financial welfare of the English houses on the Continent. He arrived at St Omers from Liege and appears to have remained there until at least the close of 1618, when he returned for a while to what was still the temporary noviciate at Liege. Before long, thanks to Fr Cresswell's care, the critical situation had at all events taken a turn for the better: and one may suppose that the improvement continued during the further years of Fr Cresswell's residence.

A subject of some delicacy, the treatment of Mistress Mary Ward whilst at Saint-Omer, calls for some attention before this discursive chapter ends. A definitive and fully documented Life has yet to be written of that very remarkable and saintly woman, and of the trials and bitter opposition she met with whilst founding the Institute of the Blessed Virgin, now happily prospering in many parts of the world.[19] At the age of twenty-one she had left England in 1606, following a call she knew not quite whither. It brought her to Saint-Omer and to the door of the English College, with a letter of introduction from the Jesuit Superior in England, Fr Holtby, to Fr Flack, still Procurator of the College. It is a strange but easily verifiable fact that the founders of religious communities for women have frequently—one might be tempted to say, almost invariably—been directed at first by Providence to a priest who either misuses his power as director or at least misdirects the founder's energies. So at all events it would appear, if judged on human

---

[18] Memoriale spettante al Sem° di S. Omer, 2 January 1616 (Archives of Eng. Coll., Rome, Scritture 6-20).
[19] For what follows cf. M. C. E. Chambers, *Life of Mary Ward* (London, 1882), Vol. I passim; P. Guilday, *The English Catholic Refugees on the Continent, 1558-1795* (London, 1914), Chapter VI.

standards. To learn obedience is without doubt a fruitful but sometimes nerve-racking preliminary to the exacting of obedience from others. Mary Ward assuredly found it so. As she tells us herself, she asked at the porch for Fr Flack and received instead, not indeed the proverbial scorpion, but Fr George Keynes, the "Spiritual Father" of the boys. From him she discovered that arrangements had been made, even before her arrival, for her entry amongst a community of Belgian Poor Clares, not as an enclosed choir nun but as one of the lay sisters whose main occupation was to go out daily into the town to beg alms and food. It is true that she would not be the only Englishwoman in the convent: but her future life had been arbitrarily decided upon—like that of a marriageable daughter by a contemporary paterfamilias—before ever Fr Keynes had seen her, still less discussed with her such a delicate matter as her vocation. Fr Flack arrived later on the scene, but appears to have left the matter in Fr Keynes' inexperienced, imprudent hands. It is to the immense credit of Mary Ward that in spite of her repugnance she accepted the situation as being "the will of God"—a phrase used by Fr Keynes which, however, as events proved, was in sore need of some careful distinctions.

In less than a year Mary Ward left the convent, convinced that God had other plans for her. Fr Keynes, who for a couple of months acted as her confessor, became convinced that he had made a grave mistake. Being a pious and honest priest he told her so; and after several months of prayer and painful disquietude she had recognized the fact. Her plan was now to buy or build a convent of Poor Clares for English ladies. It took two years to achieve this result—the details need not concern us—in the shape of a newly built convent and church in the little town of Gravelines, half-way between Calais and Dunkirk. Meanwhile, with the help of friends, especially of Bishop Blaise and Fr Schondonch, a house was found in Saint-Omer where a number of young postulants, together with five English nuns from Mary Ward's previous Walloon convent, began in earnest to live the severe life they had chosen. One of the five nuns was elected Abbess, and the postulants, including Mary Ward, were informally clothed in the habit of choir novices about Christmas 1607.

With the permission, it is stated,[20] of the Vice-Prefect of the English Mission, Fr Baldwin, who himself had assisted Mary Ward to secure the Placet of the Archduke for her convent at Gravelines, Fr Roger Lee gave the full Spiritual Exercises of St Ignatius to the Saint-Omer community and remained their ordinary confessor. Readers of Fr John Gerard's Autobiography will know of the many services Roger Lee as a young man was able to render to that intrepid Jesuit, who ever held him in high esteem. He had been Minister at St Omers for four years and was destined to remain in that post for another four. If one may trust Fr Gerard's judgment, he and his Rector were more or less carrying the College on their shoulders. Besides other innovations he introduced with much success the practice of giving the Spiritual Exercises to the older boys.[21] Mary Ward seems to have found him on the whole a wise confessor and director: "a man truly apostolic", she wrote of him, "and much illumined and favoured by God".

However, in May of 1608 an extraordinary experience, soberly and humbly related by herself, convinced her that God had other designs for the good of his Church and of England in particular. Her Abbess considered this a temptation of the devil and told her to take a discipline every time the "temptation" recurred. Fr Roger Lee was non-committal. He was in an embarrassing situation, a Jesuit Director of a convent which the Franciscan Fathers claimed to be under their exclusive jurisdiction. And it may perhaps have worried him that there was—and still is—a rule of the Society forbidding Jesuits to undertake the charge of religious communities of women or act as their ordinary confessors. In a few years time the General was to demand a strict observance of the rule, and Mary Ward's friend, Fr Gerard, suffered considerably in consequence. Nevertheless, as past and present history has shown, it was never

---

[20] Chambers, *op. cit.*, I, p. 168.   [21] Cf. Foley, I, 457, 464 seqq.

a law of the Medes and the Persians. If the facts are chronicled aright,[22] the English Vice-Prefect of the Mission and the Belgian Provincial were of different opinions as to the exceptional circumstances of the present case.

Mary Ward left the convent with the utmost reluctance, yet leave it she did about Easter 1609, trusting courageously that God willed it so. Her companions a few weeks later, having finished their noviceship, moved to the now completed convent in Gravelines. In accordance with the preference of the Abbess to be subject to Franciscan jurisdiction rather than to that of the local Ordinary, Fr Schondonch managed to arrange the matter to her satisfaction. Henceforth the English Jesuits, probably to their satisfaction as well, relinquished all direction of the English Poor Clares.

After some months in England Mary Ward was back again in Saint-Omer in 1609 with some young companions similarly dedicated to the service of God and warmly devoted to their leader. They established themselves in the Grosse Rue (the lower part of the present Rue Carnot), where a combined boarding and day school for girls was started. Two years later her doubts—but by no means her difficulties—came to a conclusion. "Being alone, in some extraordinary repose of mind", she wrote autobiographically, "I heard distinctly, not by sound of voice, but intellectually understood, these words, 'Take the same of the Society' ": or, as she wrote confidentially to Fr John Gerard in 1619, "Take the same of the Society. Father General will never permit it. Go to him."[23] Her adoption or adaptation of the rules of the Society of Jesus for the purpose of her Institute raised even greater opposition than previously she had met with. A very odd woman, some thought her. She had left two convents within the space of two or three years: of the second convent she had herself been the foundress. Decidedly odd, it seemed, and so of course it was. The ways of God are often decidedly odd; they are not as our ways. Now these "English Ladies" in the Grosse Rue

22 Guilday, *op. cit.*, p. 166.   23 Chambers, *op. cit.*, I, 283-4.

were aping the Jesuits, said the hostile critics. Exemption from enclosure they were demanding, perhaps exemption from the duties of choir, government by a Superior General. . . . Who ever heard of such dangerous concessions allowed to any convent of women? The attachment of the English Ladies to the English Jesuits at St Omers and the spiritual services they received from them had already suggested the name of "Jesuitesses": the very name was abhorrent to the Society. And now more than ever, with gathering momentum up to the suppression of the Institute in 1631, Mary Ward and her companions shared the opposition, even the bitter dislike and intrigues, of certain English Catholics which for many years had been the lot of the Society of Jesus. But the full story of these years remains as yet unwritten.

Not that the young Institute was ever destitute of friends as well as enemies. The good Bishop of St Omers, Jacques Blaise, was ever its friend, approved the rules of the Institute, and was always prepared to go out of his way to give help and encouragement. Like Fr Schondonch, he had a warm heart for the English and a very fervent zeal for the conversion of their country. The Archdukes, Albert and Isabella, were very friendly too. And of course the English Jesuits at the College and the English Ladies in the Grosse Rue had but one heart, if one may so express it. They were both engaged in the same work, the education of English youth. And it is likely enough that some of the boys at St Omers had sisters—not to mention other possible attachments—at the neighbouring convent. Bishop Blaise bears testimony to the work of the Fathers:

For the most part they usually confessed to Rev. F. Roger Lee, a true Jesuit, filled with the Spirit of God, who as far as the Institute [S.J.] would allow him (and no further, as we are able to attest) ministered to them from the beginning with the warm approval of good men. Nor do these ladies demand at the hands of the Fathers of the Society aught but the services these render to the rest of the faithful: they go to the Church of the English Jesuits for confession, communion, and sermons, they apply to them for exhortations, direction and the ministry of the sacraments, and no more.[24]

Fr Roger Lee's non-committal attitude had gradually changed to approval, then to a warm sympathy, and in course of time to something approaching enthusiasm for their Institute. His exhortations to the community assembled in the Grosse Rue, of which several extracts are given in Chambers' *Life of Mary Ward*, display an increasing tenderness towards his hearers and a sympathetic understanding of their trials present and to come; a constant insistence too on the acquisition of a solid, practical piety without any "frills". "Solid" is a word that recurs over and over again in these addresses. There seems no reason to doubt that he was a very wise and saintly director of souls. It was certainly the firm conviction of Mary Ward (or "Maria della Guardia", as Vitelleschi insisted on calling her) that her director exercised on occasion extraordinary, perhaps miraculous, cures both of the body and of the soul. It is sufficient here to note that even her ascription of such gifts to Fr Lee is a strong testimony, apart from other evidence, to the holiness of his life and the influence he exerted on those around him.

Fr Schondonch and Fr Lee, as has been suggested, were the two pillars of the College during these years. It was probably with a view to easing his work that about 1612 he was relieved of his office of Minister to become the Spiritual Father of the College. But consumption was eating away his life. In 1614 he was sent to Louvain in search of a better climate. The Rector at Louvain, Fr Henry Silisdon, records his presence there in a letter of 3 September 1614:[25] he adds however that "His harte is so fixed upon his work of St Omers, as I finde myselfe to have little hope of his stay heere with contentment". His disease growing yet worse, his Superior decided to send him to his native country, as a last hope of recovery. England,

---

[24] Quoted by Chambers, *op. cit.*, p. 286.
[25] S. Arch., Anglia IV, No. 21.

however, he never saw again: he managed to reach Dunkirk towards the close of 1615, and there he died. The story of St Omers would indeed be incomplete without some account of this fine priest's "solid" work and influence both inside and outside the College walls.

From the scholastic point of view the year 1614 was a most memorable one for both community and boys. That October, at the beginning of the school year, the separation of the two Colleges was accomplished: from that time forward St Omers became self-contained, the boys no longer going for their classes to the Walloon College. The new arrangement may well have been a relief to the latter, as it certainly was to the English Fathers, who for many years had been looking forward to such a consummation. It would serve no good purpose to conceal the fact—even did one wish to do so—or at least the very strong impression, that the initial sources of friction noted in a previous chapter had by no means diminished as the English College grew in size and fame. The faults were most probably on both sides, as usually is the case. And the differing national temperaments and habits, Walloon and English, did nothing to improve matters. No doubt the communities of the two Colleges did their best on the whole, as befitted dutiful religious, to love one another "in Domino". There is naturally more doubt about the attitude of the boys in this respect. "You English are proud and need to be humbled", a Walloon Rector had retorted in the years gone by to a remonstrance from the English College. It was perhaps true enough: the difficulty arose as to how to enforce the lesson. To take one interesting instance, which evidently was known in the town and commented upon, the English boys were clever or hard-working enough to carry off a disproportionate number of the awards distributed annually each September. As these prizes were usually paid for by one or another of the wealthier friends of the Walloon Fathers, it must have been rather galling to watch these English boys walking off, year after year, with so many of the prizes meant mainly for their Walloon

schoolfellows. It might almost be considered as misappropria-
tion of funds!

The Annual Letters of St Omers make allusion more than
once to the striking successes of the boys in their classes. Such
reports might be taken as little more than pious or patriotic
propaganda, were it not that there is some corroboration from
Walloon sources as well. There survives a Register of the
Walloon College,[26] recording the results of the various
examinations—usually as many as eight or nine a year for each
of the five classes—and the final prize list. For each examination
a list is given of the first eighteen or sixteen boys in each class.
Incidentally, the order of names is recorded after the fashion
common to the Jesuit schools of the period—a fashion which
with modifications persisted at Stonyhurst until comparatively
recent years. The first two boys were "Imperators", Roman
and Carthaginian, followed in succession by two "Praetors",
two "Tribunes", and either twelve or ten "Senators" according to the size of the class. The Register, in so far as it includes
English boys—to each name the place of origin is added—
begins in January 1612 and ends in December 1613. A little
arithmetic discloses the fact that in eighty examinations held
amongst the various classes there were but five occasions when
an English boy did not come either first or second on the list,
and frequently both "Imperators" were English. The list shows
likewise in the "Senatorial" ranks a very generous admixture
of English names. There is no particular reason to suppose that
these results were at all exceptional.

In spite of these registered successes no English boy appears
in the final prize lists. The reason as given is revealing. In 1610
it was that all English boys were excluded for the first time from
the Distribution of Prizes at the Walloon College, which took
place that year on 7 September—the day before the solemn
opening of Fr Schondonch's new church. Why? The garrulous
Hendricq amongst others got hold of the story, and he was not
the man to keep it to himself. Some "personnage de qualité",

[26] Arras, Archives du Pas de Calais, MS. II. D.2.

he tells us,[27] had pointedly remarked that last year the English had secured most of the prizes, to the considerable discouragement of the boys of the town and neighbourhood. The quaint explanation offered was that boys who in an English school would be in Rhetoric (or whatever the top class might be called) were placed in Poetry or Syntax at the Walloon College, and similarly a Syntaxian in England became a Figuritian. This of course was an excuse which implied either a lower educational standard in England—and thus of no validity as an excuse—or a discreditable lack of judgment in the allocation of boys to appropriate classes on the part of the Prefect of Studies. Anyhow, the remark served its purpose. The Canons of the Chapter who on this occasion were donating the prizes made it a condition that none of the prizes be bestowed on English pupils. The condition was accepted, possibly with some alacrity.

The sequel must be given, so characteristic of Fr Schondonch's native reaction (he was a Fleming) and typical too of the religious functions that so frequently enlivened the lives and the faith of the local inhabitants. Just a week later, on the feast of the Exaltation of the Holy Cross, a considerable ceremony was staged. The Abbot of St Bertin celebrated pontifical High Mass in the English church, crowded to its full capacity. Several notable prelates and priests were present by invitation, including the Commissary General of the Franciscans in Belgium, two Abbots and several representatives of other religious Orders. Later there was formed a procession, which first wound its way out into the street and thence into and around the garden, decorated for the occasion in the familiar continental fashion with paintings and emblems and other pious devices. In the rear walked the Abbot, richly vested, carrying a statue of Our Lady of Montaigu. The garden, as Hendricq noted on a similar occasion, was "like the 'hortus conclusus' of the Blessed Virgin". The Abbot came to a halt in front of an extemporary shrine or small chapel erected in the

27 J. Hendricq, op. cit., II, pp. 261-263.

middle of the garden. There he deposited the statue and sat down: the current Annual Letter tells us that of two seats he chose the "Sedes Sapientiae", leaving the "Thronus Salomonis" to the Commissary General. Sixteen College boys proceeded to declaim some short praises to the Blessed Virgin in twenty languages, "from Hebrew to Irish". Then the assembled boys cried out three times with increasing urgency, "Sancta Maria, ora pro Anglia"—a cry that moved many to tears, as well it might. But this was not the end. A few addresses of welcome to the Abbot and other distinguished guests and then, with a garden-full of visitors as spectators, the Rector produced his trump card, as it were, presumably a surprise to most. A distribution of prizes took place. "Au milieu de ce jardin leur furent donnez des beaux livres selon le degré ou classe ou ils estudioient". And so back to the church in the order in which they had come. Subsequently—or perhaps previously—the Abbot of St Bertin and various guests were entertained by the Rector to dinner—one of those entertainments, it may be, that the General would presently frown upon, as leading to the bankruptcy of the College. Fr Schondonch must have gone to bed that night well satisfied, if not chuckling to himself.

In 1614, then, the time was quite ripe for the separation of the two Colleges. Fr Herennius, the Provincial, had recommended the separation to the General and the latter granted the requisite permission "ad iuvenum bonum et consolationem parentum". He stipulated however that the classes were to be only for those living in the College. The Walloon College, like the great majority of other Jesuit Colleges in Belgium to which at that period no *pensionnat* was attached, catered for day-boys or day-students and only for such. For the English College to admit Belgian day-boys would be to "raise altar against altar", as Fr Oliver Manare once expressed it. There were already enough occasions of friction without the addition of yet another.

Whether Fr Aquaviva was as wise in another enactment of his is perhaps less sure. In an endeavour to preserve unity and mutual charity he decided that the five masters required for the classes in the English College should be Walloon masters. The disappointment was the greater in that Fr Blacfan, the present Vice-Prefect of the English Mission, relying on the local Provincial's assurance, had already selected his English masters. Fr Henry More, for instance, was to have taught Rhetoric, and Fr Stanton for a similar purpose had been recalled from England. The Rector at Louvain, who is our informant, was strongly of opinion, as was Fr Gerard, that

> if union be required both at home and abroad and the comfort of the Children's parents or their profit, it is certainly requisite that they be English Masters. Fr Schondonch hath written a very good letter to this effect, but, God forgive him, he had written before to the Provincial for French masters, which he afterwards repented him self of.[28]

So for once in a while Fr Schondonch did not show himself quite "totus Anglus". However, it was acknowledged that the Provincial, Fr Herennius, had done much for St Omers and that he was a good friend. Fr Silisdon, much interested in the matter, comforted himself with the thought that "to introduce English next yeare will bee no great difficulty, at least one or two". One or two certainly were introduced some time in the course of the next five years: and in 1619, though it could not have been foreseen, the whole difficulty vanished with the erection of the English Mission into a Vice-Province of the Society.

An incident that occurred this same year may be added, since it concerns that very loyal Catholic—loyal to Faith and King—Colonel Sir Henry Gage of Haling House, Surrey. After six, perhaps seven, years at St Omers he left Rhetoric in the September of 1614, intending to follow a course of philosophy at the English College, Rome. The Annual Letter (1614) tells us how in the course of his journey he "fell into a fever" at his lodging in Basle. The local Protestant doctors

---

[28] Fr H. Silisdon (Louvain) to Fr Thomas Owen (Rome), 3 September 1614; Fr J. Gerard (Liège) to the same, 26 September 1614 (S. Arch: Anglia IV, Nos. 21 & 23).

were summoned to attend him. "Two or three times they opened a vein in his arm, which became infected (or 'was injected')[29] with poison so that he could not use or even move it." There is here some suggestion at least of medical malpractice, although medical incompetence could be a sufficient explanation. At a critical moment there chanced to arrive at the same lodging a Catholic doctor, who took charge of the youth, treated his arm successfully, took him along to Cologne and restored him to perfect health. Evidently this ex-Rhetorician was in no great hurry to complete his journey. About a year later, however, in October 1615, he entered the English College and followed the three-year course of philosophy as originally intended. It is of course well known how after more than twenty years of soldiering on the Continent —in 1638 the English regiment under his command was helping to defend Saint-Omer from the French—Colonel Gage crossed over to England in 1644 to fight for his King. Before the end of the year he was appointed Governor of Oxford in place of Sir Arthur Aston, to the latter's intense chagrin. But within a few weeks in the course of a skirmish near Abingdon he was shot through the heart and died in the arms of his Jesuit friend and confessor, the future martyr Blessed Peter Wright. Here again suspicion is aroused by the Roman register, the *Liber Ruber*, which has added a few lines in praise of the Colonel's later career. "He was killed near Abingdon", we read, "and, as it is believed, treacherously." There must have been at least such a rumour, now of course unverifiable, derived possibly from the fact that, as Clarendon puts it, Sir Arthur Aston "hated him perfectly". "A Man of great wisdom and temper", concludes Clarendon, "and one among the very few soldiers who made himself to be Universally lov'd and esteem'd."[30]

[29] There seems to be a doubtful reading here—"brachium veneno *inficitur*" or "*injicitur*". The point of the story is rather lost unless the latter reading is the true one.

[30] For the above, see Litt. Ann., 1614 (A. IV. 13 [1], p. 234); *Liber Ruber*, p. 177 (C.R.S. xxxvii); Clarendon: *History of the Rebellion* (1704), II, 407, 426-7.

4

INSTITUTIONS AND CUSTOMS

O F the various Provinces of the Society of Jesus the Belgian Province was outstanding, if not unique, in the speed with which it increased and multiplied. It was in 1542 that Jesuits first arrived in Louvain—eight Spaniards they were, expelled from Paris when war broke out between France and Spain. By 1564 they had become a separate Province. Thirty-four years later, when the "Archdukes"— the Infanta Isabella, King Philip's daughter, and her husband the Archduke Albert—were beginning their long Governorship, the number of Jesuit houses had increased to fifteen Colleges, and the number of Jesuits to more than 450. In 1612 this Province of 28 Colleges and 1,000 Jesuits was split on a linguistic basis into two. The English noviciate in Louvain became part of the northern or "Province Flandro-Belge": the establishments at St Omers, Watten and (after 1615) at Liège were attached to the "Province Gallo-Belge".[1] As may have been gathered already, it was by an unusual kind of "gentleman's agreement", backed however by the ordinances of Aquaviva in 1598, revised in 1600 and again in 1606,[2] that the authority exercised over the English houses was shared between the Belgian Provincial or Provincials and the "Prefect of the English Mission"—Fr Persons himself until his death in 1610, followed by Fr Thomas Owen (1610-18) both as Prefect of the Mission and as Rector of the English College in Rome.

The influence of these Belgian Jesuits grew with the growth of their Province. Strong opposition, as so often, was encountered in the earlier years. Opposition indeed, though usually of a less stormy character, was never absent. Had it ceased altogether the Jesuits would have examined their consciences to discover

[1] Poncelet, I, pp. 415, 427 seqq.
[2] Cf. L. Hicks, *loc. cit.*, pp. 174-176.

what was amiss. They were in the forefront during the prolonged years of politico-religious war that followed the Calvinist iconoclasm of 1566. But above all they were pre-eminent in the wide field of education.

> The excellence of their method of pedagogy, the care they exercised in education and physical culture, the familiarity and gentleness of their dealings with pupils, the wholesome, pleasing appearance of their Colleges, so different from the unhealthy and slovenly schools hitherto in vogue—all this caused them to be considered as model educators.[3]

This Jesuit "method of pedagogy", common to every Jesuit College, was regulated by the *Ratio Studiorum* of 1599, the fruit of some thirty or forty years of practical experiment and trial. When in 1614 Aquaviva granted permission to St Omers to become self-contained and independent of its next-door neighbour, one of the conditions laid down was that the College should continue to take the *Ratio* as its norm of education. Why so obvious a condition was included it is scarcely worth while to guess. As a former Prefect of Studies and a former Rector at Courtrai, it is likely that Fr Schondonch may himself have contributed amongst others to the final revision of 1599. This is no place for a lengthy dissertation on the merits or demerits of the *Ratio Studiorum*. Yet something must be said of the seventeenth-century system of Jesuit education at St Omers, so different in some respects from that of our own days. The modern Jesuit school, although still faithful to the general principles enunciated some centuries ago and repeated in later revisions, has tended gradually to adapt itself to changing currents of thought and to the exigencies of examinations. There were, of course, no public examinations nor any School Inspectors at St Omers. We should indeed be mistaken did we suppose that the *Ratio* enshrined a static, changeless system of education, imposed

---

[3] H. Pirenne, *Histoire de Belgique*, IV (Bruxelles, 3 ed., 1927), p. 369. A useful summary of the very varied and successful activities of the Belgian Jesuits in the early seventeenth century is given in this volume, pp. 361-378.

absolutely by authority to be obeyed *ad literam* at all times and in all places. No doubt in the earlier years its provisions would have been strictly adhered to. A new regulation has something in common with the proverbial new broom: and one must remember that the *Ratio* had been promulgated only two years before the installation of Fr Schondonch as Rector of St Omers. But the Generals of the Society usually left it to Provincials and Rectors to accommodate the details to local conditions, although reserving to themselves the right to approve or repress. After the manner of a living organism rather than of an embalmed mummy, the *Ratio* has ever been capable of growth and in need of acclimatization, without sacrifice of its essential character.[4]

Faced with the need of choosing between the older, traditional methods of teaching derived from the Middle Ages, and the classical humanism which had come into favour with the Renaissance, the Society of Jesus had opted decisively for the latter. Not indeed that it was so unintelligent as to throw overboard the experience of past ages or to derive no profit from study of the differing methods employed in contemporary schools. Yet the basis and the emphasis of the Jesuit system was humanistic, "modern". That revolution, intellectual, moral and social, which is known as Humanism had gradually spread westwards from Italy and in the course of the sixteenth century had firmly established itself in Belgium and the neighbouring countries, England included. Humanism in the grammar schools of the period—before the end of the century they were calling themselves "Colleges" in rivalry with the Colleges attached to the Universities[5]—had as its aim or ideal the culture of the whole man, the perfection of culture being the right use of reason and of its expression, the spoken word: "ratio et oratio". The end was to be attained mainly by the

[4] Cf. F. de Dainville, s.j., *La Naissance de l'Humanisme Moderne* (Paris, 1949), p. xii.
[5] Paul Bailly, s.j., in article "Collèges" in *Établissements des Jésuites en France*, edit. Pierre Delattre, s.j., Vol. I (Enghien, 1949), col. 1410, note.

fruitful study of the ancient classical authors, Greek and Latin. Aristotle, among the Greeks, would be the best of models for the cultivation of the mind, of the reasoning faculty. For the spoken word Cicero, "orator of orators", was without rival.

For the Jesuits it was only in a comparatively few cases that the full course of education as conceived by St Ignatius was feasible; that the student should pass on from the humanities to philosophy and so to the prince of sciences, theology. More usually, as at St Omers, the course consisted of five "schools" or classes, occasionally six, forming a graded hierarchy, each "school" with its definite objective to be attained before the pupil could advance further.[6] The lower classes, known to the *Ratio* as the three Grammars—Lower, Middle and Upper— were very commonly given distinctive names. The lowest class at the Walloon College, as the Register from 1612-1614 shows, was termed Figures, whence in due course one progressed to Grammar, Syntax, Poetry (outside Belgium more usually Humanities), and finally to Rhetoric, the crowning glory of the humanist ideal. St Omers used much the same nomen- clature. Later on, about 1632, St Omers added a sixth "school", but was never consistent in giving it a permanent name. The two lowest classes were sometimes Rudiments and Figures, or Upper and Lower Rudiments, or Great and Little Figures. By the time that St Omers had reached a final resting place at Stonyhurst we find yet another school in being, known as "the Elementaries" or Elements.

Rhetoric, as has been said, was the final class in these "scholae inferiores". At the end of his five or six years at school the Rhetorician would or should have reached his humanistic journey's end and become an adept in "eloquentia latina"— Fr Schondonch, an ardent hellenist, would most probably have added "eloquentia graeca" to that popular phrase. But he was

[6] The division into classes was of course no novelty, though often the division was determined by the subject studied rather than the proficiency of the student. What was new in the Jesuit system was the regulated curriculum, each class dovetailing into the next so as to form part of a predetermined and unified system. Cf. P. Bailly, s.j., *loc. cit.*, col. 1418-19.

F

expected to be more than just eloquent. Père Dupont, s.j.
(Pontanus), himself a distinguished orator and educationalist,
speaking of that indefinable influence on manners and character
which comes from contact with the great minds of classical
antiquity, explains that

> the name "Humanities" has been given to this study because
> out of such as devote themselves to it intelligently it makes
> men who are polished, polite, gentle, pleasant, at ease in their
> intercourse. The word "humanus" indeed, means all that.[7]

The cultured Rhetorician, of course, might have been all
that, and just that—as pagan as the classical authors on which
he had been reared. Most of the contemporary lay schools,
however, professed a Christian humanism, epitomized in the
phrase "wisdom and piety"; but they had come under the
subtle influence of Lutheranism or Calvinism. The Belgian
Jesuits—let us confine ourselves to Belgium—set out to fight
heresy with the weapons of their adversaries. Indeed, the Jesuit
Ratio has been criticized on the ground that it exaggerated the
methods of the renaissance humanists. Whether that be so or
not, it was the Jesuit *Ratio* that won the battle. Whilst the
numerous lay schools grew more and more empty, the Jesuits'
classes were chock-full.[8] It should be unnecessary to add that
they aimed at something more than the preservation of the
Faith and the extirpation of Heresy. True to their motto,
"Ad Maiorem Dei Gloriam", they made it their main endeavour—as other Catholic schools of course were doing, each
in its own way—to produce not only Catholic but the best of
Catholic gentlemen, possessed of a supernatural culture and
inspired by the love of God.

This in brief was the religious and cultural atmosphere that
surrounded St Omers from its infancy. But if this exiled
English school had for twenty-one years grown up under the

---

[7] Pontanus, *Progymnastata Latina*, I, p. 320, quoted by J.-B. Herman, s.j.,
La Pédagogie des Jésuites au XVI Siècle (Louvain, 1914), p. 205.
[8] Pirenne, *op. cit.*, IV, p. 371.

shadow of the Walloon College, and in the course of them had, almost unconsciously, adopted some, though certainly not all, of its educational habits, yet from the beginning and now more than ever in its independent manhood, its outlook was focused beyond Belgium on the English shore. On a clear day, it was said, from the top of the old Abbey tower at the Watten noviciate could be just descried that same English shore, perhaps the white cliffs of Dover: the which, as St Paul expressed it in another connection, is said by way of allegory. Humanism had taken as deep a root in England as in the Netherlands. Renaissance grammar schools abounded, as classical in aim as was the case across the Channel, and with a strong religious and anti-Catholic bent. At the period of which we are speaking, the early years of the seventeenth century, even apart from official persecution, the Jesuits as a body and Jesuit education in particular were in England and in the Netherlands anathema to a certain section of Catholics. In both countries a minority of the secular clergy was strongly, at times violently opposed to all things Jesuit. Was it perhaps a pre-concerted movement? It was evidently a losing battle that any English Catholic school, whatever the particular brand, could fight against the schools in England, public or private, so long as persecution continued and schoolmastering was proscribed. We have seen that ten Elizabethan pounds a month became in 1581 the penalty for maintaining an unauthorized schoolmaster. An Act of 1603 (1 Jac. 1, c. 4) increased the penalty to forty shillings a day (at least £1,200 a month in post-war value). Furthermore, any subject of the King sending his child to a "Jesuit College or foreign seminary" to be "instructed, persuaded, or strengthened in the Popish religion" forfeited £100 (£2,000?) for each offence, and the person so sent was disabled to inherit or enjoy any real or personal estate in England. What could Douay and St Omers effect, faced with such crippling enactments? And yet the seminaries in Rome and Spain were mainly fed from these two schools, and continued, inadequately indeed but with dogged perseverance, to smuggle into England a yearly quota of priests prepared to hazard their lives in the service of their Divine Master. That was the greatest achievement of the seminaries and the schools: an achievement beyond all reckoning. Many others too there were, not priests but laymen of every rank of society, who by their influence, their example, their staunch courage, sometimes by their heroic death, added their honourable but often unrecorded share towards the preservation of Catholicism throughout these penal years. It is time to take note, so far as information is available, of the manner of education in use at St Omers and to gather what can be gleaned of its success. For of the success and renown of St Omers there is ample testimony from many quarters; and the credit for much of it can justly be given to Fr Schondonch during his sixteen years of rectorate.

That the humanist ideal of rhetoric was cultivated there assiduously is made clear by Fr Henry More in his History of the English Province,[9] and his account can be supplemented from other sources. Father More was a boy at St Omers during Fr Schondonch's earlier years as Rector; and being a talented youth he could no doubt speak from personal experience. In his terse Latin he gives us his opinion of his old Rector: an ideal schoolmaster, he calls him, both by nature and by training. Evidently Fr Schondonch did at least some coaching. From the beginning of their schooling the more talented boys were set to learn Greek as well as Latin; and the Rector delighted to listen to and encourage their early efforts to talk in that language. Latin, it may be noted, was taken for granted. It was the official language of the College, in the classroom and usually outside it, though some condescension was shown to the beginners. This was no Jesuit innovation; it was common enough at this period in English and continental schools, as it had been during the Middle Ages. But to return to Fr Schondonch. When these pupils were sufficiently grounded in Greek grammar and vocabulary, they read some of the "easier parts of

[9] H. More, p. 163. He was a boy at St Omers probably from 1602 to 1607.

the Greek New Testament or of Isocrates, Chrysostom and the like. Sometimes they translated from Greek into Latin, sometimes from Latin into Greek." In Grammar or Syntax they were exercised in what were called Disputations. One boy would support the "thesis" or subject for debate, first in Greek and then translate into Latin, his opponent disputing the argument in similar fashion. At first the subject was announced in advance; by the end of Syntax, however, they were expected to debate extempore. At the top of the school the Poet or Rhetorician should have been an expert debater, but with his mental faculties more developed by this time and his language more fluent, cultivated, classical. If his masters were faithful to the *Ratio* and knew their business, they had used the classical authors with the emphasis on education rather than information: not as a mere quarry of facts historical, grammatical, philological or what-not, but as models in an art class, to be examined, appreciated, imitated, even improved upon, if possible, in subsequent compositions. The result of such studies, a Rhetorician's culture of mind and of his critical faculty, his good taste, his "humanism", would normally be put to a keen test in these Disputations.

These friendly Greek and Latin debates, usually in the schoolroom, were often staged more formally during dinner or supper in the refectory, where the boys together with the Jesuit Community provided a critical audience. A contemporary account of a St Omers dinner is given by a certain renegade and spy, James Wadsworth by name, who before his apostasy had been a student at the College for four years, he tells us, having arrived in 1618 at the age of fourteen. Though he is far from being an admirer of "that most Antichristian fry the Jesuites", his description, flavoured with mockery, seems nevertheless to be based on actual experience.

After the boys have ranged themselves awhile, the Rector and Fathers enter, the elder says Grace himself, or ordains another, which being done, he placeth himself at the upper end of the Table, the others in their order. All this while the

Students' mouths are shut, not from eating, but speaking, bestowing their ears upon six other of their companions disputing three against three in two pews overthwart the other, of such things which may rather help digestion to the Fathers than benefit their own understandings . . . and this dispute begins and ends with their dinner.[10]

The same procedure, he says, was followed at supper, six other disputants occupying the two "pews" or pulpits. It is however most unlikely that such disputations occurred daily: for at the rate of twelve or even six disputants a day from the upper classes, the frequent recurrence of each boy's turn would have been almost intolerable.

It is evident that at St Omers, as elsewhere, the *pièce de résistance* of the curriculum was Latin, with Greek coming in a very strong second. Fr Schondonch did what he could to enhance the prestige of Greek, as we have seen, for instance, in the Disputations already mentioned. The Custom Book of St Omers offers indications of the same endeavour. Three rooms, one learns, were set apart for indoor recreation, where the boys without distinction might recreate themselves at the statutory hours, "but always in Latin, unless they prefer Greek" (p. 31). So too the Litany of Our Lady might on occasion be sung by the sodalists "at one time in Greek, at another in Latin" (p. 120): and so on. Fr Schondonch, it must be admitted, was to some extent exceptional in his enthusiasm for Greek—especially as a language to be spoken as well as read. Père Poncelet cites several letters of the General to the Belgian Provinces rebutting the objections to the study of Greek received about this period from various Jesuit Colleges. One may recall that St Ignatius himself was a little suspicious of Greek: and so too was one at least of his first companions, Nicholas Bobadilla, who at the University of Paris abandoned his plan of studying Greek when he noticed that in many cases

---

[10] J. Wadsworth, *The English Spanish Pilgrime* (London, 2 ed., 1630), pp. 15-16. The spelling is modernized. For Wadsworth, father and son, see *Dictionary of National Biography*.

"qui graecizabant, lutheranizabant".[11] Fr Schondonch at least was troubled by no such qualms.

Apart from the classics the curriculum seems singularly empty, so far as secular studies are concerned. The usages of the Jesuit Colleges in Belgium during this early seventeenth century are not easy to discover in their smaller details; and in the absence of evidence it is only by inference that one can conjecture what was taught at St Omers. Natural Philosophy or "Science", as we know from the *Ratio*, was relegated to a later course of higher studies, to be taken in the second year of Philosophy.[12] An amorphous subject it was in those days, sometimes known as "Physics", not yet differentiated into its present-day subdivisions. Some of the works of Aristotle were the text-books in use in Jesuit and other contemporary schools. Mathematics too, theoretical and applied, was taught in the Philosophy course, except perhaps some elementary Arithmetic. Clavius, the celebrated Jesuit mathematician (d. 1612), considered that mathematics was too often an object of contempt or ridicule in the eyes of Jesuit professors, and offered various suggestions with a view to emphasizing its importance and indeed its necessity as a complement to Natural Philosophy: but he was content to leave the subject to be dealt with by the Philosophers.[13]

It may be noted in passing, that although the English Seminary at Liège had been established for the training of Jesuits, yet for some ten or twelve years a later experiment was tried of admitting a number of laymen—some of them perhaps ex-Rhetoricians from St Omers—to live in the house as "convictors" and attend the lectures in Philosophy. Something similar, indeed, became the custom at Stonyhurst from its

[11] Mon. Hist. S.J.: Bobadillae Monumenta, p. 614.
[12] The course of higher studies (*scholae superiores*) comprised three years of philosophy followed by three or four years of theology. Students in the philosophy course were listed as "Logici", then "Physici" and finally "Metaphysici".
[13] See his comments in Monumenta Paedagogica (Mon. Hist. S.J.), pp. 471 seqq.

early days until the middle of the First World War: but in this latter case the lectures were for the lay Philosophers alone, and delivered in the "vulgar tongue", the only language they could follow. At Liège the experiment was somewhat reluctantly sanctioned by the General, who in fact had been presented with a *fait accompli*. He was fearful of arousing a fresh controversy with Louvain University, always jealous of its prerogatives. When in 1635 Fr Henry More succeeded Fr Blount as English Provincial, the General took the opportunity of suppressing this "convictus iuvenum" as he called it. At that date it numbered about forty lay Philosophers.[14]

If Natural Philosophy and Mathematics were cold-shouldered in the "scholae inferiores", History and Geography fared little better. They were taught, as in other schools, mainly as adjuncts to the classical authors that were being read. But though these subjects were not taught *ex professo* at this period —by the eighteenth century, in Belgium at all events, they had gained a place in the official curriculum—they were not necessarily neglected altogether. There appears to have been a certain amount of "free" time both in the schoolroom and in the study place: and at such times the boys, especially the older boys, were actively encouraged to read and write English prose and poetry, or modern history, or other subjects according to each one's particular turn of mind. There is no reason to suppose that this course was not followed at St Omers. Indeed, it is a very reasonable guess that these English boys were either taught or strongly encouraged to study the history of England or at least the history of the English Reformation with which they were so closely and so lamentably concerned. At St Omers, as a later chapter will show, music was particularly favoured, Fr Schondonch being himself a keen musician. The public exhibitions of the St Omers choir, often in combination with orchestra or drama, proved incidentally

[14] Vitelleschi to Rector of Liege (Fr Owen Shelley), 23 November 1624; to Provincial, 18 August 1635; to Fr T. Southwell, 29 December 1635 (Ep. Gen. I, 208, 413ᵛ, 423).

to be of considerable propaganda value and attracted un-numbered visitors.

From the curriculum of St Omers one may turn with more assurance to what is known as *The Custom Book of St Omers College*,[15] and gather from it what can be learnt of the daily life of a St Omers boy. With the exception of a few later additions recording particular ordinances of Provincials and similar notes, the Custom Book is the creation of Fr Schondonch, written down, no doubt, in the course of years, and arranged and amplified during the last year or two of his life when ill health began to confine him to his room. Actually, the "Customs of the Seminary of St Omers in Church and Refectory" are dealt with, month by month, in less than thirty pages. The remainder comprises Rules and "Observanda" in the refectory, dormitories and elsewhere: also, at considerable length, matters connected with the Sodality B.V.M.—instructions for the Director, meditations, considerations and various "Exercises" for the sodalists. With the later addition of "Rules of the sodalitie . . . erected in the Englishe seminarie . . . in St Omers. Anno Dñi 1629" (pp. 213-290), more than half the volume is concerned with the Sodality.

Obviously from these many pages of regulations and customs one can here but select what seems of greater interest or importance; remembering however that rules and customs set down in writing sooner or later may become obsolete although still remaining, as it were, "on the statute book". No less true is it that a written rule may sometimes suffer a change in the course of its daily application. Not the least interesting in the volume is the horarium or time-table, some details of which may perhaps arouse a laugh or shiver when compared with one's own memory of school.

[15] S. Arch., MS. C. II. 19. This copy was made at the instance of Fr L. Willaert, s.j., a small 8vo volume of 378 pp., being itself a copy mainly in the hand of Fr Henry More and written in 1620. This Louvain MS. 160 was borrowed during the First World War and so escaped destruction: but it perished in the Second World War when the Library was again burnt in 1940. The Stonyhurst copy is thus probably unique.

The hour for rising was 5 a.m. both in summer and winter—summer being hopefully standardized as a period from 1 May to 29 September (Michaelmas), however fickle might be the weather. On Sundays and Feast-days a "long sleep" till 5.30 was allowed. But there were many boys who in their keenness for study voluntarily rose earlier, we are told: the Annual Letter for 1615 reports that perhaps half the school rose earlier than need be, either for study or for prayer. It became even necessary to make a rule that none should rise before 4 o'clock —a rule which nowadays would scarcely be needed. By 5.30 a boy would or should have washed, dressed, made his bed, and spent a quarter of an hour in meditation. There was no time for dawdling! Mass followed, celebrated, strangely enough, in the "Athenaeum" or Study Place, where was an altar although presumably the Blessed Sacrament was not there reserved. (Somewhere else in the house was a domestic chapel.) An hour of Morning Studies ended at 7 o'clock when the boys went down silently, class by class, to the Refectory on the ground floor.[16] Breakfast must have been of a decidedly continental character: at 7.15 and no later the Prefect moved them on to their schoolrooms, where for another quarter of an hour "they recite their lessons"—lessons by heart, one might suppose—"to the decurions" until the master arrived to take charge of his class. The "decurio" or "censor" was a boy official appointed in each class, one of whose duties is clear from the sentence just quoted. His main duty, at least in many Jesuit and non-Jesuit schools,[17] as a reporter of breaches of discipline has already been referred to. For it was a Walloon decurion, though referred to by Fr Flack by the title of "syndic", who in the early years had foolishly reported Ambrose Rookwood for speaking in church, thereby causing a minor "international crisis" between the English and the Walloon Fathers. Since the

[16] The custom of an hour's study before breakfast survived at Stonyhurst until 1893, when the order of study and breakfast was reversed.
[17] The employment of such informers, *exploratores*, was customary at the University of Paris as well as in the contemporary Lutheran and Calvinist schools. Cf. Herman, *op. cit.*, p. 114.

Ratio made allowance for local custom when recommending this unpleasing function, lack of evidence allows at least the hopeful surmise that at the English College the duties of a decurion were considerably curtailed.

To return to the time-table. At 7.30 the master arrived, the decurion subsided and the First Prefect, patrolling the corridor, departed in peace. Schools lasted until 10 o'clock—a long session of two and a half hours. In so far as St Omers followed the practice of other Belgian Colleges, an hour was devoted to the correction, either publicly or individually, of themes, and another hour to Latin authors, with the emphasis on style or grammar according to the class. The last half hour, says the St Omers Custom Book, was set aside for "Academies".

These literary societies, voluntary almost by definition— the term must be an echo from the numerous and popular *Accademie* of Italy—were at St Omers as in other Jesuit Colleges recruited from "pupils distinguished for their talents and their piety".[18] Only members of the Sodality were eligible, according to the Custom Book (p. 89), although the *Ratio* allowed for exceptions. The two Academies (one for Rhetoric and Poetry, the other for the rest) were in fact the literary complements or counterparts of the two sodalities established in 1609 with the declared purpose of promoting greater holiness of life together with greater progress in studies. "Studies" would mean for the most part classical studies. If we can believe James Wadsworth, already quoted, morning schools lasted "until nine and better ... after which time the Prefects and Masters leave the schooles & the Students of the three under schooles go up to those of the upper, which read to them Greeke till tenne" (p. 15). But this statement raises more doubts than it solves. Was Greek alone the daily food of the Academies? The *Ratio* provided a far wider choice of fare. And what business had the Prefects in the "schooles" alongside of the Masters? Above all, if the three lower classes adjourned to the schoolrooms of Rhetoric and Poetry, what happened to those non-sodalists who were

18 *Ratio Studiorum*, Regulae Academiae, 1.

therefore not members of the Academies? The answers are not
apparent.

The Study Place succeeded the schoolrooms for an hour until
dinner at 11 o'clock. Studies however did not begin until
10.15, the first quarter of an hour being of the nature of an
interval when some talking—in Greek or Latin, of course—
was permissible and the "necessitates naturae" might be
attended to. After dinner there was recreation for about an
hour. In summer the first half hour was dedicated to music in
one of the four Music Halls, the enthusiast Fr Schondonch
presiding as often as his engagements allowed. In winter the
seance was transferred to the first half hour of recreation after
supper. At 12.30 the boys returned to the "Athenaeum"
where, after another necessary interval, they studied for an
hour. Schools followed from 1.45 till 4.30, the last half hour
being again dedicated to Academies. Another interval of
fifteen minutes and then what would now be called Night
Studies until supper at 6.30. After recreation came another half
hour of studies until at 8.30 the boys, it would seem, knelt by
their desks for a quarter of an hour whilst some form of Night
Prayers was said ("leguntur Litaniae et fit examen con-
scientiae") before they retired in silence to their dormitories.
There some short points for the morrow's meditation were
read—"they shall be read twice, in a clear voice"—and at 9
o'clock or thereabouts the candles were extinguished and
another day died in its sleep.

A fairly strenuous day, it will be admitted. Five and a half
hours were spent in the schoolroom and almost as much in the
Study Place. By modern standards these long hours of work
may well appear excessive, and the whole time-table ill-
arranged. The afternoon especially is fearsome to contemplate.
Even granted some free periods of study, the fact remains that
from half past twelve to half past six, with two short intervals,
the boys were continuously at work. It will have been noticed
that there was no provision made for even the pretence of a
meal between dinner and supper. Afternoon tea was of course

out of the question: it was an unknown institution and an unknown beverage. At some later period—for time-tables change in the course of two centuries—a standing meal in mid-afternoon must have been introduced, adequately named "Bread and Beer", for it was nothing more.[19]

Not every day, however, was so austerely ordered. Tuesdays and Thursdays were half holidays, when, as James Wadsworth describes them,

> ... dinner ended we march forth of the Colledge by 2 and 2, Father Thunder carrying up the reare untill we are distant about a mile from the Towne, where we walke, or play at ball or bowles or other such games, till the clocke and our stomackes strike supper time, whence repairing to the Colledge, rost mutton is our provision being not ordinary.[20]

On Sundays and Feast-days, after a long sleep and about an hour devoted to pious reading in the Study Place, the boys attended the 7 o'clock Mass in the College church. Elaborate rules are laid down in the Custom Book as to the manner in which they should descend from their gallery to the Communion rail and return in similar order, class by class. There would on occasion be High Mass at 10, with the College choir and orchestra in action: and in mid afternoon, it seems, they returned to the church for Vespers. During the summer months there followed recreation until supper: but at the approach of winter with its dark evenings the last hour or more before supper was spent in the Study Place. Finally, about 8 o'clock, the church filled again for the singing of the Litanies of Our Lady—sung with such devotion, says Hendricq, that people flocked to the service "en sorte que le plus du temps l'esglise est trop petite".[21] But two years later, in January 1614, in order to avoid "aucunes insolences commisses par aucuns mauvais garchons" during the service, the hour was changed to

[19] Afternoon Tea took the place at Stonyhurst of "Bread and Beer" as late as 1908.
[20] Wadsworth, p. 17.
[21] J. Hendricq, *op. cit.*, II, p. 350. He is writing of 1612.

5 o'clock, to the greater satisfaction both of the College and congregation.[22]

But it is high time to introduce Father Thunder, whom Wadsworth has already mentioned, the Prefect of the boys—for some years the only Prefect, and later, after the addition of two others, known as First Prefect. "The office of Prefect", wrote Fr Schondonch in a preamble to his "Rules of the Prefects", "is one that demands a man of grave and mature mould and of a genial disposition. For the character of English boys is such that in my opinion there is scarcely any other nation more easily induced to excel in virtue and learning and to submit to domestic discipline." That at all events was Fr Schondonch's experience, and Fr Thunder evidently answered to his requirements. Kentish-born, he was a boy at St Omers in its early days; for at the age of nineteen and not later than October 1596 he had gone thence for his higher studies to the English College, Rome, leaving it after three years in order to enter the Jesuit noviciate. It was in 1602 or possibly in the previous year that he returned to St Omers, at first as a student of theology, though probably giving a helping hand to the Prefect then in office. In 1603 he succeeded him as "Praefectus studiosorum", was ordained, and continued in that office until his death in September 1638. By that time he would have become almost legendary. There must have been many a story told of him when some of his "Old Boys" met and waxed reminiscent. But alas, the memory of them is lost. When he left the English College, Rome, he left it, so the *Liber Ruber* notes unexpectedly, "with the sweet odour of edification". And when he died, says Foley, he had won the affection of all "by his admirable candour and piety". His retention of office for so many years is itself good evidence of success. The jaunty Wadsworth speaks of "Father Thunder who appointed Chambers and Studies, makes them render account of their studies, keepes houres of study and recreation, and exercises many of his claps upon their breeches." As to that last clause

22 *Ibid.*, II, p. 462. Cf. Litt. Ann., 1614 (S. Arch., MS. A. IV, 13 (1), p. 232).

one may suspect, if not hope, that Master Wadsworth was a recipient of some of those "claps". It is surely worth adding that, apart from his record tenure of office, he was exceptional too in being the author of a Latin book of devotion, *"Locupletatio Animae*,[23] The Enriching of the Soul, or How to offer one's self daily to God by acts of virtue", a work published in 1634 and probably at the College Press, though with the imprint of Paris as a "blind". No other work of this devotional kind (if one may venture to guess) has had a First Prefect as its author. All in all, the foundation and fostering of a strong tradition of work and prayer, though certainly encouraged and influenced by many Fathers, would seem to be due in particular to the enthusiasm—in its fullest sense—of three wise men: to Fr Schondonch during his long reign of sixteen years, to Fr Roger Lee in the earlier years of that rectorate, and to Fr Thunder, whose firmness, prudence and sense of responsibility—that "cordata gravitas" which Fr Schondonch demanded of his Prefects—would have grown more and more impressive with his ever-lengthening term of office.

No attempt will be made here to summarize the many rules and regulations relating to the Study Place, the Refectory, the Dormitories and so on. Reading through them one can sense something of the heart and spirit of their author, the meticulous care of detail combined with breadth of mind whereby he strove to mould his dear English boys to that exacting pattern of virtue and sound learning which he knew they would need on their return, whether as priests or as laymen, to a Jacobean England. Flemish by birth and upbringing he had been able and willing to adapt himself to English ways, to acquire to some extent an English outlook upon life. But it is clear from some of his regulations that he was not quite "totus Anglus". How could he be? As well imagine Fr Flack or Fr Thunder "totus Belgus". The excessive surveillance, for example, whereby the boys were almost continuously under the alert observation of

---

[23] Nath. Sotvellus (Southwell), s.j., *Bibliotheca Scriptorum Societatis Iesu* (Romae, 1676), p. 332.

one Prefect or another was a continental custom born of over-scrupulosity, perfectly familiar to a Belgian and equally abhorrent to modern English modes of thought—which are not quite the same, however, as those of three hundred or even one hundred years ago. But it must be conceded that the Rector's hands were often tied by the regulations framed in 1600 by the two Italian Cardinals and ordered to be firmly enforced.

Like his Franciscan friend and fellow townsman, Bishop Blaise, Fr Schondonch was all afire for the re-conversion of England to the Catholic faith. It was an objective, an ideal that was the inspiration of his Custom Book. He felt it his duty to educate these English youths to as near to heroism as was practicable. God in his singular providence, he says, has set apart these "very noble and gifted youths" (*nobilissimam et ingeniosissimam hanc iuventutem*) for the conversion of their country; and he warns his Prefects that they will have to answer to God for any negligence in their duties. When the bell sounds for the end of recreation, silence is at once to be observed, "not only because that is befitting, but in order that these boys, born and destined to distinguished service, may learn in their tender years the lesson of self-control". It became the custom that in the refectory—at the end of supper, according to Wadsworth—one of the disputants read in Latin the Martyrology of the morrow; and at the mention of any English saint all removed their caps and the passage was repeated.[24] Then the special English Martyrology[25] was read by a boy in the opposite "pew", and listened to with heads again uncovered. We have it also from Wadsworth—how he would have disliked to be quoted in such a connection!—that

[24] Custom Book, p. 49; Wadsworth, p. 16. From this and other rules it is clear that the boys wore some form of cap both inside and outside the house. Wadsworth (p. 12) speaks of "cassocks" and of hats "that might almost shadow all". Not a biretta at all events.

[25] This no doubt was the *English Martyrologe*, compiled and printed at the College Press by the Rev. John Wilson in 1608, the first year of the press. A second edition appeared in 1640 and a third in 1672.

the Vespers and the Litany of Our Lady, sung in the church on Sundays, were directed in intention towards England's conversion: and that there was "written on their Church and Colledge doores in great golden letters, *Iesu, Iesu, converte Angliam, fiat, fiat*".

Some of Fr Schondonch's regulations would be still familiar to Stonyhurst boys of the present day. Indeed, in some cases one might find him surprisingly modern. All sodalists, for instance, must learn to serve Mass; and "when at a Sodality Mass, all will say together according to custom in one tone and with suitable pauses (*per cola*) the Confiteor, Misereatur, Suscipiat, &c.". The fairly modern innovation of a "Dialogue Mass" at Stonyhurst and elsewhere is evidently but a revival of a former custom. The Holy Week services were very similar to what Stonyhurst boys have been used to for some 160 years. There were a few "Good Days", one such occurring on the feast of St John Chrysostom (27 January) for "the more skilled and more diligent in the Greek language". Another was for the "musicians" (*musici*) and altar-staff on 22 November, feast of St Cecilia. On such occasions they were freed all day from schools and sat at a special table at dinner where they were served, in addition to their normal portion, with one "antepast" and "postpast".

That brings one to the subject of food, so close to the heart and diaphragm of a boy. Did the Diaries or "Ministers' Journals" of the period survive—they were all confiscated at the suppression of the Society in 1773—one would probably be able to form a fairly adequate idea of how the boys were fed; for the Father Minister was the man responsible. For lack of them one can do no more than quote what Wadsworth had to say on the subject:

> Now let us come to the Collegiates or Students, and their diet. First they are served in by seven of their owne ranck weekely and by course [i.e. by rotation], and according to seniority each man hath first brought him a messe of broth which is the antepast: afterwards halfe a pound of beefe

which they call their portion, after an aple, or peece of cheese for their postpast, bread and beere as they call for it.[26]

The above is presumably just a specimen of a normal meal, including both antepast and postpast; for Wadsworth was unlikely to flatter either the diet or the Jesuits who provided it. Soup, meat of one sort or another, fruit or cheese, and presumably vegetables according to the season: on particular occasions possibly a pudding or something similar as an additional "postpast"; all this sounds likely, even apart from Wadsworth's statement. Much of it, no doubt, would be the produce of the farms on the Watten property, dispatched regularly by barge along the canal to within a few hundred yards of the English College. Breakfast consisted of "a peece of bread and butter, and beere as pleaseth him"—home-made beer, which we may be confident was not too strong or heady. Beer was the beverage, it seems, common to every meal; so was it in Stuart England, either beer or ale, at meals and not less in the intervals between them. Sobriety, as some one has observed, was not an English virtue. In a St Omers Catalogue for 1609 one of the nine Jesuit laybrothers is listed with the office of "Braxator" (Brewer) and "Pistor", which might mean Miller or Baker and in this case means probably both. The cook too was always a laybrother. After such a breakfast at 7 o'clock a boy might well be more than ready for his dinner four hours later. Only a rash man would attempt to gauge the limits of a boy's appetite: yet it would need a stalwart stomach to devour "a halfe pound of beefe" between antepast and postpast. Doubtless however Wadsworth was merely taking a flying guess at the weight; for he liked to be definite, even at the cost of accuracy.

Slovenliness was Fr Schondonch's *bête noire*, and dirt or untidiness appalled him. Everything must be done "modesté", with due decorum and in orderly fashion. There must be no slouching or bad manners during meals. The boys are to sit "erecto corpore"; and the Rector's presence with his Community at meals would have ensured the observance of his

26 Wadsworth, p. 19.

orders. Certainly vigilance in such matters was needful; for English table manners even in the later seventeenth century were atrocious. They went from Study Place to Refectory, from Refectory to Schoolrooms, from Schoolrooms to Study Place in crocodile fashion, two by two like animals into the Ark: and they went in silence, or so the rule prescribed. Fr Thunder was there to see to it. St Omers was in this but following the custom of the country. Everything too must be "mundissima", spotlessly clean, in Sacristy, Study Place and everywhere else. Classes are encouraged to vie with one another in keeping their respective sections of the Study Place tidy and free from every trace of dirt.

As to personal cleanliness one must take account, of course, as in other matters, of the standards of the age and country. We are not to think of modern hygienic standards nor of modern sanitation: but we are not writing of the Middle Ages —"the thousand years without baths", as Michelet once called them. One should remember nevertheless that water was not yet "laid on" to the houses nor to the town: it had to be conveyed laboriously from river or canal. Of baths there is no mention at all in Fr Schondonch's Custom Book, though it is impossible to conceive that the boys had none. The matter was perhaps left to be arranged by Fr Thunder. But it is likely that baths were not too frequent. At all events the boys were expected to come down from the dormitories in the mornings "washed and combed". On a later page the regulation is repeated: "Having washed their *hands* they proceed in silence to the Athenaeum". One must leave it at that, in hope that it was not just that and no more. There is incidentally a quaint rule concerning the dormitories, furnished with cubicles and curtains as is still the custom. No boy without permission may visit his dormitory during daytime; but "on certain days the boys may be allowed during the summer to cleanse their beds from fleas and vermin: such dirt is not to be tolerated in the household".[27] Vermin indeed! There comes to mind a passage

[27] Custom Book, p. 25.

in the Psalms—"non timebis a terrore nocturno", which Miles Coverdale instinctively translated, "Thou shalt not be afraid for the bugges by night". Admittedly this standard would cause a shock to any right-minded Government Inspector of these days. It was far otherwise in the seventeenth century. Indeed, as has been noted earlier in this chapter, the Jesuit Colleges in Belgium were considered superior in this as in some other ways to the "unhealthy and slovenly schools" of that period.

The story of Fr Schondonch's Rectorate would indeed be incomplete were no mention made of the Sodality of the Blessed Virgin Mary. A considerable part of the Custom Book is concerned with rules and instructions and suggestions for its well-being and efficiency. Thirty years before the foundation of St Omers a young Belgian Jesuit, Jean Leunis, was teaching the lowest class—Figures, presumably—at the Roman College. He it was who there first laid the foundations of what grew swiftly into a world-wide organization. His practice was to assemble some of his more devout pupils before they returned home (they were of course all external students) for the purpose of honouring Our Lady, Mother of God, by certain pious exercises. The idea quickly caught on: boys from other classes sought permission to join in the devotions. Within a year the number had grown to about seventy and some regulations had been found necessary.[28] The example of the Roman College was soon followed in other Colleges of the Society. In Belgium the Jesuit College at Douai claimed to have been the first in its Province to establish a Sodality (1572). Twelve years later, at the instance of the General, Claude Aquaviva, Pope Gregory XIII, by his Bull, *Omnipotentis Dei* (5 December 1584), gave a canonical status to the parent Sodality in Rome, the "mother and head" of all Sodalities of Our Lady, and placed it under the official charge of the General of the Society. Authority was given him to erect and aggregate to this Roman

[28] Mon. Hist. S.J.: Polanci Complementa, I. p. 471. The beginnings of the Sodality in Belgium are given by Poncelet, II, chapter xii.

"Prima Primaria" a similar Sodality in any or all of the various Jesuit Colleges and to communicate to them the privileges and indulgencies granted by the Pope to the Prima Primaria. The General's powers were extended in 1587 by Pope Sixtus V to all houses of the Society whether Colleges or not. The number of Sodalities was no longer restricted to one only in each house; a division of an existing Sodality into two or more was now both permissible and much needed.

It was in 1609 that a Sodality at St Omers was thus affiliated to the Prima Primaria. A copy of the Diploma of erection, printed in the later eighteenth century and still preserved in the Sodality Chapel at Stonyhurst, gives the date, 16 March. By this date, of course, most Jesuit Colleges, probably all of them, had established Sodalities for their students. Several of them, including the Walloon College at Saint-Omer (1582), had Sodalities even before the Bull of Gregory XIII: and after extended facilities were made available by Sixtus V, the number of Sodalities increased almost yearly. Why then was St Omers so late? The answer is somewhat obscure, although it may be surmised that the rivalry between the Walloon and the English Colleges may in part supply the reason. However that may be, one may read in the Annual Letters that "for many years" the Rector had petitioned in vain for leave to erect a Sodality; that at last, probably in 1607, the Provincial, Père François de Fléron, had given his consent; but that "since it could not be done in any other way he wished that all the boys be gathered into one Sodality". The Provincial presented the College with a statue of the Blessed Virgin, made of wood from the famous shrine of Montaigu, and with much ceremonial installed it on the altar in the Study Place. We are told that the increased devotion of the boys was such that at bedtime there were many who needed Fr Thunder's authority to move them from their knees before the statue and send them to bed.[29]

Nevertheless, if this "Sodality" included all the College

[29] Litt. Ann., 1606, 1607, 1608 (Moguntiae, 1618), p. 649.

boys, it was a Sodality only in name. The whole idea of a Sodality, of an association of carefully selected persons voluntarily dedicating themselves to a more perfect way of life, was thereby destroyed. Fr Schondonch, with his previous experience of Sodalities whilst Rector at Courtrai, must have been disappointed. He at least would have known the reason for this substitute of a Sodality proper, whatever it may have been. There was a very flourishing Sodality under the care of the Walloon Fathers: and it is not unlikely that it was for the sake of the Walloon Sodality and its claims of priority that Père de Fléron framed this compromise, hoping to satisfy both Colleges. In a somewhat similar situation at Liège a few years later, where "vested interests" were at stake, it was decided by the General that in the English Jesuits' Church the feasts of Jesuit Saints were to be publicly celebrated, not on the feast-day itself as at the Walloon Church, but on the Octave day or within the Octave.[30] That may have been the arrangement likewise at St Omers.

But if this be the explanation of Père de Fléron's action, he evidently knew not the ways of Fr Schondonch. How the Rector managed it is not recorded. But, as we have seen, some two years later, on 16 March 1609, there was established and affiliated to the parent Prima Primaria a Sodality in the fullest sense, under the title of the Assumption of Our Lady—a Sodality with which the present Sodality at Stonyhurst rightly claims unbroken continuity. Almost at once Fr Schondonch divided the Sodality into two. The First Sodality was open to members of the three higher classes, the Master of Rhetoric being its Director; whilst the two lower classes, Grammar and Rudiments, were eligible for the Second Sodality, directed by the Master of Grammar.

The Sodality, in Fr Schondonch's view, was no mere gathering of selected boys for the purpose of periodical prayer-meetings and the singing or reciting of Our Lady's Office. There were prescribed times for such, it is true. On Saturdays,

[30] Vitelleschi to Fr Knott, 24 October 1626. (Ep. Gen. I, f. 247.)

for instance, the sodalists met to recite together the Litany of Our Lady. Every Sunday, too, they assembled to form a kind of study circle on some spiritual topic proposed by the Director or the Prefect of the Sodality. Fr Schondonch gives several model conferences in brief, to illustrate the manner in which these various subjects might be expanded: in these meetings "every member should be ready to say what he thinks whenever he is asked for his views by the Father or the Prefect". Each conference, however, is to end in a practical "Resolution", whether the subject concerns the avoidance of sin, or good conduct (which includes good manners), or the study of Christian doctrine. He is not content with generalities but, like that well-known devout author, Alphonsus Rodriguez, he "descends to particulars". In the church, for example, the "Aula Dei", God's Presence Chamber, the good sodalist will be ashamed to kneel on one knee only, to come late to service, to fall asleep during the sermon, to talk to his neighbour, or to befoul the floor with spittle—this last a well-deserved reflection on contemporary Jacobean manners. The sodalist, in short, is expected to live a more perfect life, to be more alert to his own shortcomings and the correction of them, more sensitive to the presence of God and his gifts of grace, more appreciative of His Mother's help and protection. A few prayers were prescribed to be said on rising, and when going to bed three Paters and Aves, followed by the "De Profundis" for those who had died. Although they did not sing the Office of Our Lady they were enjoined to say it privately, at least on Sundays and festivals, "in Greek or in Latin as best suited them".

Much therefore was expected of a sodalist, even if much was left to individual effort and initiative. One should look for nothing less. And it must not be forgotten that the majority of the boys at this period were "church students", with the prospect of priesthood in due course and the English Mission. Incidentally a pleasant ceremony took place on the yearly occasions—usually 15 August, feast of the Assumption B.V.M. —when a party of youths set out for the seminaries in Rome or

Spain to begin their higher studies. After a very special meal
at a special table in the refectory they said their good-byes and
for some way were accompanied on their journey by the whole
school. Thereafter one of the Fathers continued with them
and, when reasonable, a few others—a brother, it might be, of
one of the travellers. These lodged with them on the first night,
returning next morning to the College.[31] Surely a pleasing and
practical gesture of comradeship.

Most, if not all, of Fr Schondonch's rules and recommendations for the sodalists were dictated during his last illness.
At one point of his dictation he evidently felt he was at death's
door. "What I think on this subject", he said, "I will here
dictate from my bed of agony, in which I was expecting today
that I would breathe my last breath." They were his views on
loyalty to King and Prince, well worth quoting if only they
had been expressed more briefly. Sympathy they deserve, says
he in effect, not harsh criticism nor reproaches. Evil counsellors
abound, and often a King is not his own master, to do as he
would wish to do. If Kings or Princes are hostile to Catholicism,
they need our prayers: when they receive the light of faith they
will see as we see. (The Rector's eyes are evidently on King
James.) If they command us to die for our religion, let us
readily obey. Did they have the knowledge that we have, they
would do no less.[32]

But whatever Fr Schondonch recommended to his sodalists
—frequent Confession and Communion, mutual charity, a
prudent choice of friends, and so on—all was focused on one
practical and impressive end, the conversion of England. And
that of course was a very "live" subject in the reign of King
James I, as it had been in the previous reign. Either as priests or
laymen the great majority of St Omers boys, sodalists or not,
would presently return to live in England or at least would
make the attempt. Both journey and journey's end were
perilous. These youths needed a robust faith, a fine courage, a
character well equipped to withstand the lure of appeasement,

[31] Custom Book, p. 200.   [32] Ibid., pp. 143, 145.

the temptations of flesh and blood. Surreptitious letters from home that had managed to reach their destination would tell them of the persecution, of the fines and seizures and imprisonments, if no worse, of their parents and friends—some of them, no doubt, like Fr Thomas Garnet, "Old Boys" of St Omers. The conversion of England was for them an immediate issue, a phrase to conjure with.

The aim of the youths being trained in this family is different from that of youths from other schools. The latter frequently have in view ecclesiastical or civil posts, such as may add to the honour of their parents' distinguished families or, if they are of lesser account, may win them renown. But the young men here, however noble be their families, look first and foremost to the conversion of England, each in his own degree. This indeed is why their friends have sent them there: in the first place that when they return home, where the Catholic religion and right living is so hotly persecuted by the heretics, they may stand strong in faith and stedfast in virtue. And secondly, that amid so much false doctrine which they will have to face in England, they may see the right path themselves and lead the way for others. In a word, it is piety and learning that they set themselves to acquire.[33]

This with much else was dictated to some unknown amanuensis during the last few months that remained to the Rector; and three years after his death it was neatly copied out by Fr Henry More, who himself was destined some thirty years later to occupy the same post of Rector. Fr Schondonch died on 28 January 1617. There survives an account,[34] written on the following day by the Rev. John Wilson, the secular priest who presided over the College printing press. The Rector had been in poor health for some two years, suffering from a combination of ailments of which asthma was one component. For many months he had had to keep to his room and latterly to

[33] *Ibid.*, p. 87.
[34] De obitu Patris Schondonchi (Audomari, 29 January 1617). A copy is in S. Arch., MS. A. IV. 12 (2), pp. 257-264.

his bed. Two or three days before he died the boys sent up a request for a last blessing from their well-beloved Rector. They were summoned to his room where for a good quarter of an hour, until his strength failed him, he addressed them, speaking of his love for England and of course exhorting them to virtue and hard work. The writer of this obituary goes on to recite the virtues and gifts which this exceptional Rector possessed in plenty. It may be more profitable to translate the only bit of autobiography which Fr Schondonch allowed himself in his Custom Book. For those who are aware of the unhappy contentions in England amongst some of the missionaries, secular and regular, which at this period were hindering the united efforts of the rest, the quotation may come as a surprise. His mind goes back to 1601, the year of his appointment as Rector.

Sixteen years have gone by since I entered upon this present office. Already I had heard talk of some dissension or other between certain members of the English nation. I summoned those in the house and asked them whether they knew anything of such quarrels. They too had heard that here and there were some who were at odds with one another; but with such they neither had nor wished to have any connection. Then said I: Then I too have found for myself here a haven of peace; for I detest such wrangling and quarreling amongst the descendants of the saints. So it has come about that during all these sixteen years I have lived here with the good Fathers of the Society as it were in Paradise. No national quarrels either in word or writing have found their way into this house or been mentioned.[35]

So passed a great Rector, a great character, at the age of about sixty-one. He had his faults, no doubt, and limitations —what man has not?—but they are unrecorded, in any case overshadowed by the fine work he so successfully performed in setting this English College quite firmly on its feet. He ran into considerable debt in the process, and continued to build and to

[35] Custom Book, p. 144.

buy until obedience forced him to stop. The prohibition was understandable, and the Rector's urge to share expenses with posterity was no less so. He was indeed a man of considerable resource and persistency of character, who would gently but firmly thrust his way through a crowd of difficulties till he reached his objective. On occasion one might almost be tempted to imagine that he suffered, as did Admiral Nelson, from the disability of a blind eye. What is quite certain is that he was not only a learned humanist but also and especially a devout and most zealous religious. The condition insisted on at first for political reasons by King Philip of Spain that St Omers must be governed by a native of the Netherlands must have been a sore disappointment to the English Jesuits concerned. Fr Schondonch at all events was a man after their own hearts: he loved the English, and it is not too much to say that they, both Community and boys, loved him. It was thus by great good fortune—which is a pseudonym for Providence—that St Omers was governed so long by a Flemish Rector. "The best and greatest Rector this College has ever known", wrote one of the Fathers in 1613; when one looks back on the long history of St Omers, there appears no reason to alter the wording.

5

THE FIRST ENGLISH RECTOR

THE obsequies of Father Schondonch were carried out with great solemnity—with too great solemnity, thought the General, although he recognized therein a testimony to the affection in which the late Rector was held by both Community and boys. Fr Joseph Creswell, still at St Omers, became the Superior for a few months until in April a new Rector was appointed.

This third and, as it turned out, the last of the Belgian Rectors was a man of about forty years, a Walloon, native of Lille, whose name has sometimes been given as Fr Philip Dentiers—as by Foley, in the wake of Dr George Oliver—but which perhaps was more probably Dennetiers. That at all events is the spelling in an old St Omers Catalogue for 1618-19, as also in the drafts of the General's letters addressed to him as Rector. Few Rectors would have found the post an easy one to fill in succession to a man of the calibre of Fr Schondonch. It does not seem that Fr Dennetiers was of those few. One burning question with which he had to deal was the nationality of the Masters. Aquaviva in 1614 had insisted on Belgian Masters and had persistently refused to alter this arrangement. When towards the close of 1615 the 7th General Congregation elected Fr Mutius Vitelleschi as his successor, renewed attempts were made to obtain the desired permission. It was in vain. The General was prevented, he said, by the 21st Decree of the recent Congregation, which disapproved of any tendency leading to exclusive nationalism. The new Rector soon found himself at odds with the English Fathers who were now asking that at least the Prefect of Studies should be an Englishman. Indeed, he wrote to the General in just the opposite sense, explaining that Belgian Masters would not easily submit to the orders of an Englishman. The Belgian Provincial wrote too, but using the same argument in favour of appointing a full English staff. The only result was a warm letter to the Provincial characterizing that particular argument as reprehensible. Let them look up the 21st decree of the 7th General Congregation. A year later the kindly Provincial, Père Herennius, returned to the subject. He asked if he might appoint English Masters for the upper classes, the plea being that the English Fathers needed "exercise" in poetry and rhetoric. Of course the General understood well enough the reason for these requests. The English and the Walloons did not mix successfully: they would be happier apart. But he felt that his hands were tied: there was that 21st decree of the 7th General Congregation. So he answered cheerfully that the difficulty was easy of solution: let the Provincial, if he wished, appoint English Masters for the upper classes of the Walloon College![1] The subject was not pursued. The problem however vanished next year when the "English Mission" of the Society, now increased to about two hundred members, was formally erected into a Vice-Province, becoming thus independent of the Belgian and other Provinces which had hitherto taken such kindly care of the English Jesuits. Fr Richard Blount, the local Superior of the Jesuits working in England, was chosen to be the first Vice-Provincial. This decision of Vitelleschi solved many problems; for the English Jesuit Mission had by this time grown out, as it were, of its more youthful clothes, and become at least semi-independent, with a noviciate of its own at Louvain since 1607, and a house of studies, later transferred to Liège. The death at Rome in December 1618 of Fr Thomas Owen,[2] the successor of Fr Persons as Prefect of the English Mission, may have helped to hasten the General's action.

Of the internal history of St Omers during Fr Dennetiers' rectorate there is not much to be recorded. Fr Creswell had

[1] Vitelleschi to Herennius, 29 July 1617; 12 August 1617; 29 September 1618 (Rom. Arch., Gallo-Belg., III, ff. 66, 70; IV, f. 86).
[2] Foley in his notice of Fr Thomas Owen (VII, 562) has sadly confused him with Fr Owen Shelley, whose brother was Cyprian Shelley, not Cyprian Owen.

been commissioned to do his best, as a competent man of affairs, to improve the finances of the English houses in Belgium, all of them apparently in debt. At St Omers, the most in need of him, he spent several years, with some excursions to Louvain and Liège: and his efforts met with at least partial success. It was in 1618 that Fr John Floyd[3] by wish of the General came to reside at St Omers as a controversial writer: and there he remained until his death more than thirty years later; a prolific author in an age of prolific religious controversy. Many a story was told of him, especially in his later years: one such is preserved by the anonymous author of *Florus Anglo-Bavaricus* (p. 51) to illustrate his absorption in his studies. With a candle in his hand he had gone to consult a book in the St Omers library. So intent was he on his research that he became oblivious to time and place and all things else. Meanwhile the candle in his left hand burnt lower and lower until the flame reached his hand. He did not notice it. In the event the nerve or muscle of his index finger was so burnt and contracted that never again could it be fully extended.

It was about 1621, so one learns from the Annual Letter of that year, that the Rev. John Wilson, the priest in charge of the College Printing Press, made himself responsible for the enlargement of the church, which already after only some dozen years had become too small for the growing number of worshippers. A chapel was added, dedicated to St Thomas of Canterbury, patron saint of the College, which almost doubled the seating capacity. The sacristy was enlarged; a larger room in the house was allotted to the sodalists and fitted up for their convenience; and a part of the grounds was enclosed by a wall and levelled so as to provide a place apart from the playground where the Fathers could recreate in peace. Not for the first nor for the last time, he added to his many benefactions by

[3] Fr John Floyd (*c.* 1572–1649) was one of the boys who began their education at Eu in Normandy. He joined the Society of Jesus in 1592, and subsequently became a learned theologian and controversialist with some twenty works to his name or pseudonym.

paying this year the cost of the prizes presented to the "first six" of each class or "school". Such generous donation of prizes was a common practice at the Walloon College, and it became no less common at the English College. Two years later it is recorded that the Provincial, Fr Blount, was the donor: and for the next twenty or thirty years at least the custom prevailed, the donors, probably for reasons of political safety, usually desiring to be anonymous.[4] Of those few whose names are given was Sir George Wintour of Huddington Court, the baronet grandson of that Robert Wintour who paid on the scaffold for his complicity in the Powder Plot. When a young man he had wished to become a Jesuit, and at a later period had intended to bequeath much of his money to the Society. Fr Blount and other friends dissuaded him from the former course: and as for the legacy, he died in 1658 leaving a debt of £4,000. Another donor was that devout and respected prelate, George Chamberlain, Bishop of Ypres, half English, half Flemish, evidently a friend of the English Fathers. The only other name mentioned is that of a certain "R.D. Joannes Carltonus", an English secular priest.

That same Annual Letter of 1621 ends with a lively story of a youth recently converted to Catholicism on the Continent, who returned after a while to his family in England, only to meet with the concentrated fury of his father. Angry expostulations met with no success: the youth remained firm in his newly-found faith. His father's temper, like certain inferior wines, did not improve with keeping. On a memorable occasion at dinner this irate parent, foiled in argument and losing all control, picked up a plate and threw it at his offspring —who nimbly dodged it. It was fielded possibly by the butler. Then the furniture came into action; for the father jumped up from his seat, drew his sword and chased his son around the dinner table with murderous intent. Chairs no doubt, flung in his path, impeded his progress until finally he was held back

[4] Registrum Audomarensis Anglorum Gymnasii (B.M. Additional MS. 9354).

by the attendant servants. The situation must have remained tense, even menacing, until the resolute youth quietly absconded, made his way across the Channel and sought and obtained admission at St Omers.

Vitelleschi had stipulated when erecting the Vice-Province that Fr Dennetiers should remain as Rector until such time as the Archduke should be willing to allow an English Rector to replace him. That arrangement was apparently not to the liking of Fr Creswell, a man whose ways were often unpredictable and not less so as he grew old. For one reads[5] of his making some sort of approach to the Bishop of Saint-Omer with a view to the Rector's removal from office. Naturally the General was not pleased when he was told of this interference, though not unduly alarmed. He trusted, no doubt, to the good sense of the Bishop, and did not trust in vain. Fr Dennetiers continued his rectorship.

The new Vice-Provincial began his first official Visitation of the continental houses a few months later, in the spring of 1620. Vigorous, downright, practical, courteous in manner, he won golden opinions from all he met. Both Provincials of the Belgian Provinces, after discussing with him their business, wrote separately to Vitelleschi in warm praise of him. The Vice-Province quickly began to take definite shape and rapidly to increase in numbers. England was divided by him into Districts—"Colleges" or "Residences" according as the number of Jesuit missionaries was greater or smaller—a Rector or Superior being placed over each. Scattered as they must needs be in various Catholic homes, the Jesuits had at least a Superior to whom they could now have more immediate approach in their perplexities and who in turn could supervise and direct their activities. In those troublous days this was the nearest approach to the regular life of a religious that was practicable in England. Only on the Continent was it possible to live a full community life.

It is Belgium that is here our more immediate concern.

[5] Vitelleschi to Floyd, 26 October 1619 (Ep. Gen., I, f. 114ᵛ).

To complete the organization of the new Vice-Province there was need of another establishment, in addition to a noviciate and a house of studies, where after ordination the Fathers would be able to spend their third or final year of noviceship—the Tertianship, as it is called—which precedes a Jesuit's solemn vows. The generosity of Lady Arundel, the pious and beneficent widow of Blessed Philip Howard, Earl of Arundel and Surrey, made possible the project. Vitelleschi's approval was given in the spring of 1621, and the House of Tertians began to function in the autumn of the following year. Various changes too of personnel resulted from Fr Blount's Visitations. Fr Creswell amongst others was moved, not unexpectedly, from St Omers, to become Superior at Watten, as yet no more than a residence. The appointment, one may note, was found to be not entirely suited to his age and health and character. Two years later, in the autumn of 1622, he went to Ghent, to be the first of a long line of Instructors of Tertians: and there he died in the following January.

Fr William Baldwin (1562-1632) is of greater interest. Towards the close of 1620 he was appointed Rector at Louvain, the house of studies that in another three years was to migrate to Liège.[6] Either late the next year or very early in 1622 he received another appointment as the first English Rector of St Omers College. For more than one reason he deserves some detailed mention. A Cornishman, with all that that implies, he had studied at Oxford and at Rome, where he was ordained in 1588 as a secular priest. Two years later he became a Jesuit novice in the Belgian noviciate at Tournai. In the January of 1595 we find him setting out for Spain in the company of a batch of six St Omers boys: his alertness in maintaining his disguise under the assumed name of Ottavio Fuscinelli has

---

[6] The theologians and philosophers from Louvain (pace Foley, VII, p. xlviii) moved to Liège, together with their Rector, Fr Owen Shelley, at the close of 1623, whilst the novices from Liège moved to Watten. General to Blount, 14 October 1623; ibid. to John Norton, 30 December 1623 (Ep. Gen., I, ff. 183, 187ᵛ).

H

been noted in a previous chapter. On this occasion his im-
prisonment in the Bridewell lasted but a few weeks. But in
1610, whilst on a journey from Brussels to Rome as Vice-
Prefect of the Jesuit mission, he was kidnapped by the Elector
Palatine, handed over to James I as a supposed accomplice in
the Powder Plot and confined for eight years in the Tower of
London. Banished from England at the instance of Count
Gondomar, the Spanish ambassador, he lived and worked in
Brussels until his appointment to Louvain. Fr Dennetiers was
now asking the General to be relieved of his office: at the same
time Fr Blount was suggesting the need of an English Rector
for St Omers. The General gave at once his consent, provided
however that the Archduke could be persuaded to sanction
such an arrangement. An "outstanding" Rector, he agreed, was
wanted for the post: he approved of Fr Baldwin as one fulfilling
that requirement.

It was not so much the Archduke Albert as the *échevinage*,
the town councillors of Saint-Omer, whence arose the opposition. The Archduke indeed, when approached by Fr Blount,
was not unfavourable to the idea of an English Rector for an
English community. On 25 June 1621 he wrote to this effect to
the Governor of Saint-Omer, asking him to ascertain the views
of the local magistracy. But meanwhile, it seems, rumours of
Fr Baldwin's nomination had spread through the town, and
the English residents—to say nothing of those at the College
—were delighted. Fr Blount had prematurely relieved Fr
Dennetiers from office and had appointed an English Jesuit as
temporary Vice-Rector. All this the town councillors considered as provocative: their consent was being presumed
before they had assembled to consider the matter. So they stood
on their dignity and fought the proposal tooth and nail. Their
main argument was based on a fallacy. They maintained that
in accordance with the Spanish King's letter of 4 March 1594,
the charge of the English Seminary must always be in the hands
of a Belgian Jesuit, a subject of the King. It is true that in a letter
of this date to the Bishop of Saint-Omer the King had men-

tioned such a condition, Spain and England being then at war:
but the "always" was a gloss of the town councillors. As Fr
Flack bears witness,[7] neither in the official letter of 4 March to
the Archduke Ernest nor in the "Letters Patent of the Foundation" of the following May (recapitulating the King's "whole
intention") is there any mention either of the nationality of the
Rector or of any limit to the number of scholars admissible.
Subsidiary arguments adverse to Fr Baldwin were based on the
danger to the town in wartime of an establishment entirely
staffed by Englishmen.

What impression these arguments made on the mind of the
Archduke Albert it is impossible to say. A few weeks after his
letter to the Governor, on 13 July, the Archduke died, and the
whole duty of governing the Spanish Netherlands devolved on
the Archduchess his wife, the Infanta Isabella. After a decent
interval Fr Blount repeated his request, supporting it with
varied reasons—an English Rector, for instance, would better
understand the scholars, would afford greater confidence to the
parents and would attract more financial aid to the College,
still in debt to the tune of 80,000 livres. Fr Baldwin, he added,
is "a man well known to your Highness". He was; and the
Infanta wrote handsomely in his favour in letters dispatched
both to the Bishop and to the Governor of Saint-Omer. But
the *échevins* only increased their protests. The English College
and grounds, they declared, covered an immense area, surrounded by high walls behind which five or six thousand
soldiers could easily be hidden. The 120 scholars were nearly all
old enough to bear arms. And there, but a few miles away, was
another English Jesuit house at Watten, from whose high
tower signals could be sent to an enemy fleet operating in the
English Channel. The thing was becoming childish. Eventually
—to shorten the story—the friendly Infanta wrote on 16
November to the Council of Saint-Omer that in this particular
case ("pour ceste fois"), knowing Fr Baldwin as she did, she

[7] Hist. Mem., pp. 16-17. The Letters Patent in this MS. are dated 19 May,
but the actual date appears to be 6 May.

dispensed the Father from any previous condition in force, and asked them to accept his nomination as Rector. Fr More adds to this her assertion that his qualifications were such that she would have no qualms in entrusting him with the whole administration of the Netherlands. At a meeting held on 14 December the town councillors accepted their defeat, whilst registering her own reservation that it was "seulement pour ceste fois et au regard du P. Beaudouin". Two years later Fr Blount endeavoured to induce the Infanta to make permanent what was as yet but a particular exception; but his success was not complete. Her Highness went so far, however, as to authorize Fr Baldwin by Letters Patent to make choice himself of the English Father whom he would wish to be his successor. Her diplomatic tact secured the result hoped for: the nationality question never again cropped up.[8]

Of events directly concerning St Omers College during Fr Baldwin's ten years of office not very much has come down to us. It must have been a short while before his arrival that some talk arose in the town as to the refusal of the College to admit a boy on the recommendation of "Dominus Personius", brother of Fr Robert Persons—perhaps that George Persons of whom we have heard in an earlier chapter. Two hundred crowns had been offered for the youth's education as an "alumnus"; and the reply had been given that "alumni" were not admitted at St Omers but only "convictors", i.e. such as paid a yearly fee for their board and lodging. It "seems unworthy of the Society", wrote the General when he heard of the incident. And so it was, if in fact this was the whole story: the family of the Founder had surely some claim to be heard. Yet the Rector, presumably Fr Dennetiers, was but obeying, although somewhat woodenly, an order issued six years earlier by Vitelleschi himself, that in view of the heavy debts incurred

---

[8] For the details cf. Bled, pp. 13-18; H. More, p. 378; Vitelleschi to Blount, 24 April & 21 August 1621, *ibid.* to Baldwin, 8 January 1622 (Ep. Gen., I, ff. 136ᵛ, 143ᵛ, 150).

by Fr Schondonch no "alumni" were in future to be admitted until the College should become solvent.[9]

The College was still in debt. Fr Blount, as has been said, put the debt at 80,000 livres, or about 8,000 Jacobean pounds. The main cause was the chronic failure of the Spanish pension granted by Philip II and his son. It was a situation that repeated itself over and over again during the next century and a half. Nevertheless the number of boys the College was able to support remained fairly satisfactory. To give such statistics as are available: whereas in 1610 there were 135 boys (about twenty had left that summer for Rome or Spain, but forty-eight had been admitted), in 1620 the total "was greater than usual, especially towards the end of the year". Four years later, in 1624, the number is reported as being less than in the preceding year: it was "under 140 in all". Twenty-four had left for the higher studies—admittedly an unusual number: eight "convictors" had gone to join the band of lay philosophers at Liege, and seven had joined the Jesuit noviciate at Watten. Thus thirty-nine at least are accounted for as having left during the autumn vacation, whereas not more than thirty had entered the College. From the point of view of numbers St Omers reached its apogee in 1635 when 200 were on the roll-call for some months: but the war on the Continent and increased persecution in England soon reduced the total again to about 140.

Great hopes had been entertained on the accession of Charles I that the persecution of the Catholics would die down. In spite, however, of his marriage contract Charles was forced by Parliament—not too unwillingly just then, exasperated as he was with the French entourage of the Queen—to approve a "Proclamation for recalling his Maiesties Subjects from the Seminaries beyond the Seas, and putting the Lawes against

[9] Vitelleschi to Blount, 22 January 1622 (Ep. Gen., I, f. 150ᵛ); Arch. of Eng. Coll. Rome, Scritture 6-20, "Coll. Audomaren. 1616", dated 2 January 1616.

Iesuites and Popish Priests in execution" (4 August 1625).[10]
Three years later, in 1628, the penalty decreed against persons
either going or sending children to the continent, there to be
"Popishly bred", was forfeiture for life of all goods and chatels,
lands, rents and so forth (3 Car. 1, cap. 2). But even at the close
of his old father's reign, when the "wooing" of Spain was
changed resentfully to war, together with an increase at home
of the tempo of official repression, the effect on the number of
arrivals at St Omers was noted in the Annual Letter of that
year. As it chanced, six or seven youths accepted by the
Rector were intercepted that summer of 1624 and imprisoned.[11]

It may have been noticed that the flow of students from
St Omers to the seminaries was still considerable. Twenty
would perhaps be about the average number travelling each
year to Rome and Seville and Valladolid. In 1610, as we have
seen, the number was "about twenty". But there were exceptional years, as in 1613, when "forty more or less of the alumni
were sent this year to Spain and Italy, and only slightly fewer
were for health's sake sent back to England". One may suppose
that this latter course was followed partly for the sake of the
financial health of the College; for Fr Schondonch by that date
had fallen deeply into debt. And yet, adds the annalist, "I have
scarcely noticed any loss of boys in consequence". In spite of
constant vigilance at the English ports, newcomers—presumably "convictors", paying the full fee—were almost as many as
ever. In 1621 twenty-four youths went off in August to the
seminaries. The total for that year is given as "nearly 120": but
such totals are deceptive since they probably represent the
numbers present, not at the close of the school year, but at the
end of the calendar year.

In the following year, 1622, there were twelve students who
set off from St Omers for the seminary at Seville. Thereby
hangs a long tale, told by one of them in about 30,000 words and

[10] Cf. Gordon Albion, *Charles I and the Court of Rome* (London, 1935),
p. 79 note.
[11] Litt. Ann., 1624 (S. Arch., A. IV. 13 [1], p. 350).

by another, James Wadsworth no less, in little more than 3,000.[12] The accounts in bare substance agree, but Wadsworth varies very considerably in the details, often colouring his narrative, as one might expect, to his own taste and advantage. The anonymous author, more direct and objective, inspires far greater confidence. The experiences of that voyage were evidently too much for Wadsworth's waning faith. When at last they reached Seville, "taking my leave I left them, being not willing to tast any more of their discipline". This future pursuivant apart, the anonymous narrative, often vividly told, is of considerable interest as a commentary on that colourless statement, so constantly repeated, that such and such a number "was sent this year to Spain to pursue their higher studies".

The ages of these twelve students ranged apparently from about eighteen to thirty-four; an indication indeed of the indefinite age-limit laid down by Rectors in these difficult times. They set out from St Omers on 7 August, reaching Calais the same day. Whilst waiting to sail they took the opportunity of purchasing a stock of provisions for the voyage, as a supplement to the ordinary fare provided by agreement with the Captain. An ample supplement it would seem: "mutton pies, turkey pies, live turkeys, capons, pullets &c, with manchets, wines, strong waters, preserves, Conserves, candies, and many comfortable spices for makeing brothes and sauces". A welcome change, no doubt, from the antepasts and postpasts of the College. Their ship was a "Dunkerker" of 200 tons, Captain John Collatt, with a crew of twenty-two "tall fellowes for service and guards", being armed with fourteen pieces of ordinance, two "Murderrers" and the customary small arms. Their vessel formed part of a fleet of eight ships that sailed down the English Channel, all flying the French

[12] S. Arch., *A Relation of the Journey of 12 students from the English Colledge at St Omers in Artois to the English Colledge of Seville in Spaine An. Dni 1622 stylo novo*. This is a MS. of eighty-three foolscap pages in a hand probably of the later seventeenth century. It has been printed in the *Month* (with certain omissions) for December 1879, January, March, July 1880. For Wadsworth's account, see *The English Spanish Pilgrime*, pp. 30-42.

colours. A week or so later, off Cape Finisterre, a Dutch man-of-war hove in sight, concentrated its attack on the Dunkerker (whilst the rest fled) and captured it after a valiant resistance. The Hollanders, famished after some weeks of rationed bread and water, proceeded to make short work of the youths' stock of provisions. However, when discovered to be English, the youths themselves were kindly treated and, though robbed by the crew of most of their money, they were transferred to another captured ship and allowed to proceed on their journey. They had now to live on bread which was calculated, says the writer, to have gone mouldy and been rebaked several times during the past three or four years, and on a pittance of water "such as even now I abhor to describe". As a luxury they were allowed the occasional delicacy of a "gnawne beef bone". There ensued a violent storm, vividly described: by the time it had subsided their ship was within a day's sail from Plymouth.

September 1 found them again in the vicinity of Cape St Vincent, tired to death of the sea and in some danger of death for lack of food and water. They had been driven at times to sip sea-water, but soon discovered that "it both searched our entrails and augmented our thirst". Here they were stopped by the flagship of a Dutch fleet. The Admiral, however—a man "like some rich-nosed brewer in his red cap and waistcoat"—after some questioning, allowed their ship to continue on its way. Two days later they reached harbour, under the fort of Cape St Vincent.

The Lord had further trials for these poor youths. Their request to land was refused: another day's sail, they were told, would see them at their journey's end. Scarcely had they left harbour when they were captured by a small Turkish vessel, without resistance of any sort; for the captain and crew were Anabaptists and fatalists. Prevented by weather from passing through the Straits of Gibraltar, the Turks decided to make for "Sallee" (Salé), a nest of pirates on the west coast of Morocco, a few miles north of Rabat. The troubles of the "Twelve Apostles", as they had jeeringly been called, were at this time not so much material as moral. The food, for instance, though coarse was now plentiful. But what utterly upset them was the attempt of a perverted Turk to satisfy his unnatural lust. On a second occasion, after he had contrived by false accusation to have the youths chained hand and foot, he might have accomplished his foul purpose had not their wild shouts brought down the watch to investigate. In the event the Turk was made to feel the rope's end and the youths were freed from their fetters.

At Salé the question arose, were they to be considered as prisoners awaiting ransom or as slaves? With the help of a kindly lawyer the matter was settled, at least in theory, by the local Governor. The twelve were all Englishmen, the King of England and the town of Salé were bound together by treaty, and therefore the twelve were not to be treated as slaves. A ransom of 1,000 Barbary ducats, or £300, was agreed upon. Eight of the students were to travel to Spain and four to remain as pledges for the ransom. Later, on good advice from one who knew the Turkish tricks, it was decided that all must leave together, else the four left behind would never gain their freedom. It must suffice here to say that after nearly a month of varied adventure a French Catholic merchant, factor for a firm in Cadiz, took them aboard his ship, which on 8 October managed to slip out of harbour under cover of darkness. This Frenchman, already gravely ill when they sailed, was put ashore at the small town of "Marmora", a Spanish enclave, where a priest was in time to visit him before he died. After many hazards and escapes from one pirate after another they reached Tangier on 28 October. Previously, when in fear of Turkish pirates they had anchored for some days at a place named "Marache" (probably "Larache", El Araish), Wadsworth and another of the students, Peter Edwards,[13] tired of such delays,

---

[13] The Valladolid Register (C.R.S., XXX, p. 146) makes it clear that the Peter Edwards of the MS. (p. 60) is the *alias* of Amesius Eveleigh. Wadsworth, giving the "true names" of the twelve, calls him "Evely". This student turned up at Valladolid, already ordained at Seville, in 1627, and,

left the others "without even a farewell" and made their own
way to Spain.

Passing over the renewed sufferings of the ten students,
the scarcity of food and especially of water, and what the
author thought to be a cunning way of catching some of the
"vermin" (lice, to be precise) that so bothered him, we find
them presently at Gibraltar. Once on Spanish ground, which
they kissed in exuberant joy, they decided to trust the sea no
more but to travel to Cadiz by land. This they did, although
they had not reckoned on their feeble state of health which
barely survived the journey. Cadiz they reached on 9 November after five days of travel. Here they interviewed John Bravo
de Laguna, the principal of the firm for which the kindly
Frenchman at Salé had acted as factor. Loans made to these
ten at Salé and at Gibraltar were duly settled by means of
another loan from the British consul. But of the £300 ransom
John de Laguna had no record, though his books recorded the
sums paid for about 150 other prisoners of the Turks. There
were other indications too that the French factor had paid the
equivalent of the ransom out of his own private purse. The rest
of the journey was made in comparative comfort. On 14
November 1622, fourteen weeks from their setting out, "we
arrived at our long-desired home, the College of St Gregory,
in the street called Calle de las Armas at Seville". How many
others had experiences of a like nature of course one cannot
tell. These certainly were not the only students to be captured
at sea by the Turks or predatory Moors, though their stories
may not have been written up in such close detail. Drastic
adventures of this sort must have served as a very realistic
introduction to what so many were later to endure in the
English mission field.

Fr Baldwin had been Rector but a year when on 21 January
1623 the General wrote to Fr Blount announcing that the

strangely enough, began again a course of philosophy. Four years later he
became troublesome (*inquietus*) and was dismissed. Cf. C.R.S., XXIX,
p. 217.

English Vice-Province had now become a Province and that Fr Blount was to govern it as Provincial. This was no mere change *honoris causa*, nor had it been brought about without considerable preparation. Early in his Vice-Provincialate Fr Blount had taken the necessary preliminary step of gaining the consent of the Archduke Albert for uniting the English Jesuit houses in his territory to a "foreign" Province. Both the Archduke and, after his death in 1621, the Infanta Isabella had expressed their favour and support for the scheme. In the spring of 1622 Fr Blount summoned an assembly of forty Fathers at the French Embassy in Blackfriars to draw up a Memorial to the General giving reasons for their petition to be erected into a Province. It would indeed be difficult to think of any reason for such a step which this local "Congregation" omitted to mention. Nothing that the Society of Jesus according to its Institute required for the erection of a Province was lacking. The number of subjects was steadily growing and by now was as much as 240, of whom 190 were priests, including 56 professed Fathers. The numbers in England and in Belgium were almost equal, with the difference that those in England were all priests, whereas on the Continent those preparing for the priesthood were about as many as those already ordained. In addition to the continental establishments, three "Colleges" or "Districts" had been financially founded by anonymous benefactors, and others were promised as soon as assurance could be given that certain current rumours were untrue. Here was a strong point for the petitioners. For a report, says the Memorial, is being spread abroad by some enemies of the Society, both clerical and lay, that the Vice-Province so recently erected is no more than an experiment, that the English Jesuits are not considered as genuine sons of the Society, and that at the latest when the General, Fr Vitelleschi, dies, the experiment will be abandoned. Nothing will more adequately prove the falsity of such rumours than the erection of the Vice-Province into a full-fledged Province. Of the generosity of benefactors some lines are worth quoting. Although the benefactors were mostly

English families, the Belgian houses at St Omers and elsewhere were in due measure deeply indebted to these generous friends.

> Nowhere have benefactors shown greater love towards the Society than those whom we have in England, especially when we consider that they could give nothing at all to the Society without running the risk of losing their lives and of confiscation of all their goods. And yet, notwithstanding the danger, they have not ceased to do good to the Society during the whole course of the persecution. Their resources were drained by constant payment of fines; they were forced, amongst other burdens, to pay two thirds of their yearly income for professing their faith and to support themselves and their families with the third part alone; and they needed also to make many presents (so many as to be scarcely credible for those who lack the experience) in order to buy off the harassing visits of pursuivants and countless other officials. . . . These benefactors not only have received the Jesuits into their houses and provided everything that was needed, but also have founded houses for the Society, first of all in a foreign land, and then in England itself, with a boldness almost beyond belief and in the teeth of difficulties far greater. . . . Indeed it is certain that there are many benefactors, each of whom has lost on account of the Society enough to found an excellent College. . . .[14]

No doubt this Memorial was inspired if not actually written by Fr Blount, whose experience of the English scene extended already to more than thirty years of missionary work. It was taken to Rome by the elected delegate of the assembly, Fr Henry Silisdon,[15] who arrived there in November. In the following February he returned to Belgium in company with

---

[14] A translation of the Memorial (from Rom. Arch.) is given in a privately printed periodical, *Letters and Notices*, vol. xviii, pp. 344 seqq. Cf. H. More, pp. 445-6, 450.

[15] Fr Henry Silisdon, *veré* Bedingfeld (c. 1583-1659), was at this time Rector and Master of Novices at Liege, whence at the close of 1623 he moved with his novices to Watten, holding the same post until 1632. He was subsequently appointed Provincial (1646-1650).

Fr John Gerard, bringing with him the formal reply to the Memorial he had presented.

Even before the assembly of the Fathers in April 1622 it had been decided that the Vice-Provincial (as he then was), living of necessity in great secrecy in England—it still remains a guess where exactly were his headquarters—was too remote from Belgium to be able efficiently to govern directly the two halves of the Province. There was always considerable risk at the ports of being suspected and arrested as a priest. That the Provincial should run a double risk when making his yearly visitation of the Belgian houses was justly considered an unnecessary danger. A "Vicarius", or Vice-Provincial as he soon came to be called, was appointed, who should take charge of the houses in Belgium as the Provincial's delegate, though in due dependence under his higher authority. The first to fill this office was Fr Silisdon. It became evident, however, that the duties of a Rector and Master of Novices were incompatible with those of a Vice-Provincial. So a year later another capable Father was chosen to succeed him, Fr Edward Knott,[16] who for one reason or another did not cross over from England till the close of 1624. This arrangement did not hinder the Provincial from visiting the continental houses from time to time when he saw fit to do so; for Fr Blount was not only a brave but also an astute man, more than a match for any pursuivant. During almost half a century of missionary life he never once was caught.

In view of the difficulties of communication between England and the Continent it was likewise decided that one of the Jesuits in London, in addition to his other work, should act as agent for St Omers College. His duties were more than those of a recruiting officer: he managed too some of the finance of

[16] Fr Edward Knott, *veré* Matthew Wilson (1582-1656), was already a priest on entering the Society in 1606. He was twice Vice-Provincial in Belgium, for the second time (after three years in the Clink) from 1632 to 1634. He was also twice Provincial, 1639-1646 and 1653-1656. A number of controversial works were the product of his learned pen. "The most learned man in England", said George Con in 1637 (Albion, *op. cit.*, p. 278).

the College, school fees in particular. For many parents it was
easier and far less dangerous to pay their debts to this agent
than directly to St Omers. Incidentally it was also easier, no
doubt, in this way to secure in some cases a prompter payment
of the fees.

An important addition to the social life of St Omers was a
country house (known as a "Villa House"), yet another gift of
that generous "Maecenas", the Rev. John Wilson, head of the
St Omers College Press. It was a small property of a little
under four acres, situated some three miles from the College
in or near the village of Blandecques. It was acquired in 1626
—a house and garden with a fish pond, a large orchard and
meadow "watered in one part by a river and on another side
protected by a foss or ditch".[27] The river Aa—that same mono-
syllabic river which here curves westward to flow past the
walls of Saint-Omer—ran close behind the house. A convenient bathing place there may have been, if bathing was
allowed: and being plentifully stocked with trout, the river
may well have supplied an extra "portion" to the boys'
dinners according to the skill and success of youthful fishermen.

It has been said that only during the summer months did the
boys spend their monthly whole holidays at Blandecques—or
Blandyke, to give the place its anglicized name. Thus Fr
Gerard in his Centenary Operetta, *Oliver Cromwell and his
Table*—

And once a month in summer-time, but not in winter
      weather;
'Tis there we play the live-long day, and take our sport
      together;
Blandyke its name, and ever the same we gratefully remem-
      ber;
Blandykes come round, as they are bound, from April to
      September.

It is not worth making the small point that summer-time at St

[17] Litt. Ann. 1626 (Foley, VII, 1164): *Stonyhurst Magazine*, January 1882
(Vol. I, pp. 73-75).

Omers, at least in Fr Schondonch's day, began in May, not in April. Fr Gerard is applying to the St Omers of 1648 the evidence which, as shall be seen, is derived from a Liege Journal of about 1780. In point of fact there is no available evidence to show that the custom of St Omers in this respect remained unchanged for so long a period.

It seems reasonable at least to suppose that the boys went there on occasion during their short summer vacations and on various "Good Days". It is possible that they spent their weekly holidays and their monthly holidays likewise at Blandyke. One must leave it at that. By the time that the College in its series of migrations had arrived at Stonyhurst in 1794, a Blandyke had changed both in name and in fact into a "Month Day". But after several decades the older name survived, and still survives in a truncated manner, a Blandyke being now a far rarer event than of old.[18]

Under the year 1631 Fr Julius Caesar Cordara[19] has noted that at St Omers a "new Sodality" had recently been formed; and he quotes at some length an enthusiastic appraisal, written by one of the Fathers there, of the resulting increase of fervour and devotion to the Mother of God. In point of fact there was no question of a new Sodality, but of newly revised rules for the existing Sodality, drawn up in 1629 and confirmed over the signature of the Rector, Fr Baldwin, on 7 September of that year. These rules, seventy-five pages of them, are an addition to the Custom Book of St Omers, so frequently referred to. It would seem that the Sodality rules or customs previously in

---

[18] In 1925 the length of the Easter Vacation was increased and several Blandykes were omitted by way of compensation. As to the name, it has been argued with much probability that "Blandyke" (the Flemish "Blandijk" = White Bank) rather than "Blandeques" was the name commonly used at this period. Flemish was spoken at Saint-Omer up to about the end of the sixteenth century.

[19] J. C. Cordara, s.j., *Historiae Societatis Jesu Pars Sexta*, Tomus II, p. 514 (Romae, 1859). This volume, still in manuscript at the suppression of the Society, was lost but finally found in Bavaria and published with some additions by Fr Ragazzini, s.j., more than seventy years after Cordara's death in 1785.

vogue were considered to be of too general a nature to be altogether adequate to the conditions now prevailing at St Omers. Had the first fervour perhaps begun to show signs of wear? Fr Schondonch had adopted the rules drawn up by Aquaviva for general use, without making much use of the permission "to make particular Rules which for the varietie of countries or persons every Congregation should think most convenient" provided that they were consonant with those general regulations.

Thus the Preface. The Director of the Sodality—likely enough that devout man, Fr Francis Foster, a future Master of Novices and Provincial—would probably have been the prime mover, but assisted and urged on by the officials of the Sodality, that is to say, the Prefect, Assistants, Council and others. The Director's part is fairly evident in the Preface, but the voice fades out, so to speak, at its end, and we are given only the names of his cooperators; "The most unworthy servants of our B^d Ladie, ye officers at this present of her holy Congregation: *Prefect*—Richard Walwine: *Assistants*—William Worseley, Jhon Manners: *Secretarie*—Raph Russell: *Consultours*—William Watson, William Gaskin, Henry Harcourt, George Smith, Jhon Cooper, Peeter Whittaker". In addition to these were two representative sodalists apiece out of Rhetoric, Poetry, Syntax and Grammar. One may note that of the two Grammarians one, "William Waring" (Barrow was his real name, and Harcourt another *alias*), born at Weeton, near Kirkham, and baptised on 10 March 1608/9, became a Jesuit and a victim of Titus Oates. He was martyred at Tyburn in June 1679 and was beatified, as Blessed William Harcourt, by Pope Pius XI in 1929. All these boys were allowed to be present "at ye receaving of ye Rules and customes which immediately followe". These were ceremoniously handed over to the Sodality by the Rector at the end of his Mass on the eve of the feast of Our Lady's Birthday.

The rules in question are copious, minute, even meticulous; unsuited in some cases to the modern sodalist, although

1. Fr Robert Persons, s.j. Founder of St Omers
from an old print

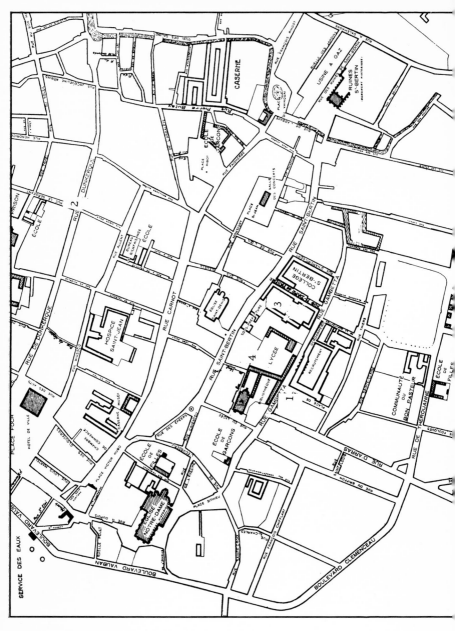

2. Modern Street Map of Saint-Omer

(1) Maison de Bergues: "Mr George Persons' corner house", on Place de l'État.

(2) Rented house in Tenne Rue (Rue de Dunkerque). Rue Le Sergeant did not then exist.

(3) St Omers College. Printing Press and Church, now the Sous-Préfecture.

(4) Walloon Jesuit College: now Lycée, Bibliothèque and shell of Church.

L'Église Notre-Dame was a Cathedral until the close of the eighteenth century.

seemingly they were to the liking of these seventeenth-century officials who shared in their making. But the details are not likely to interest the general reader. It is noticeable that the Prefect of the Sodality is given very extensive authority: he would seem to have been only something less than a Head Prefect or "Head of the Line". Evidently there was a tightening up of discipline. Recruits for the Sodality were most carefully selected, with the result (says Cordara's informant) that there was considerable competition to gain the votes required for admission. If any sodalist was observed to give bad example, he was (apart from the normal College discipline) publicly reprehended at a Sodality meeting: if he showed no signs of improvement he was expelled from the Sodality. There were those, we are told, who would voluntarily perform some public penance at these meetings, or who would ask the Director's permission for private penances—penances that sometimes transgressed the bounds of prudence. Thus a party of sodalists, we read, had recently asked the Rector for leave to make a pilgrimage *nudis pedibus* to a shrine of Our Lady six miles distant from the College. Permission was granted for the pilgrimage but not for the bare feet.

The Rules, as has been said, were drawn up for the particular benefit of the St Omers Sodality: they were "proper" rules in the Latin sense of that word. In and out of study time, in the Study Place ("when they pass *through* the studie place they must allwayes keep their hatt of"), in the Refectory, in the dormitories, in fact wherever they may be, there are rules or earnest suggestions for their behaviour. Even their personal appearance is provided for. After ordaining that a sodalist who is known to have become an idler at his studies must be admonished, perhaps given a penance by the Director, and at the last resort, if no amendment ensues, be suspended or even excluded altogether from the Sodality, the rule continues:

The same also is to be observed with thos who without expresse licence from Superiours shall presume (contrarie to the order of this Colledge and not without greate signe of

J

vanitie) to nourish long locks, and weare theyr hayre cutt of an extraordinarie fashion.

But however detailed or harassing some of these rules may now seem to be, it is reasonable to suppose that those who framed them knew well enough the capacities and limitations of those for whom they legislated. And from every account that is extant one gathers that the rules justified themselves in their result. The spirit of Fr Schondonch's apostolic zeal was still abroad, and was welcomed by many a subsequent Rector or Director, not least by Fr Baldwin who gave these rules his approval and his blessing.

Fr Baldwin's eleven years as Rector were for the most part uneventful. The troubles and dissensions which at this period were agitating the Catholic body—and not least the Jesuits—in England seem to have found no echo at St Omers. There was no particular reason why they should. If the Rector was criticized it was on account of a "nimia facilitas", as Vitelleschi put it, an over-indulgence to the boys, inducing a certain relaxation of discpline. It may have been so, though there was always Fr Thunder in the offing, whose weighty presence would have done much to restore the balance. As the years passed the Rector's health began to fail. He had led an adventurous life, had suffered much during his years of imprisonment in London, and he was growing old and prematurely feeble. Younger men, with younger ideas, critical as always of the *status quo*, were replacing their elders. Amongst the latter Fr Flack, now nearing seventy, who had watched the growth of St Omers from its cradle, was moved in 1629 to Ghent, to become Rector of the house of Tertians. The assignment proved less successful than had been hoped, and after three years he returned to St Omers, ending his life there in December 1637 at the age of seventy-six.

But he made history before he left Ghent. On the night preceding the feast of Blessed Aloysius Gonzaga, 1632, he was at death's door and suffering excruciating pain from a disease of stone, entailing a total stoppage of function. The doctors had no remedy to offer: all he could do and did do was to implore his friend and fellow novice, the Blessed Aloysius—already beatified, though seven years his junior in age—to alleviate his almost intolerable suffering. Early next morning, which was 21 June, after a General Confession in preparation for death, he made a vow, at his confessor's suggestion, to present to the chapel a well-beloved reliquary (*lipsanotheca*) in his keeping, if only he might be relieved of some of the pain. His friend responded generously. Within the space of an Ave Maria Fr Flack was, so to speak, delivered of two large stones, and the pain at once subsided. An hour later he was in the chapel giving thanks to God and his benefactor. The news of course reached Vitelleschi, who wrote more than once for a full report from Fr Flack and others.[20] Everything that would help to establish the miracle he wanted, for preservation in his archives—not the stones, of course, but the accounts concerning them.

It was in 1629 that with the cooperation of Fr Baldwin the General was able to bring to an end what was a more or less amicable dispute between the two houses of Liege and Watten. It deserves some notice, if only on account of a local shrine once famous but now no more than a memory. The subject of dispute was what on both sides was then regarded as an authentic and wondrous relic, the hair of the Blessed Virgin Mary. The sumptuous reliquary containing the hair had come to Watten in 1097 as a gift from Clemence Countess of Flanders, wife of the crusader Count Robert II, who had brought it back from Jerusalem. The Canons of Saint Augustine had built a church and had dedicated it to Our Lady in honour of the relic: it had become in the course of centuries a famous place of pilgrimage. But by the time that Bishop Blaise handed over the Abbey to the English Jesuits the church was little more than a ruin, the pilgrimages had gradually ceased. This ancient relic he gave, it would appear, to Fr Schondonch, who in his turn presented it to Fr John Gerard, then resident

[20] Fr Flack's own statement is printed in More, pp. 461-2.

at the noviciate in Louvain. Fr Gerard was always partial to
relics. When the Jesuit noviciate moved in 1615 to Liège, Fr
Gerard and the relic went with it. But it did not return home
to Watten when the noviciate moved thither: it remained at
Liege, perhaps a present from Fr Gerard, himself no longer
there. *Hinc illae lachrymae*. The Jesuits renovated the church,
and the local inhabitants wished to renew the pilgrimages.
A worthy lawyer of the name of Morael or de Morales, a
former *Maire* of Watten, made himself the spokesman of the
would-be pilgrims and interviewed Fr Silisdon, the Rector
there. A long correspondence followed between the two
Rectors; Fr Robert Stafford maintaining the "rights" of Liege
against Fr Silisdon, behind whom loomed the fiery Watten
lawyer, with much to be said for his demand that the relic be
returned to Watten, its home for centuries. The question
presently became more urgent, for de Morales, exasperated,
was threatening legal proceedings. Both parties appealed to the
General, Vitelleschi, who after due enquiry decided that the
relic must be quietly conveyed to St Omers, whence it was to
be taken by Fr Baldwin to Watten and restored to the church.
An affidavit, *in verbo sacerdotis*, dated 16 July 1629, declared
that Fr Stafford had handed over the relic, and the whole relic,
to Fr Baldwin, who was present at the signing and added his
own signature. The latter returned quietly with it to St Omers:
but the rest of the journey was delayed until 8 September. It
proved to be far from quiet.

By request of de Morales and his supporters a public procession, so dear to the Belgian heart, was organized. Printed
leaflets were distributed by them in the neighbouring villages,
announcing the date and time of the procession: and they
asked especially that the College boys should accompany the
relic to Watten. This they did: it was Our Lady's birthday and
a whole holiday. Down the Rue Saint-Bertin they went, a short
distance to the water's edge, where they embarked on barges
suitably draped for the occasion. Thirty or more vessels had
come onto the river to greet the relic on its approach to
Watten. There they landed, and the procession moved on to

the parish church at the foot of the hill, where High Mass was celebrated, probably with the St Omers choir in full throat. Thence with more chanting they climbed the winding road up the hill to the noviciate which crowned the summit: and so at length the relic came to rest in the former Abbey church.[21]

Although the pomp and circumstance were not to the General's liking (he had expected the restoration to be quietly arranged and carried out), yet he expressed his admiration of the piety and the devotion shown to Our Lady by boys and populace. What were the General's views—or Fr Baldwin's, for that matter—as to the authenticity of such a relic one will never know. The wise man will withhold judgment in such a matter until he had a basis of good evidence before him. What we do know is that both these Jesuits were emphatically keen to promote devotion to the Mother of God, of which this relic was at least a symbol.

In 1631 the General was looking round for a successor to Fr Baldwin. The latter's memory was gradually weakening, the work was getting rather too much for him. Not that anything had gone wrong. On the contrary, the Rector was paying off some of the debt on the College, the number of boys was increasing—three years after his death the total had risen exceptionally to 200—and the General was congratulating him on the flourishing state of discipline and studies. Nevertheless, he thought, a new Rector seemed called for, and in February 1632 it was settled that Fr Thomas Worsley would be the best choice. Thanks to Fr Baldwin's charm of manner and his friendship with the Archduchess, the succession of an English rather than a Belgian Rector was not challenged. At this date Fr Knott was on his way back from England. He had gone there "for his health's sake" early in 1629, had been intercepted at an English port and had spent some three years in

[21] MS. History of Watten ("Compendiosa Narratio" &c. ut supra), ff. 69, 71-72: Baldwin to Vitelleschi, 21 July & 27 October 1629 (S. Arch., Anglia IV, nos. 78, 79): Vitelleschi to Silisdon, 22 December 1629 (Ep. Gen., f. 307ᵛ).

prison. English prison life, he learnt, was a poor substitute for a convalescent home. He now resumed his post as Vice-Provincial in Belgium, and after visiting St Omers declared his opinion that Fr Baldwin was still fit to continue as Rector; that his eminent services to religion, past and present, constituted a strong argument for his retention in office. Fr Baldwin, however, settled the matter himself a month or two later by departing for heaven. He died on 28 September 1632, evidently to the great regret of his Community.

He is memorable as the first English Rector of St Omers. Unlike Fr Schondonch, he had had little experience of boys and College life until his appointment to this College. He had lived an active life and in his time played many parts—including the part of "Ottavio Fuscinelli". A slippery fellow, thought his captors in 1610, who took him from Heidelberg to Juliers, west of Cologne, with a heavy chain wrapped round and round his body, his right arm only free. A further precaution was another heavy chain, six yards in length, that trailed behind him, so that an assistant was needed as a kind of train-bearer. Adaptable by nature and by grace, he soon settled down at St Omers, proving an efficient and at the same time a most kindly Rector.[22]

---

[22] Fr John Morris, s.j., a very careful historian, criticizing an article in the *Stonyhurst Magazine* (IV, 932 seqq.) in a brief and characteristic letter to the Editor, Fr Gerard, wrote: ". . . how funny for the writer [Fr Gerard himself], and Br Foley before him, to turn Fr Baldwin into his phonetic *alias* Bawden" (16 November 1892).

6

THEATRE AND PRINTING PRESS

THIS chapter is after the manner of an interlude, inasmuch as it deals with subjects not easily fitted into the more or less chronological sequence of this history. It is concerned firstly with music and drama, and secondly with the beginnings and the development of the St Omers College Press.

What was the musical reputation of the College in later times one cannot say, for scarcely one of the few surviving documents of those days refers to the subject. It is to the rectorate of Fr Schondonch that one must look for the reason why St Omers so quickly achieved fame, both in the town and far beyond, for its musical and dramatic performance.

The oft-quoted Custom Book of St Omers College (p. 27) enumerates four music "halls". The first, over the Refectory, was mainly for singing or for stringed instruments. The second and third were set apart for the teaching of psalmody and Gregorian chant: whilst the fourth room, apparently a room connected with the theatre balcony ("aula pensilis supra theatrum"), was reserved for those learning instrumental music. On Sundays and feast days the full orchestra practised for an hour in the morning, from 9 to 10 o'clock. Its members would obviously form a select body of proficients. From singing practice whenever it occurred no boy was allowed to absent himself without permission, especially during the half-hour after dinner (in winter after supper), with Fr Schondonch present to encourage the singers, perhaps also to conduct the singing.

Of instrumental music Fr Schondonch has a good deal to say that deserves quotation: indeed, his enthusiasm leads him far beyond the bounds of a code of rules. And, as will be noticed, the list of the instruments used by this orchestra of the first decade or two of the seventeenth century is itself of considerable interest.[1]

1. The music of the viols alone—the "whole consort" as it is called—is highly to be esteemed and the students are to be carefully trained in this.

2. But the combination of instruments of various kinds, called in English the "broken consort", is much more delightful for the reception of guests and persons of distinction, especially if the tunes are well chosen and pleasant.

3. In the broken consort these are the more suitable instruments:

> The bass viol, or viol da Gamba,
> The lute or, wanting this, the orpharion,
> The treble viol,
> The zither,
> The flute.

Add a tenor viol (violina) and a bassoon for greater effectiveness and charm.

4. The music of wind instruments is full of majesty, especially for Church services, for the reception of persons of high rank and for the theatre. Such instruments are the hautbois, which is well suited to boys as it does not overtax them, and the recorder. But the former is more majestic.

5. Other wind instruments demand more lung-power, such as the sackbut and the cornett.

6. One may recommend too the instruments with metal strings, to be plucked, not with a plectrum as the zither, but with fingers and thumb; such as the orpharion, the psal-mallett, recently invented in England and presented to us by the inventor, the Irish harp (if there is some one who knows how to play it), and the Italian theorbo, which has strings of gut.

7. Besides these, the organ and the harpsichord are well suited and add grace to church music.

[1] Custom Book, pp. 29-30. The translation is taken, with a few minor changes, from W. H. McCabe, "Music and Dance on a 17th-Century College Stage," pp. 314-15 (*Musical Quarterly*, xxiv, July, 1938).

Thanks to the encouragement given in both vocal and instrumental music, St Omers soon became almost a fashionable resort of visitors, so the Annual Letter of 1609 tells us.[2] But many came from sheer love of good music whenever choir or orchestra was to be heard: and such occasions, even apart from the Church's liturgy, must have been rather more frequent than a modern Prefect of Studies would care to countenance. Processions there were in plenty, reception of distinguished guests, who were no less plentiful, and of course the various plays performed in the course of the year, especially the great "actio" in August at the close of the scholastic year.

An incidental result of this popularity was the gift of new instruments. Amongst others there is mention in this same Letter of 1609 of a unique instrument presented by an unnamed English gentleman, no doubt the psal-mallett referred to above. The donor was the inventor, who had had it made and insisted that it should be the only one of its kind. Seven years earlier in 1602 one reads of two other gifts; an organ "of considerable value", presented by Bishop Blaise, and a harpsichord, the English donor of which preferred to remain anonymous.

Before the arrival of Fr Schondonch, apart from a vague reference or two, there is record of a minor play or "dialogue", of which the script strangely enough is now to be found preserved among the Salisbury archives at Hatfield.[3] It was "a brief dialogue, exhibited on the feast of St Thomas of Canterbury [29 Dec.], patron of the English, in the year 1599 at Saint Omer". This dialogue, written of course in Latin, is stated to consist of a prologue, nine short scenes and an epilogue.

With the advent in 1601 of Fr Schondonch St Omers got quickly into its stride. Within a year the College made a hit with a tragedy perhaps entitled *Humphrey*—at all events about a Mercian General of the name of Humfredus who, according to Bede, refused to confess his sins and died in despair. As was

[2] S. Arch., A. IV, 13 (3), 361 seqq.
[3] Hist. MSS. Comm., MSS. of the Marquis of Salisbury at Hatfield, IX, 420.

usual, the author would have been some Jesuit on the staff. The play was produced in honour of the new Bishop of Arras who for a month had been at the College, making the Spiritual Exercises of St Ignatius in preparation for his consecration: and its success was such that it was repeated a second and apparently a third time.[4]

Amongst other visits of distinguished guests the Annual Letter for 1604 records a visit of the "Vice-Admiral of England" together with the Duke of Frias, Constable of Spain, who was negotiating a peace with England. They were entertained at dinner and for their delectation a small play of some sort was acted in the refectory during the meal. They were delighted, so we read, with both play and dinner: it was at least a novel experience for them. At the end the Vice-Admiral raised his glass "ut mos est patriae", and proposed the health of King James, to which the boys would no doubt have given a loyal response, presumably in small beer.[5]

To what extent music had a part in these early productions is not clear. But that it had some part at this period, as it certainly had in later years, may perhaps be inferred from Fr Schondonch's reference to the music of wind instruments as being suitable "for the reception of persons of high rank and for the theatre". In connection with the reception of distinguished guests one must remember that music and acting entered into the Jesuit system of education. So it was from the beginning and so it has ever been. That may account, at least in part, for the frequent occasions on which choir and orchestra were called upon to display their talents. Geographically Saint-Omer was an obvious stopping-place for those travelling to and from the Continent by way of Calais; and for Englishmen especially, though by no means exclusively so. The fame of St Omers was an added attraction. Hence, as has been said, a fairly constant stream of visitors, clerical and lay, statesmen, scholars, soldiers and others, both Catholic and non-Catholic. The cost of

[4] Litt. Ann. 1602, printed at Antwerp, 1618, pp. 684-86.
[5] Ibid., 1604, p. 683.

entertainment added not a little to the mounting debt incurred by Fr Schondonch in his varied projects—a debt which was increasingly a source of worry to his Superiors, but which seemingly worried Fr Schondonch not at all.

When, in October 1609, the Papal Nuncio in Flanders, Archbishop, later Cardinal Guido Bentivoglio, spent a whole day at St Omers, he sent to Rome a most flattering report of his visit. He had come, as he told the boys, in obedience to the express wish of the Holy Father who was deeply interested in the preservation and increase of religion in England. It was for him a full day: Mass, followed by a procession[6] to the accompaniment of singing voices; in the afternoon a formal concert; later an address to the boys in their study-place; supper in the refectory, enlivened by an impromptu debate in Greek and Latin between four selected youths; and after supper "I was again entertained with sacred music, to my infinite delight". That he was greatly impressed is very clear. "During the whole of my visit I truly seemed to be in Paradise and among angels", he wrote. And he was not, as might be thought, an old man "dreaming dreams" (as the prophet Joel expressed it) but a young man seeing visions of the probable destiny of many of these boys—"persecution, afflictions and martyrdom". Though already a Papal Nuncio he was but thirty years of age.

Perhaps one may be pardoned for adding another quotation from this letter, even if it goes beyond the scope of this chapter: for such first-hand impressions derived from visitors to the College are all too scarce.

> The Rector is a native of this country, and he rules these youths with the utmost charity, discretion and wisdom, and is regarded not so much as a Superior as a father. . . . These

[6] In the procession, he writes, "I wore a cope that once belonged to King Henry VIII, and which is preserved here as a rich and rare memorial" (Bentivoglio to Card. Borghese, from Saint-Omer, 18 October 1609; cf. Foley, VII, 1153). If this is the cope well known to connoisseurs as the Henry VII cope (Henry VIII apparently took this and other copes with him to the Field of the Cloth of Gold) it reached St Omers at a very early date in the history of the College.

youths may be said to be the flower of the English Catholics: many are noble, and some are sons of heretics or at least such as through worldly policy only, exteriorly follow the times, and for their creed worship their own temporary interests. Among the rest I saw a youth, son of the King's private secretary. His father, although passing for a heretic, nevertheless provides amply for his son's education here under the name of his mother who is a Catholic lady. Many more parents who are true Catholics do the same. . . . I conclude my letter by recommending this Seminary to your Eminence's protection with all my heart and soul.[7]

That the St Omers theatre knew no language other than Latin is not entirely true. In 1613 was staged *The Triumph of the Cross* with full costume and elaborate scenery. The subject of this sacred tragedy was the loss of the True Cross and its recovery by the Emperor Heraclius—a favourite theme in many of the Jesuit Colleges on the Continent. What was unique in this production at St Omers was that it was not written in Latin but in English: "omnia Anglicé", says the Annual Letter.[8] The success of an English play produced before a mixed audience of Englishmen and Belgians would be difficult to gauge. No other instance is recorded of such an exceptional departure from the rule set down by Fr Schondonch himself in his Custom Book.

There was however no ruling against the production of Greek plays: and it would have been unlike Fr Schondonch to neglect an opportunity such as the stage provided of promoting the study of Greek. So on the arrival in September 1612 of Don Rodrigo Calderon, ambassador extraordinary of the King of Spain to the Archdukes, he was welcomed to the College with a Greek play, the name of which is not stated.

Une comedie en grec qui estoit en substance les Erreurs et heresies du Roi d'Angleterre, lequel enfin par la misericorde de la Vierge Marie, et des Saints qui ont floris et esté mar-

---

[7] Bentivoglio's letter (as above) is partly translated in Foley, VII, 1152-55.
[8] Litt. Ann. 1613 (S. Arch., A. IV. 13 [1], 263).

tirisez en Angleterre, se retourne au giron de l'esglise abjurant ses Erreurs et recoit absolution.[9]

This too seems to have been an experiment that was not repeated.

An experiment of quite another kind was made during the Lent of 1614 when scenes from Christ's Passion were represented in the College church in the form of *tableaux vivants*. Above the high altar, perhaps on a temporary platform, was enacted in dumb show each Sunday evening an appropriate scene.

> On the first Sunday, dressed suitably in red clothing and wearing a beard ... one of the boys represented our Lord in the Garden, praying and agonizing. He said no word but, without any affected mimicry, he portrayed the trembling, the weariness, the sorrowing of Christ, raising his hands heavenwards or folding them or moving them about: thus most expressively did he instil into the minds and hearts of the spectators a sense of this sacred passion.

And so on the following Sundays might be witnessed the betrayal of Christ, the scourging, the crowning with thorns, the carrying of the Cross, and finally on Palm Sunday the crucifixion, or rather, the nailing to the Cross. In the opinion of the saintly Father Feck this series of "live" scenes increased the devotion of the College boys no less than of those who crowded and over-crowded the Church on those occasions.[10] This experiment too was not, it seems, repeated, although something of the same sort took place in connection with the Lenten sermons of 1630 in the church at the neighbouring village of Watten, and with equal success. Half-empty benches soon became full: the large church was packed to the doors.

Both Church and State were pleased to honour St Omers College with their interest and approval. The visit of the Nuncio at the express wish of Pope Paul V was a great event

[9] Hendricq, *op. cit.*, II, pp. 426-7. The date was Thursday, 13 September 1612. In this year he says there were 160 boys at the College (*ibid.*, p. 349).
[10] Fr Thomas Feck in S. Arch., A. IV. 13 (1), pp. 230-1.

in the life of this young College. No less an occasion and probably more exciting for the boys was the visit in the autumn of 1625 of the Infanta Isabella herself, King Philip II's daughter, and now, since the death of the Archduke Albert, the sole sovereign or governor of the Spanish Netherlands. She had come on official business to Saint-Omer, accompanied amongst others by the unpopular Cardinal de la Cueva and the Genoese General Ambrogio Spinola, the two most powerful servants in the Netherlands of the Spanish King. The Cardinal sang Mass in the College church with choir and orchestra in fine fettle. Two days later came the Archduchess, with Spinola and a galaxy of nobles in her train. After Mass they were shown round the College, doubtless by her friend Fr Baldwin in person. They were present later at an elaborate masque, the *dramatis personae* of which included most of the College boys. The masque was evidently written for the occasion, the prosperous reign of the Archdukes Albert and Isabella being thinly disguised under the classical allegory of Saturn and Astraea.

Cardinal de la Cueva had been unable to be present, and at his request the masque was repeated that same evening for his sake. The Cardinal arrived in company with the Bishop of Saint-Omer and some of those who had already attended the previous performance. Rather characteristically the Cardinal demanded yet a third performance—a request which Fr Baldwin felt it impolitic to refuse. Three days later therefore, having again said Mass in the College church, the Cardinal dined in the refectory and in the afternoon attended this repetition of the masque. At dinner, it is recorded, he asked that he might witness one of the customary debates in Latin and Greek. He himself proposed the subject to be debated and was lavish in his praise of the manner in which the debaters fluently acquitted themselves of the task.[11]

In the Jesuit theatre the plays, as has been noted, were normally in Latin and home-made, written by one or other of

[11] Cf. Foley, VII, 1162-64.

the masters. It was the master of Poetry, occasionally of Rhetoric, who was responsible for at least the final "actio" of the school year, in early August. But besides this "tragoedia solemnis" with its accompanying Distribution of Prizes to the first six of each class there were lesser occasions for less solemn performances—the *comoedia*, the *declamatio*, the *dialogismus* and so on, acted some with costume and scenery and some without, some in the theatre and some in the class-room, as prescribed by the *Ratio Studiorum*. These lesser plays were produced in connection with the several "Compositions" or written exams, each of which resulted in a revised order of places in class, read out by the Prefect of Studies and introduced by a well-known formula, "quod felix faustumque sit"—a formula that survived at Stonyhurst as late as the early twentieth century. These plays, or at least the more important of them, took place usually in the afternoon but occasionally in the evening with the aid and at the expense, one must presume, of innumerable candles.

As in other Jesuit schools, so at St Omers there was always a religious, supernatural background to these plays, more or less prominent according to the character of the play and the skill of the composer. The themes chosen were taken from the Bible, from the lives of saints and martyrs, from pagan antiquity and Christian sources. It has been noticed that at St Omers the history of the Byzantine Emperors proved a useful and much frequented quarry. More obviously the playwrights made use of English or British history. The Venerable Bede and even such "modern" sources as Camden or Stow were requisitioned to provide material for plots. *Rosa Candida et Rubicunda* (1623), lamenting the fate of King Henry VI during the Wars of the Roses, *Odoardus Varvici Comes*, or Edward Earl of Warwick (1642), which deals with the rebellion of Perkin Warbeck, and *S. Augustinus Angliae Apostolus* (1653) are examples taken at random.

Beyond a doubt both drama and music were educational in purpose. The plays were written to exercise the actors in Latin, declamation, gesture, deportment and so on. Quite important and yet secondary was the artistic quality of the production. And at the back of it all, as of course in every branch of study, lay the intention, the endeavour to instruct the boys in their religion and increase their interest and devotion—to prepare them, in fact, for life, present and future. Needless to say, the utmost care was taken to safeguard the morals of players and audience. Presumably with this in view the *Ratio Studiorum* of 1599 forbad the impersonation of female characters on the stage. To this regulation exceptions were sometimes allowed in special circumstances; but one does not hear of any exceptions of the kind being asked for or granted at St Omers. In fact this restriction continued for some three centuries and embarrassed the Stonyhurst stage for many a decade, when home-made plays had given way to presentation of the works of English playwrights.

If all this solicitude for the purity of morals, however good in intention, appears to the modern mind as excessive and uncalled for, it must at least be remembered that Jesuit drama in its origin was a much needed reaction to the scandalous uncleanness of the fifteenth-century stage in many countries, even in such quarters as the Papal Court of Leo X and other renaissance Popes. The Jesuit decision to write their own plays involved the obvious disadvantage that a master, however good a scholar, might be an inferior playwright. No doubt the authors of the *Ratio* foresaw the problem and chose what seemed the lesser evil. The problem is comparable to that which forces a decision whether to adapt a building to an entirely different purpose or to build afresh from the foundations to one's heart's desire. For the study of the classics in school the *Ratio* almost of necessity adopted the former course. Hence various editions of the classics either expurgated or partly rewritten. For the theatre the second alternative seemed preferable. And if the success of this venture during at least the first hundred years of the Society be a guide, one gathers that the right alternative was chosen. Incidentally it is to be observed that the "modern mind" or the "public opinion" of a post-Christian society, whatever one may understand by such terms, is not of necessity the fittest or final arbiter in the field of religious and moral education.

With few exceptions, as for instance when in 1624 at a day's notice the Rhetoricians wrote and staged a play to greet the Governor of Artois, the authors were Jesuit masters. The minor plays and "dialogues" were usually written by masters of the lower classes. But it should be noted that normally a new master, whatever his abilities, was put in charge of the lowest class and continued in subsequent years to teach the same set of boys. Five or six years later he would be teaching Poetry or Rhetoric and probably entrusted with the task of writing and producing the "Grand Action" at the Prize-giving in August. This system whereby a master "went up" with his boys had of course its disadvantages, from either point of view. For the master it had at least a certain pedagogical value; and incidentally he was thus provided with the opportunity of becoming practised in the art of writing plays. At the worst there were other masters who might be called upon to come to the rescue.

Fr McCabe has made a provisional list of nearly a hundred plays produced in the course of St Omers' history, and some others could be added.[12] With one exception they are Latin plays—a language that presented no particular difficulty to the boy actors nor to many in the audiences of those days. But there must also have been many others whose Latin was either rusty or non-existent. These would have had to be content with what they could see and appreciate, the glamour of the scenery which was often quite elaborate, the skill and grace of the actors, the dancing, and the programme with its "argumentum" describing tersely the plot in Latin, but sometimes translated into French. It says much for the popularity of the St Omers theatre

---

[12] Twenty-two seventeenth-century copies of these are in S. Arch., MSS. B. VII, 23; B. VI. 10, 22, 23. There are others elsewhere, e.g. three MS. plays by W. Banister, s.j., in the B.M., Addit. MS. 15204, which can all be dated 1664.

K

that even the larger hall was often too small for the townsfolk who at times struggled in vain to find standing room.

Very few of the authors can be identified. Before he was ordained Fr Maurice Newport (*veré* Ewens), a minor poet, was responsible for a tragedy in 1641, but the subject is not mentioned. So too a certain "P(ater) Clarcus" in 1623 and again in 1655. Best known, however, as a playwright was Fr Joseph Simons, who published five of his tragedies in 1656 at Liège[13] where he was at that period Professor of Sacred Scripture. Indeed, one of his plays, *Zeno*, attracted the attention of the anonymous author of *The Imperial Tragedy*, published in London in 1669, a play very obviously adapted from the Jesuit Latin original, although with omissions and such additions as the introduction of female characters and a slight love interest.[14]

Fr Simons' known plays were however written and produced at St Omers at an earlier period, during the rectorship of Fr Baldwin. He was teaching at the College for four years, from 1621/2 to 1624/5, when three of his tragedies were produced, one of them, *Theoctistus*, at the close of a school year. He returned later in 1629 or 1630 after ordination to be Prefect of Studies for two or three years. In 1631 *Zeno* was staged at the August Distribution of Prizes. Much of his later life was spent at Liège as Professor of Philosophy, Sacred Scripture and Theology in turn. We shall meet him again as Provincial in England in Charles II's time.

Three of these printed plays, as their titles suggest, make use of Byzantine history for their plots. *Vitus* tells the legendary story of the boy saint, patron of actors and dancers—invoked too, one gathers, against such diverse and distressing cases as

---

[13] Josephi Simonis Angli, *Tragoediae Quinque* (Leodii, 1656). Reprinted in 1657, 1680, 1697. The five plays are *Zeno* sive Ambitio Infelix, *Mercia* sive Pietas Coronata, *Theoctistus* sive Constans in Aula Virtus, *Vitus* sive Christiana Fortitudo, *Leo Armenus* sive Impietas Punita. Fr Simons' real name was Emmanuel Lobb. Foley and others persist in calling him Simeon or Simeons.

[14] W. H. McCabe, *The Imperial Tragedy* (Philological Quarterly, XV (1936), pp. 311-314).

over-sleeping and madness of man or dog—whose death in the days of Diocletian is commemorated on 15 June. Staffordshire provides the background for *Mercia* with its simple plot, derived from Stow's Annals and from Camden. All except *Vitus* are stated to have been staged likewise at the English College, Rome. *Zeno*, evidently the most popular, was acted "at Rome, Naples, Bologna, Parma, Spain and elsewhere, many times" before this first edition of the plays was printed.

Zeno provides a good example of the manner in which music served the purposes of the playwright. It begins with music ("clangentibus tubis, tympanis sonantibus"); there is a dumb-show or "Scena Muta" in two places, an Interlude between each of the five Acts, there are songs and dancing. In this respect it is more musical than are the other four plays, two of which are without Interludes: but without doubt the musical tradition in the College was fully recognized and strengthened in these and other less-known plays. As Fr McCabe has observed, music in Fr Simons' plays was employed both incidentally, as in the Interludes and occasional ballets and songs, and also structurally, where the music contributes to the dramatic framework of the play, as in the musical dumb-shows and certain other ballets.

Of the actual musical notation for the plays produced at St Omers there is, if we mistake not, but one surviving example. It is to be found in a manuscript of *Zeno*, being the notation for the brief song of a boy-lutenist, sung at the bidding of the dejected Longinus, seated in his tent.

> Astrorum jubar
> Mundo salubres fundit ex alto faces:
> At si minaces igne sanguineo comas
> Trahens, Cometa regnet, heu quantum solo
> Instat malorum. (Act II, sc. 1.)

So too did the boy Lucius in Shakespeare's *Julius Caesar* (IV, 3) sing and play to the humour of Brutus in his tent. But that Fr Simons was influenced in any way by contemporary

English drama or by Shakespeare in particular is quite uncertain.

Some decades later we come across the name of William Banister, the only other playwright whose name appears to be preserved. His real name was Selby, of the Biddleston family in Northumberland. Educated, as was Fr Simons, at St Omers, he was master of Rhetoric in 1664—probably in the school year of 1664-5. His three plays, *Jephte*, *Andronichus* and *Perseus et Demetrius* all bear the date of 1664, which must be the calendar year, since the last of the three was produced at the August Prize-giving when the author would have still been master of Poetry. After a year or so at Liege studying theology he returned in bad health to St Omers (or "Flamsteed", as his uncle, William Blundell the Cavalier, calls it), and died a month or two later at Watten in December 1666, not yet a priest. There is no wisdom in supposing that these three plays are better or worse than those that are anonymous or that have not survived. But it is a relief to come across a name. Anonymity bears always a maimed, truncated appearance, lacking the completeness and responsibility provided by a full title-page.

There can be no denying that some of the St Omers plays, interwoven as they were with music and dancing, must have been unduly long. One recalls a note in the Walloon Diary under October 1612, when in honour of a new Abbot of St Bertin a comedy was produced at the English College. The diarist added the cold comment that it lasted from three in the afternoon until nearly half-past seven! Complaints on this score in succeeding years finally induced the Provincial, Fr Blount, to issue in 1631—a few months before *Zeno* was acted that August—a series of "Observanda" which he wished to be strictly followed.[15] The regulations were mainly concerned with the length and the number of the plays.

Tragedies and comedies, he declared, were not to exceed two and a half hours or three at the very most. He was asked to allow at least the "Grand Action" in August to be an exception; but he was obdurate. For lesser plays ("declamatoriae actiones")

[15] Custom Book, p. [25] seqq.

he considered an hour and a half amply sufficient. This was interpreted or "annotated" seven years later by the succeeding Provincial, Fr Henry More, as meaning that the maximum of three hours including everything—Interludes, ballets and incidental songs and music—whilst the play itself, stripped of its accidentals, might occupy two hours or preferably less. The limit set for less solemn occasions should be understood in a similar fashion.

As for the number of plays of lesser account, it was enacted that six plays might be—in fact, must be—produced in the course of the school year in addition to the "Grand Action" in August. For each of the six were assigned definite months and definite classes responsible for the production. To three of them the general public might be invited: the other specified three were for home consumption.

There is much too concerning the "declamationes", into the details of which it would be tedious to enter. The chief interest is to discover the connotation of that term—a far-reaching term which might be applied to almost any exercise of oratory. It included the "dialogues" or debates in the refectory, already described, and somewhat similar exercises carried out in the classroom as if in a law court, the remainder of the class criticizing or acting as a jury. Sometimes a boy would recite his own composition in prose or verse before his critical audience; or he would declaim a passage from a Latin poet or from a speech of Cicero. As for the "declamatoria actio", it was something of a hybrid—a single scene, it would appear, perhaps set off by some simple scenery, and performed by not more than seven boys. The emphasis, however, was heavily on the oratory rather than on the acting.

There was thus for these minor oratorical exercises a wealth of choice, as may be gleaned from a perusal of the rules of the various masters, from Rhetoric downwards, as detailed at considerable length in the *Ratio Studiorum*. The general purpose of these frequent exercises was not only to cultivate the art of oratory or poetry but also to form the habit of self-help. In a carefully graded system the boy had to learn whilst growing up; not just to sit back and imbibe information from his master, but very actively to educate himself under his master's direction and supervision.

The St Omers College Press now claims our attention.[16] It was to some extent a "secret" press in as much as the volumes issued bore usually either no imprint or a faked one. It continued the series of presses that began in 1580 at Greenstreet House, East Ham, with the printing of Fr Persons' *Brief Discourse* and two other of his works carrying the false imprint of "Doway by John Lyon". Next year appeared Campion's famous *Decem Rationes*, printed at "Cosmopolis", an ingenious *alias* for the Hall at Stonor Park, buried deep in the woodland of Oxfordshire.[17] Thence to Rouen where Fr Persons, with the help of George Flinton and later of Stephen Brinkley, established a press that lasted for perhaps four or five years. Here, besides a few other books, were published the first two editions of his *Book of Resolution*, later re-named *The Christian Directory*, reprinted innumerable times in the course of the centuries.

There followed a lull as it were, lasting for twenty years or more, during which period most if not all of the Jesuit books destined for England were printed either at Antwerp or in the town of Saint-Omer where François Bellet since 1602 had been granted a monopoly of the printing trade. His business, however, was so seriously injured when in 1608 the English College set up its own printing press that in the following year, his trade with England now practically lost, he moved his printing works to Ypres.

It has been told already how towards the close of 1608 that

---

[16] Much of what follows is derived from a series of articles by Fr C. A. Newdigate, s.j., "The Printing Press of the English College at St Omers", contributed to a private periodical, *Letters and Notices*, Vols 27 & 28 (1922, 1923). And cf. (by the same author) *The Library*, 1920 (July & October) and 1926 (December).

[17] Cf. R. J. Stonor, o.s.b. *Stonor*, pp. 243 seqq.

kindly prelate, Bishop Blaise, on one of his many visits to the College, was shown the new "print-house"—"a small house with a printing press together with all accessories, which we have recently set up and certainly very handsomely".[18] Whether it was Fr Persons in Rome or Fr Schondonch who originated the idea is uncertain and of no great importance. One may be sure that once the project was afoot, they both were enthusiastic to make the venture a success. Of course that meant far more than installing a press in a suitable and convenient building. All sorts of transport difficulties had to be overcome. Knowledgeable and trustworthy agents were needed at Antwerp and some more southern ports. Captains of coastal vessels must be induced to run the risk of landing illegal cargo on the English coast. And of course there remained all the complexities of distribution to select booksellers or agents in London and the provinces. The illegality could probably have been construed from one or other of the Elizabethan Acts of Parliament. In any case by virtue of an Act of 1605 (3 Jac I, Cap. 4) the importation, printing, buying or selling of any Popish books written in English involved seizure and was punishable at the rate of forty Jacobean shillings a book.

St Omers was most fortunate in securing a competent man to take charge of this department. For the best part of forty years the College Press was in the hands of Mr John Wilson, a Staffordshire man who at the age of about twenty-seven, and apparently a convert to Catholicism, entered the English College, Rome, in November 1603, was ordained during the March of 1605 and three months later left for the English mission-field in accordance with his College Oath.[19] The only other piece of information concerning his earlier life is that whilst at Rome he acted as secretary to the Rector there, namely to Fr Persons.[20] That however is interesting, for it explains the choice of this secular priest as a suitable manager of the St Omers Press. It must have been on Fr Persons' warm

---

[18] Litt. Ann. 1608 (S. Arch., A. IV. 13 [3], p. 381).
[19] C.R.S., Vol. 37 (*Liber Ruber*), p. 133.   [20] H. More, p. 248.

recommendation that Fr Schondonch placed him in this responsible position. The terms on which he was engaged are unknown.

The press must have begun its work many months before the premises were so proudly shown to Bishop Blaise. It may well have started in 1607, for at least five works issued from this "print-house" dated 1608, and no slender volumes at that. Besides two books in quarto in reply to King James I, one by Bellarmine, the other by Persons, there was a third of similar format—a "sturdy volume" it has been well called—wherein under the pseudonym of "John Brereley, Priest" an enlarged edition of *The Protestants Apologie for the Roman Church* spread itself over 850 pages and a little more. That book was not printed in a day! By 1608 too John Wilson himself had compiled and now printed his *English Martyrologe* with a Supplement comprising an important catalogue of English martyrs from the days of Henry VIII to the time of printing—just in time to include as his last entry the name of Fr Thomas Garnet, protomartyr of St Omers, who was hanged at Tyburn on June 23.

The heyday of the College Press coincided with the presence of John Wilson as its head or manager. The Civil War in England and the several contemporary invasions of the Netherlands by French armies were amongst the causes that brought the press in 1642 to a temporary end. Both before and after this date some collaboration has been observed between St Omers and printers in the town, such as Charles Boscard who in 1610 succeeded Bellet, and the Englishman, John Heigham, who issued books from Douay but no less from Saint-Omer where his son, also named John, was about 1630 a student at the College. It would appear that although most of the books bearing the imprint "at St Omers for John Heigham" were printed for him by Boscard, yet in a few cases it was the type of the College Press that was used.

Many of the works printed by John Wilson were controversial and frankly propagandist. It was a controversial age and

English Jesuits amongst others were busy producing books in refutation of no less busy Protestant divines. Few such Jesuit books were written at this period that were not printed at St Omers College and destined for a secret, precarious English market. But scarcely less numerous were devotional works of one sort or another, written or translated, and not infrequently in need of a second or third edition. Even by this press alone —and of course there were others—Catholics were provided with a wide choice of ascetical reading: and when Mass and the sacraments were a matter of such difficulty and danger, they needed all the help they could derive from such literature. Some of the tattered volumes that have survived are some small evidence of the use to which such books were put. Translations of works by St Augustine, St John of Avila, Luis de Granada, Luis de la Puente, Nicolas Caussin and many another occur in the list of books that issued from the St Omers College Press.

Usually such translations were the work of Jesuits, but not quite all. That errant knight, Sir Tobie Mathew, is a case in point. A wanderer in Europe he certainly was; but he had reason to be so, for he was exiled three times—the last time in 1640 at the petition of both Houses of Parliament. He was a priest, ordained apparently in 1614 by Cardinal Bellarmine, although his ordination was kept a secret. For services rendered he was knighted in 1623—this Catholic priest who refused to take the hateful Oath of Allegiance and was legally guilty of high treason! King James, had he known more than he did, would not have been amused. But to return from this digression. Between 1619 and 1622 Sir Tobie had at least three of his translations printed at the College Press, the best known being his version of St Augustine's *Confessions*. From the same press appeared in 1619 *The Widdowes Mite*, and in 1622 another precious book, also of his own composition, *Of the love of our only Lord and Saviour Jesus Christ*. No doubt his friendship with the Jesuits and his generosity towards them were not unconnected with this choice of a printer. It may also perhaps account for the mistaken notion that he was himself a Jesuit.

His last days were spent in the Jesuit House of Tertians at Ghent: and on his death in 1655 the whole Society was ordered by the General to offer up three Masses for the repose of the soul of this benefactor, "Dominus Tobias Matthaei"[21]— a title that would not be accorded to a Jesuit.

There is ample testimony to the widespread success reaped by the diffusion of such literature amongst Englishmen, even amongst opponents of Catholicism. To cite one instance, the Annual Letter of the English Province, speaking in particular of Jesuit controversial authors, has this to say:

Their productions in pamphlet form, written in the vernacular tongue, are circulated throughout England with the most happy results. They effect what could scarcely be done by priests, for to persuade a Protestant to forsake his sect and be reconciled to the Church is a capital offence, and the fear of the law makes Protestants shrink from the very mention of a priest; so that it is both a difficult and a dangerous matter to treat with them about religion. But nothing is easier than to call their attention to a new book, which they eagerly accept and devour, especially if, as is sometimes the case, it contains an attack upon some famous Calvinist preacher or prelate.[22]

Of a "certaine notorious Jesuite" (identified as Fr John Fisher, veré Percy) John Gee, once a Catholic if only in name, wrote that "Myselfe have seene greater stores of books in quires [i.e. unbound] at his chamber than I ever beheld at any stationers warehouse about Pauls; he having two or three large roomes filled out with heapes in this kinde to the very top".[23] Allowing for the usual exaggeration we may take it that Fr Fisher was an active agent in spreading Catholic literature. Indeed these "books in quires" may have been, as has been

[21] General to Provincial (Fr Knott), 14 August 1655 (Ep. Gen., II, f. 167ᵛ; cf. I, f. 520ᵛ). The General must have taken Sir Tobie's name to be Matthews. The date of his death is usually given as 13 October. The General's informant may have been incorrect; but the letter of 14 August presupposes an earlier date for Sir Tobie's death, probably July at latest.

[22] Translated by Foley, VII, 1076.

[23] John Gee: The Foot out of the Snare (London, 2 ed., 1624), Appendix.

suggested, either wholly or in part a stock of Fr Fisher's own works of controversy, nearly all of which were printed by John Wilson.

From 1635 when France, now at war with Spain, began to harass the Spanish Netherlands the output of the College Press declined. There were other troubles, too, famine and pestilence not least. The financial state of St Omers was particularly grave; and the consequent economies applied, no doubt, to the printing press as elsewhere. The number of volumes issued became fewer and fewer. In 1640, according to a list compiled by Fr Newdigate, only three are known to have been printed, two in 1641, and the next year only one. Then a long silence, not broken until 1672, and then it was but to print another edition of Wilson's *English Martyrologe*. Not until the last decade of the century did the press really become active once more. Of this second period, however, more will be said in a later chapter.

The last one hears of Mr John Wilson is in September 1645, when the Prizes were presented yet again by this "optimus Maecenas". On at least two previous occasions he had been no less generous. By this date he was seventy or nearly so. Without doubt his death, whenever it occurred, must have provided the opportunity to sing his praises without reserve: but whatever was then written has perished or been lost. Of the man himself one does not gather much, though of his generosity something is known though probably not all. He it was who from his private fortune or possibly his printing profits provided the money for the enlargement of the College church and sacristy, for the purchase of the "Villa" at Blandyke and for other improvements. Half a century later the memory of this "great benefactor" was still green. It well deserved to be, and does so still.

7

WARS WITHOUT AND TROUBLES WITHIN

THE successor of Fr Baldwin in the autumn of 1632 was Fr Thomas Worsley. Four years later he gave place to Fr Thomas Port (*veré* Layton), during whose ten years of office, first on trial as Vice-Rector and then Rector (1637), there were several difficult decisions, as we shall see, that had to be made. For the later years of his rectorship were complicated by financial troubles arising not only from the Franco-Spanish war and the ravages of French troops in the Spanish Netherlands but also from the Civil War in England. In 1646 most of the Rectors in the Province were changed by the new General, Vincent Caraffa, in consequence of an order from Pope Innocent X. His Brief, *Prospero felicique statui* (1 January 1646), published about a week before Caraffa's election, ordained that a General Congregation of the Jesuits should be held every ninth year, and that the term of office of all Superiors except the Master of Novices should in future be limited to three years. The first part of this decree remained in force for a hundred years, though it suffered several exceptions, until it was abolished in 1746 by Benedict XIV. But the limitation of office to three years, with the proviso that eighteen months must elapse before a Superior could be appointed to another similar office, was first suspended and then revoked by Alexander VII in 1658. A tiresome business it must have been for Generals and Provincials to keep count. To the conscientious Fr Michael Alford, the historian, Rector of the Derbyshire District, the succeeding General, Francis Piccolomini, wrote in August, 1650:[1] "This triennium business may be a comfort to Rectors, but it is a great nuisance and worry to me: but it can't be helped, it's a cross to be welcomed. So please add up the time you were Vice-Rector or exercised acts of juris-

[1] Piccolomini to Alford (*veré* Griffith), 6 August 1650 (Ep. Gen., II, f. 131).

diction, plus the few weeks you spent in making the Visitation of two Colleges in England, and the rest of the time, if any, will settle when your triennium ends." It had become a mere question of mathematics.

The more immediate successors of Fr Port were therefore subject to the provisions of the Brief. It will be convenient to list them here: Fr Edward Courtney (*veré* Leedes), a future Provincial; Fr Henry More (1649-1652), a former Provincial; Fr Charles D'Arcy, *veré* Thompson (1652-1655). His successor was Fr Thomas Babthorpe, brother of Barbara Babthorpe, the friend and companion of Mary Ward whom she succeeded as Superior General of her Institute. Father Thomas was appointed Rector in March 1655 and was later addressed by the General as Rector: but he had fallen ill at Munich when on his way to Rome as elected representative of a Provincial Congregation. He never reached Rome, and it is very doubtful if he ever reached St Omers, although Dr Oliver dates his rectorship as from 16 February 1656. He died on 20 October of that year. Be that as it may, Fr Port was appointed Vice-Rector until in December he was given another assignment as Rector at Ghent, when another Vice-Rector, Fr John Stephens (*veré* Poyntz), carried on for a few months. In April a Rector was at last installed—Fr Henry More (1657-1660). He had been recalled to Belgium some months previously so that he might have leisure at Liege to complete his history of the Province. This second term as Rector, however, did not hinder him from finishing his work which, after censorship at Rome in 1659, was published at Saint-Omer (though not at the College Printing Press) in the following year.

But St Omers must not be left in an historical vacuum. In the December of 1633 died the friendly old Archduchess, the Infanta Isabella, worn out with work and worry and her personal austerities. The "reign of the Archdukes" had ended with the Archduke Albert's death in 1621: yet in reality King Philip II had from the beginning so clogged their apparent independence with conditions and secret clauses that they differed little from the Governors their predecessors. The Archduchess had continued for some dozen years as Governor, a deputy of her nephew, Philip IV (1621-1665), with not much more than the trappings of sovereignty to console or irritate her. For Ambrogio Spinola continued as before to direct the military operations in the North against the United Provinces, whilst that ambitious, unpopular personage the Marquis of Bedmar, Cardinal de la Cueva, was mainly responsible, at least in practice, for carrying out the wishes of Philip IV in the political sphere. Both of them, however, had been recalled before the Archduchess died, the Cardinal in 1629. His haughty bearing and high-handed conduct had re-created a violent anti-Spanish nationalism. His successor, the Marquis d'Aytona, a friend of the English Jesuits (his nephew seems to have entered St Omers about 1632), would have done much to soothe the angry Netherlanders but for the intransigent attitude of Philip IV and his advisers.

As successor of the Archduchess came the young Don Fernando, brother of King Philip IV and known as the "Cardinal Infant". The cardinalate had been imposed upon him when nine years old, but his *métier* was that of a soldier. He soon had an opportunity of displaying his valour and his considerable skill as a commander; for in the May of 1635 war with Spain was declared by Catholic France, acting in alliance with the Protestant United Provinces. France, in other words, took its place definitely in the Thirty Years War.

The Spanish Netherlands was now attacked both from the North, where the Cardinal Infant commanded in person, and from the South. Saint-Omer and the other frontier towns prepared at once to strengthen their defences. All available hands were needed. From a note in the Register of the "First Six"[2]

---

[2] *Registrum Audomarensis Anglorum Gymnasii* (B.M., Addit. MSS., No. 9354); a register of the "First Six" in each class in their periodical examinations ("Compositions")—for whom a Good Breakfast was probably the reward—and of the yearly prize-winners, from 1622 to 1670. Notes are added here and there.

we learn that on the declaration of war the St Omers boys quitted their schoolrooms and at the request of the magistracy worked for a whole month by relays upon the city walls, helping like the rest to build new fortifications or repair the old. A pleasant change, no doubt, for most of the boys, although probably not for the Prefect of Studies, even though no public examinations loomed ahead.

A strong French army entered the Netherlands that summer, but Saint-Omer was not yet in danger. Pestilence however—bubonic plague, typhus or what you will—swept over that part of Belgium, as at this same time it raged in England and elsewhere. In Saint-Omer alone there are said to have been some 8,000 deaths. Throughout 1636 the dreaded scourge continued and well into 1637. The death-carts trundled monotonously with many halts from house to house through silent streets. Providentially St Omers College escaped infection. But in numbers it had declined from 200 boys at the peak of 1635 to 115 by the end of 1636. Not only the plague but war and rumours of war in the vicinity of Saint-Omer were naturally reasons for caution on the part of many English parents. Rumours indeed of all sorts were rife in Saint-Omer itself. On one occasion the futile accusation was made to the Court of Brussels that the English College had become a danger to the city garrison; that in some subtle manner French troops from across the frontier were likely, under the guise of English Jesuits, to gain admission into the city. The Annual Letter for 1636[3] is not very clear (how could it be?) as to how this feat was to be accomplished. Yet certainly the authorities were so credulous of the rumour that they seriously planned to confine the community and boys within the College walls, or in other words to place them under house arrest. Before that order, however, was put into execution the Rector had managed to obtain commendatory letters from Cardinal Barberini, the Cardinal Protector of England, and from

[3] S. Arch., MS. B. I. 15 ("Fr Glover's Extracts"), I, p. 17. The summary given by Foley (VII, 1166) is unreliable.

Cardinal de la Cueva, far away in Spain. The Rector's strong protest, backed by the two Cardinals, proved sufficient to secure a withdrawal of the proposed order.

Although a European war—the Thirty Years War—had been in progress since 1618, it was not until the intervention of France in 1635 that the annual "missions" to the seminaries in Rome and Spain became a serious danger. But now, says the writer of the above Annual Letter, a new and more expensive route had to be developed. It was decided to send the students first to England, for reasons which are left unexplained. Hitherto the journey to Seville or Valladolid had been by sea from Calais down the French and Spanish coasts; and to Rome by an overland route via Munich or through France to Lyons and beyond. With France already girt for war, this latter route had now grown hazardous. The new plan, one may suppose, was for both parties to slip across to an English port, risking the obvious danger of arrest by pursuivants, and there re-embark on an English or neutral vessel bound for a Spanish port. For the Roman party there would remain a journey across Spain to the Mediterranean and another sea voyage to Italy. Certainly, whatever may have been the precise details, the plan involved considerable risks, even though considered the lesser of two evils. Of the first batch so sent in 1635 one of the youths[4] was arrested on landing in England and confined in Dover Castle. Was it at St Omers that this prisoner had developed his musical talent? At all events the Governor of the Castle, the Earl of Suffolk, offered him the post of music master to his children—provided of course that he would take the oath of Allegiance and Supremacy. Master Baines politely declined the honour: he was not to be caught so easily as that. A few weeks later he eluded his guard, escaped from the Castle and by devious ways was able to return to St Omers. Next

---

[4] William Baines (veré Simpson), as is evident from his replies when he reached Rome in December 1636 at the age of about twenty-five. He was at St Omers c. 1629-1636. Later he left the English College to become a Benedictine (Foley, VI, 334-5).

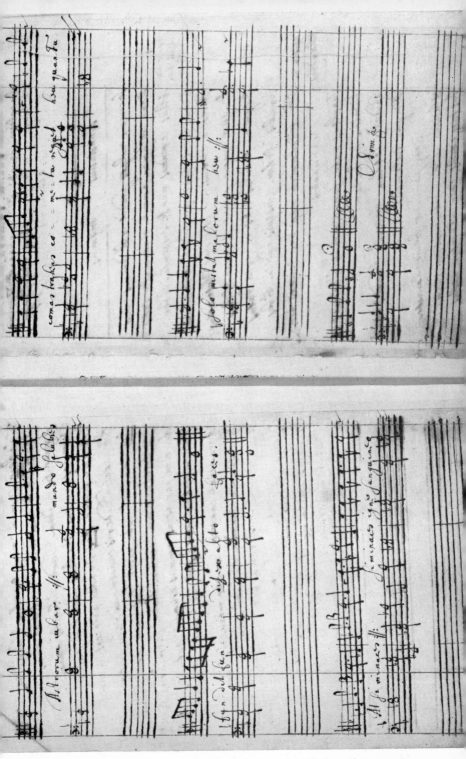

3. Notation for a song in Fr Simons' *Zeno*, Act II, Sc. 1 (*see* p. 137)
(B. M. Harleian, 5024)

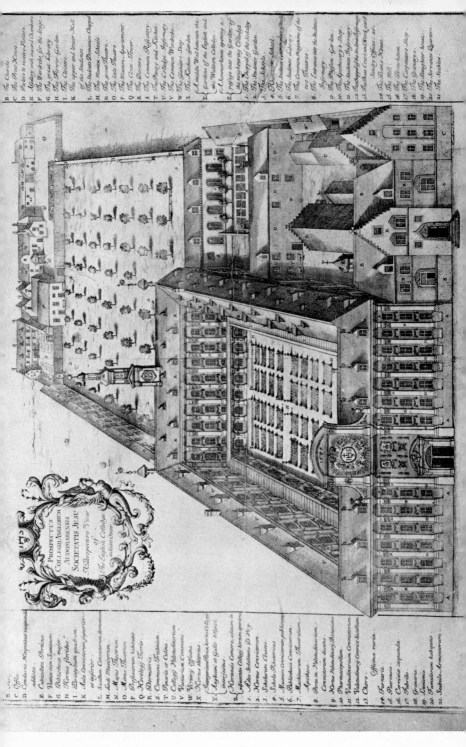

4. Engraving by Montbard of St Omers College as it was in 1689

year he fared better and reached the English College at Rome in time for Christmas Day and its festivities.

In 1637 a French army invaded Artois in retaliation for the invasion of Picardy by the Spaniards in the previous year. But the fighting and devastation was away in the direction of Arras and Douai. In 1638, however, Saint-Omer was a main objective. On 25 May Gaspard de Coligny, Marquis de Chatillon, encamped at Blandecques (Blandyke) with an army of 25,000 men, and Saint-Omer was soon surrounded. Fortunately the siege lasted no longer than six weeks before it was raised. But the devastation and pillaging in the surrounding countryside—including Watten and Blandyke—caused widespread ruin and misery.

Before the blockade was completed the Rector, Fr Port, was able to evacuate some forty of the younger or more delicate boys under the charge of a few masters. These were sent to Ghent, where the local Bishop most kindly lent them a large country house on the outskirts of the town, doing all he could to make them comfortable. And not unmindful of the native habits of youth he gave them a house-warming in the form of a sumptuous meal of some sort (*lautissimum epulum*)—what in Lancashire might have been called a "rare do"—which was graced by his own presence and that of the local Spanish Governor of the Castle.

The remainder, numbering nearly 100, if the Jesuit community be included, were divided or re-divided in three classes. They carried on as best they could, although the noise of the bombardment often drowned the masters' voices. At times, when the "pyroboli exitiales (*vulgo bombi*)" were dropping dangerously near, a quick retreat to the cellars upset the lesson in hand. To obtain the protection of God and His Virgin Mother, public prayers were said, the Blessed Sacrament was exposed, processions were organized to various churches in the city or privately within the College precincts. Although serious damage was done in the vicinity of the College, the building itself was not more than grazed. From the point of view of

L

victuals, the writer tells us, the Father responsible had been wise before the event and had laid in a stock enough to last almost a year. A little scepticism may here perhaps be lawful. In twelve months the weevily flour would surely have been uneatable.

The Jesuit house at Ghent was overcrowded these days. Not only had a swarm of small boys from St Omers settled upon the house until the kindly Bishop could make other arrangements for them, but about two dozen novices from Watten, with their novice master, Fr Robert Stafford, arrived unexpectedly about the same time, the beginning of June. It became a very tight fit, for the house was not a large one. To afford breathing space it was soon settled that the eight tertian Fathers should disperse and end their third year of noviceship without delay. The novices remained there till about the end of the year, for the noviciate at Watten had been occupied by the military, the farm and fields devastated and much of the timber burnt. There was at all events reason for gratitude to God that the house itself had not been burnt down as had the village of Watten at the foot of the hill.

The young St Omers boys had been able to return earlier, soon after the raising of the siege. Then as an aftermath there arrived another kind of pestilence, described as a fever or sweating sickness. The havoc wrought in the surrounding countryside had filled Saint-Omer again with homeless peasants, many of whom had driven into the town the cattle or other animals they had been able to rescue from the French soldiers and marauders. Disease was rife. All that summer of 1638 and throughout most of the winter the epidemic raged. Once again thousands in the town are said to have died and the College did not escape. An early victim was Fr Thunder, whose death on 12 September ended, as has been noted in a previous chapter, a long life of devoted service to St Omers. In the course of the winter the fever had spread so rapidly and widely throughout the College that novices from Watten (they had by this time returned from Ghent) were summoned to help in the nursing of the sick. In addition to Fr Thunder four other Jesuits succumbed to the epidemic and two College boys. Fortunately a return to the normal routine of studies became feasible in the early spring.

From the Annual Letter of 1639 we hear of yet another wave of refugees into the town after the siege and capture of Hesdin by the French. For many months some hundred of these received bread and soup at the College three times a week, whilst at least twenty of the most needy were fed each day. The dwindling financial resources of St Omers must of course have been further strained by this exercise of Christian charity. Finally, we are told, when war and pestilence had receded for the time being, a silver statue of Our Lady and Child was presented in thanksgiving on behalf of the College to the famous chapel of Notre-Dame des Miracles, situated in the centre of the town, the *Place du grand Marché*. There was of course a procession from the College to the handsome chapel standing majestically alone on the open *Place*. Here the statue was solemnly dedicated by the Bishop of Saint-Omer, Christophe de France, and placed on an altar at which he subsequently said Mass in the presence of his youthful congregation. In a short speech—of course in Latin—one of the Rhetoricians expressed the gratitude of St Omers to our Blessed Lady for her protection of the College, and added graceful thanks to his Lordship for his cooperation and kindness.[5]

From a letter of Vitelleschi to the Rector it would seem that in the spring of this year the College boys were again at work on the fortifications of the town. Possibly, however, he is referring to the siege of the year before, when certainly the students from the Walloon College had been called upon for similar work. At all events the General thoroughly approved, in spite of the interruption to studies that was involved. Such

---

[5] S. Arch., MS. B. I. 15, I, p. 68. For a history of this chapel see a brochure by Canon Georges Coolen, *Saint-Omer et Notre-Dame des Miracles* (Saint-Omer, 1951). The statue does not seem to have survived.

work, he says, is a debt owed to Saint-Omer, the good favour of which you enjoy.[6]

To go back a few years. The Provincial, Fr Blount, was growing old and diseased and finding the burden of office almost too heavy to bear. Superior of the English Jesuit Mission since 1617, then successively Vice-Provincial and Provincial, he was approaching his seventieth year and anxious for a successor to be appointed. No one else, it seems, shared his views on this subject. As delegate of a Provincial Congregation in 1633 there was sent to Rome the Rector of the Lancashire District, Fr John Worthington—we have met him before when in 1584, a small boy of eleven, he suffered from a violent gastric upheaval in the presence of a Royal Commission. The delegate was expressly charged by Fr Blount to petition earnestly at Rome for a change of Provincials. This he did, as an act of obedience. He added, however, his own personal opinion that the English Province still needed his prudence, his experience, his grasp of administrative affairs. And amongst other "postulates" or requests handed by him to the General was one from the Rector of St Omers, Fr Worsley, "that for as long as may be we may enjoy the continued government of our Father Provincial".[7]

Vitelleschi, though in no wise lacking in sympathy for Fr Blount, held out for another two years. A successor to such a man was not easily to be found. At length in the August of 1635 he released the Provincial from office, appointing Fr Henry More in his place. Within a few months the new Provincial had crossed to Belgium where the plague was raging: there was plentiful work awaiting him. As far as St Omers is concerned, he came to the conclusion—or was it Vitelleschi that did so?—that Fr Worsley was not 'cut out' for a Rector. Tentatively he suggested Fr Blount as a suitable substitute. The General disagreed, but approved of the experi-

[6] *Établissements des Jésuites* &c. (ut supra), IV, col. 837. Vitelleschi to Port 25 June 1639 (Ep. Gen., I, f. 493).
[7] Ep. Gen., I, ff. 386-387.

ment of appointing Fr Port as Vice-Rector for some months. The experiment proving successful, early in 1637 his appointment as Rector was made public. In England Fr Blount became one of the Consultors of the Province. On 13 May 1638 he died in his seventy-fifth year, most likely in London, and was buried, no doubt by special favour, in Queen Henrietta's chapel in Somerset House, a chapel served by "Her Majesty's Capuchins". Vitelleschi had put almost implicit trust in him —in his judgment, in his obedience. "Here comes Father Blount", said Robert Catesby on one occasion, "everybody's favourite, but has no favourites himself."[8] His death, be it said briefly, meant the incalculable loss to the English Province of a really great man.

About a year after his death, in the autumn of 1639, Fr Knott succeeded Fr More as Provincial; and almost at once arose an outcry, engineered by a party in England hostile to the Society. Fr Knott, a notable controversialist, some three years previously had published a book or booklet in defence of the Catholic faith in support of some earlier works of his, *Charity Mistaken* (1630) and *Mercy and Truth or Charity Maintained* (1634). His book of 1636 (presumably *A Direction to be observed by N.N.*, meaning Chillingworth) had been made the occasion of an attack on the author, whose anonymity deceived nobody. And when Fr Knott became Provincial the attack was renewed against "this man and his brood". Protestants were again encouraged to take umbrage at the "insult" to their religion: even the King, it was thought, was likely to take action against the Jesuits and banish the author from the Kingdom. Vitelleschi was alarmed. Had he known in time of the gathering storm, he wrote, he would never have made the appointment. But to remove Fr Knott now, as if he were in any way guilty, would be unjust.[9] The new Provincial, however, who had crossed to

[8] *Ibid.*, I, ff. 412ᵛ, 419, 438. J. Morris, s.j., *Troubles of our Catholic Forefathers*, Series I, pp. 202–204.

[9] Cf. Vitelleschi to Père Suffren (Confessor in London to the Queen Mother), 14 January 1640 (Ep. Gen., I, f. 501ᵛ); T. Hughes, s.j., *History of the Society of Jesus in N. America* (London, 1907), Vol. I (Text), pp. 71–72.

Belgium to make his official visitation of the houses, was ordered to remain there for the time being, with Fr More acting as Superior in England during his absence. It was not until 1643 that it was considered safe for Fr Knott again to cross the Channel. Meanwhile his proximity to St Omers— —if indeed he did not make the College his head-quarters— was opportune, for the problems that continued to arise there could be referred to him without undue delay or possible interception at an English port.

The perennial problem of St Omers was of course financial. There is nothing astonishing or unique in that! It is an endemic disease of most Colleges. In point of fact St Omers was an endowed College, in the sense that its support was partly based on the promise of an adequate yearly pension guaranteed by the Kings of Spain. The misfortune was that the payments came fitfully, in parts, and often not at all. During the decline of Spain under Philip IV the situation worsened. Officials, lay and clerical, were often careless, if not worse than careless; and in any case money was scarce and needed for other purposes. Minor economies were made by various Rectors to lessen the burden of debt which Fr Giles Schondonch in the first instance, not without some justification, had left for posterity to deal with. At Seville, to give an instance, there was usually a Jesuit Father acting as agent for St Omers and for the English Province in general. He had little to do in this respect and had a laybrother to help him do it—both of them at the expense of St Omers. Fr Worsley, with the General's help, managed to remedy this waste of money and men.

Yet the College was always struggling to keep its head above water. In view of the long-continuing war and the consequent rise in prices, in addition to the decrease in the number of boys, the suggestion was made in 1641 that the fee of these convictors should be raised to a more economic level. The suggestion was possibly carried into effect, although there is no explicit statement that it was. But the question of the rise or fall of the yearly "pension" seems insoluble for lack of sufficient evidence.

Several years later, in 1658, the subject was raised again; and the Provincial was told to consider the opinion advocated by some Fathers that the fee should be not less than 250 florins, to be paid in advance by half-yearly instalments. The failure of a parent to observe this regulation would result in the son or sons being sent home without more ado. Yet if a local florin was equivalent to two shillings or thereabouts in nominal value, this proposal was but a return to Fr Blount's original prescription of £25 as the standard fee for convictors. Again it is uncertain what conclusion was reached by the Provincial. It is to be hoped that he gave some consideration to the parents' point of view and to the serious difficulties and hardships that in England would attend the full enforcement of such a regulation. It may be added before this subject is dismissed that more than a hundred years later, when in 1773 the College, then at Bruges, was suppressed, £25 was still the normal fee for older boys and £20 for the younger.

The year 1640 ushered in the centenary of the Society of Jesus, to be celebrated in each Province and College as each thought fit. For the Flemish (Flandro-Belgic) Province there was published from the Plantin Press a large quarto volume of 950 pages, a flamboyant and rather unpleasing production. But further south at Sint-Omer and elsewhere the Jesuits, though not less enthusiastic, met the occasion somewhat more calmly. The Annual Letter of St Omers, written in baroque Latin, is full of ardour but tells us little except for the several performances in the College theatre. Each class produced during the course of that year a Latin "tragedy" (a somewhat loose term), the series beginning in February with a "splendid tragedy" written and acted by the "school" of Rhetoric. To these five—for the fall in numbers had reduced the classes from six to five—was added a sixth and even more spectacular play at the close of the school year in August, a play in which members of every school or class took part. A general demand for a repeat performance had to be refused; for on the first occasion the many gate-crashers had so ruthlessly packed the hall beyond its normal capacity that a second performance, it was feared, might give rise to a veritable riot or mob fight in the street outside.

A further venture was a set of Latin poems written by the Rhetoricians, which commemorated the fruitful apostolate of St Ignatius and his first companions. Another set, for which Poetry was responsible, eulogized the work and wanderings of St Francis Xavier. These two sets were displayed in the entrance hall, pinned or otherwise fixed to the walls. May we here note in passing that *"affixio carminum"* in the text of the Annual Letter is the happy emendation of what our copyist carelessly or tactlessly misread as *"afflictio carminum"*—a meaning that was surely far from the mind of the author! Rhetoric and Poetry, it is evident, were busily engaged this year in studying the lives of St Ignatius and St Francis Xavier, and to some profit. In September all Rhetoric with one or two exceptions entered the Jesuit noviciate at Watten.[10]

But tragedy was not far away—real tragedy, in no wise theatrical. In mid-May a French army invested the neighbouring town of Aire, capturing it on 27 July. When news of the siege reached Watten, community and novices fled for safety to their "Refuge" in Saint-Omer, a house, it would seem, not far from the English College: and there they stayed for about six months until Aire was re-taken by the Spaniards. One afternoon in June a party of novices went off for a walk to the other side of the river. No doubt they had chosen a direction considered free from danger. That same afternoon, as it chanced, one of the St Omers masters, a young Jesuit of

---

[10] Litt. Ann., 1640 (S. Arch., A. IV. 13 [1], pp. 288 seqq.). The plays acted this year were, in order of classes: *Geminus Alcides* (SS. Ignatius and Francis Xavier); *Sanguis Sanguinum*; *Gonsalvus Sylveira*; *Aloysius sive Saeculi Fuga*; *Fratrum Discordia Felix* (St Stanislaus); and in August *Haeresis Triumphata sive B. Ignatius Soc. Jesu Fundator*. Apparently another tragedy, unnamed, was acted in June by Rhetoric, making seven plays in all. Cf. W. H. McCabe, "The Play-List of the English College of St Omers", an article in *Revue de Littérature Comparée*, No. 66 (Avril-Juin, 1937), pp. 366-367 with the references there given.

twenty-five years, not yet ordained, Henry Poulton by name,[11] took his class for a walk in the same direction. It turned out to be a rash adventure for both parties. Unexpectedly a troop of French cavalry scouring the countryside came down upon them. The novices got off lightly, for the quest of these marauders was for money; and they soon discovered that, like all novices, their prisoners were penniless. They contented themselves with stripping six of them of some of their clothing —in the circumstances, as Jesuits at all events will realize, a very poor substitute for cash. The soldiers then espied Mr Poulton's small boys who were seeking safety across the river. Some, however, got into difficulties in the water and three of them were drowned. Mr Poulton himself was overtaken on the bank whilst assisting one of his charges. He was struck with their swords, dazed, probably wounded. In the event he fell into the water and shared the fate of his three pupils. The news when it reached the College must have cast a deep shadow over the centenary celebrations.

Towards the close of the year 1640, yet another menace was added to the troubles, and not least the financial troubles of St Omers. In England the Long Parliament was reluctantly summoned in November by Charles I: and with the Puritans now firmly in the saddle and as strongly opposed to the King as was the King to them, civil war seemed almost inevitable. As is well known, it began in the August of 1642. Thanks to the moderation of the King and the influence of his Queen Henrietta and of the ambassadors of some Catholic countries, persecution of the Catholics, though it had never ceased, had for some years been less intense. Fines for recusancy were still frequent: they were a source of revenue for the impoverished royal treasury during the eleven or twelve years during which

---

[11] His *alias* at St Omers, both as boy and master, was Matthew Palmer. He was of the Poulton family of Desborough, Northamptonshire, a well-known St Omers name. No less than fifteen Poultons became Jesuits. Henry had entered Watten as recently as 1635. Cf. Foley, I, 616-618. And see Litt. Ann. (Watten) 1640 (S. Arch., B. I. 15, pp. 80-81).

Charles refrained from summoning a Parliament. Other vexations and impositions there were too; but since 1628 when the Jesuit Fr Arrowsmith and Mr Richard Herst (or Hayhurst?), a Lancashire farmer, were executed at Lancaster without the King's previous knowledge, no Catholic had been put to death for his religion.

These ghastly prosecutions and hangings were resumed by the Long Parliament. During the first four years of its sessions (1641-1644) one may read of sixteen Catholics, both priests and laymen, who gave their lives for their faith, apart from others who died in prison. Amongst them were two former St Omers boys, Thomas Holland (1615-1621) and Ralph Corbie or Corbington (1613-1619). By a bitter irony of circumstances Fr Holland certainly, and possibly Fr Corbie as well, were at least partly indebted for their martyrdom to two contemporaries of theirs at St Omers, James Wadsworth (1618-1622), by now a pursuivant, whom we have met before, and the notorious Thomas Gage,[12] the apostate Dominican whose enmity to Jesuits was insatiable. Both these martyrs were beatified in 1929 by Pope Pius XI.

One gathers from their first biographer, Fr Ambrose Corbie, S.J.,[13] who was at school with both these martyrs, that Thomas Holland was the sort of boy, not particularly clever but bright and cheerful, dependable, solidly pious, who would be an obvious choice as a boy prefect. In point of fact he was more than once elected Prefect of the Sodality—an office which had

---

[12] For his activities cf. C.R.S., XI, 572-3; G. Anstruther, O.P., *A Hundred Homeless Years* (London, 1958), pp. 158 seqq. and passim. He was apparently a priest in 1619 (*ibid.*, p. 123); yet a contemporary account of Holland's trial (S. Arch., Anglia, V, No. 11) states that Gage claimed they had been "school fellows five years together", and that Holland "acknowledged to have studied with him beyond sea". Gage's assertion is inconsistent with the date given of his priesthood. According to D.N.B. he was sent to Spain in 1612 to study under the Jesuits; but it is more than likely it was to St Omers he went, where his other three brothers were educated.

[13] *Certamen Triplex* (Antwerp, 1645), a small volume, written anonymously, containing the lives of the three Jesuits (Fathers Holland, Corbie, Morse) who had suffered at Tyburn since the assembly of the Long Parliament.

some similarity to that of a Captain of the School or the Stonyhurst equivalent, Head of the Line. Ralph Corbie, as described
by his younger brother, was seemingly of a more reserved
nature, utterly straightforward, and simple in the best sense of
that word. A characteristic that had its compensations was his
distaste for money. "As soon as any money was given him, he
handed it over to his younger brother." Both of them were
students for the priesthood at Valladolid when Prince Charles
arrived in Spain to "woo" the Infanta Maria. Holland, a
graceful speaker—he had been a prominent actor on the St
Omers stage—was chosen to "spout" a speech prepared for
him, welcoming the Prince to Madrid on behalf of his fellow
students. Thereafter he entered the English Jesuit noviciate in
1624, as did likewise Ralph Corbie, already a priest, in this or
the following year.

Fr Holland was for a few years a Prefect at St Omers,
subordinate, no doubt, to Fr Thunder. In that office he acquired
much the same reputation, his strict discipline overshadowed by
his kindly, sympathetic manner. In 1625 he crossed to England:
his native air, thought his doctor, might be a remedy for his
poor health. (It is amazing to note how many priests were
sent over to England at the risk of their lives "for their health's
sake".) Not much is known of his seven years of missionary
life. But the need of concealment certainly did not improve his
health, for he suffered considerably in head and stomach. Some
of his work was in London in the very centre of danger. Often
at night or early morning he would venture out in various
disguises, his skill as an actor and mimic and his fluency in
four languages enabling him to avoid detection. Detected he
was, however, at length and arrested on 4 October 1642. At his
trial "Captain" Wadsworth, Thomas Gage and a certain
Francis Newton, a professional priest-catcher, tried their best
to prove him to be a priest, but lamentably failed. It made no
matter. The jury found him guilty, somewhat to the surprise
even of the presiding judge. The usual sentence was pronounced and the usual butchery followed on 12 December,

with two thieves to share his fate. Thanks, however, to the disobedience of Gregory the hangman, Fr Holland was dead before the butchery began.

Fr Ralph Corbie after two years at Ghent had gone to England in 1632, three years earlier than Fr Holland. A report from his Superior, perhaps from Fr Flack or from Fr Michael Freeman who succeeded him that autumn as Rector at Ghent, was far from enthusiastic over his prospects. His abilities, wrote the Superior, are quite mediocre, and he lacks judgment and prudence: he is considered ill fitted for missionary work. It is possible to lay too much emphasis on this report, for it is possible that his Superior's judgment as to his rather silent subject may have been at least in part mistaken. Indeed, Fr Ralph's twelve years of work, first in Yorkshire and then in Durham, belied his Superior's forebodings. He toured the countryside on foot—later his infirmities obliged him to ride—visiting more especially the poor farmers and labourers, with whom he delighted to share a meal. "He was commonly called ye Apostle of ye Cuntry", wrote his fellow missioner, Fr Robert White. Not quite a week after the royalist defeat at Marston Moor he was captured near Newcastle by Parliamentary soldiers on 8 July (O.S.) 1644 and shipped to London. His examination at Westminster was short, since he had already admitted to being a priest and Jesuit. The rest followed according to custom. The last scene at Tyburn was on Saturday, 7 September, the eve of Our Lady's traditional birthday, and probably the anniversary of his entrance into the Society. Like Blessed Thomas Holland, he and his fellow martyr, Blessed John Duckett, a secular priest, were allowed to hang till dead.

The Corbie family of County Durham is an interesting one. All four brothers were educated at St Omers and were all admitted into the Society of Jesus. One of them, Richard, died whilst still a boy there and was allowed to take his vows on his deathbed. Ambrose was the only one to survive Ralph, though not for long, dying in 1649. Their two sisters became

Benedictine nuns at Brussels. Finally their parents arranged to follow their children into religion. Gerard became a Jesuit laybrother at the age of seventy and died at Watten in 1637 after five years of total blindness. His wife was professed in 1633, aged eighty, at the Benedictine Abbey in Ghent. It is recorded that no Jesuits from the neighbouring House of Tertians were allowed to be present at her profession. Sister Benedicta, as she now became, was distressed, and the Lady Abbess complained to the General that the Abbey was harshly treated. Vitelleschi, though he had issued severe orders against any excess in priestly services rendered to nuns, admitted willingly that the local Rector had obeyed them woodenly and unwisely. Sister Benedicta lived to her hundredth year, a most holy and mortified religious, "saying dayly a world of prayers", as befitted the mother of a martyr.[14]

Heavy thunder-clouds of war seemed once more to be moving in the direction of Saint-Omer when, a month or two before Fr Corbie's death, the noviciate of Watten was again occupied by French troops. Watten, it may be recalled, was but some five miles distant from the College. The fine church of the noviciate was converted into a stable, part of the buildings was destroyed and the estate despoiled. The community fled once again to their "Refuge" in Saint-Omer, and the Rector and Master of Novices, Fr Francis Foster, travelled to Paris in quest of financial help. His hopes in the English Queen and in Cardinal Mazarin were apparently without much practical result.

But it was not only Watten that was in financial straits. Twelve months later, in fact, the crisis loomed so menacingly that Fr Knott, the Provincial, sent circular letters to several other Provinces begging their assistance, in particular for the houses of formation in Belgium. The whole Province was *in extremis*. In this year, 1645, it numbered 334 persons, of whom some 200 were in England, woefully hindered in their

[14] Litt. Ann. 1637 (S. Arch., MS. B. I. 15, p. 43); Foley, VII, 167; C.R.S., XIX, 54-56.

work for lack of that assistance which under the present Parliamentarian persecution their Catholic friends could now no longer afford. For a similar reason the Belgian houses were in distress. Prices were high; and living as they did in an alien land, these "foreigners" could not hope to subsist on alms or to be allowed much credit from the local tradesmen. The Provincial had eighty subjects for whom he wished to find suitable work in other Provinces. It is a melancholy story.

At St Omers, by reason of the Civil War in England and the continued fighting and pillaging in Artois, the number of pupils rapidly declined. What with Graveline captured and the French at Watten, the town was in constant fear of another siege. By 1642 the number of boys at the College had dropped to 104, with the prospect of still fewer boys in the immediate future. Debts were steadily increasing. What was to be done? Nothing was done, nothing perhaps could be done at the time. But two years later there seemed to be no other recourse than to send some boys away. By the June or July of 1644 we read that nearly all of Rhetoric and Poetry had left—some perhaps of their own accord, to join the Royalist forces in England. There was no play that autumn, and at the prize-giving, postponed to the beginning of the next school year, only three classes were represented. In 1645 the number had sunk to a mere twenty-four, whilst the Jesuit community in the course of three years had been economically reduced from twenty-nine all told to just a dozen. As for the boys, they were divided apparently in two classes: some had been sent away and no new boys admitted. With this miserable remnant of twenty-four the closing and ruin of St Omers became a subject of much discussion.

If one enquires whether those sent away returned to an England in turmoil, the answer is not clear. Writing to the Rector, Fr Port, in August, Vitelleschi agreed that to send boys straight back to England would be dangerous for them, and shameful from the Jesuit point of view; that it would be wiser to send them to neighbouring Jesuit schools. "My advice", he adds, "is to keep them at the College as long as it is possible to do so." But no doubt it was a matter for parents to decide. The probability is that some returned to their homes in England and some did not.

Somehow or other St Omers managed to survive. There appears to have been some confusion in the process, or at least some conflict of opinion as to the means to be employed. Fewer boys were arriving and some were sent away. Yet talk there was—possibly it was more than talk—of lowering the fee in order to attract more arrivals. Whatever may have been the method or methods adopted, the crisis was gradually overcome. In January 1648 the Rector reported that the numbers had increased to sixty, "although by reason of the misfortunes we have recently suffered, we have no Rhetoric or Syntax and very few in Poetry". The rest, he says, are in the three lowest classes. "But for the war we could manage to weather the storm. Yet we fear even greater trouble in England; and here too we have no better hopes, for it is likely that the enemy will besiege us."[15]

By the end of 1649 there were five classes with about ninety boys to fill them, and a community of twenty including seven lay-brothers. There was no Poetry this year, but, as the Annual Letter explains, Rudiments was split into two divisons, the lower of which catered for new boys from England knowing little Latin and less Greek. It is edifying to learn that the ex-Rector, Fr Port—his post had been taken in 1646 by Fr Edward Courtney—though getting on in years and in failing health, had at his own humble request been appointed to cope with this lowest and no doubt rather tiresome class. It was, as it chanced, in the September of this year 1649 that the veteran scholar, Fr John Floyd, was called to his reward at the age of seventy-seven. He had attended a Provincial Congregation held, not for the first time, at St Omers rather than in England, and died on the day after the close of the proceedings. He did not die of any known disease but just flickered out like a lamp that

15 S. Arch., Anglia V, No. 30.

has exhausted its oil. By this date the College had definitely turned the corner on the road of recovery, both in numbers and efficiency. There was of course much leeway to be made up. The small number of boys, and the scarcity of older boys in particular, had had their effect on the studies and the discipline and morale of the school. Under two good Rectors, Fr Courtney and Fr Henry More, convalescence was fairly rapid. By 1651 St Omers resumed its normal course of studies with its six classes and 110 boys. The total henceforward never rose much above this figure except in 1685 when, as we shall see, it stood for a while at 180.

The French incursions into the southern parts of the Spanish Netherlands had meanwhile continued with unremitting vigour. By 1643 most of the towns and territories in Artois had been wrested from the Spaniards, and there remained but a remnant, sometimes known as *Artois reservé*, a region comprising the two towns of Aire and Saint-Omer with their territorial dependencies. It was a salient that sooner or later was bound, in view of a degenerating Spain, to fall into the hands of the French King. But not as yet, even though in 1647 a plot was laid by some townsfolk (but happily discovered in time) to open the gates of Saint-Omer to the French Maréchal de Gassion. By this time, however, the United Provinces in the North had grown weary and suspicious of their alliance with France which now, under the direction of Mazarin, was aiming at the direct annexation of the Spanish Netherlands and might thus become an unwelcome next-door neighbour. At the Peace of Munster (January 1648) the United Provinces settled their differences with Spain, very much to their own advantage, and left France in the lurch. Before the end of the year the Thirty Years War petered out to an inglorious end.

This side of the story may be carried a little further. The Treaty of Westphalia which in October followed upon the Peace of Munster in no wise deterred the young Louis XIV and Mazarin from their policy of annexing the Spanish Netherlands, nor King Philip IV from defending as best he could what remained of his far distant possession. This Franco-Spanish war dragged on for another ten years. In 1657 Cromwell joined in the fray on the side of France, and an Expeditionary Force crossed the Channel. Later that year both French and English troops were in the vicinity of Saint-Omer. A document of 1659 describes how

> last year this house [Watten] suffered very serious damage when an army of French and English for fully eleven days encamped in the house and surrounding grounds. During that period grain of almost every kind was laid waste, various flocks and herds were driven away, timber cut down, everything ruined. The cost of repairs will not be less than 8000 crowns.[16]

The novices fled at first to Ghent since their Refuge in Saint-Omer was at that time occupied by a tenant. But the tenant presently withdrew: it was not till the autumn of 1660 that the Watten noviciate was able to receive them once more. Saint-Omer, though obviously nervous and on the alert, was not attacked at this time. But marauding bands of soldiers, French and English and even Spanish mercenaries, were "living off the country" to the great distress of the countryside. In the June of that year (1658) the decisive battle of the Dunes, followed by the capture of Dunkirk, led almost inevitably to the Treaty of the Pyrenees (November 1659) whereby *inter alia*, Artois, with the exception of *Artois reservé*, was formally ceded to France. It was not till another twenty years or so had passed that Saint-Omer changed perforce its nationality.

The vicissitudes of Saint-Omer and its future prospects, although of course connected with the history of the English College within its walls, are no substitute for what one would like to know, the intimate life of the boys and masters during this period. Would that there survived some letters of boys to

---

16 *Catalogus Tertius Rerum . . . in Provincia Angliae* (E. P. Arch., f. 854). Cf. Ep. Gen., II, ff. 196ᵛ, 197, 199, &c.

M

their parents, some unofficial and uncensored revelation of the domestic scene, however trifling it might be! What, for instance, was the food like? That is a subject on which the normal boy of any period would willingly dilate. What games did they play in their playground or when they went crocodiling, two by two, into the country beyond the town? Or had the custom of crocodiling fallen into disuse? What sort of books were they allowed to read in their spare time, and what *did* they read? For one gathers from some letters of the Generals that these two questions need separate answers. Were they ever allowed to smoke, and did some of them ever seek uncovenanted occasions for evading the law? As to this last point it would not be very rash to venture a guess, even though history is silent on the subject. Truth to tell—but tell it not in Gath—it was the Jesuits, not the boys, about whom we hear in this connection.

The matter came up as early as 1636. To King James I, writing his *Counterblaste to Tobacco* in 1604, smoking seemed a "filthie noveltie . . . the black stinking fume thereof neerest resembling the horrible Stygian smoke of the pit that is bottomlesse". His courtiers thought otherwise, thanks to Sir Walter Raleigh and his propaganda. Vitelleschi's "counterblaste" was by comparison mild: but he considered the use of tobacco, especially pipe-smoking (*per tubulos sorbendi*), involved a considerable waste of time and did not make for edification. "Your Reverence", he wrote to the Provincial, "must take care to remove this abuse or so to moderate it that all may understand that its use is permitted only for some clear need on the advice of a doctor and with approval of the Provincial."[17] Amongst a group of youths, some of them over twenty years of age and many of "gentle birth", would it be strange, even at this early date, if a custom of absorbing, *per tubulos* or otherwise, this noxious weed had also grown familiar? It may even be that the Jesuits picked up the habit

[17] Vitelleschi to Provincial (Fr Henry More), 2 August 1636 (Ep. Gen., I, f. 441^v).

from the boys. However, it will be better perhaps to keep to solid facts, even if they be somewhat indigestible.

Such scanty information as can be gathered concerning the period of the Civil War and Commonwealth reaches us mainly from the other side—the Olympian side. It seems clear, for instance, from various replies of the Generals that the reputation of St Omers for its success in studies had temporarily declined to some extent since the spacious days of Fr Schondonch. Greek was said to be languishing and music still more so. Discipline, according to some reports, was in need of being tightened up. To what extent these criticisms were valid it is impossible to say. But in view of the difficulties and disturbance resulting from the invasions of the French, and later from the Civil War in England, it would be surprising if some temporary decline had not developed. The seminaries in Spain and in Rome complained at times of the poor quality of the students provided by St Omers. Some of them, wrote Caraffa, can't even talk Latin properly! The explanation may be the limited choice of students during these embarrassing years, and the selection of some older ones—"late vocations" one might almost call them—who had not done the full five or six years' course. In 1641 the Prefect of Studies, Fr John Turner, wrote that interest in Greek had decreased ever since the commentaries of the Fathers of the Church, to the exclusion of "profane writers", had begun to be explained in the Refectory. Vitelleschi, forgetting the far distant days of his youth, replied that he really could not understand why this should be. Surely the Fathers of the Church were learned men and eloquent? However, he concludes graciously, take counsel on the subject and order what seems best.

Early in 1648 an official Visitor was appointed by the General, Caraffa, to make a general survey, spiritual and temporal, of the several houses of the two Belgian Provinces. The four houses of the English Province on the Continent were to be included. The Visitor was Fr Alexander Gottifredo, an Italian, who had but recently acted as Visitor of the Naples Province.

One of his suggestions has survived the ruin of time. It was that in view of the scarcity of novices at this period the two noviciates of the Belgian Provinces together with the English noviciate at Watten should be amalgamated into one. The Master of Novices (who was always Rector as well), his "Socius" or assistant, and the Minister of the combined noviciate would be representatives of these three Provinces. True it was that Watten was almost empty of novices for some years. In 1644 the Provincial had decided that no novices should be admitted for the coming year, to the disappointment of candidates for the Society, so largely recruited from St Omers. Gradually the prohibition was able to be relaxed; meanwhile a few candidates were sent to such neighbouring Provinces as could find room for them and the means to support them. The Visitor's plan may have been a good one from the economic, but scarcely from the social, point of view. The Provincials concerned disliked the idea and said so. Finally the scheme was given up by the General, a little while before he died in the June of 1649.

A Visitor's appointment by Jesuit law lapses with the death of a General. Strangely enough Fr Gottifredo continued his Visitation, his subsequent actions as Visitor becoming thus invalid. The new General, Fr Francis Piccolomini, therefore appointed another Visitor, Fr Florent de Montmorency, a distinguished Belgian Jesuit who had been Vicar General during the recent interregnum. His task was to complete the Visitation rendered nugatory by the curious mistake of his predecessor. As for Fr Gottifredo, after Piccolomini's short "reign" of eighteen months he was himself elected General in January 1652. His tenure of office was far briefer, for he died within less than two months, in the following March.

One other miscellaneous note may be added before this chapter closes. In 1658 the Cardinal Protector of England, Barberini, decided that a new and more detailed *questionnaire* must be completed by all students intending to continue their ecclesiastical studies at the English College in Rome. The

Rector of St Omers, Fr Henry More, objected to some of the questions as being more intimate and inquisitive than was necessary. Nevertheless the Cardinal Protector's order stood; nobody was to be sent to Rome "without previous, accurate and full information". If in a particular case, wrote the General, there is anything which for good reasons you think should not be answered by the student, omit it and write the answer yourself. It seems that the boys agreed with their Rector; for next year there was something of a slump, few boys wanting to go to Rome that autumn. Very well, said the General, they should not and indeed cannot be forced. He added, rather haughtily, those who come here *receive* a benefit, do not confer one. The effect of this last remark was somewhat spoilt by the postscript: "Try and persuade some of them to come". Fr More must have tried, and tried successfully. The Register of the English College, as annotated by Foley, shows but a slight decline in admissions from St Omers.

8

ST OMERS VERSUS OATES

IN 1660, 8 May, Old Style, Charles Stuart was declared the rightful King of England. The Clarenceux King of Arms proclaimed in London the happy event "ritu solemnissimo, pompâ magnificentissimâ, plausu incredibili", as Fr George Gray, the Provincial's "Socius", enthusiastically reported. Fr Gray might have made a good living as a journalist. Some dozen letters of his, dated 1660,[1] are full of choice morsels of news which he thinks his General in Rome would like to read. We hear, for instance, of the three royal palaces—Whitehall, St James' Palace and Somerset House—being unceremoniously cleared of their Cromwellian residents and made ready for the King's own use. General Monck is preparing to set out for Dover to greet His Majesty: and Mrs Monck, the blacksmith's daughter, "with her own hands is at work on the (royal) bedspreads, linen sheets, blankets, silk hangings" and the like.

As were most English Catholics of the time, this good Father was full of loyalty and excitement; full too of confident hope that with the arrival of the King all would be well, the Catholics allowed to live in peace. Had not Charles declared at Breda his desire for religious toleration? And was he not Catholic, if not in fact at least in sympathy and by conviction? Mr Thomas Whitgrave of Moseley Hall and his Chaplain, Fr Huddleston, had helped to convince him, at least temporarily, of the soundness of the Catholic claims. And four or five years later that truant Jesuit, Fr Peter Talbot, had involved himself in politics with the same ultimate end in view.[2] Hopes

[1] S. Arch., Anglia V, Nos. 50 seqq.
[2] For his persistent disobedience the General, Caraffa, finally dismissed him from the Society in 1659. Ten years later he was consecrated Archbishop of Dublin.

were high, on the Continent as well as in England. A period of religious peace would surely be reflected at St Omers in a growth of numbers and a lessening, if not an extinction, of debts. Alas, in spite of Charles' good will and more than one Declaration of Indulgence for tender consciences, the reign is memorable for the most bitter and harassing persecution of Catholics that they had yet experienced.

As to the perennial debts of St Omers, something was done to decrease them during the efficient and popular rectorship of Fr Richard Barton who after four years as Provincial ruled the College from 1660 until his death in February 1669. The sister of Fr Barton (veré Bradshaigh, of Haigh Hall, near Wigan), one may note in passing, had married Nicholas Blundell of Crosby, making her brother in due course uncle of that well-known personage William Blundell, the much-suffering "Cavalier". The General, Paul Oliva, had fallen in love with St Omers, "that noble Seminary", as he called it. "I love that place", he told the Provincial, and made of him two requests—to appoint a competent Procurator in London for the business of the College, and to induce the Fathers scattered throughout England to "favour" that establishment and assist in securing a prompter payment of College fees.[3] To the succeeding Provincial, Fr Joseph Simons,[4] who had just reported on his official visitation of the College he expressed his "incredible happiness" at receiving so good a report. Do all you can, he tells him, to promote the study of the classics, especially of Greek; encourage the custom of disputations in Greek and Latin in the refectory; and let the Rector stir the enthusiasm of the disputants by the offer of prizes. As for the masters who were bearing the burden of daily drudgery, they must be sent oftener to the country villa—Blandyke—and provided

[3] Oliva to Provincial (Fr John Clark), 24 January 1665 (Ep. Gen., II' f. 271ᵛ). In view of the infirmities of the aged General, Goswin Nickel' Fr John Paul Oliva was elected perpetual Vicar General, and on Nickel's death (31 July 1664) automatically succeeded to his office.
[4] Oliva to Jos. Simons (veré Emmanuel Lobb), 15 September 1668 (Ep. Gen., II, f. 308ᵛ).

there with better fare, as is done in other Colleges. Fresh air and relaxation they need, that they may return renewed in mind and body for the work ahead. The masters aforesaid would surely have been in full sympathy with such a proposal.

It was during Fr Barton's rectorship, in the September of 1667, that there died in the College a boy of about fourteen named Edmund Mathews, though known at St Omers by his *alias* of "Poins" or Poyntz. His family, it is almost certain, hailed from Tipperary. He is mainly of interest—at least from the viewpoint of the history of the College—in that his death was the occasion of a manuscript account, nearly fifty pages long, with the title "The relation of Edmund Poins",[5] from which one may gather here and there something of the customs of this period. Customs are sometimes long a-dying: or were they the ghosts of some of these that seem to have haunted Stonyhurst in its earlier years?

But something should be said of the boy himself. After two and a half years at the College, first in "Little Figures" and then in "Greater Figures", he had been promoted to the school of Grammar just a month before his death. His natural abilities are overshadowed in this biography by his supernatural piety and gift of prayer. Yet from some of the incidents related it is clear enough that he was not just a museum-piece but quite human and alive, keen and expert at games and of considerable promise as an actor. As a literary effort, however, his biography makes dreadful reading, being written in a pietistic, sickly sentimental style that tends to nauseate the reader. The author fortunately is anonymous, although obviously one who knew the boy well during his terms at St Omers. His only excuse, if excuse it be, is that the account was written for the perusal of a nun ("For the use of S^{tr} Hellen with leave of Superiours"). Of Sister Helen's taste in literature of course one cannot speak.

No doubt the College boys played several games according to the season. The only game mentioned in this account by

[5] The account has been printed in C.R.S., III, pp. 60-81.

name is "trap-ball", a game at which young Poyntz was "very dexterous". The trap, as described by the knowledge-able Strutt,[6] was a fixed contrivance not too unlike a wooden slipper pivoting in the middle between toe and heel. The striker with his short, broad bat strikes the "toe" from above, whereupon the ball resting in the heel is projected into the air and must be hit before it reaches the ground. The dexterity required would presumably vary with the width of the bat and be conditioned by the rules of the game, which as likely as not were home-made.

There is however a possible allusion to some form of hand-ball where it is counted amongst Edmund's virtues that when on an occasion a companion "would have bought of him the Place he had (as they call it) in the line for to play at ball", he offered him the "Place" but refused to accept the "sugar plum" (or plums) which served as the barter price. At all events a similar custom of "touching in" or "bagging a place" for handball and sometimes of selling it to another—not at all necessarily for sugar plums—prevailed in earlier days at Stonyhurst and was, it seems, peculiarly associated with handball and with no other game. The "line" above mentioned is almost certainly the term used at St Omers for playground, as quite certainly it was once at Stonyhurst and is still in use, though with a slightly extended connotation.

Master Edmund Poyntz was admitted into the Sodality of Our Lady on his death-bed: otherwise, having joined the school of Grammar but a month ago, he would have had to wait "some months" until the normal time (perhaps 8 December) for Grammarians to be admitted.[7] On his death-bed too he was conditionally admitted into the Society of Jesus— conditionally, in view of some uncertainty as to whether the Rector had power to admit so young a boy even *in articulo*

[6] J. Strutt: *Sports and Pastimes of the People of England* (London, 2 ed., 1810), pp. 99-100.
[7] Grammarians continued to be eligible for admission at Stonyhurst until 1852 when a separate Sodality for younger boys was formed.

mortis. There are several references to "the Sodalitie", meaning the boys' chapel, which served also as the meeting place of the Sodality B.V.M., as it did at Stonyhurst until 1859 when a separate Sodality Chapel was opened. For here in "the Sodalitie" this devout youth would say his many prayers, though not yet a Sodalist. And here too the boys assembled each morning for "the Common Masse (as they terme it)", apparently at half past five, a half hour after having been summoned out of bed.

This chapel was presumably on the ground floor, since we read of the gravestones of those who were buried there. Relics of the Saints abounded—Fr Thomas Cary would have seen to that, for he was a great devotee and connoisseur of relics and reliquaries. Relics, says our author, "like to a crowne or diademe of glory did environ our Bl Saviour upon the Alter"; but not only there. In a more "obscure" part of the chapel were kept some relics of "the glorious virgin Martyr Saint Martina": and early in 1666 Edmund's brother and his cousin, both named George and both of them dangerously ill, were "very strangely cured" at her intercession. Hence the vogue and popularity of St Martina at St Omers. To this day at Stonyhurst there is said on her feast, 30 January, a public "Mass for Health" with some solemnity. Edmund and the two Georges seem to have paid particular devotion to some of the less-known Saints. Witness the devotion of "our saintly child" to St "Encratides" or Encratia—a saint with a better claim to actual existence than the Bollandists will grant to St Martina—whom at some Father's suggestion he adopted as his patroness and invoked in every need. "In every theme he made, was written in his fairest hand, 'Ad maiorem Dei, Deiparae et Sanctae Encratidis gloriam'."

What else in this manuscript is to be gleaned of the customs in use three hundred years ago? The mention of "Composition Days" would certainly have meant much to Stonyhurst boys, even sixty years ago or less. In Edmund Poyntz's year in Greater Figures there were five Compositions during

the school year,[8] and a final examination before the summer
vacation, on which depended a prize and promotion to a
higher class. Edmund, one may note, was amongst the "First
Six" in all but one of these Compositions, and so was entitled
to the appropriate reward—probably a Good Breakfast or a
"postpast" or something of the sort. The term "Study Place"
was then in use as it still is, and probably other "Places" as
well (such as Shoe Place, Washing Place, etc.), the term being
but an Anglicized pronunciation of the French word. The
standard of classical studies must have been high. After a year
in Greater Figures this boy of fourteen "spoke Latin well for
one of that school"; could "interpret David's psalter out of
Greek into Latin" in public during dinner, and was "pretty
forward for interpreting Greek authors". Greater Figures and
Rudiments, be it remembered, were variant names for the
same school or class.

Finally an anecdote told by our anonymous author conveys
some incidental information. The summer of 1657 was more
than usually hot, and it was thought "unhoulsome" for boys to
sleep so many in one dormitory. It was therefore decided that
one class should sleep in the Watten Refuge nearby, not now
occupied by novices though a few Fathers were residing there.
The choice fell upon Greater Figures, in which was Edmund
Poyntz: "and it was a divertisement gratefull to little children
to go in the evening to the Refuge and returne to the Colledge
in the morning, their Master accompanying them". Here "the
great silence which is kept in our Colledge at these howers"
was neither exacted nor expected of these small boys. Edmund,
however, considered it more fitting to observe the silence customary at the College, always went straight to the chapel, "and there
expected the saying of Litanies of the Saints" before bed at
9 o'clock. This "greater silence" and Night Prayers in the

---

[8] The number of Compositions (written examinations) had varied in
different years, sometimes as many as eight occurring in the course of the
school year. From 1658 the number seems to have been reduced to five,
excluding the final examination (possibly oral) at the end of the year.

form of the Litany of the Saints, even for the youngest boys, dates back to the days of Father Schondonch: a Jesuit custom which the boys were made to share.

As early as February 1663 a toleration bill, sometimes known as King Charles' First Declaration of Indulgence, was introduced in the House of Commons. The cavalier majority forced its withdrawal, and procured instead a Proclamation, dated 9 April, ordering all "Jesuits and priests" with certain exceptions to depart from the kingdom before 14 May.[9] There was a panic. The Provincial reported to the General in May that many had already retired to France or Belgium, whilst those who remained were taking immediate precautions for their safety. A month later and the "recent edict" had turned out to be rather a damp squib.[10] In the years that followed there were alternations of hope and despondency. Charles on the one hand, although intellectually convinced (as some would have known), was politically unwilling to declare his convictions: on the other hand the country at large and in particular the majority of Parliament were in ever-increasing opposition to any relaxation however slight of the penal laws. The antagonism grew in strength when it became known not only that the Duke of York's wife, Anne Hyde, Lord Clarendon's daughter, but that in 1669 the Duke himself had been received into the Church by the Jesuit Provincial, Fr Joseph Simons.

The hopes and still more the fears of the Catholics in England were of course shared by the Jesuits abroad, even though they were on the safer side of the Channel. Apart from obvious religious motives, the material prosperity of St Omers depended on a satisfactory complement of pupils and on the prompt payment by parents of the fees. For lack of such the College was reduced to such penury that according to Fr Basil Langworth, Vice-Rector for some months in 1672, he must needs

[9] C. S. P. Dom. 1663-4, p. 106.
[10] S. Arch., Anglia V, No. 64: E. Courtney (Provincial) to General, 8/18 May 1663; No. 65, *ibid.* to *ibid.*, 12/22 June 1663. He signed his name "Courteney". The Latin, "Courtnaeus", accords with the pronunciation, not with his spelling.

reduce the number of pupils either by sending some prematurely to the English College in Rome, or by returning them to their homes in England. The General, Paul Oliva, replied[11] that the decision had better be postponed to the following year—when, as the Annual Letter notes, sixteen students left the College to continue their vocations elsewhere.

During these years the numbers had gradually been falling from an unexpected peak year of over 150 boys (1670) to 120 (1674), where the total remained fairly stationary for awhile. In 1672 the College was some 20,000 scudi (nominally about £5,000, in modern values at least £50,000) in debt, owing mainly to the failure of parents to pay the fees. As for the Spanish pension, a statement of annual payments from that source [12] shows that in the course of twenty-five years, from 1660 to 1684 inclusive, 1,517 florins had been received out of 250,000 fl. due. No wonder therefore that in 1679 the General himself, and one or two Provincials likewise, contributed unnamed sums of money to relieve this "noble seminary" in its distress.

All this notwithstanding, St Omers was maintaining its reputation as well from an academic as from a religious standpoint. Fr Thomas Cary, successor of Fr Barton as Rector (1669-1672), had spent the best part of twenty years in the College as master and Director of the Sodality before his rectorship, in which office he ended his days. Himself a man of singular piety, with a special devotion to the Saints and their relics, he had the gift of educating souls as well as minds, if one may so express it. No doubt there were others too with at least similar if not equal skill. From the Annual Letters of this period one gathers there was great competition amongst the boys to be admitted into Our Lady's Sodality. Many boys too, even the younger ones, with full liberty of choice had taken to the habit of fasting on certain special days, such as the eve of St Ignatius' feast—a fast which was not more than a Jesuit

11 Oliva to Langworth, 23 July 1672 (Ep. Gen., II, f. 341).
12 S. Arch., A. IV. 13 (2), pp. 107 seqq.

custom. In past years, we are told, such voluntary fasting had become almost a joke—and a pretty thin joke at that!

Studies likewise have flourished, especially, it is added, has Greek regained its former prominence in the school. Young boys as well as older ones talk fluent Greek from the refectory "pulpit". Boys in Grammar dispute in public and extempore in Greek and Latin, to the astonishment of visitors, including some non-Catholic visitors from England who had come purposely to verify reports of what was being done at St Omers. (We are returning in spirit to the days of Fr Schondonch.) Fr Edward Courtney is cited as a witness. He was the "Grand Old Man" of the period, who had been a boy at the College some sixty years earlier—he would have been a Rhetorician in 1618-19—had taught classics there, and later been its Rector. In his old age, after having been twice Rector in Rome as well as Provincial, he obtained leave to retire to St Omers and prepare for death, which came to him six years later in the October of 1677. He is quoted as having expressed his utter astonishment at the fluency of the boys in Greek and Latin, and at their unexpected erudition.

From these same Annual Letters one may pick up some odds and ends of information that will bear relating. During the rectorship of Fr Cary, for instance, on occasion of an epidemic in 1669 a substantial relic, the arm of St Thomas of Hereford, was publicly exposed in the "Sodality" with remarkable results. This relic, it is known, reached St Omers in September 1668, after having passed through several hands in the course of the preceding cenuturies. It is of interest that a somewhat similar relic of this Saint, which came to Stonyhurst from Holywell in 1835, was believed to be this same "arms-bone". That particular relic, however, has been lost ever since the suppression of the Society in 1773: what Stonyhurst possesses is a *tibia* or shin-bone.[13]

We read too of a visit to the College in 1670 of the Governor

[13] Cf. J. Morris, s.j. in *The Month*, XXV, pp. 112-126; *Acta Sanctorum*, October, Vol. I, p. 540.

of the Spanish Netherlands—probably the young Comte de Monterey—in whose honour an almost extempore play was staged at short notice. It is easy for a chronicler to comment that the Governor was delighted with what he saw: but deeds are a stronger testimony than polite words. The Governor was evidently a man of broad views: he asked that the boys be granted a week's holiday in his honour. One can imagine a perturbed expression on the Rector's face on receiving such a wholesale request: what the Prefect of Studies said remains unwritten, certainly unprinted. The account does not indeed explicitly state that the request was granted, though in the circumstances a refusal would have been difficult. For the request was backed up by a very generous gift, a gift of no less than 300 "aurei" or golden crowns, nominally equivalent to about 900 florins, for the purpose of providing the boys with an extra-special "feed". Remembering that 250 florins or thereabouts was considered sufficient to keep a scholar at school for a year, one can appreciate the generosity of the gift. It should have been enough and more than enough to feast the boys for the whole week that was asked for.

Like the Treaty of Westphalia, so too the Peace of the Pyrenees (1659) had little effect on Louis XIV and his designs on the Spanish Netherlands. In 1660 he married his cousin, the Infanta Maria Teresa, eldest daughter of Philip IV of Spain: and on the latter's death five years later he saw his way to claiming, through his wife, at least a partial succession to his father-in-law. He was delayed in the execution of his plans, first by the Anglo-Dutch war (1665-1667) and then by the Triple Alliance formed against him early in 1668. The resulting Peace of Aix-la-Chapelle, however, left him in possession of several towns in southern Flanders. In the course of the next ten years Belgium was the seat of war on both its northern and southern frontiers. Holland, Louis XIV's main opponent, was invaded in 1672 but saved itself by the memorable expedient of opening the dykes. For another five years Louis fought with

success, although gradually opposed by most of the European
states. By 1678 his treasury, exhausted by the vast expenses of
war and not a little bribery, brought him to a standstill. On
10 August 1678, the Peace of Nijmegen (Nimègue) was
signed by France and Holland, and on 17 September by France
and Spain. Spain, the ally of the Dutch, again paid most of
the costs of the war by what was handed over to the French.

We must go back a little. In the course of the campaign of
1676 Aire was besieged and quickly captured by the Maréchal
d'Humieres. In Artois *reservé*, therefore, Saint-Omer alone
remained in the hands of the allies. Next spring Louis himself
took command of the army which after no more than a week
of siege forced Valenciennes to capitulate in mid-March.
Thereupon the King divided his forces, sending his brother,
the Duc d'Orleans, with one part to besiege Saint-Omer
whilst he led the other half to an attack on Cambrai. By this
date the Duc d'Orleans had married again, his first wife
Henrietta, the beloved sister of Charles II, having died
mysteriously—whether from poison or from peritonitis one
can't be sure—a few weeks after her well-known visit to Dover
in 1670.

The fall of Saint-Omer was inevitable unless relieved by its
Dutch ally. The Duke's head-quarters were established at
Blandyke; and nearly all the information available from Jesuit
sources is concerned with the damage done there to the Villa
house. So serious was it that the cost of repair was estimated
at more than 600 crowns—a considerable sum for an impecuni-
ous College. Watten also seems to have fared badly. As late as
January 1680, a memorandum of the Provincial, Fr John
Warner, is to the effect "that Watten church shall be cleered
of ye corne with all possible speede".[14]

Of the siege itself one need only note that it lasted about
twenty-five days. An attempt was made by William of

[14] Litt. Ann., 1677 (S. Arch., B. I. 15, p. 323) signed by Thomas Harcottus,
i.e. Fr Whitbread; *Letter-book of Fr Warner* (Cambridge Univ. Library, MS.
Ll-1-19, f. 86).

Orange to relieve the town. At Mont Cassel on 11 April after a severe struggle with heavy losses on both sides the Dutch and Spanish troops abandoned the field, and the Duc d'Orleans returned to Blandyke. On 20 April the town finally capitulated. Louis XIV entered Saint-Omer on 1 May, stayed that night at the Bishop's Palace and left next morning after hearing Mass at the Cathedral and paying a visit to "the principal religious establishments". Whether the English College came within that category one is left to guess.[15] Next year in accordance with the peace terms of the Peace of Nijmegen (September 1678), Saint-Omer and all Artois were formally and permanently ceded to the King of France.

It is to be doubted whether the townsfolk of Saint-Omer were unduly grieved by this change of allegiance. Spanish rule in the Netherlands had usually been resented, sometimes violently so. If the Annual Letters are a fair criterion, it was the financial aspect that mainly agitated the minds of the College authorities. Intermittent as had been the payment of the Spanish pension, it now seemed that even the hope of payment was gone for ever. The Spanish ministers at Brussels refused to pay anything to an institution now subject to a foreign King: and Madrid, even if it would, was unable to find the money. The bleak prospect of yet another financial crisis was dispelled, however, by an ordinance of Louis XIV dated from St Germain en Laye, 21 February 1680. Thereby His Majesty was pleased to grant an annual pension of 6,000 livres

> pour estre par les dicts Peres de la Compagnie de Jesus employez en l'entretient et augmentation des bastiments du dict College et a celui du nombre suffisant des Peres et Regents pour eslever et instruire dans la Religion Catholique Apostolique et Romaine dans le dit College Cent gentil-hommes Anglois au moins les quels ils seront tenus d'y recevoir nourir et entretenir sans priejudice neantmoins des pensions que les parents de dicts gentilhommes pourront

---

[15] For this paragraph cf. Reboulet, *Histoire du regne de Louis XIV* (Avignon, 1744), pp. 209-211; Derheims, *op. cit.*, pp. 343 seqq.

envoyer et faire tenir volontairement aux dicts Peres ainsy qu'il s'est praticque iusques a present. . . .[16]

This yearly sum of 6,000 livres or £600, graciously granted by Louis XIV, was the equivalent almost exactly of the 2,000 golden crowns named by King Philip II in his Letters Patent of 6 May 1594.

Thus in 1678, half-way between the foundation of St Omers and its forced migration in 1762, the College changed of necessity its allegiance from Spain to France, whilst remaining always loyal in rightful love and allegiance to its English homeland and King Charles II. What is no less important, 1678 saw the beginning of the notorious "Popish Plot", or more correctly "Oates' Plot", which for a few years wrought havoc among the English Catholics. Of the plot itself and its many ramifications there will be not much to say unless it be to make clear the part played by St Omers in the course of it.

There is more to be said of Titus Oates, that lecherous and dedicated liar who for some six months was a pupil at the College. How such a man came to be accepted by Fr Richard Strange, the Provincial, remains a mystery beyond reason. It is however reasonable to presume that all the sordid details of Oates' earlier life were not known to him as they became known to subsequent investigators. Expelled from Merchant Taylors' School, from Cambridge and from a chaplaincy in the Royal Navy, he was as poor as a dormouse. Hoping to better himself, he abandoned for a while the Protestant ministry and turned Catholic, being received into the Church in April 1677 by an ex-Jesuit of the name of William Berry, *alias* Hutchinson, an unstable, eccentric priest, charitably supposed to be suffering from "bats in the belfry". Of the sincerity or insincerity of this conversion it is impossible to be quite sure. (In the course of Lord Stafford's trial Oates stated that his conversion was but a pretence. Had it suited him, however, he would as easily

[16] A notarial copy of the original is in the Archives of the English College, Rome (Lib. II, f. 178), for a transcript of which I am indebted to the kindness of Rev. A. Kenny.

have stated the opposite.) A week or two later he set off for Spain. Under the name of Titus Ambrose he was admitted as an ecclesiastical student in the English Seminary at Valladolid, and after about five months was expelled on 20 October (N.S.) "ob pessimos mores" and returned to England.[17]

Having somehow won over the Provincial by his entreaties and tears of repentance (it was discovered later that he possessed the gift of weeping at will), he was sent to St Omers, where he arrived on 10 December. Not only did he come as a prospective pupil, but also as a possible candidate for the Society. (What a devastating "Jesuit of Fiction" he would have made!) The authorities at the College were loath to accept him.[18] He was a man of twenty-eight, an entire stranger, and neither by birth nor manners nor learning did he seem fit to associate with the youths of whom they had the care. However, as "Titus Ambrose" had the backing of the Provincial, they were more or less powerless. The "new boy" was placed in Rhetoric. Henry Thornton, then in Syntax, deposed later that Rhetoric was assigned to him "by reason of his age and upon no other account; he might have gone elsewhere . . . for any great store of learning he had". He was given too a separate table in the refectory, between the boys' tables and the Fathers' table. "He pretended", according to Will Parry (veré Conway) that "he could not diet as the rest of the young students did; and therefore obtained leave to sit alone at a little table by himself. . . ."[19] As there is good reason to suppose that all in the refectory fared alike, one is left to guess the Rector's real reason for this "privilege".

In the January of 1678 Fr Thomas Whitbread (alias Harcourt)

[17] Valladolid Register (C.R.S., vol. 30, p. 173). The Gregorian Calendar (New Style, or N.S.), in use in at least the Catholic States abroad, was ten days ahead of the Julian Calendar (Old Style, or O.S.) in use in England. Since the question of dates is of importance in this chapter and some confusion may arise, the dates will be given according to the New Style or according to both.

[18] Florus Anglo-Bavaricus (Liège, 1685), p. 93.

[19] Cobbett, State Trials, 10; 1109, 1111.

succeeded Fr Strange as Provincial, and presently crossed the Channel in June to make his official visitation of the Belgian houses. By this time it would appear that Oates' reputation had spread beyond the College walls. At all events William Gerard stated in 1685 that "it was discoursed of all over the town that when the Provincial came he was to be dismissed". The rumour proved to be true; for after learning the facts of the case Fr Whitbread ordered him to depart. He had, as we shall presently see, made himself a laughing-stock for his companions—quick to give offence and to take offence; a boastful liar, unobservant of the rules, and so on. It is said of him[20] that when more than usually harried in the course of the day—boys in a crowd can at times be very cruel—he would at night in the dormitory, unmindful of the rule of silence, loudly intone some imprecatory psalm by way of revenge, probably to the further amusement of his hearers.

We come to something more serious. When his entreaties had no effect on Fr Whitbread and he saw himself soon to be reduced to a state of intolerable poverty, he told some companions that he must become either a Jesuit or a Judas. The Provincial's reaction when he heard of it was to tell him to hurry. Fr Stapleton, the author of this part of the *Florus Anglo-Bavaricus*, here relates an incident which had better be given as he tells it:

> On the eve of his departure, late at night, he was found in the Sodality (Chapel), leaning on his elbows over the altar like a priest at Mass. Asked what he was doing there he replied, "I am saying farewell to Jesus Christ". The words might be taken in a good sense: yet for understanding them in a sinister sense there stood the evil character of the man and the arrogant posture of his body—so much so that somebody made the comment, "Oates has said farewell to Christ in the sense of having nothing more to do with Him".[21]

Early next morning, 23 June, Oates set out for England. He had of course paid nothing for his six months at St Omers. At

[20] *Florus Anglo-Bavaricus*, p. 93.   [21] *Ibid.*, p. 94.

his departure, as the Provincial testified,[22] he was given a good suit of clothes, a periwig, and £4 for his pocket—a very generous sum in those days—which Oates promised to repay but did nothing of the kind: his repayment took the form of a savage revenge.

Fr Whitbread's visitation had taken him to the Jesuit seminary at Liège in the month of July. A well-attested account exists of an exhortation he gave to the students, preparatory to a renewal of their vows on the feast of St James, 23 July.[23] Apropos of the feast he enlarged on our Lord's answer to the request of St James' mother (Matt. xx, 22)—"Can you drink the cup that I am to drink?", and the stout reply of the two sons, "*Possumus. We can.*" And if persecution should arise (he asked), as so easily it might, could they face the consequent dangers, false betrayal, the hardships of prison, the rack, false evidence, unjust conviction, the atrocious ignominy of Tyburn? The answer in each detail must be, "*Possumus. We can.*" The earnestness and vividness of this exhortation was long remembered. And when a year later the heroic answer was given by the Provincial to all these questions, the rack excepted, this exhortation seemed almost a prophecy of his future martyrdom. Evidently the threat of Titus Oates—either Jesuit or Judas—had not been forgotten. On 4 September 1678, Fr Whitbread wrote from St Omers, "Tomorrow I begin to move towards England".[24] About five weeks later, on 8 October (or 28 September, Old Style), Oates and his associate, Ezrael Tonge, appeared before the Privy Council and launched the famous, the infamous plot.

Titus Oates after his departure from St Omers appears to have gone straight to London—a journey of about four days. During the following months there was much coming and going between the inventors and the patrons of the plot. Oates for a while was playing a double game. He frequented

22 Cobbett, *State Trials*, 7; 358.
23 Cf. Foley, V, 235 seqq., who prints it from an Oscott MS.
24 S. Arch., Anglia V, No. 88.

the company of the Jesuits, begging their assistance, ingratiating himself with them as best he could. On the Provincial's return —he and his Socius had both caught the fever at Antwerp where it was raging—he repeatedly renewed his petition to be admitted into the Society. At a later stage he began to threaten. He let it be known that unless he was admitted as a Jesuit, or at least was paid an annual pension, he would see to it that the Fathers were accused of high treason. Meanwhile with the fanatical Ezrael Tonge, Colonel Blood, famous for his attempt on the Crown Jewels, and a certain Digby, a bankrupt merchant (Fr John Warner, however, calls him a lawyer), he was busy concocting the details to be inserted in his *True Narrative of the Horrid Plot*. The finishing touches to this romance, we are told, were given in "Aula Vulpina" or Fox Hall (Vauxhall). Here at frequent intervals could be seen the coaches of certain noblemen—members of the Green Ribbon Club, one may suppose, and perhaps Lord Shaftesbury himself—who had come to confer with the plotters. Indeed, this Vauxhall lodging came to be known locally as the "Plot-house".[25]

Of the Plot in general this much may be said. There was undoubtedly a plot contrived against the Catholics in general and the Jesuits in particular. For Titus Oates it provided both an instrument of revenge and a means of livelihood. Incidentally, as it turned out, it was the road to fame: no history of this period can omit the story of his Plot. Because of the prevailing anti-Catholic temper of the times this vicious plot might have succeeded in its object without extraneous help. But its extraordinary success was due to the powerful support, aided by political influence and propaganda, that it received from such men as Shaftesbury, Buckingham and their republican supporters.

The exclusion of the Catholic Duke of York from the throne was no doubt the immediate aim of Shaftesbury. More positively, the Duke of Monmouth, Lucy Walter's son, was to be King in place of the rightful heir. But the attempt to

[25] *Florus Anglo-Bavaricus*, 95-6.

declare Monmouth legitimate was quickly and effectively frustrated by the personal intervention of King Charles himself. Would the crowning of Monmouth have brought to a natural end the intrigues of Shaftesbury or of the Green Ribbon Club? Until the elusive problems arising out of the history of the Rye House Plot have been more fully investigated there can be no certain answer. Shaftesbury indeed was dead by that date; but "the evil that men do lives after them". As for that trenchant publicist, Sir Roger L'Estrange, he at least was troubled by no doubts: "There was indubitably a Republic Plot. . . . But the Plot was to be called a Popish Plot. . . . The True Protestants were to kill the King, and the Papists to be hang'd for't."[26] Titus Oates, it is probable, knew beforehand of the Rye House Plot, and, to use Maitland of Lethington's famous phrase, was "looking through his fingers", ready, if called upon, to perjure himself yet again.

"The history of the interval betwixt Otes'es Damnable Discovery and (if the conceit be not too trivial) the Discovery of Damnable Otes"[27]—Sir Roger was nothing if not frank—concerns us here in connection with the St Omers "Old Boys" who suffered during that interval, and the younger ones who came over to London as witnesses in some of the trials. Two "Old Boys", Fr William Ireland, Procurator of the Province, and Fr John Fenwick who acted as Procurator in London for the affairs of St Omers, were the first to be arrested, within a few hours of Oates' declaration of the Plot before the Privy Council. Fr Ireland, in company with his lay secretary, John Grove, and a Benedictine laybrother, Thomas Pickering, were tried for high treason at the Old Bailey on 27 (or 17, Old Style) December 1678: all three were condemned and presently martyred at Tyburn. Fr Ireland had an excellent alibi for his defence; but it was not till six years later that Oates' evidence was abundantly proved to be perjured. Is it significant that Oates had at once made sure of the two Procurators, and of

[26] *A Brief History of the Times*, Part I (London, 1687), p. 159.
[27] *Ibid.*, p. 33.

course of their papers and whatever money there was in their rooms? He and his fellow priest-hunters were never averse to what they would probably have described as perquisites.[28] On the following night he broke illegally into the house of the Spanish ambassador and but for the latter's intervention would have arrested Fr Whitbread and his Socius or assistant, Fr Edward Mico, both of them still suffering from a severe attack of fever. For the time being he had to be content with their letters and papers, brazenly seized: and with a few blows aimed at Fr Mico by one of the escort he proceeded elsewhere on his quest. At a later date both Fathers were taken to Newgate, but Fr Mico never recovered, dying in prison that December "not so much from the fever as from the blows of a musket inflicted on him by a brutal soldier".[29]

Fr Whitbread, the Provincial, was spared for a more gruesome but none the less coveted fate. On 23 June (N.S.) 1679 he was tried at the Old Bailey, Chief Justice Scroggs as usual presiding. With him were four other Jesuits, cited as William Harcourt, John Fenwick, John Gaven *alias* Gawen, and Anthony Turner,[30] all of them educated at St Omers with the exception of Fr Turner. London excitedly flocked to the court, anxious to catch a glimpse of five live Jesuits awaiting their trial and condemnation. And Oates had indeed risen to the occasion. Here was the Provincial of these fearsome Jesuits, Fr William Harcourt, Rector of the London District, and the Procurator of St Omers. The Procurator of the Province, Fr

[28] Of Sir William Waller, the priest-hunter, the Lord Chief Justice remarked with grim humour during Oates' trial for perjury: "We all know Sir William Waller was wonderful good at the fingering of gold; he us'd to take away broad pieces as Popish relics, because of the crosses upon them". (Cobbett, 10; 1225.)

[29] Litt. Ann., 1678-79 (S. Arch., MS. B. I. 16, p. 39).

[30] These five Jesuits were beatified in 1929, with the same nomenclature as given above, not quite consistently. Fr William Harcourt, also known as Waring, was in fact Fr William Barrow, a Lancastrian born at Weeton-cum-Prees in the Fylde. Fenwick was an *alias* of Fr Caldwell, whilst Gavan (or Gawen) and Turner were the true names of these two martyrs. For their trial, cf. Warner's History of the Plot (C.R.S., vol. 47, pp. 109-112).

Ireland, had already been hanged, drawn and quartered some months before. But if Oates hoped thus to throw the English Jesuit Province into confusion by lopping off the heads, he soon learnt his mistake. On receiving news of Fr Whitbread's arrest, the General, making an excellent choice, appointed the Rector of the Liege seminary, Fr John Warner, to be Vice-Provincial. In England Fr Edward Petre was given temporary charge—a charge carried out with competence, even from his prison in Newgate. A year later, after Fr Whitbread's death, Fr Warner became Provincial. He had sent over to England two Jesuits to look after the financial affairs—Fr John Baker, born in Spain, and a laybrother, Br. Beaugrand, a native of Ypres, neither of them subject to arrest in England.[31]

We return to Scroggs and the trial of the five Jesuits. For this trial a number of St Omers boys had been sent over by the Vice-Provincial as witnesses for the defence. In fact several of them had been in London some months earlier on behalf of the five Catholic Lords in the Tower,[32] whose impeachment would have taken place in April or May but for continual disputes between Lords and Commons on questions of procedure. A cardinal point in Oates' presentation of his case was his sworn statement that he had left St Omers and come to London for a week or two, in order to be present on 4 May (24 April, O.S.) with various professed Jesuits at a "consult" held at the White Horse Tavern in Wild Street, off Drury Lane. It was there, said he, that he had learnt the details of the "horrid plot" to assassinate King Charles, to massacre the Protestants, to bring over a French army of 50,000 men, and so on.

---

31 *Letter-book of Fr Warner*, ff. 5, 75ᵛ. Foley, *op. cit.*, quotes from the Letter-book a letter of 14 June 1680, as reporting Fr Baker's "escape from England", whereas Fr Warner reported the very opposite. Fr Richard Petre, he says, "ex Insula evasit ob adversam valetudinem" and Fr John Baker "eo penetravit" (f. 21ᵛ).

32 The Earl of Powis, Viscount Stafford, and Lords Petre, Arundell of Wardour, and Belasyse. Eventually it was Stafford only who was impeached and condemned (December 1680). Lord Petre died in prison; the remaining three were released early in 1684.

The facts were different. A "consult"—one of the customary triennial Congregations of the English Province—had indeed been held on that date: not however at the White Horse Tavern or any other tavern but in the private apartments of the Duke of York in St James' Palace. To advance such a fact would, of course, in the circumstances have brought about the ruin of the Duke: such a defence was out of the question. Another objection was that Titus Oates was neither a Jesuit nor a priest, still less a Professed Father—professed, that is to say, of a special fourth vow in addition to the usual three vows of religion: and only such professed Fathers and Rectors of Colleges were eligible to attend the Congregation. But a more damning fact and far safer defence was the absence of Oates from London at that date. For with the exception of one night at Watten he had not slept outside of St Omers from his arrival in December 1677 until his dismissal on 23 June of the following year. Here then seemed the appropriate opportunity to prove the perjury of Oates by the cumulative evidence of his companions at school.

In point of fact the testimony of St Omers had been given six months earlier, but "beyond the seas" and therefore not admissible as evidence in an English Court of Law. Lord Castlemain, defending himself from detractors after his acquittal of high treason in 1680, stated:

> Protestants in Court can testifie, that being sent to St Omers about Christmas '78 to know whether Mr Oates had been there all April and May as was asserted in Mr Ireland's Tryal, they found it confirm'd by the whole Colledge, and saw fourteen of the chief Scholars . . . make Oath before the City Magistrates, That the said Oates never lay out of the Colledge from the 10th of Dec. '77 to the 23 of June following, but one night at Watten. . . .[33]

He added that this "certificate" was in the Court during the trial.

---

[33] *The Earl of Castlemain's Manifesto* (1681), pp. 94-5.

According to Fr Warner's history of the Plot, fourteen boys gave evidence at the trial of the five Jesuits. The Annual Letter of 1678-79 (perhaps his authority) says the same. But in the contemporary printed record of the trial not more than nine boys are cited as giving evidence, with the addition of three other older witnesses, of whom two can be identified as Jesuit lay-brothers. Three others from Watten—the gardener, the mason and a bargeman—and two laybrothers from Liege gave testimony contradicting Oates' statements as to what Jesuits had (as he pretended) travelled with him to England towards the close of April. At least three boys had been arrested soon after their arrival in London. Their examinations—for what they are worth—were taken on 8 May (N.S.) before Sir William Waller. A petition of the Lords in the Tower is on record, dated the following day, asking for the discharge of Christopher Towneley, Henry Hall and Daniel Gifford, whom they had sent for "from beyond the seas" as being very material witnesses but who had been imprisoned "upon suspicion of being a priest".[34]

Fr Morgan's Annual Letter of 1678-79 tells a story of two other young boys, brothers, who were arrested in London. They had by chance met Titus Oates (known to them as Sampson Lucy) whilst they were out for a walk; and the younger one "commented" on the impudence of Oates in pretending to have been at the "consult" in the previous year when all the while he was at St Omers. Oates, brazen-faced, had them arrested. In the pocket of one was found a letter for Fr Edward Petre, address and all. Here was more valuable prey than were two young boys. Fr Petre was duly captured,

---

[34] For the examinations see Fitzherbert MSS. in Hist. MSS. Comm., 13th Report, Pt. 6, pp. 149-152. The petition of the Catholic Lords is in Cobbett, *State Trials*, 7; 1263. Towneley became a Jesuit, was ordained, but died soon after, in 1692. Gifford or Giffard (*vere* Coulster) also entered Watten, but left after some ten months. A son of Sir Joseph Coulster, he had been maintained for nearly seven years at St Omers by Col. Charles Giffard, well known as the royalist officer who after the battle of Worcester guided Charles II to White Ladies.

and though he defended himself vigorously before the Privy
Council he was of course committed to prison.

It must have been a hard ordeal and have required very
considerable pluck on the part of these boys to stand up in a
packed court of hostile and jeering spectators and say their say.
Being Catholics they were not allowed to give their evidence
on oath. Oates was inclined at times to ask incriminating
questions: "Was not the witness a priest or Jesuit?" But the
Lord Chief Justice drew the line here and disallowed such
questions as these. That is not to say that Scroggs was at all
tender towards either the witnesses or the prisoners at the bar.
Vituperation of one kind or another was a common, almost
customary, adjunct of trials at this shabby period of judicial
practice: and Scroggs provides an extreme example of such
practice.

Inevitably a long series of witnesses all testifying that Oates
was with them at St Omers when he swore he was in London,
and supporting their assertions by recollection of incidents of
College life—all this must have tended to shake the confidence
of judges and jury in Oates' word. So at least one would have
thought. But justice in the seventeenth century had a meaning
different from its meaning today. Certain legal forms, the
accessories of a Court of Justice, had to be observed. But the
verdict, especially in these cases of treason, was as often as not
predetermined on political grounds. "In those days", writes
Mr Pollock,[35] "state trials were not merely impartial inquiries
into the question whether or no certain persons had committed
certain acts . . . they were life-and-death struggles of the King
and his government against the attacks of those who wished to
subvert them."

These five Jesuits—and many others too—were accused of
plotting to murder the King and subvert the Protestant
Government. Charles, it is true, did not believe a word of it;
but he had promised a strict enquiry. Parliament, or at least
most of its members, appear to have believed in a plot; and

[35] John Pollock, *The Popish Plot* (London, 1903), p. 286.

the country at large was wildly fanatical in its belief. Shaftesbury and his colleagues, intent on the exclusion from the throne of the King's Catholic brother, did everything in their power to fan the fury of the "mobile", the London mob, into a raging fire. Sentence of death on the five Jesuits was assured. Had they been acquitted, Scroggs might well have been torn limb from limb.

The evidence given by the St Omers boys was consistent, though not without mistakes. They were all positive about the months that mattered. How could they know? How could they not know? Did he not sit daily at meal-time at a table apart, between Community and boys? He was a marked man. His face, his figure, his accent and conversation and the uncouth oddities he indulged in made him the butt of the whole school. He must have added considerably to the hilarity of his companions: when conversation flagged or monotony was creating a sense of boredom, there was always old Sampson Lucy's leg to be pulled.

Said Anthony Turberville at a later trial: "I saw a little boy beat him up and down with a fox's tail. Indeed, my Lord, all his actions were very remarkable. . . . I was a person then the youngest in the whole company, and Mr Oates being very abusive to me, I did what became me to right myself upon him."[36] Two days before the date of the famous "consult" Oates was walking in the College garden with Thomas Billing, as he had earlier in the day with Dick Blunt (veré Burnaby).

So I was with him walking a little while [continued Billing] and then this Blunt and one Henry Howard [i.e. Haggerston] were playing one with another, throwing stones at one another's shins. At which he was displeased and said, if they would not be quiet, he would go tell the Rector. Howard was hasty, and spoke angerly to him, and said, if he would not be quiet, he would beat him. But Mr Oates persisting, and daring of him, says he, "What, do you dare me?" and

[36] Cobbett, *State Trials*, 10; 1131.

comes up to him, and throws up Mr Oates his heels. Upon that Mr Oates lookt very fretfully upon him, and withdrew himself into the Infirmary.[37]

Evidently the practice of reporting to the authorities for such trivial reasons was not looked on with favour at St Omers.

Another lamentable instance may be cited, as told by William "Parry" (Conway) of Flintshire, who was a witness at this trial—he was in Poetry—and again in 1685 as a Jesuit in his first year of theology, although he did not advertise the fact. Asked at that latter trial how he remembered that Oates had been at St Omers in the March of 1678, he explained that on the Thursday in mid-Lent "the scholars had a peculiar recreation which they call 'Sawing of the witch', and Mr Oates was among them; and I was one of them that broke a pan about his head for recreation".[38] One cannot but feel some sympathy here for Sampson Lucy, vile perjuror though he was. But possibly the pans used in this strange game were made of some frail material: else a broken pan strongly suggests a broken head. Certainly it was a "peculiar recreation"!

As might be expected, the witnesses were not uniformly expert. William "Parry", for instance, became flurried and seemed unable to distinguish between New Style and Old Style. Master Cox asserted at first that Oates had left the College in July, whereas the others said correctly that it was in June. He then began to hedge, and parried Scroggs' persistent questioning as best he could. He saw he had made a mistake. Scroggs however made the dubious point that if the witness was mistaken in one date, his memory of more important dates was unreliable. "You hear how he delivers his evidence; it is as if he had been instructed."

Mr John Pollock, the chief modern writer who believes in

---

[37] *The Tryalls . . . of Thomas White, alias Whitebread . . .* (etc.) London, 1679, pp. 55-56. Or Cobbett, 7; 370. Haggerston and Burnaby both entered the noviciate at Watten, the latter leaving it before taking his vows. Haggerston died, a Jesuit priest, in England in 1714.
[38] Cobbett, 10; 1110.

the existence of some form of Popish and Jesuit plot—he thinks, for instance, that they were Catholics, if not Jesuits, who murdered Sir Edmund Berry Godfrey—has gone further than Scroggs: he asserts definitely that the St Omers witnesses were "very cleverly parroted".[39] Such a statement is as easy to make as it is difficult to discuss. What exactly is meant by parrotry? The dictionary would have it to be the unintelligent repetition of another's words; yet lack of intelligence is by no means a characteristic of these witnesses. One needs, surely, to be realistic in such a matter. When news of Oates' monstrous accusations reached St Omers, and still more when those selected to give evidence had been told, what would the boys have done? They would of course have discussed the matter *ad nauseam* among themselves, compared notes, remembered this and that, until the life and adventures of Sampson Lucy at the College had become almost a collective memory. It is quite probable that the Rector or somebody in authority gave the selected party audience, warned them of the dangers they might well encounter in London, confirmed dates—those for instance of Oates' arrival and departure: they would long ago have worked these out roughly for themselves—and advised them, possibly, that a date clothed with an incident relating to it carries more weight than a bare date. No doubt he added his blessing. And then the final arrangements in London before the trial. "Well, I'll tell them about when the old ass sat down amongst the orchestra when we had that play, and refused to budge." "All right, then I'll tell them about his reading aloud on Sundays in the Sodality", and so on. Something of the sort is surely natural, and sufficient to explain the background of the St Omers evidence. If this is parrotry, so be it. More definite instruction *might* of course have been given to the boys, however unnecessary it would have been. But neither Scroggs nor Mr Pollock nor anyone else can do more than guess: the Recording Angel is beyond our reach.

If one has lingered somewhat on this subject of parroting, it

[39] J. Pollock, *op. cit.*, p. 345.

is because Mr Pollock has made a graver charge against these boys, and indirectly against their educators.

> No doubt can exist [he writes] on the subject of Oates' repeated and astounding perjuries. It is as little open to doubt that the witnesses who were opposed to him at this trial were almost equally untrustworthy. . . . If his infamy remains undisturbed, the unctuous indignation with which it was denounced by the Jesuits, at the very moment when they were employing means as unhallowed as his own to contro-vert his statements, at least entitles them to a place by his side in the pillory of history.[40]

The St Omers boys could not be called perjurers, for they were not on oath. So they are just a set of liars, to say nothing of the Jesuits at their back.

For so serious a charge Mr Pollock offers a certain amount of evidence. It is at least worth sampling. He refers, for example, to the evidence of William "Parry" as given by Cobbett:

> *Parry.* He did not stir from the college till the end of June; and never went out but a day or two, as I know of.
>
> *L.C.J*(ustice). Not as you know of; but might not he go, and you not know of it?
>
> *Parry.* I am sure of it.
>
> *L.C.J.* How can you tell?
>
> *Parry.* Not a Scholar goes from thence to England but the whole college rings of it.
>
> *Gavan.* And then, my Lord, when they go out, they go in secular clothes, that none must know when any person leaves the college.[41]

There! says Mr Pollock (p. 343) in effect: Parry's lie is immediately contradicted by Fr Gavan from the dock. Yet if so, how strange that this Jesuit, dedicated to falsehood, should correct a lie uttered in defence of the prisoners! Had Mr Pollock, however, referred for confirmation to the con-temporary printed version of the trial, he would have seen his

[40] *Ibid.*, 344-345.   [41] Cobbett, 7; 363.

mistake. For Cobbett has accidentally omitted one small word which changes the whole sense. Fr Gavan's intervention really runs as follows: ". . . when they go out they go in Secular Cloaths, that none *but* must know when any person leaves the Colledge".[42] There is much virtue in that "but".

Another sample may be taken from the examination of three St Omers boys, already mentioned, who amongst others were arrested "upon a suspicion of being a priest" and examined on 28 April (8 May, N.S.) by Sir William Waller, "Shaftesbury's plot-monger" as he has been called. What reliance can be placed upon everything contained in these examinations is a matter of opinion. Mr Pollock clearly has no doubts. But we may waive this question aside for our present purpose, which is merely the correct interpretation of a sentence in one of them. Christopher Towneley, it is made to appear, added to his other lies by deposing "that Parry, Palmer and Gifford were all absent from St Omers while Oates was an inmate of the College. At the trial Gifford, Palmer and Parry were produced to give evidence of their personal knowledge that Oates had been there the whole of the time. No credence whatever can be given to such witnesses."[43] Not unnaturally one looks up the reference supplied; and what do we find? ". . . hee further saith Mr Parry, Mr Palmer, Mr Stapylton, the two Jacksons, and Henry Palmer, and Charles Gifford, now prisoners with him, were all absent from the colledge, and believeth that all those come to bee evidence for the Lords in the Tower".[44]

Mr Pollock has obviously mixed up the dates. Parry and his companions quite evidently had come over from St Omers, as had Towneley, in 1679, expecting to give evidence in favour of the five Catholic Lords in the Tower. The impeachment of these Lords, timed for April or May, did not take place as expected. Parry's examination is not printed. Gifford and Palmer, both examined by Waller on the same day as was

---

[42] *The Tryalls . . . of Thomas White, alias Whitebread* (as above), p. 48.
[43] J. Pollock, *op. cit.*, p. 344.
[44] Fitzherbert MSS. (as above), not "pp. 361, 364, 366" as stated, but p. 352.

O

Towneley, state that they had been at St Omers with Titus Oates in 1678. There is no contradiction whatsoever in what they admitted to Waller and what they testified at the trial. What then was Towneley's meaning when he told Sir William Waller that his fellow prisoners were "absent from the colledge"? He was speaking of the present time, not of 1678 when they were all with Oates at St Omers. If there is a difficulty, it lies in Waller's unhappy English; for that they were now "absent" was self-evident. What else can he have meant if not to inform Waller that they had all come from St Omers and from no other place?

Enough has been said of these unwarranted accusations. What meanwhile was happening at St Omers? They were aghast, of course, at the effrontery of their former companion, now turned perjurer to his very considerable financial profit. Many of their families and friends were in prison or in dire danger of imprisonment on his account. What most moves me, wrote the Vice-Rector, Fr Thomas Stapleton, is the peace of mind of the boys. "For though they hear of their parents and relatives being thrown into prison, and are themselves in danger of losing their inheritances if further action is taken against them, yet they remain cheerful, speak of their parents as fortunate to be suffering for Christ, and hope that they themselves may some day suffer the same fate. For that they are already beginning to prepare."[45] The persecution, he says, had produced a change, spiritually for the better although materially for the worse. Indeed he feared that unless pecuniary aid came soon, the question of closing down the College would again arise.

At this crisis, in fact, the boys excelled themselves. Fr Morgan's long Annual Letter and Fr Warner's History of the Persecution and his manuscript Letter-book bear ample testimony of this. Rumours that the College was to be closed

---

[45] Stapleton to ——, 20 January 1679 (S. Arch., Anglia V, No. 90). Fr Stapleton became Rector a week later, on 27 January.

had got about. There were those in England, Catholics as well as Protestants, who would have rejoiced to hear of the ruin of this Jesuit stronghold. Fr Warner indeed admits that there was something to be said for the closing of the College. The older edicts had to some extent been revived, prescribing severe penalties for parents sending their children abroad to be educated in the Catholic faith, or for aiding those already sent. If school fees could not be paid, was not the situation hopeless? However, Providence came presently to the rescue. There were unexpected benefactions from well-wishers living on the Continent. And before long many of the more devout parents, even some who had hitherto been remiss in their payments, found secret ways of transmitting money across the Channel. For they dreaded the danger to which their sons would be exposed if sent back to England. When in 1680 a royal annual pension was granted by King Louis XIV, the future existence of St Omers was assured.

The Vice-Provincial's decision in 1679 that the College was to remain open was greatly influenced by the attitude of the boys themselves. Did they return to England they would be confronted with the oaths of Allegiance and Supremacy, and asked to declare solemnly their disbelief in Transubstantiation and other Catholic beliefs. "Not a single one out of all their number thought of returning to his native land: all preferred to beg alms from door to door, or to enter the service of some nobleman in any capacity whatever rather than trust themselves into such a manifest danger of losing the Faith while uncertain of their own constancy."[46] They had frequently discussed this matter among themselves, and this was the prevailing notion of what course they would follow if need should be.

But what of the rumour of closing the College? This problem too they considered, evidently with a practical realization of the difficulties involved. In 1679 they numbered about 150:

[46] Warner, *History of English Persecution of Catholics* . . . (&c.) (C.R.S., vol. 47), p. 235.

add the Community and servants and the number would be not far short of 200. One morning early in 1679 a deputation of older boys waited upon the Procurator or Bursar of the house. With the money available, they asked, for how long will the provisions last? Three months at most, replied Fr Busby. The deputation was ready with a suggestion. "Then give us just bread and butter for our meals. We shall be quite content with that, and the food will last for six months." They expressed their conviction that God would come before long to their aid and in his own wise way would answer their prayers.

Of the fervour of the boys' prayers—and of their efficacy—there can be no doubt. Indeed they had good reason to pray, and only prayer remained, as they well knew, for many who were suffering the violence of persecution. There were of course prayers publicly recited every day; and in the church the Blessed Sacrament was exposed each Sunday, the boys "watching" every half-hour in sets of four. It was settled that the members of the Community should fast each Friday whilst the persecution lasted. Nearly all the boys of their own accord followed this example. In fact it was with great difficulty that a few of the youngest could be persuaded to act otherwise. Fr Warner notes that when the *Gazette* (the only normal source of information) announced the day for the trial of the Lords in the Tower—false news, as it chanced—the boys decided to petition that a day be set aside for intensive prayer before the Blessed Sacrament exposed. So from 5 a.m. until 8 o'clock in the evening relays of four boys relieved one another in the church or chapel. One boy, incidentally, was noticed to have spent two continuous hours on his knees in prayer. Nor was this the only occasion when the boys took it upon themselves to ask for a day of prayer. One result of this fervour of spirit, together with an increased sympathy with the Jesuits in this period of trial, was the increase of vocations to the Society. Whereas ten was perhaps about the average number admitted yearly to the noviciate, this year (1679) as many as twenty-two were accepted—sixteen at Watten and six others for whom places were found in neighbouring Provinces.[47]

We return to the witnesses from St Omers. On 24 June (N.S.), the day following the trial of the Five Jesuits, Mr Richard Langhorne stood his trial, and a number of boys from St Omers were again called to testify that Oates was far from London on the day of the "consult". Langhorne was the legal adviser of the Jesuits in London. Though he is not known to have been a boy at St Omers, his sons had been there—Richard, Charles and Francis. The two last mentioned were studying for the priesthood at Valladolid whilst their father was being tried and condemned to death. Charles in fact was there when Oates made his short and unpleasant sojourn in that house of study.

Seventeen witnesses from Belgium gave their evidence, the same for the most part as had been given the previous day. They cannot all be identified since several are merely referred to in the report as "4th Witness", "5th Witness", and so on. In the course of the trial there appeared unexpectedly the Earl of Castlemain, not to give evidence but to complain to the Judges of the conduct of the mob outside. "Some of the witnesses", he stated, "that were summoned here for the Prisoners (sic) are so beaten and abused without, that they dare not come to give their Evidence, for fear of being killed."[48] Scroggs and the other Justices professed much concern at this news, but they do not appear to have taken any measures to deal with the trouble. "If your Lordship will but tell us who they are . . . we will take care for the punishment of them; for we will show ourselves just and fair." Scroggs must surely have been aware of the futility of so conditional a guarantee. This intervention of Lord Castlemain came shortly after the St Omers contingent had had their say. One may wonder how the mob had treated them at the previous trial: it would appear that they suffered some unspecified violence. At all events on this second occasion

[47] *Ibid.*   [48] *Tryal of Richard Langhorn Esq.* (London, 1679), p. 44.

the boys just possibly had taken what precautions they could. On the appearance in Court of their first witnesses, Oates seemed agitated.

> *Dr Oates.* My Lord, here are Papists come into the Court with their Swords on.
> *L.C.J.* They will not draw them here.
> *Lord Mayor.* 'Tis well enough, 'tis well enough, Dr Oates, you are safe enough here.[49]

The "5th Witness"—evidently Master Cox—again gave evidence, as he had done the day before. He was again brimful of eagerness even if at times somewhat muddle-headed. He was sure, however, that Oates was at St Omers on 1 May (N.S.), that is to say, three days before the "consult" in London. "The first day of May there was a great Feast, SS. Fortunatus and Gordianus, and then I saw Mr Oats four days, and he was there all the Month of May."[50] As to St Fortunatus—there are listed fifty-seven Saints of that name—we know little. When St Omers migrated to Bruges in 1762, the "noble large shrine" or reliquary which enclosed his relics was deposited temporarily with the English Carthusians at Nieuport, and was seen no more, as Fr Charles Plowden tells us in his account.[51]

The relics of St Gordianus are of greater interest, since they now repose beneath the altar table in the Stonyhurst Sodality Chapel. Unlike many another relic, this can be traced back, with the help of several attestations, to the Roman cemetery of S. Cyriaca whence in 1667 the Bishop of Porphyrium took them, evidently at the request of Thomas Eccleston, a youth who next year entered the noviciate at Watten. Himself a native of Lancashire, he destined the relic for the Jesuit Lancashire District, whenever England should again become a Catholic country. Meanwhile the "Sodality" of St Omers was to be their resting place. After nearly a century at the College

---

[49] *Ibid.*, p. 29.
[50] *Ibid.*, p. 34. Cobbett (7; 454) misprints the date as 1 March.
[51] C. Plowden, s.j., *Destruction of the Colleges at Bruges, 1773*, App. II (S. Arch., A. III. 21).

and shorter sojourns at Brussels, Bruges and Hengrave Hall, they reached Fr Angier, the missioner at Bury St Edmunds. In 1862, it seems, the relics were "translated" to Stonyhurst and with much pomp and ceremony placed in the position they now occupy. A new reliquary, ornate and gilded, supplied the place of the original "richly wrought silver shrine" which seems to have vanished.

When, about a month after Langhorne's trial, the case of Sir George Wakeman, the Queen's physician, was due to be tried, King Charles is said to have hinted to Scroggs that it was time to call some sort of halt to Oates' perjuries. A conviction of the Queen's physician on the charge of attempting to poison the King might well spell ruin to his Queen. Scroggs took the hint and summed up accordingly; to the intense annoyance of the Green Ribbon Club Sir George was acquitted. Henceforth one could never feel quite sure of the result of these trials. Convictions followed, of course, but acquittals too, as in the case of Sir Thomas Gascoigne, of Mrs Cellier and of Lord Castlemain. At Castlemain's trial on 3 July (N.S.) three or four St Omers Old Boys were called as witnesses. But actually the favourable verdict resulted, not from any rejection of Oates' lies, but from disbelief in the no less false evidence offered by the villainous Dangerfield, the only other crown witness. It was agreed by the Justices present that in a case of high treason there must be two witnesses whose evidence the jury were willing to accept.

Lord Castlemain (husband of the notorious Barbara Villiers) had for many a year been a friend of the Jesuits. From 1672 at latest he seems to have resided off and on at the English Jesuit Seminary in Liège:[52] and in 1678 helped very materially in the acquisition for the students there of a Villa house near Chèvremont. Three years later, as Fr Warner tells us, he had retired from England to the Watten noviciate where he could remain in peace and safety until the times should be less troubled. In

[52] See for instance the evidence at the trial of Lord Stafford given by Lydcott, his secretary, an Old Boy of St Omers (Cobbett, 7; 1432).

the course of his trial he too was accused of what Mr Pollock calls "parroting" the witnesses from St Omers: but of that enough has already been said. It seems true, however, that he paid some or all of the costs of the witnesses whilst they were in London, found them lodgings and kept a watchful, kindly eye on their interests.

Fr Whitbread and the three other St Omers Old Boys martyred in July 1679 and beatified in 1929 have already been mentioned. Several others there were, such as the Provincial's "Socius", Fr Edward Mico, who died either in prison or as the result of brutal treatment by their captors: but it is not feasible to mention each St Omers man by name. Nor indeed is it possible at present even to distinguish who among the many victims of Titus Oates, priests and laymen, were educated at St Omers and who were not. Something nevertheless should be said of three beatified martyrs—two secular priests[53] and one Jesuit—who must be added to the previous eight.

One of the secular priests, Fr John (or perhaps William) Plessington, born near Garstang in Lancashire, was executed at Chester in July 1679. He had worked on the English mission for some fifteen years, residing mainly at Holywell and later at Puddington Hall near Chester, the home of the Massey family. Little is known of the details of his capture or of his trial. It seems clear, however that he was condemned rather for his priesthood than for any part in the fabricated Plot.

Three days later at Cardiff suffered Fr Philip Evans, s.j., Welsh to the marrow-bone. Witness his love of the harp and the Welsh songs with which he would cheer his fellow prisoner, Mr John Lloyd. He had been in Rhetoric at St Omers in 1664-5: and then or earlier had been a member of the orchestra and choir. After four years on the mission he was arrested in December 1678 at the house of Mr Christopher Turberville of

---

[53] For the identification of the two secular priests as St Omers men, see Warner's History of the Plot (C.R.S., vol. 47, pp. 137-38; vol. 48, p. 335). A short account of each is in Stonyhurst Magazine, vol. 32, pp. 108-111, 238-240.

Sker, in Glamorgan. At long last his accusers managed to procure a woman and her daughter to swear to the priesthood of both these Fathers. Arnold, a fanatical priest-hunter, produced also an apostate dwarf for the purpose of implicating Fr Evans in the "Plot", but the presiding Judge apparently ignored him. Perhaps he disliked dwarfs in general, or it may be that he objected to the dwarf's perjuries as being too obvious. Another two months elapsed before the sentence of death was put into execution. Fr Evans and Mr Lloyd (a secular priest) were now allowed more freedom: in fact the former is said to have been playing a game of tennis when he received news that he was to die next day. Never did a more nonchalant and cheerful martyr go to his reward. He was thirty-four when he died.[54]

Of the other secular priest, now Blessed Thomas Thwing, little is known apart from his trial and condemnation. Born at Heworth in the North Riding, he had gone for his higher studies from St Omers to Douay where (presumably) he was ordained in 1665. His missionary life seems to have been centred in his native county. The Northern "subsidiary" to the Oates Plot, known sometimes as the "Yorkshire Plot", with Robert Bolron as its managing director, manufactured the evidence that led to his death. Bolron and Maybury, former servants of old Sir Thomas Gascoigne until their dismissal from Barnbow Hall for thieving, concentrated their vengeance upon the Gascoigne family But by the time Mr Thwing was tried at the York Assizes, Sir Thomas and his relatives had been acquitted. How Mr Thwing, although a nephew of Sir Thomas, came into the affair is uncertain. Whether for complicity in the bogus Plot (which in his speech from the scaffold he stoutly denied) or for his priesthood, a charge he proudly admitted, or perhaps on both counts, he received the usual sentence.

---

[54] Cf. T. P. Ellis: *The Catholic Martyrs of Wales* (London, 1933), pp. 117-123; Fr Morgan's Annual Letter for 1678-79 (ut supra), pp. 64-68; Warner's History of the Plot (C.R.S., vol. 47), pp. 296-298.

October 23 (or November 2, N.S.) was the date of his actual martyrdom.

All this while, and during all the period of his Provincialate, Fr Warner had been forbidden by the General to cross over to England, in spite of repeated requests. His information was derived from his correspondents there, not least from Fr Edward Petre, now Rector of the London District and acting as Vice-Provincial for England; an active, zealous man, busy from morning to night—"tanquam apis argumentosa", as Fr Warner expressed it. As the months passed, the Provincial noted in his letters the gradual slackening of the persecution, although there were not wanting attempts to stir the warm embers into flame. The credit of Titus Oates was also losing ground. Nevertheless the sinister activities of a few Catholic priests, secular and Regular, were causing him anxiety. None of these need concern us here unless it be Dr John Sergeant, a notable government spy, who in October 1679 informed the Privy Council that at least one of the "Five Jesuits" martyred in the previous June had died "with a lie in his mouth". It was the old stale story of the so-called Jesuit doctrine of regicide, with Fr Gavan as the latest exponent.

Not content with this accusation, Mr John Pollock has seized the occasion to add another charge—a story which (so he tells us) caused laughter at the time. Sir William Waller, says he, arrested Fr Gavan "in the stables of the Imperial ambassador, where he was hiding with a woman who passed as his wife, and their son".[55] He cites his evidence in a footnote. Fortunately there is no need to linger on this disgraceful calumny. Major Malcolm Hay has printed out in full Mr Pollock's two references, one of which is in plain French and the other in plain English. And he has proved to the hilt that neither document makes any such accusation: the originator of it is Mr Pollock himself. "His misinterpretation of the texts", writes Major Hay severely, ". . . can be accounted for only in two ways; either he does not understand French, or his in-

[55] J. Pollock, *op. cit.*, p. 201.

tellectual faculties suffer from some peculiar derangement whenever he has to write about Jesuits."[56]

In spite of the attempts of Titus Oates, Bedloe, Dr Sergeant and others to blacken the name of the Society of Jesus, its reputation in England fared none the worse amongst the Catholics. Writing from St Omers in July 1681, soon after the triennial "consult", held this time on the Continent and apparently at Ghent, Fr Warner tells the General:

> ... Not for the last forty years have there been more boys at this Seminary than now: and yet but yesterday three more arrived, and in a few days eight more are expected. I have sent over to the (English) mission quite a number of priests; the few that remain will follow. Had I another twenty to dispose of, I could not satisfy the demands of the Catholic gentry who ask for Jesuit chaplains. So it is clear that their devotion to the Society has not cooled—indeed it has increased wonderfully. Scarcely one has deserted us and many have recently attached themselves to us. To God be the praise and honour and glory.[57]

Not for the first or the last time, he ends with his usual request: "I beg your permission to cross over to England".

Fr Thomas Stapleton's rectorate was highly successful, despite the repercussions of the storm that raged across the Channel. A quiet, genial man, a disciplinarian rather by grace than by nature, at first he had shown himself too kind—if that be possible—or at least too lenient. But he soon discovered that his apparent weakness was being abused; and taught by experience and by his Provincial's forceful advice, he learnt to temper mercy with justice, kindness with firmness. He was rewarded by the exceptionally fine spirit that pervaded the College at this time. There was, it would seem, little left to be desired, whether in regard of piety or studies or discipline.

Towards the close of 1681 he took the opportunity of starting the Confraternity of the "Bona Mors" not only

---

[56] M. V. Hay, *The Jesuits and the Popish Plot* (London, 1934), p. 6.
[57] Warner to Oliva, 29 July 1681 (*Letter-book of Fr Warner*, f. 35).

amongst the boys but also amongst those who frequented the College Church.[58] This was a Confraternity which owed its first erection in 1648 to the then General, Vincent Caraffa. Unlike the Jesuit Sodality of Our Lady from which women as yet were rigorously excluded, this Confraternity was open to both sexes: no doubt, however, the College boys would have met separately in their own "Sodality". A Register of enrolments still survives, dating from 1782 and continuing fitfully until 1886, about which time, one may suppose, the Confraternity as such came to an end at Stonyhurst. The public "Bona Mors Devotions", however, continue to this day in the College church.

In November 1681 died that great General, John Paul Oliva, to be succeeded seven months later by Fr Charles de Noyelle, a saintly Belgian who for twenty years had, as one of Oliva's Assistants, been concerned with the affairs of the English Province. By the May of 1683 the new General had had time to consider the need of appointing several new Superiors whose normal term of years had by now run out. For although Pope Alexander VII had reversed the order of his predecessor that Rectors must be changed every three years, this triennium of office had become the normal, though by no means the invariable custom—and so remained for many a year. On this occasion Fr Warner was succeeded as Provincial by Fr John Keynes, the late Rector at Liege. Fr Stapleton moved from St Omers to Liege to replace Fr Keynes; and Fr Warner succeeded him at St Omers. He was installed as Rector of the College on 31 July, feast day of St Ignatius.

---

[58] Vicar-General to Stapleton, 13 December 1681 and 27 February 1682 (Ep. Gen., II, ff. 416, 418ᵛ).

9

FR WARNER AND THE FIRE OF 1684

THE new Rector would have been an interesting man to know. He had entered the Society as a priest, had taught theology for some years at Douay before his entrance, and afterwards for five years at Liege. From the English mission he was summoned to Liege as Rector at the beginning of 1678. Just a year later, after Fr Whitbread's arrest he was appointed Vice-Provincial and presently Provincial of the English Province. A copious controversialist, he was better versed in theology than in the Ciceronian Latin of some of his contemporaries and elders. As Provincial in particularly difficult times, and as Rector of St Omers (1683-1687) he was in his element; for he was an organizer and liked to get things done —and well done. As his letter-book shows, his sense of humour was all his own. When a certain Rector, for instance, had confused his Procurator's (or Bursar's) accounts by spending unexplained sums of money in gifts to the poor—to his poor relatives, surmised the Provincial—and on that count petitioned the General for a change of Procurators, Fr Warner agreed that the new Procurator proposed would do as well as any other; he added casually if not very cryptically, communing as it were with himself, "Caiphas was the person to be blamed, but it was Malchus who got his ear cut off".

In January 1684 Fr Warner sent to de Noyelle his first report, a favourable one, on the state of the College.[1] The household all told numbered 214, composed of 178 boys, 26 Jesuits including nine laybrothers, and ten servants. Amongst the boys there was plenty of keenness both in prayer and studies. He had made some changes in the time-table with the object of giving rather more free time to the scholastics (non-priests),

[1] *Fr J. Warner's Letter-book* (Camb. Univ. Library, MS. Ll.1.19), f. 56ᵛ (31 January 1684).

and had provided more and better fires. The impetus given to the school by his competent predecessor, Fr Stapleton, is still running its course.

Already however has begun a series of complaints concerning the personnel of his staff which continue off and on for the rest of his rectorate, and indeed for many a decade even though subsequent Provincials proved to be more accommodating. Like many another, Fr Warner had his preferences. Fr Edward Petre, for one, was a firm friend of his. They had several qualities in common, not least their capacity for, and love of, hard work. The new Provincial, on the other hand, was evidently not a personal friend. A certain incompatibility of temperament divided them, at least on the natural plane. As Fr Warner knew and the General soon discovered, Fr Keynes, for all his good will and supernatural piety, was a very obstinate man. It would be vain to shirk the fact, which explains, though indeed not fully, the Rector's continual and fruitless petitions for a competent and permanent staff. At the moment Fr Warner is in quest of an efficient Minister. A few months later we find him complaining of the frequent changes of the Prefects of Discipline; within three months there had been six changes of Prefects. "It is generally agreed", he writes, "that the men given me are such that it would be difficult to find any more incompetent in the whole Province."[2] This, be it noted, was during what would now be called the second or Easter term. Next July it was the turn of the Prefects of Studies, of whom three had succeeded one another within about three months.[3] And so it continued, in spite of some severe remonstrances to Fr Keynes from the General. No doubt the Provincial explained his reasons for all these drastic changes—his letters have not survived—but it is evident that they did not convince the General.

The accounts of these various permutations are sometimes not without a tinge of humour, however annoying they must have been to the Rector. There was sent to him, for example,

[2] *Ibid.*, f. 59ᵛ; 29 March 1684.   [3] *Ibid.*, f. 62; 25 July 1684.

as a Prefect a certain Fr William Janion for whom no suitable post could be found on the English mission. A sociable man, athletic and odd, he neglected his prefectorial duties, according to Fr Warner, preferring to join in their games or chat with them without limit of time: fond too of displaying his strength by carrying or hurling heavy weights about the place, to the admiration, no doubt, and amusement of his young spectators. When admonished he would promise due amendment, but forget his promise on the first opportunity. What, asks the Rector, am I to do with a feckless man like that?[4] Brother Hewitt, on the other hand, was a treasure, the best tailor in the Province, satisfactory in every way, indeed indispensable. Yet he was taken away from St Omers and sent to Paris, where he was to act as "socius" or companion to the Procurator there. "Strange it is", writes Fr Warner with commendable restraint, "that to the loss of this Seminary the Provincial should send this man to Paris, where his occupation will be only to accompany the Procurator, to clean his shoes and make his bed—duties which don't seem of such importance that another less needed man could not be found."[5]

In spite of these harassing changes of staff the College by all accounts was flourishing. By the beginning of 1685 the number of boys had slightly increased to 181. Charles II was now more firmly settled on his throne than ever, the Oates' Plot was fading into the distance and Catholics were again hopeful and expectant. The King's death on 6 February was for them a calamity, even though James, Duke of York, already reinstated in his offices despite all Test Acts and Exclusion Bills, stepped peaceably enough into his royal brother's shoes. At least for the time being the prospect for St Omers of a continued influx of new boys into the College and of school fees more easily and promptly paid was never so bright.

A long letter of Fr Warner to the General, dated 7 January 1685,[6] gives interesting details of certain aspects of College

---

[4] Ibid., f. 62^v; 25 July 1684.   [5] Ibid., f. 64^v; 12 September 1684.
[6] Ibid., ff. 67-68^v.

life as seen from the official point of view. (No doubt some unofficial commentaries would be no less welcome, but alas they seem not to exist.) It is now not much less than a hundred years since the foundation of St Omers and still the spirit of Fr Schondonch is abroad and very much alive. We have heard from time to time of certain lapses from the high standard attained in earlier days. The vogue of Greek was reported to be on the decline, that of music to be almost dead, and so on. But when attention was called to these "seasonal" defects attention was usually paid, and apparently with gratifying results. Yet if in discipline or in application to studies the College, like any other institution, had its ups and downs, one does not read of any adverse comments on the spiritual standard of the school. During the crisis of the Oates Plot the morale of the boys was almost beyond praise—an unexpected reaction which the "Salamanca Doctor", had he known of it, would have deeply deplored.

When Fr Warner wrote his report he made it clear that St Omers, in his opinion, was still at the top of its form. He has been much impressed and edified to see how attentively the boys serve Mass or assist at it, how they take every occasion to make voluntary visits, often protracted visits, to the Blessed Sacrament. He goes on to explain to the General something at least of the educational methods of the College whereby religion and learning, and in that order, were unobtrusively combined, with the aid of grace, to produce cultivated, dependable, solid, devout Catholic gentlemen. He instances the numerous plays, most of them tragedies and all of them of course in Latin. They were, as we know, for the most part home-made and written with a moral end in view, to show forth God's Justice, God's Mercy, His Providence over His creatures, His Kindness, His Love. Such plays were accepted as a matter of course in Jesuit schools: the boys delighted to act in them, and visitors crowded and crushed to witness these spectacular entertainments. That they were not without their salutary effects is clear enough. In the case of St Omers Fr

5. Bl. Thomas Whitbread, s.j., Provincial. Martyred at Tyburn, June 1679

From a portrait formerly at the Watten noviciate, now at Stonyhurst

6. Bruges: The House of the Seven Towers
From Sander: Flandria Illustrata (1641)

7. Liège: The English Jesuit Seminary
From P.-L. de Saumery: Les Délices du Pais de Liège, *Tome I* (1738)

Warner quotes the Bishop (or Bishop-elect) of Ypres, apparently a fairly constant visitor at these plays and often to be seen
at them with tears in his eyes, who told him he had never sat
through a College play without gaining solid and lasting profit.
One gathers that, tears apart, the Bishop shared with the
audience—and the actors too—something of that catharsis,
that motion or emotion of the spirit, which tragedy tends to
inspire.

Then there were the debates, the "disputations", in the
refectory. At dinner on Sundays and feast days the subject
set for debating was a pious one, chosen from the gospel of
the day, from some Saint's life or similar subject in accord with
the feast. At supper on these days either a boy read a passage
from one of the Greek Fathers of the Church, which another
rendered into Latin, or else there was a sermon preached. On
other days of the week the set subject had a wider range.

> Yesterday [writes Fr Warner] at dinner two from the school
> of Rudiments disputed in Greek with one another for about
> a quarter of an hour. During supper a Grammarian trans-
> lated a passage of St Chrysostom from Greek into Latin;
> and then, whilst another read a Latin extract, he turned it
> into Greek. Subsequently he gave accurate answers to
> questions of etymology, parsing and so forth that were put
> to him. Yet this Grammarian was only 10th in his school.

Of course when Rhetoric or Poetry entered the field they
aimed at less easy quarry. Anacreon, Hesiod, Pindar were
subjected to similar transmutations, questions concerning the
various Greek dialects presenting no difficulties.

A fortnight before this letter was written, at about eleven
o'clock on the night of 22 December 1684 a devastating fire
had swept through part of the College, although not before
every boy had been safely evacuated. Nothing seems to be
known as to how or where the fire originated. A previous
letter reporting the disaster to de Noyelle is lost. But the
second part of the Rector's long letter of 7 January, already

P

cited, contains an account which has not hitherto appeared in print.

About the fire which occurred here on December 22nd last I wrote to your Reverence a fortnight ago. It destroyed a very fine portion of the Seminary, including the kitchen, dispensary, refectory, a large hall in which lesser plays are produced, the Community recreation room, the procurator's room and one entire dormitory, not to mention furniture of various kinds. Yet by God's goodness nobody at all suffered any bodily harm. We are thus full of gratitude to God that the disaster involved no personal injuries. The workmen all declare that the inner walls (*parietes*) were so slender and weak that it is a wonder, what with the weight of the audiences filling the theatre, that the floor had never given way. That could not have happened without much loss of life and great injury to our reputation. The fire halted at the Guardian Angels' Chapel on one side and at my room on the other, though in both places there was plenty of combustible material. He however who sets limits to the sea set likewise a limit to the fire. The result is that what remains of our building is sufficient to accommodate the boys, and no change in their religious or scholastic exercises needed to be made. Only my catechetical talks to the Brothers were interrupted, for lack of a place in which to give them. . . .

I hope there will be erected a more handsome, certainly a stronger building and one more suited to our requirements. His Excellency the Internuncio at Brussels has promised to write on the subject to His Holiness. Père de la Chaize is in hopes of getting something from the French King; and certain English gentlemen have given substantial alms. *Spes in Deum non confundit*. From the customary alms that we give to the poor I have not allowed any diminution, indeed I have ordered them to be increased; for I have full confidence in Him who said, "Give and it shall be given to you".

An earlier letter to the Internuncio in Brussels[7] adds a few

[7] Warner to Internuncio (Brussels), 28 December 1684 (Nunziatura di Fiandra, t. 75, ff. 5-6). A copy of this letter has been kindly supplied by Fr G. Anstruther, O.P.

minor details. Although none of the boys was seriously injured, their clothes or their hair had in some cases been burnt or singed. They were now inconveniently cramped for room. A few had written home asking not to be recalled on this account: they were well content, said they, and the thought of Jesus Christ born in a stable was their consolation.

Since no sketch or engraving exists of the seventeenth-century building for which Fr Schondonch was mainly responsible, it would be profitless to attempt any mental reconstruction of the building or to estimate the extent of the damage suffered. It is clear, however, from this and other sources that the boys' dormitories were at the top of the house, that the secondary theatre had a room, probably the main theatre, below it, and that the refectory—and no doubt the kitchen—occupied some part of the ground floor. The Custom Book of St Omers told us no less.

Hopes of repairing the damage without running into debt were shared by both General and Rector. There were many offers of help, direct and indirect. The Governor of the Netherlands took an interest in the matter, as did the Internuncio. Other neighbouring Provinces of the Society sent contributions; and, as Fr Warner notes, he received assistance from some English friends of the Jesuits. The only definite sum mentioned was that contributed by Louis XIV at the suggestion of Père de la Chaize—a generous gift of 4,000 scudi (nominally about £1,000). In the spring of 1686 the Rector paid a short visit to England; but he appears to have collected more promises than cash. Nevertheless towards the close of his rectorate he was able to tell de Noyelle—

I hope my successor will soon be announced. Who he is I know not, nor do I greatly care. Enough for me that I hand over to him a College in far better state that I found it. Its income has increased, a good house has been purchased, and I leave as much petty cash as I found on arrival, although the building has cost more than 17,000 scudi [some £4,250].

Various debts are owing to us: we don't owe a farthing to anybody. To God be the praise.[8]

The only restriction of importance that the General had insisted on was his injunction to build with an eye to utility rather than to "magnificence". The time would come, he hoped—James II had by now ascended the throne—when there would be no more need for a Seminary outside of England.[9] He was over a century ahead of his time! The builders, it would seem, took at least three summers to complete their job. The plans had been approved of course by the Provincial before the work was begun. But at some later stage a halt apparently occurred, and an appeal by Fr Warner to the General. What exactly was the point at issue is obscure, but a spanner had somehow been thrown into the works. The Provincial explained that though he had praised the plans he had not approved them; to which plea de Noyelle replied that he was making a distinction without a difference.[10] The spanner was removed from the works and the wheels again revolved. In the autumn of 1686 the builders were still at work: thereafter the subject is not mentioned.

Fr Warner, as has been said, was happy in the thought that no personal injuries had resulted from the fire. It was six months later, during the course of reconstruction, that one of the workmen went down into some subterranean cavity where he was overcome by poisonous gas. He had just time before collapsing to call for a priest. Though the danger was evident, a young priest, Fr Smithers, Procurator of the College, who presumably was near at hand, quickly descended to the fatal spot. He is said to have been in time to give the man at least conditional absolution before he himself collapsed and died, a notable martyr of charity.[11]

Here we would break the thread of the narrative and hark

[8] *Warner's L-book*, f. 72; 25 August 1686.
[9] Ep. Gen., II, f. 453ᵛ; 28 July 1685.
[10] *Ibid.*, f. 455; 11 August 1685.
[11] Litt. Ann., 1685 (S. Arch., B. I. 16, p. 100).

back to a statement of Fr Warner in 1686, already quoted, to the effect that he was leaving the *College* in a far better state than he had found it. Hitherto St Omers has been referred to in official correspondence between the Generals and the English Province not as a College but as a Seminary. The yearly catalogues, such as survive, giving the General the list of resident Jesuits or of the state of the finances of St Omers, are headed "Seminarium Audomarense".[12] The term "College" may have been used by Fr Warner inadevertently, or possibly not—one can never be quite sure of him. But it was just at this period that St Omers was getting tired both of the term and of its implications. Why that was so we may see in a moment. Certainly from 1693 (incidentally the centenary year) a catalogue boldly used the heading "Collegium", and then adds a little timidly, "It may legitimately be termed the seminary of our Province, since almost all the members of the Province derive from there". This sop to Cerberus was repeated once or twice in subsequent catalogues but was soon discarded entirely. In the eighteenth century St Omers became almost without exception "Collegium Audomarense". The Generals continued to refer to it as a Seminary.

This question of names is in part a constitutional one. A Jesuit "Collegium" in earlier days catered only for external students. There were, it is true a few *pensionnats*, viewed with disfavour by the Society or at best with a grudging tolerance. But these were not Colleges, *internats*, in the modern sense: they were *maisons de famille*, hostels or boarding houses, presided over by a "Primarius" in due subjection to the Rector of the near-by College whither the students went daily to their classes. Up to 1614 when St Omers became self-contained, this establishment had many of the characteristics of a *Pensionnat*. But it was even then an anomaly. The conduct of the school, financial and disciplinary, was entirely separate from that of the Walloon College, and its Superior, Fr Schondonch, was, at

---

12 Audomarum—need it be said?—is the Latin name for Saint-Omer.

least officially, by no means a Primarius but a Rector in his own right. Such an exception, one may well suppose, was a consequence of the special circumstances of the school and of the wise recommendations of its founder, Fr Persons.

After 1614, however, St Omers became as self-contained as any of the English grammar schools of the period. It combined the functions both of a Jesuit "College" and of a *pensionnat*. The school in fact was to all intents and purposes a boarding school or *internat* in the modern sense of that term. True it is that the Constitutions given it in 1620 by the Cardinal Protector assumed that it was what might now be called a *petit séminaire*: but it was not so. It was founded for Catholic boys whose education as Catholics was prohibited in Elizabethan England. The founder obviously hoped that many of these boys would in due course return as priests to the assistance of their afflicted countrymen: and indeed a large majority, especially in the earlier years, embraced the ecclesiastical state. But although the St Omers Registers have long been lost, we know that from the beginning there were those who preferred to live their lives as laymen, and their number increased with the years. After 1614, in fact, St Omers became, from the Jesuit point of view, not only anomalous but unique. When in 1617 the question arose as to whether its Rector was entitled to take part in the Gallo-Belgic Provincial Congregation, to which triennial assembly the Rectors of the Province were *ex officio* summoned, the General decided against his admission. That house, he said, was not a College of the Society nor founded as such: and if *per accidens* it had five classes under Jesuit masters and a church in which the ministries of the Society were carried out, yet it was in reality only a seminary.[13] That is to say, it had to be either one or the other, for lack of a wider

[13] Vitelleschi to Jean Herennius, 24 July 1617 (summarized in S. Arch., A. IV. 17, p. 59). For the question of *pensionnats* see Poncelet, II, 29-36; P. Delattre (edit.), *Les Etablissements de la C. de J. en France*, I, col. 1434-1437. In France, even as late as 1760, there were but 13 *pensionnats* out of a total of ninety-eight Colleges.

classification. *Per accidens*, however, it was either both or neither!

And why this pother about a name? Because if the College boys were all to be ranked as seminarians, St Omers would be no more than a reserve of young ecclesiastics awaiting their turn to proceed for their higher studies to Rome or Spain. Of Spain there is less mention in the letters either of the General or of Fr Warner. But the English College at Rome at this period was, one gathers, in the doldrums and sadly in need of promising recruits. More and more the Generals had been demanding a regular yearly supply of youths, the pick of the school, who would help to revive the good name of that Seminary. The supply however did not always equal the demand either in quantity or quality. There would then result a mild reproach and a persuasive appeal—"nothing but the best is worthy of your seminary" . . . "a little more energy and surely St Omers will live up to its former reputation" . . . and so on. Both Provincial and Rector would have liked to meet fully the wishes of the General, evidently ill at ease and anxious about the future. With perhaps a few exceptions those only were eligible for the Roman "mission" each August who had completed their studies. But these Rhetoricians were becoming increasingly hesitant: volunteers for Rome were not easy to find.

The College Oath demanded of all students entering the Venerable English College in Rome was the main difficulty. Its wording had been revised from time to time by Propaganda. No doubt as a result of similar prompting Pope Alexander VII issued a very formidable decree, dated 20 June 1660, to which was appended a new form of oath, or rather series of oaths, obligatory for all alumni of Pontifical Colleges.[14] Not only must they swear to enter no Religious Order, to be ordained and then to spend their whole lifetime in the appropriate mission field as directed by Propaganda; but no alumnus, whether he be expelled from the College or leave for reasons

[14] *Bullarum Romanarum Collectio*, tom. 6, pars. 5, pp. 78-80.

of health or for any other reason, is ever during his life exempt from his oath of serving on the missions if called upon, and of not entering a Religious Order. In such cases he must report to Propaganda every two years, or each year if he is residing in Europe. Finally he must take an oath to keep his oath. All this presupposes that the alumnus has failed to obtain from the Holy See express leave in writing to act otherwise. For a while there was found a way of escape by entering the College, not as an alumnus, but as a "convictor", paying the full yearly maintenance fee. Not every one, of course, could afford the expense: and that route was blocked by the Cardinal Protector, Cardinal Howard, in 1684 if not earlier, by his order forbidding the admission of such convictors.[15]

The main purpose of this stringent oath, as far as England was concerned, was thus to secure an increased supply of secular clergy for that country. All other exits from that College were barred. It was obviously not intended to bar the front entrance as well, yet the oath was becoming for St Omers a distinct obstruction on the doorstep. St Omers was of course not the only possible source of supply. But the English secular clergy, writes Gasquet,[16] after several unsuccessful efforts to oust the Jesuits and obtain the control for themselves, had lost interest in the establishment; and Douay refused to send students to Rome. Hence the urgent appeals from the Generals to St Omers to come to the rescue.

Perhaps a little wearied with reiterated demands for more recruits, Fr Warner in the last year of his Provincialate had stated briefly to de Noyelle a point of view which has not always been allowed for. The General had asked for nine or ten youths to be sent in 1683; and as usual they must be of the best, "the pick of the bunch". To this the Provincial replies[17] that not more than three or four had as yet given their names to

[15] C.R.S., Vol. 40 (*Liber Ruber*), p. 103.
[16] A. Gasquet, O.S.B.: *History of the Venerable English College, Rome* (London, 1920), pp. 114-115.
[17] *Warner's L-book*, f. 42ᵛ.

Fr Stapleton, the Rector. More perhaps will volunteer in time, he adds soothingly.

Yet it is not so easy to send many to Rome, for they are frightened by the Oath that will be required of them. They don't mind knocking at the door and being welcomed inside. What they don't like is for the door to be so closed and locked behind them that it cannot again be opened except with the consent of the one man who is determined never to accede to such a request.

A year later and again came a request, although a more moderate one. Fr Warner, now Rector of St Omers, could speak with more direct and intimate appreciation of the difficulties to be faced. His reply is illuminating, and may be helpful towards an unbiassed solution of a very vexed question.

I have your Reverence's letter of March 25th in which you tell me to see that some students be sent to the College in Rome. I have done and will do what I can that these be numerous and of the quality your Reverence requires. To that end I have made an appeal to the boys in the College and I have also written to our Fathers in England and to the Benedictines, telling them that if they have any suitable candidates they may send them along.

Otherwise it is not merely difficult, it is impossible for this seminary to have to provide six or seven each year for Rome. True, we have here a large number of boys. But most of them are below the age of eighteen or in the lower schools; or they have not an attraction to the ecclesiastical state; or they are boys we have accepted out of charity, whose parents can't afford the expense of the journey to and from Rome. All these are excluded by the regulations of the English College. Of the remainder there are 43 who are knocking for admission to the Society. I shall never gain the consent of these to go to Rome as long as the College Oath remains in force. Nor can their confessors do anything *tutâ conscientiâ* to persuade them to go. Where then am I to find candidates each year for Rome?

We shall of course do our best and try still harder to

increase the number of suitable volunteers. Yet it is Rome itself that is blocking the way and creating difficulties for us. It is also a fact that this seminary was established for the needs rather of the Society than of the English College in Rome, according to the intentions of the founders. It would therefore be well to recommend to the Fathers in England and especially to the Provincial that they should look elsewhere for candidates to join those who will be leaving from here.[18]

It need not be supposed that this candid statement of Fr Warner put an end to the demand for volunteers. The gentle Fr de Noyelle acknowledged the difficulty of the situation: but, as he said, he was quite unable to obtain the alteration, still less the removal of the College Oath. So he relied on the zeal, the industry, the prudence and other virtues of the Rector to provide a sufficiency of candidates. A few years later de Noyelle's successor, Thyrsus Gonzales (1687-1705), the well-known opponent of Probabilism, was less gentle. He enacted that no novice should be accepted into the English Province in any year until six students had been found prepared to undertake the journey to Rome. There is no evidence of any consequent improvement, and five years later the order was withdrawn.[19]

In spite of his preoccupations, Fr Warner kept a watchful eye on England and what was happening there. He even had time, or made time, to write a controversial work defending Catholic doctrine against the aspersions of the Bishop of Winchester, George Morley. The Duke of York on being presented with a copy—probably by his friend Fr Petre—was so pleased with it that he arranged for copies to be presented anonymously to each of the Protestant Bishops.[20] The Rector has much to say too of the continued machinations of Titus Oates and of certain "false brethren"—Dr John Sergeant, of

[18] *Ibid.*, f. 60; 25 April 1684.
[19] Gonzales to Provincial, 10 January 1693; 15 March 1698 (Ep. Gen., II, f. 524 and 574).
[20] *Warner's L-book*, f. 58ᵛ; 1 March 1684.

course, in the pay of the Government, Fr "Munson" or
Anderson, a Dominican, Fr Philip Gage, recently dismissed
from the Society and now a renegade "wretched, pitiable,
poor, in rags, begging from door to door".[21]

The decline and fall of Titus Oates is duly reported to the
General. By 1684 he had definitely fallen, although his fangs
had not as yet been drawn. In March of that year Fr Warner
has this story to tell—

> The famous Oates, once the oracle of the Protestants but
> now the laughing-stock of everybody, even of urchins, not
> long ago sent letters to the King's Secretaries. To both of
> them he wrote that he had business of extreme public import
> to communicate, provided that he could visit them in safety.
> This however he could not do unless provided with an escort,
> so violently was he greeted when he appeared in public, not
> only with abuse and execration, but with rotten eggs and
> stones as well, so that his life was not infrequently in danger.
> Such treatment, so unworthy of his merits, he neither could
> nor would endure.[22]

For answer he was told, if he had anything to disclose, to
disclose it to the nearest Justice of the Peace. Mr Secretary
Jenkins was reported by him to King Charles himself for so
off-hand a reply to his petition. "If I must perish for serving
your Majesty and the Government", wrote the Saviour of the
Nation, "I humbly pray that I may perish quietly, and starve
in peace, and not be put into a Bear's Skin in order to be
worried by Popish Dogs."[23]

On 10 May, whether in bear's skin or not, he was put into
the Compter and then into the King's Bench prison, charged
at the suit of the Duke of York under the statute known as
"De Scandalis Magnatum". When on 11 June the case came
before the Chief Justice, Sir George Jeffreys, presiding with a
jury of fifteen, the defendant neither appeared nor was represented: it became a Writ of Enquiry for damages. A wealth

[21] *Ibid.*, f. 49ᵛ; 14 March 1683.   [22] *Ibid.*, f. 59; 29 March 1684.
[23] Quoted by Jane Lane, *Titus Oates* (London, 1949), p. 299.

of witnesses made it clear that "Popish Dog" would have been
the mildest of epithets applied by Oates to the heir to the
throne. Traitor, son of a whore, rogue, devil were some of his
terms of abuse. The jury assessed the damage at the usual sum
of £100,000 together with twenty shillings costs.[24] Oates had
expected no less: at least the costs would have been within his
means! He returned to prison—escape to the Continent was
thus prevented—with at all events the assurance of permanent
board and lodging and of safety from flying stones and rotten
eggs.

Twelve months later, on 8 and 9 May 1685, in Westminster
Hall Titus Oates was tried for perjury. By now the Duke of
York has changed his title to King James II: he had been
crowned a few weeks previously, on the feast of St George.
But this trial was no sudden surprise for Oates. A bill of indictment had been found against him in the previous November:
a month or two later three counsel had been assigned to him
at his own request.

To Fr Warner the Provincial had given the task of looking
for witnesses, "even from the Society" who could testify to the
presence of Oates at St Omers on the crucial day, 24 April (or
4 May, N.S.) 1678, when he swore he was in London attending
the "Jesuit Consult". "I have asked the Provincial over and
over again", wrote Fr Warner, "to decide whether it be lawful
or expedient for Jesuits to take part in the trial as witnesses
where there is in question the shedding of blood"[25]—not death,
of course, but a possible mutilation of Oates' ears. Presumably
Fr Warner settled this point of Canon Law for himself. Under
the date 15 November we find the Earl of Sunderland writing
to a number of former St Omers boys signifying His Majesty's

---

[24] Mr Ogg (*England in the Reign of Charles II*, Oxford 1934, p. 651), basing
his comment on the evidence of the first of eleven witnesses, says, perhaps
seriously, that Oates was convicted "as a premature advocate of the penny
post". He adds that Judge Jeffreys "addressed the accused with scathing
emphasis as *Mr* Oates". Oates was not present at the trial. Cf. Cobbett's
State Trials, 10; 125 seqq.

[25] *Warner's L-book*, f. 66ᵛ; 6 December 1684.

pleasure that they repair at once to Roger L'Estrange, a Justice of Peace for Middlesex. And L'Estrange is directed (2 December) to take on oath their information as to the presence of Oates at St Omers on the day in question.[26] The trial had been fixed for 6 February but was postponed in consequence of the unexpected death of Charles II two days earlier.

There were two charges of perjury chosen for the trial: Oates' statement that he was present in London at the "Jesuit Consult", and his statement, made likewise under oath, that he had met Fr Ireland in London in August and September 1678. It is the former indictment that mainly concerns us here, since it was the evidence from St Omers, now accepted at its proper value, that convinced the jury after no more than fifteen minutes that the accused was guilty. It seems to be generally accepted that he was given a fair trial, and that Jeffreys, irritable by nature and chronically irritated by the painful disease of the stone, nevertheless restrained himself admirably in the circumstances. For Oates with malice prepense did all he could to obstruct the proceedings and rouse the Chief Justice to anger. He had finally decided to make his own defence. His witnesses however were of little avail.

To prove his presence in London in April 1678 he had subpoenaed the witnesses of six years ago, Sir Richard Baker the physician and his household. But Sir Richard had had a bad night and begged to be excused; his housekeeper and his coachman foolishly contradicted one another. Smith the schoolmaster and the old Dominican priest, Matthew Clay, so it transpired, had perjured themselves under threat of death if they refused; whilst the querulous Mr William Walker, an ancient Minister, was doubtful of the precise year. All he could remember was that "in Leicesterfields . . . I saw the elm trees budded forth as big as a hazel-nut". Oates on one occasion tried to prompt his witness, but Jeffreys quickly pulled him up. Altogether it was a disappointing defence.

Of the twenty-two witnesses from St Omers only three, it

[26] C. S. P. Dom., 1684-5, pp. 210, 230.

seems, had given evidence in 1679. By this time, of course, the
contemporaries of Oates had left the College: he had been sent
away, it may be recalled, in the June of 1678. Of the three just
mentioned, two had by now become Jesuits.[27] Henry Haggerston ("Howard") and William Conway ("Parry"), both of
whom we met in the previous chapter, were in their first year
of theology at Liege. No doubt they enjoyed this break in their
studies. They certainly now showed a good deal more sparkle
and confidence in themselves when they were questioned.

> *Attorney Gen.* Mr Haggerstone . . . were you at St Omers in
> the year 1678, with Mr Oates?
> *Haggerstone.* Yes, I was, my Lord, I had the honour to be of
> the same bench with the Doctor of Salamanca.
> *L.C. Justice.* You mean you were of the same class with him?
> *Haggerstone.* Yes, my Lord, of the same class. . . . He spoke
> unto me on the 25th of April . . . he spoke of an indis-
> position he [Hildesley] had, for which he prescribed him
> a medicine of poppy, and he thought it would do his
> business effectually.
> *L.C.J.* Who said so?
> *Haggerstone.* The Doctor of Salamanca; he was called
> Sampson Lucy in the college: and likewise he forbid him
> to chew tobacco, which he used to do very much. He was
> called Titus Ambrosius, he had twenty names.[28]

In addition to these two young Jesuits three others can be
identified. Clement Smith, who like Haggerston had been in
Rhetoric with Oates, was now a second-year theologian; and
Robert Beeston, a future Provincial, was almost at the end of
his three years' course of philosophy. Cook, who declared
himself to be the tailor at St Omers, can be no other than the
laybrother, Br James Cook, of about thirty-five years of age.
He too had previously been a witness at the trials of the five

[27] Foley (VII, 359) would make the third, Martin Hildesley, a Jesuit also,
identifying him with Francis Hildesley, s.j.: but even a comparison of dates
puts this out of the question. And Martin, as he says himself, was in 1685
living in London.—"I am of the Inner Temple."
[28] Cobbett's *State Trials*, 10, col. 1112.

Jesuits and of Richard Langhorne. And there may be two or three more.

The final sentence on the two indictments was undoubtedly severe—floggings, pillories on five days yearly for life (24 April, the day of the Jesuits' Consult, was one of them) and imprisonment for as long as he lived. The sentence was not without precedent; and it must be remembered that some thirty or more innocent people had been sent to their death in consequence of his calculated lies, and countless others had been imprisoned or impoverished. Mr Justice Wythens, who pronounced the sentence on behalf of the Court, expressed his regret that he could not pronounce a shorter and deadlier sentence. But perjury of course was not a capital offence, even though the gallows awaited a convicted pickpocket.

Four years later, after the Revolution of 1688, Titus Oates had quitted Newgate prison and was in receipt of an annual pension from the Dutchman, William III. In 1693 he married a lady of the name of Miss Rebeccah Weld: Lord Ailesbury may have been exaggerating when he called her "a heap of flesh and brandy"; at all events her dowry was £2,000. By 1705, when Oates died, his fame as the "Saviour of the Nation" was little more than a memory. Nothing is recorded of his last hours: but if he did not save the nation but rather plunged it into turmoil and disruption, one may yet hope that at least and at last by God's mercy he saved his own soul.

Amongst the books which Fr Warner, both as Provincial and as Rector, found time to write, his history of the Plot, now printed in Latin and English,[29] is the only one that seems here to call for mention. When Provincial he had asked Fr Stapleton to write such a book; and some progress had been made, at all events in gathering documents and notes. At the Provincial Congregation held at Ghent in 1684 Fr Warner himself had been proposed as the most suitable person to undertake the task; but the Provincial and his friend Fr Lucas for reasons best known to themselves—and probably to Fr

[29] C.R.S., vols 47 and 48.

Warner—had objected. Finally in the July of 1685 the General wrote, asking him in his "spare time and leisure hours" to write a history of the Plot. It was a request that could scarcely be refused. With the help of the documents from Fr Stapleton —some of them the property of Lord Castlemain—the work was finished in about a year, and by January 1687 was ready, it would seem, for the press. In the previous August he had told the General: "I have finished the History of the Persecution. When your Reverence has appointed a new Provincial I will show it to him: meanwhile I will revise and polish it as much as is in my power".[30]

If Fr Warner was waiting for a new Provincial before submitting his work to the censorship which the Jesuit rule requires, he would have had to wait till the summer of 1689. Scarcely however had he finally completed his History when he was asked for by James II to act as his confessor. After attending the Provincial Congregation of 1687 held in London and probably in March, he made a final visit to St Omers and then returned to London where he took up his new duties some time in April. Fr Michael Constable, the Minister, took his place temporarily as Vice-Rector until in the following April he was formally installed as Rector. It is thus probable that Fr Warner brought with him to London the manuscript of his History and left it behind with much else when he made his adventurous escape to St Germain on the eve of the Revolution. That at least would account for the presence of the manuscript in the library of Cambridge University. The much maligned Privy Councillor, Fr Edward Petre, effected his escape about the same time.

Indicative of the loyalty of the St Omers boys to James II and the house of Stuart was their excitement on hearing of the birth (10 June 1688) of a son to Queen Mary of Modena. The

---

[30] *Warner's L-book*, f. 72; 25 August 1686. For most of the above see C.R.S., vol 48 (as above), pp. 522-524, where also it is noted by the editor, Prof. Birrell, that the information acquired by Fr Stapleton concerning Titus Oates and his activities was worked up by him to form Part II of the *Florus Anglo-Bavaricus.*

small Prince of Wales—later "James III" or the Chevalier St George—would have been gratified had he known of the rejoicings and the procession through the town, carried out in his honour. Coincidentally, as the result of some youthful manoeuvre or other, the bells of various parish churches rang out the good news, to the exceeding annoyance of the Town Council. The young ringers were fined and the *Procureur de la Ville* was dispatched to demand an apology from the Rector, Fr Constable, which of course was promptly made.[31]

A catalogue of 1689 records that forty-six Jesuits had escaped to the Continent, whilst nineteen were still in prison or released on bail. The other Jesuits in England, some forty of them, were weathering the storm as best they could. At the Court of St James on the eve of the Orange Revolution were four Jesuits in addition to Fr Petre. Fr Anthony Jodici, said to be a Frenchman, and an Italian, Fr Bartholomew Ruga, were respectively confessor and preacher to Queen Mary of Modena. The King's confessor, Fr Warner, has already been mentioned. Fr Louis Sabran, whom we shall meet again, had at least nominally the post of chaplain to the Prince of Wales. He too escaped to St Germain-en-Laye as did the others, though not without adventure. In the company of the Polish ambassador he was surrounded by a rioting crowd at Deptford and, as he tells us, would have been shot had not the powder failed to ignite. Other perils awaited him, but at last he got safely across the Channel.[32] Four years later, about the close of 1692, his place at St Germain was taken by Fr Francis Sanders, who remained there as Superior of the small Jesuit community until his death in 1710. With him had arrived Fr Michael Constable, transferred thither at the close of his rectorship at St Omers. Of this Rector (1688-1692) there remains little record beyond a comment, as we shall see, made by his successor.

Fr Edward Petre was a priest of about sixty-two years when

---

[31] Archives de Saint-Omer, Table des Délibérations des Magistrats, Reg. HH. f. 44.
[32] Cf. Foley, V, 292-3.

Q

he succeeded Fr Constable—or rather the Vice-Rector, Fr John Swinburn—at the end of April 1693. His reputation has suffered severely at the hands of the Whigs, the contemporary pamphleteers and writers of Memoirs and Diaries, and from the Whig historians down to the present day. As material for propaganda on behalf of the Protestant Revolution Fr Petre was a godsend. Not only was he a Privy Councillor of the unpopular Stuart King whom the advocates of "No Popery" wished to eliminate; he was also a Catholic priest and hated as such. Worst of all he was a Jesuit, an object of fear and detestation to many a Protestant, as also to a small but active party amongst the Catholics themselves. The more sordid and scurrilous accusations one discards with contempt. For the rest, without holding any special brief for Fr Petre, one may legitimately ask for far better evidence of his ambition, his indiscretions and suchlike than the floating rumours spread industriously by his enemies and retailed with easy conscience by contemporary and later writers.[33] The worst that can be said of him, if we mistake not, is that he, like several others, placed mistaken trust in that exceedingly sly turncoat, Secretary of State Lord Sunderland, who professed, when it suited him, to be a Catholic and his friend.

Three months after the new Rector's induction into office he in his turn wrote a report of the College to the General, Thyrsus Gonzales.[34] Of the discipline of the boys, their application to their studies, their proficiency in Greek and Latin, and above all their piety he has nothing but praise. The masters too are keen and form a united community. The discipline, he adds, would be still better but for the too frequent changes amongst the staff. We have heard of this complaint before!

But financially he has found the College in so precarious a

[33] Some of the charges against Fr Petre have been dealt with by M. Hay, *The Enigma of James II* (London, 1938), in Chapter VI.
[34] S. Arch., Anglia V, No. 116 (28 July 1693). A free translation is in Foley, VII, 1174–76.

state that it is not far from ruin. Boys have been admitted in
the recent past whose parents were quite unable to pay their
fees; and when they left he has had to pay for their clothes and
travelling expenses. Owing to the heavy taxation of Catholics
in England, even the wealthier families are finding it difficult to
pay the very moderate fee demanded—"moderate", he
explains, since the cost of living has increased threefold whilst
the fees have remained unchanged. Even if all the fees were
fully paid (and of course they were not) the money would not
be sufficient to support the boys in the school. And since for
the last three years and more the royal pension had not been
paid, the staff and the servants had to live on an income that
was insufficient even for the boys. "I found debts amounting
to at least 10,000 florins and only sufficient money in hand to
last a fortnight." It is a melancholy picture that he draws, but
we have seen it more than once before and shall see it again in
later years. Fr Petre successfully surmounted his difficulties.

One remedy of his which, besides saving some expense,
would, he thought, improve the standard of St Omers and help
to attract more boys was what he calls a "slight" change in the
uniform. Apparently the General's consent was needed and to
gain it he enclosed a sketch of the garment thus modified: the
sketch alas is missing. Were it forthcoming it might have
saved some speculation, for the subject of the St Omers
uniforms is beset with difficulties. But the subject must be
tackled.

It may be recalled that James Wadsworth, who left St Omers
in 1622 and wrote his diatribe against the Jesuits eight years
later, has given a description, presumably correct in the main,
of the dress as worn in his day. "A Doublet of white Canvas,
Breeches and stockings that had not troubled the Weaver with
over much paines, Cassocke & stockings of the same blacke
and grave, the band precise & short, with a hat that might
almost shaddow all, and shooes correspondent." This is far
from being a clear explanation. On the presumption however
that a College boy did not wear one pair of stockings over

another pair, it is at least a possible guess that the "Breeches and stockings" formed one nether garment, the colour being unspecified; that over this underwear he wore a black cassock or soutane (with sleeves) bound at the waist with a "precise band"; and that a brimmed hat—not, therefore, a biretta— and a pair of shoes or boots completed the costume at either end. The hat, as has been noted, was worn inside the house as well as out of doors. Doubtless these clothes were made in the College tailor's shop, and would have been modelled to some extent on the contemporary Jesuit garb.

A passage in Massinger and Field's *The Fatal Dowry* (1632)[35] presents a tangential problem. The noble gentleman, Charalois, is in mourning for his father and subjected to comment—

> *Liladam.* A good dumb mourner.
> *Aymer.* A silent black.
> *Novall* (*Jun.*). Oh, fie upon him, how he wears his clothes!
> As if he had come this Christmas from St Omers,
> To see his friends, and returned after Twelfthtide.

Although the venue of this play is Dijon, it is highly probable that the reference to St Omers is to the English rather than to the Walloon College in Saint-Omer. One remembers the remark interjected by Fr Gavan at his trial in 1679—"when they go out (to England or elsewhere), they go in secular clothes, that none but must know when any person leaves the College". In any case a soutane would be a poor "disguise" even in the milder atmosphere of this period. Black however must be the colour, if the above quotation is more than a flight of imagination. So it is not unreasonable to suppose that a boy on leave of absence from St Omers—an unusual privilege— would be dressed in black doublet and hose, a sword perhaps at his side, after the manner adopted by the young witnesses at Richard Langhorne's trial. Whatever he may have worn, his unusual and perhaps ill-fitting attire sufficiently suggested the school whence he had come. St Omers, as we know, had

[35] The reference was kindly given by Fr G. Anstruther, O.P. The passage occurs in Act II, Scene 2.

entertained many an enquiring and astonished visitor. Its name and reputation would be not unfamiliar to an English audience: the allusion in the play can imply no less.

We return to Fr Petre's request for a slight alteration in the College dress—a request which aroused some controversy at the time, though the community at St Omers seems to have been in favour of the change. In the letter already quoted he tells the General that "the boys' clothes are in general so old and worn and tattered that one might mistake the house for a paupers' seminary". It is a wretched, shameful state of affairs, continues the Rector, and a very bad advertisement. Whilst Vice-Provincial for four years in England at the time of the Plot and when later for some years he lived at Court, he had learnt to appreciate the reluctance shown by many of the Catholic gentry to sending their sons to St Omers: and it was the present College uniform that deterred them. Although Fr Thyrsus Gonzales, an authoritative General, had refused the previous request for a change, the Rector, by order of his Provincial, was writing again to state his reasons.

Fr Petre's letter of 28 July was accompanied by shorter letters from his four Consultors, each of them advocating the proposed change. A month later a further letter,[36] unsigned but in the handwriting of Fr Visconti, classifies the reasons under seven heads; whence it becomes apparent what was the outer dress in use. One of these reasons is curious. Many of the English gentry have complained that boys wearing so long a cassock or gown have developed a slovenly manner of walk: they walk like rustics, not as is expected of them in polite society. The "slight" alteration asked for is evidently a shortening of the soutane—how much shorter one cannot say for lack of the missing sketch. The proposed change would save money (this from Fr Visconti, bursar as well as Consultor): it will also be neater and cleaner. How can boys be expected always to be as careful as Jesuits in tucking up their gowns to the waist whilst playing games? The ends become dirty, ragged, torn to

[36] S. Arch., Anglia V, Nos. 112-115, 117.

pieces: bits of gown are found lying about in the house. Another cogent reason is that the gown or soutane, if adequately shortened, would serve to distinguish boys from Jesuits. Visitors, even Jesuit visitors from other Provinces, can at present scarcely see any difference in the dress. As a consequence, when boys walk through the town or visit perhaps a relative, their sometimes unclerical behaviour is often taken to be unseemly conduct on the part of the Jesuits themselves.

The final reason is diplomatically given. Many other Colleges, writes Fr Visconti, such as La Fléche in France, the Colleges at Rome, at Parma and elsewhere, seek to attract the nobility and gentry to their schools, each of them knowing what best suits its needs. Had they the College uniform hitherto worn at St Omers they would never have succeeded so well. So too the English Province is a better judge of its own needs than are those who are strangers to the English character. For our part the Rector, his Consultors, the Consultors of the Province, the Provincial himself and many others agree that this alteration in dress will help to attract a better class of boy and increase our reputation and our numbers. "And undoubtedly, when your Reverence has given his consent to our petition, experience will show what a great success this slight alteration will achieve to the profit of this Seminary."

Thyrsus Gonzales began to waver. But before cancelling his previous decision, he wrote to the new Provincial, Fr Anthony Lucas, to ask his opinion. Fr Lucas was at Watten, suffering from a "continual fever", but was able to dictate an answer.[37] He agreed that the alteration should be made, adding that "the Rector is so keenly alive to the need of raising the general standard of the College that even on that score his judgment should as far as possible be accepted". The General, though reluctant, granted the request with the proviso that the change be no more than was asked for.[38] The Provincial never saw the letter, for he died on 3 October, after less than two months of

[37] *Ibid.*, No. 118.
[38] Ep. Gen., II, f. 533ᵛ: Gonzales to Lucas, 24 October 1693.

office. Four years later, in answer to a petition sent to Rome from the Provincial Congregation, Gonzales allowed that a Provincial, if he so wished, might restore the "old custom" in regard of the St Omers uniform.[39] And there the subject is dropped, at least in official correspondence.

Incidentally one may note that twenty years later the anonymous *History of the English College at Doway*, of which the real author was "Charles Dodd" (Rev. Hugh Tootell) masquerading as a Protestant clergyman, tells of the Douay College dress at that period. It was clearly not very dissimilar to that in vogue at St Omers. "Their Dress is uniform", he writes, "Black Cossacks [surely he means Cassocks], Surtouts plated [pleated] upon the Shoulders, and Collar-bands."[40]

There are a few subsequent allusions to the College uniform, and it seems best to finish the subject here. In the Stonyhurst archives there exists the copy of a Prospectus issued at Bruges after St Omers in 1762 had migrated thither. It is so extremely improbable that any change of dress was initiated there that one may take it that the Prospectus applies equally, at least in this respect, to the later years at St Omers. This is what it says: "L'habillement des Pensionnaires est uniforme, et consiste en une Soutane de drap noir, et une Robe de même étoffe". Here in addition to the soutane we have a *robe* or cloak. There are plenty of engravings of distinguished Jesuits about this period whose dress could be described in similar terms. The length of the soutane of course is not mentioned.

A Protestant gentleman, travelling on the Continent and taking careful note of the "Popish seminaries" in Flanders and thereabouts, arrived at Bruges in 1766 and apparently paid a visit to the Jesuit "Great College", then in its fourth year of residence. He informs his friend that at this College were some 175 boys, "all of them clothed in the Jesuit habit", and that the yearly fee was £25, habit included. But at the preparatory or "Little College" there was no uniform dress, the boys' dress being provided by the parents.[41] There is no good reason to doubt the accuracy of this report.

When the College again migrated from Bruges to Liège after the suppression of the Society of Jesus in 1773, the "Jesuit habit" disappeared along with the Jesuits. The uniform became colourful, presumably at the instance of the Prince-Bishop of Liège, Mgr Velbruck. To quote a printed Prospectus of 1774—

> "L'habillement de Son Altesse et des Seigneurs de Sa Cour à la campagne est celui des pensionnaires. Il consiste en un habit de drap, couleur de maron, garni de boutons d'acier."[42]

A maroon cassock, not to mention the steel buttons, is not every one's choice. Nor would such a garment be any more suitable than was the "Jesuit" soutane for a boy when playing games or walking along muddy lanes. It is quite likely that the dress was changed soon after Mgr Velbruck's death in 1784. A dozen years or so later, another Prospectus of 1797—the College by this date was at Stonyhurst—announces that

> the Sunday or holyday dress is uniform, and consists of a plain coat of superfine blue cloth with yellow buttons, red cloth or kerseymere waistcoats.[43]

The Prospectus omits to add that with the blue swallow-tail coat and red waistcoat were worn buff-coloured knee-breeches, grey stockings and a peculiar cap of leather and fur. A specimen

---

[41] *Memoirs of Thomas Hollis* (London, 1780), pp. 694-5, being a copy of a letter of an Englishman on his Travels, dated Paris, 21 March 1766.

[42] Reprinted by J. Brassinne: *Les Jésuites Anglais de Liège et leur Orfèvrerie*, pp. 71-73 (extrait du "Bulletin de la Société d'Art et d'Histoire du Diocèse de Liège", Tome 33 (1947)). *"a la compagne"* refers, one may suppose, to the less ceremonial dress worn at the Prince-Bishop's summer residence at Seraing, about five miles out of Liège, now a busy manufacturing town.

[43] See the *Ordo Recitandi Officii Divini* (ancestor of the *Catholic Directory*), for 1797, p. 8. Fr Gerard however tells us (*Centenary Record*, 1894, p. 38) that at Liege the dress was "a grey coat, yellow leather breeches, and black stockings". Unfortunately he quotes no authority for the statement. Three different uniforms in the course of less than twenty-five years seems excessive.

of the uniform still survives. In the course of half a century this vivid costume gradually disappeared. Blue coat and red waistcoat succumbed to a monotonous, bland neutralism; and the coloured knee-breeches gave way to the common or garden trouser. The vision splendid faded into the light of common day.

We return to the rectorship of Fr Petre, although there is little further information to be gleaned. There can be no doubt that he was a popular Rector and possessed a flair for finance that was greatly needed at this time. Indeed throughout its history St Omers appears to have been, more often than not, near the verge of ruin; to have passed fairly rapidly from one financial crisis to another, even if some of them may have been less acute than they were made to appear. In the late autumn of 1694 the laybrother, Cornelius Beaugrand, was arrested. Sent to London, as has been noted, in 1679 to assist in ordering the Province accounts left desolate by the arrest and martyrdom of both the Province Procurator and the London Procurator for St Omers, he had at last been caught sending money— parents' fees, presumably—by some roundabout route to St Omers.[44] That was a set-back for Fr Petre.

The College may have been similarly affected by the panic arrests that followed the Jacobite plot of 1696, a somewhat lame and broken-winged affair involving the seizure, possibly the assassination, of the Dutch King William III. Its betrayal by George Porter, perhaps a spurious Catholic, was quite in the style of his ill-famed predecessor, Titus Oates. Needless to say, the Jesuits were not forgotten. Nine of them were summarily arrested, including the Provincial, Fr William Mumford. Though after two or three months they were released on bail, the Provincial could not cross to Belgium until a year later. During the few months that remained before he laid down his office he made a formal visitation of St Omers. Strangely enough he reported that the College had declined both in piety and in studies under the Rector's "new method of govern-

44 Ep. Gen., II, f. 543ᵛ,

ing". There is no good reason to doubt his judgment, even
though one may wonder to what extent his judgment was
affected by Fr Petre's departure—no details are available—
from ancient custom. By this time Fr Petre's successor had
already been chosen. Fr William Walton was installed as
Rector in December 1697 and Fr Petre, tired and ill, retired to
Watten where less than two years later he passed to his reward.

Saint-Omer, now under French sovereignty and protection,
was saved the horrors of the aggressive war waged in Flanders
by Louis XIV during the years preceding the Treaty of Ryswick
(September 1697). At Liège indeed, where after the recapture of
Namur by the Allies vessel after vessel arrived conveying
wounded and dying soldiers by the hundred, the theologians
and philosophers did splendid work amongst their countrymen, ministering to both body and soul. It was during their
summer vacation and they made full use of the opportunity
offered them. Two years later, during the winter of 1696-97,
some of the Fathers at St Omers were busy amongst a "legio
Hibernica" (was it by chance the Irish Brigade?) which had
made the town or vicinity its winter quarters. Over a hundred
of them were converted or brought back to their duties.[45]

Time and again during these years and on many later
occasions too we hear the urgent call of the General for more
students to be sent to Rome to meet the pressing needs of the
English College. And the poor response was by no means the
fault of St Omers. "It is Rome itself that is blocking the way",
as Fr Warner had frankly declared. Not that there were no
volunteers for Rome, in spite of the College Oath of 1660: but
the supply from St Omers was seldom if ever adequate. A
certain number of youths in England could at times be persuaded to undertake this Roman journey, travelling direct
from England. In 1697, for instance, an unspecified number had
left England for Rome: the Register of the English College
(*Liber Ruber*) records the entry this year of four candidates, all
of them from Lancashire. Since these were already on their

[45] *Ibid.*, ff. 562ᵛ, 569ᵛ.

journey when the General wrote, he suggests that the one volunteer from St Omers had better wait till the following autumn, when perhaps more will have been persuaded to come.[46]

In 1702 Gonzales appealed for students more urgently than ever. The Cardinal Protector, he writes, and the Vicars Apostolic are complaining. In the whole of the three-year Philosophy course there are only five: one only survives in the second year of Theology. In all there are but twenty-two students. "There should be forty at least: in a very few years there will be none!"[47] Next year the Provincial, Fr James Blake, reported the more cheerful news that five students would be coming—though apparently but four arrived. In 1709 there were "scarcely two" for Rome: in 1711 seven were expected. One would gather that by this time the term "Seminary", although still in use by Generals when referring to St Omers College, had become an anachronism.

As every well-instructed schoolboy knows, the Revolution of 1688 was protestant and anti-Catholic. The many savage laws against Catholicism were set again in active motion: and if the rack and the halter were no longer used, the alternatives were perhaps even more effective. The glamour of martyrdom with its prospect of a speedy entrance into heaven gave place to the uninspiring tedium of life-long confinement in some insanitary, reeky prison. New oaths were substituted for those of Elizabethan and Jacobean days—an Oath of Allegiance and an Oath excluding all jurisdiction and authority of the Pope within the realm of England. To these was added the Declaration formulated in 1678 (30 Car. II, cap 1) repudiating transubstantiation and other Catholic doctrines.

The *chef-d'oeuvre* was "An Act for the further preventing the Growth of Popery" (11 & 12 W. III, cap. 4) which was to come into force on 25 March 1700. By this Act "every Popish

[46] *Ibid.*, II. f. 572.
[47] *Ibid.*, III. f. 41ᵛ: Gonzales to Rector of St Omers, 11 November 1702.

Bishop, Priest or Jesuit" convicted of saying Mass or otherwise functioning as a priest incurred the penalty of imprisonment for life. The same penalty was incurred by "every Papist keeping school, educating or boarding Youth for that purpose" —the purpose of every Catholic school. In both cases the informer was to be awarded £100. A "Popish Recusant Convict" was disabled to inherit land or property; and during his lifetime, unless he took the Oaths and made the infamous Declaration, the Protestant next of kin would "enjoy his Lands" and reap the profits. Meanwhile the Catholic owner paid double land-tax. £100 was also the reward of any informer who should "convict a Person of sending his Child etc beyond Sea to be educated in Popery".

The common informer of the eighteenth century was able to ply a very lucrative trade. Hitherto, ever since the early years of James I, a similar award of £100 had to be divided equally between the informer and the Crown; whereas after 1700 the informer was warmed up to his task by the prospect of securing the whole sum for himself. In consequence they seem to have increased like rabbits. No doubt the administration of the law grew gradually milder as the years passed by; but it was not until 1778 that these laws of William III were modified. Nevertheless some ten years earlier Chief Justice Mansfield had ruined the common informer's business by mercifully finding an unexpected but valid pretext for acquitting certain clerical victims brought before him. He demanded clear and direct evidence of a priest's ordination—an almost impossible proof for any who were not eyewitnesses—before he would convict. And failure to obtain a conviction carried with it the loss of the £100 reward.

Writing from St Omers to the General on 10 April 1700,[48] before the Royal Assent to the Act had actually been given, Fr Henry Humberston, the Provincial, is expecting "such a persecution as has not been experienced since heresy was

[48] S. Arch., B. I. 16, pp. 207-209.

set up in England. Certainly no laws more effective for rooting
out the Catholic religion have ever been passed; and unless
God hinders the execution of them, it will be impossible for
religion to survive for long in that kingdom." The Provincial,
just returned from England, was ordering public prayers
throughout the Province to supplicate God's mercy. It is thus
reasonable to expect a considerable decrease in the roll-call of
St Omers. From scattered references one can gather some at
least of the figures. Whereas in 1690 the total of boys was 134,
the number had fallen by 1700 to "about 100"; and in 1705,
five years after the passing of the Act mentioned above, the
total had dropped to 80. By 1711 however, the next year
available, the number is given as 111. Since there are always
several factors to be taken into account in the recruitment of a
school, the inference one can draw from these figures can be
but a general one. One is surprised to find that in spite of the
Provincial's forebodings the number of Jesuits stationed in
England rose steadily from some 130 in 1700 to almost 160
in 1710.

Having entered the eighteenth century we find ourselves in
a somewhat barren stretch of land as far as St Omers is concerned. A few odds and ends, however, may perhaps be worth
picking up.

There is, for instance, a rather gruesome account told by
Dom Bennet Weldon, o.s.b.,[49] who was at St Edmund's
monastery, Paris, at the time of King James II's death and is
thus an authoritative witness of the places of burial. James II
died on 16 September (N.S.) 1701: and though he is said to
have wished to be buried quietly in the parish church of St
Germain-en-Laye, it was ordered otherwise by Louis XIV.
The embalmed body, although not drawn and quartered in

---

[49] Weldon, *Chronological Notes* (1709), pp. 241 seqq. Printed at Stanbrook,
Worcester, in 1881. Cf. *The Memoirs of King James II* (83 pp., translated
from the French, 1702) which contain an account of "the Circumstances of
his death" in a letter written "from our Monastery of Chaillot, the 1st of
July, 1702" for the information of their other houses.

Tyburn fashion, was certainly "drawn". It was a common enough custom in the case of royalty, and it is far too late to protest. What remained of the body was brought the following night to St Edmund's, in the Faubourg St Germain. A few hours later—"ye moon shining very bright and cleare", as some one noted—the heart was conveyed to the Visitation Convent of Chaillot, a favourite resort of the King and his Queen. The brains were presented to the Scots College, part of the flesh of the right arm to the Austin nuns, Rue St Jacques; and in the parish church of St Germain were buried some flesh and "part of his bowels or entrails (of which the Jesuits of St Omer's had the rest)". An unsavoury gift, it may be thought; but the Jesuits were staunch Jacobites and one may be sure that this Jacobite "relic" was ceremoniously given an honourable resting-place, probably in the College Church. "What epitaph the Jesuits have framed at St Omer's . . . I have neither seen nor heard", wrote Dom Bennet. The present writer is no less ignorant.

The writer of the Annual Letter for 1708 mainly confines himself to citing examples of fervour amongst some of the St Omers "seminarians" as he calls them, which normally would be considered excessive and undesirable, even though the writer is evidently of another opinion. Some of the mortifications practised by certain boys, such as strewing their mattresses with fragments of wood or bone, or removing the mattress and sleeping on the hard boards, were fairly obviously learnt from contemporary Saints' Lives, whose authors were so often apt to place undue emphasis on the less frequented and rougher paths of holiness. Nevertheless it is clear enough that the tradition of piety was being still maintained. Parents and relatives in England needed all the prayers their children could say; and many a private visit, we are again told, was made daily to the "Sodality" or Boys' Chapel whenever the day's work allowed of it.

Special mention is made of the holy deaths of two boys, both of them received into the Society on their death-beds. One of

them is given especial praise—Robert Fitzherbert, a younger
son of William Fitzherbert of Swynnerton. His age is not
stated; but before he came to the College he had at the age of
twelve converted some "heretic" companion of his to the
Catholic faith. After a life which might seem to have been
almost Aloysian in its thoroughness he died of some dreadful
disease—the short description suggests cancer—which he
endured as cheerfully as he did the repeated incisions of a local
"chirurgeon". The other boy was Roger Petit, of whom less
is said. He had been a "difficult" boy when first he came.
Thereafter by grace and strenuous effort he too had won the
esteem and admiration of the other boys by his exceptional
holiness of life.[50]

Fr Edward Slaughter on becoming Rector (1705-1709)
decided to introduce Hebrew into the curriculum of St Omers.
He had been a Professor at Liege for several years and more
recently the Rector of that College. Hebrew seems to have
been a hobby of his. In 1699 he had published his *Grammatica
Hebraica*, which acquired some fame. But all we know of this
venture is from a letter of the General, who expressed his
approval of a "moderate study" of Hebrew, that is to say,
half an hour a day for the school of Rhetoric.[51] It is not unlikely
that Fr Slaughter himself taught the subject with the aid of his
Hebrew Grammar. Hereafter the subject is dropped. If one
may venture a guess, it is that the subject likewise dropped out
of the curriculum shortly after this Rector's departure.

The General just referred to was Fr Michael Angelo Tamburini (1706-1730), whose name in the cryptic language often
used in persecution times is transmuted into "Mr Drummer".
Similarly St Omers College appears as Blandike, or simply
B——, or Flamstead. (Why "Flamstead" one cannot say.) Fr
Tamburini, like many of his predecessors, found it difficult to
understand the character and habits of his English subjects.

---

[50] S. Arch., B. I. 16, pp. 223-225.
[51] Ep. Gen., III, f. 83ᵛ: Tamburini to Slaughter, 18 December 1706.

That is not at all surprising: Englishmen are queer folk! But he must have embarrassed Fr Thomas Parker, acting as Vice-Provincial in Belgium, and have left him wondering how to reply to some of his more admonitory letters. "It is not edifying", he wrote in the May of 1707, "that our scholastics should publicly and promiscuously join in the students' games" —he presumably has football in mind—"and it is quite intolerable that in winter time they should make use of skates and go gliding about on them over the ice: for the layfolk who are spectators it provides a most irreligious sight."[52]

It is true of course that misunderstanding by foreigners of the English temperament and way of life is probably equalled by the average Englishman's failure to understand the mentality of the foreigners with whom he may come in contact. St Omers could be called an enclave in the midst of a foreign town, but it was not a "hortus conclusus": not much that happened at the College would have escaped the knowledge and gossip of the townsfolk. "When in Rome, do as the Romans do" is a well-known piece of advice; but its application has its limits. The problem must frequently have arisen as to where to draw the line. It was no new problem raised by "Mr Drummer". Some forty years earlier, to cite one example, a General had expressed his horror—"it raises a blush even to hear of it"— that some young Jesuits in the autumn vacation had so far departed from the modesty proper to the Society as to go fishing in the river with bare feet and sleeves rolled up.[53] The General of those days may well have been justified in his admonition. It is not at all improbable that the Walloon Jesuits next door and some of the local inhabitants had been similarly shocked to see or hear of such "wanton" behaviour. Times have indeed changed, in France and Italy as elsewhere!

Since skating and fishing have been referred to, one may ask what games were in vogue during these continental days. The

[52] *Ibid.*, f. 88ᵛ: Tamburini to Thomas Parker, 14 May 1707.
[53] *Ibid.*, II, f. 291ᵛ. Oliva to Provincial (John Clark), 18 September 1666.

8. The English Noviciate at Watten, aerial view, including the
modern farm buildings near by

Photo: Studio Combier © *by S.P.A.D.E.M., Paris,* 1962

9. St Omers College today: Front view

Photo: Rev. A. Powell, S.J.

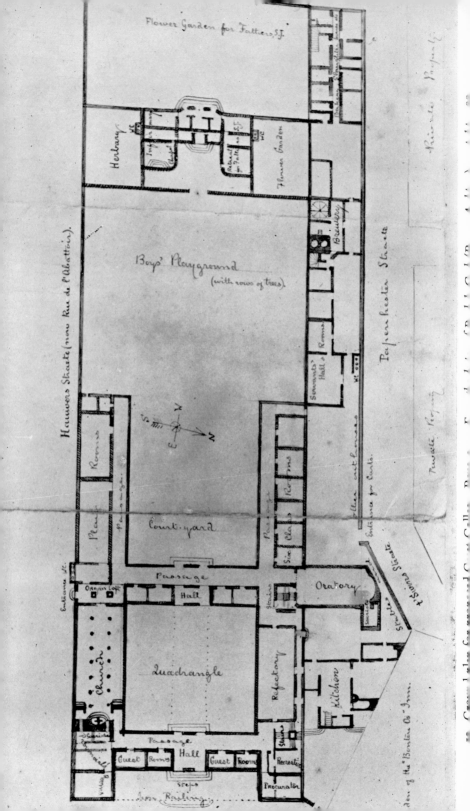

Flower Garden for Fathers, S.J.

Herbary

W.C.

Jesuit House

Chapel

Retreat for Fathers, S.J.

W.C.

Flower Garden

Boys' Playground
(with rows of trees).

Hauwers Straate (now Rue de l'Abattoir).

Flower Rooms

Plan

Passage

Court-yard

Six Class Rooms

Passage

Balcony

W.C.

Servants'
Hall &
Rooms

Garden Entrance

Entrance for Carts.

Talpenhoots Straate

Private Property

Private Property

N W S E

Entrance St.

Organ Loft

Passage
Hall

Stairs

Oratory

St. Sious Straate

Church

Sacristy

Quadrangle

Passage
Hall

Stairs

Refectory

Recreation

Kitchen

Procurator

Guest
Rooms

Guest
Rooms

Steps

Iron Railing

Ground plan for proposed Great College, Bruges. Found later ... Edinburgh University Library. (4 Miles.) 111 to 22.

answer can be but meagre, for very little information is available. Handball has been mentioned in an earlier chapter: and from the evidence given by St Omers boys at the trials connected with the Oates Plot we hear of "kittlepins" (ninepins) and of that "peculiar recreation" of the Sawing of the Witch at mid-Lent which had better be described as a pastime, as Titus Oates discovered to his cost. For the rest there is only football for which there is documentary evidence. It was played at St Omers;[54] not of course the polished game of Association football, but presumably the rough-and-tumble game, with few rules and no limit to the number of players, which reached Stonyhurst from Liege and as "Stonyhurst Football" was played there for at least a hundred years.

That cricket of one sort or another was also a St Omers game seems certain enough, even though there are, as far as is known, no documents to prove it. "There cannot be much doubt", wrote Fr Thurston in an article in *The Times*,[55] that cricket, like football, was brought over from England in the course of the seventeenth century by boys accustomed to see the game played at home. Once introduced, it was most unlikely ever to have died out: and the shape it took, despite possible minor modifications, can probably be inferred from the style of cricket in active use at Stonyhurst from the migration thither in 1794 until the eighteen seventies.

Fr Thurston, himself an ardent cricketer—he left from Rhetoric in 1874—proceeds in his article to describe the traditional game as he knew it: "Little Cricket" or "Stonyhurst Cricket" it was called. At St Omers as at Stonyhurst it would have been played in the "Line" or playground, which we take to be the "Base Court" (the anglicized form, one may suppose,

---

[54] Fr Gerard (*Stonyhurst . . . Centenary Record*, p. 25) aptly quotes from some contemporary verses:

"Tum poterant juvenes rapido, vacua atria circum,
Cursu ventosas exagitare pilas."

[55] *The Times*, 12 September 1936. The article was by permission printed later in the *Stonyhurst Magazine* for November 1936 (Vol. XXIV, pp. 47-50).

R

of the French *Basse Cour*) as marked in Montbard's engraving. The various details cannot be given here. Suffice it to say that it was played either "double-wicket" or "single-wicket" on hard ground; that the batsman, with a shoulder-less bat that slightly curved towards its thick lower end, defended his hewn stone wicket, some seventeen inches in height. The bowling was underhand: the hard leather ball bumped along the ground after the manner of "sneaks", and the batsman slogged at it as best he could.

10

A SECOND FIRE: THE PREP. SCHOOL

F R Louis Sabran came to St Omers in 1712 and was
installed as Rector in the June of that year. His father,
Marquis de Sabran, had been ambassador in London for
some years during the Commonwealth and had married an
English lady. Himself a former St Omers boy (1663-1670), Fr
Sabran had become by this time a distinguished member of
the English Province. At Liège in 1699 where he was professing
theology he had an experience which is possibly unique in the
history of the Society. In an attempt to reform the Episcopal
Seminary which for some years had been under the influence
of Jansenism, the Prince had chosen him, with the General's
consent, to take over for the time being the Presidency of that
Seminary and to occupy, together with Fr Henry Stephens, the
two chairs of theology. That measure of safety was far from the
liking of the professors and students: it was resisted violently
with every possible means at their disposal. The installation
was finally accomplished with the aid of a detachment of some
200 soldiers from the local garrison, who surrounded the
Seminary, battered down the doors that had been bolted and
chained against the arrival of the new Jesuit President, and
quelled all opposition.[1] The storm presently subsided. Until
1723 Jesuits from the English "College" or Seminary continued
to lecture on theology: but in 1708 the Presidency was handed
over to Fr Stephens, Fr Sabran having been appointed official
Visitor of his own Province as well as Vice-Provincial. He
entered on that office early in 1708 and was relieved of it in
1712, only to become Rector of St Omers.

Of his rectorate there is in general not much to remark. The

---

[1] The whole account is given in S. Arch., B. I. 16, pp. 253-340 (copy from
Rom. Arch.); cf. J. Daris, *Histoire du Diocèse et de la Principauté de Liège
pendant le xviie siècle* (Liège, 1877), I, 360 seqq.

succeeding Provincial, Fr Thomas Parker, after his Visitation of St Omers wrote in praise of the College and especially of its Rector. Less than a couple of years later Fr Sabran had restored to the capital sum all that in one or more previous rectorates had unwisely been spent. What is of more general interest is a letter-book that has survived destruction, a manuscript of 126 folios wherein Fr Sabran recorded briefly the substance of the letters received and his replies.[2] It is longer but not so vivid and self-revealing as is the letter-book of Fr Warner. The spelling is more exotic than usual, for which his French ancestry is perhaps responsible. As to the "calligraphy", at least in its literal sense, it is decidedly a misnomer: like that of Fr Warner, it is atrocious. For all that, one may find here and there items of greater interest than one might expect in the often dull routine of a Rector's daily correspondence.

The Calvert boys, for instance. There were four of them at St Omers when Fr Sabran arrived, sons of the fourth Lord Baltimore (as he became) but paid for by their grandfather the third Baron, a devout Catholic. Charles, the heir, was, it seems, in Syntax, at the age of fourteen; his brother Benedict in Grammar, and the two others, unnamed, were younger still. In November 1713, as is well known, Benedict Leonard, the father of these boys, apostatized, publicly renouncing "the Popish errors" for the evident purpose of recovering the proprietorship of Maryland with its emoluments, of both of which his father had been deprived at the Protestant Revolution of 1688. He at once recalled his sons from the College. "They went away this morning", wrote the Rector on 17 December. On the same day he records a letter to their father tactfully expressing "my greef and theirs for their going, just when beginning to gather ye fruit of their Education. (I) confide in his care, since now 'tis he must answer to God for them." A remark of Robert Harley, Earl of Oxford, is noted—that 'if the Calverts were not sent at once, not a Jesuit should stay in

[2] Letter-book of Fr Sabran, 1713-1715 (Bibliothèque Royale de Belgique, MS 4177: xerograph in S. Arch., D. II. 2).

England". The boys, it should be added, were placed in Protestant schools and presently followed in their father's wake. But at first they seem to have put up a fight. "Ye eldest", wrote Fr Coxon from London, "threatened to bee disinherited, answered he had rather loos his estate than his religion."[3] Alas, the prospect of succeeding his father as Governor induced him to revoke that solid answer of his. The family, now turned Protestant, survived for some sixty years in the direct line until on the death in 1771 of Charles' profligate son, the sixth Baron, at the early age of thirty-nine, the peerage became extinct.

Then there was the lamentable case of Mr Deale the apothecary, offspring of a mixed marriage, whom a Jesuit, Fr Ambrose Jackson, had reconciled to the Church. A post was found for him in Paris in some monastic establishment. Fr Sabran was in need of an apothecary and Deale was recommended as very suited for the post. He arrived about March 1714, after four months in Paris, where "ye Prior says he carryed himself very well—that they lookt on him as a saint". Nevertheless the Prior was willing to do without his saint. Fr Sabran for his part was evidently disappointed with this addition to his staff: after all, his need was not so much for a saint as for a competent apothecary. Mr Deale did not stay long at the College—a month or two at most—for reasons unexplained. He returned to England; and Fr Coxon, the Procurator or Agent in London for St Omers, tells the rest of the story, roughly summarized by Fr Sabran.[4]

The day after he arrived in London, the £100 which a recent proclamation had promised to informers proved all too tempting. He tried to take Fr Coxon but his intended victim was too quick for him. Then with the help of a letter for Mr Wright of Kelvedon, which (so he said) Mr Wright's son Billy had given him at St Omers, he managed to hear Mass at Kelvedon where Fr John Hanmer, s.j., was chaplain. Next

[3] *Ibid.*, f. 18.
[4] *Ibid.*, ff. 39ᵛ-40. Coxon to Sabran, 10 May 1714.

day Fr Hanmer was arrested by a "Messenger" and lodged in Newgate. But it rested with Deale to provide the vital evidence in Court, and when it came to the point, recollecting some creditors of earlier days, he hesitated to make known his presence in London. Presumably he lost thereby all hope of the £100 reward. "Not daring to appear", writes Fr Sabran, "he repents what Poverty forced him unto; so, if no Great Mischievous man back him, that affair is at an end." Not so for Fr Hanmer, who nevertheless remained in prison for several months.

The Rector was magnanimous in dismissing the case so easily. For Deale, creditors or no creditors, had also deposed upon oath to "some of the Ministry" that "Mr Sabran, who goes also by ye name of Whitmore, sent him over to poyson a great person; and several other things relating to the Pretender".

This regrettable tendency of his towards poisoning his enemies was by no means the only accusation he had to endure. The ancient charge, which had at least a hundred years of bad history behind it, of Jesuit intriguing for the control of the English College at Douay, the main educational rival of St Omers, was revived during Fr Sabran's rectorship. Indeed it was Fr Sabran himself who on this occasion was cast for the chief part. The responsibility was not his but "Charles Dodd's", who revived the subject in general terms in his short *History of the English College at Doway* and two years later in his *Secret Policy of the English Society of Jesus* (1715), wherein the two chief actors appeared as "Mr P." (Rev. Austin Poyntz) and "F.S." (Fr Sabran). The former work pretended to have as its author a Protestant chaplain to an English regiment.[5] The book seems to have appeared about November 1713; and Fr Sabran was commissioned by the Provincial to gather

---

[5] The writer's initials are given as R.C. But though at first, in accord with Dodd's evident intention, he was taken to be a parson, the deception was of short duration. "Doth not some Clergyman lurk under ye Name of ye Parson?" was the suggestion made a few weeks later.

"out of the Archivium or elsewhere authentic answers to ye chief Calumnies" which Fr Thomas Hunter would then use for his *Modest Defence* in answer to Dodd's attack. The Letterbook contains a résumé of several letters from the impatient Fr Hunter, who however was reminded that "a full and usefull answer, not a quick one, is desired". For all that, the answer was a fairly "quick one". The *Modest Defence*, wrote Fr Hunter on 23 April (N.S.) is "comd out" and he is sending some copies.

Dodd's *Secret Policy* was his reply to Fr Hunter, written in a sequence of twenty-four letters addressed to the English Provincial, obviously with a backward glance at Pascal's famous *Provincial Letters*. One is here concerned, not with the foolish subject in dispute, but merely with the accusation that Fr Sabran was implicated. For he was accused of egging on a certain Austin Poyntz, a student in 1704 at the Douay College, to gather evidence of Jansenism amongst the Professors, and of writing letters to him with this object in view. If by hook or by crook it could be proved that Jansenism was rife (said Dodd) a thorough reform would be insisted on by Rome, and the Jesuits hoped to be brought in as the reformers.

Dr Robert Witham, successor of Dr Paston as President of Douay, had his own private quarrel with Dodd and speaks of him as "magis astutus quam sincerus";[6] one may easily agree that he was astute. Why did he pick on Fr Sabran as the "main Spring" of this Jesuitical conspiracy? He must have been well aware that for several years Fr Sabran had been President of the Episcopal Seminary at Liège, placed there that he might purge it of Jansenism. Any reader of Dodd's writings can guess that he would have had his own sinister interpretation of that episode. Five years later, in 1704, there had arisen what Dodd might well have seen as a similar situation. If Douay College could be condemned as Jansenistic, a Jesuit might again become President of a clergy establishment. *Cui bono?* The advantage presumably would accrue to the rival Catholic College at St Omers: and whilst Dodd was penning his *Secret Policy* of the

[6] C.R.S., Vol. 28 (Seventh Diary), p. 72.

English Jesuits, the former President at Liége had become Rector of this supposedly envious school.

It is true that Dodd inserts a lengthy statement made by some "Confederate" of Poyntz which supplied all that was wanted from an anti-Jesuit standpoint. Two or three letters of Fr Sabran are quoted or summarized in this document.[7] Nevertheless the Provincial, Fr Parker, was advised that amongst English Catholics "the greater part here, especially of externs [i.e. non-Jesuits] are not for having the letters answered, to avoid the encrease of scandal". An answer indeed was compiled by Fr Hunter but it was never published. One copy at least survives in the Stonyhurst archives; and it is only fair to Mr Poyntz, now Confessor to the Austin nuns at Bruges, to note that in this unpublished manuscript is included a long extract from Mr Poyntz's own account of the matter—an account that differs very considerably from that of the "Confederate" quoted by Dodd.[8] Fr Sabran's own denial may here be added. He summarizes a letter received from the Provincial on 21 March 1715—

Some give out an odd story, that Mr Sabran writt formerly to Mr Poyntz or some of his compagnons att Douay College, bidding them have patience with Dr Paston's tyranny and they should be supported. Inquire if true, or he hath sayd any thing that might have given occasion to this report.

Fr Sabran's reply two days later is noted briefly: "I never writt any thing on ye subject mentioned".[9]

Turning to less unpleasant subjects, one may note that the Fr Hunter mentioned above acted as chaplain to the Shireburn family at Stonyhurst for some three years. He had been a

---

[7] Secret Policy, pp. 273-278.

[8] Hunter's Answer to the Four and Twenty Letters (etc.), pp. 277-281 (S. Arch., A. IV. 23). Mr Poyntz was anxious to print his own reply to the accusations made against himself, and Sabran was in favour of the project (f. 101). But Poyntz was persuaded by other Jesuits to drop the subject for the sake of peace.

[9] Letter-book, ff. 92, 92ᵛ.

Professor at Liege and took up his appointment as chaplain in 1706. When in 1709 Sir Nicholas Shireburn's only daughter was married to the Duke of Norfolk, he became chaplain to the Duke and Duchess, and no doubt lived wherever they chose to live—which was mostly, it would seem, in London at their town house in St James' Square. At all events, so far as Jesuit catalogues provide evidence, from 1712 until his death early in 1725 Fr Hunter was stationed in the London district, with the exception of one year. That was in 1715 when he is said to be at Rouen "with his noble patrons". On 10 April of that year Fr Sabran received the chaplain's letter announcing that "Ye Duke of Norfolck, Duchess, Mr Philip Howard, all ye family" were going to take the waters at Spa and hoped to call at St Omers soon after Easter. In the event Fr Sabran travelled to Calais on Friday, 10 May, to meet his distinguished guests, whom he entertained on the following Monday and Tuesday.

Evidently there was much fuss and bustle. "Ye badges of Earle Marshal" were in position, and a programme or "argument for our stage entertainment for ye Duke of Norfolck" had been sent to him already. Doubtless the boys would have been freed from schools. It was a "great occasion" and the Rector would have made the most of it. The guests were shown the sights of the town, including the famous Abbey of St Bertin where they were entertained at dinner. On Wednesday the Rector accompanied them as far as Watten before saying good-bye. A month or two later Fr Sabran learnt of the reception given to the Duke at the seminary at Liège.[10] There the visitors were joined by Henry Howard, another brother of the Duke, and by that strange busybody, the Abbé Strickland, whose persistent endeavours in favour of an Oath of Allegiance to George I and of Abjuration of the Stuart dynasty had for a time the qualified support of the Duke, though certainly not of the Duchess. This visit of the Duke and Duchess, but more especially of the Duchess, has its interest in that before the close

10 *Ibid.*, f. 106.

of the century the visit was returned by the total emigration of the school—with a couple of halts on the way—to her ancestral home in Lancashire.

There is a good deal in this Letter-book on the subject of "packs" or "packs of Marchandises"—packs being the cryptic word for (new) boys. Fr Coxon, the London agent for St Omers, was frequently pressed to send over more boys, notwithstanding the impoverished Catholic situation in England; and Fr Coxon was evidently a keen agent. In March 1715, for instance, Fr Sabran writes that "20 packs (have) gone hence this dead time of 6 months", and he is in hopes of replacements. He seems to have got them, for in July he says that if the five "packs" come now and two more in September, he would begin schools with over 140. At the end of September he could proudly announce, "I have in my shop 142 packs". The number had reached 146 before another month had passed. It was a considerable achievement, the roll-call during the eighteenth century averaging, it would seem, some 110 or a little less.

Another frequent correspondent was Fr William Darell, Procurator at Paris during this period. Finance of course was a main topic—difficulties connected with the payments of the royal pension to St Omers, the securing of advantages by means of the varying exchange value of bonds, and so on. A certain number of boys were from Paris and from St Germain-en-Laye or its vicinity, mostly of English or at least British extraction. Fr Darell and Fr Justiniani (veré Ayroli), chaplain to Queen Mary of Modena, were both called upon to assist in securing the College fees. That was often no light task. The families at St Germain were no better off, probably worse off, than were the Catholic gentry in England, mulcted in many cases of two thirds of their incomes yet forced to pay double land tax on the whole property. After a few months at St Germain Fr Lawson—he succeeded Fr Justiniani in the March of 1715—reported that many families "sell all to buy bread"; that the small Community of Jesuits there were living on borrowed money, their salaries unpaid for several months.[11] According to Fr Darell they were starving: but he himself, more fortunate, was living, together with his assistant, Br Thomas Smith, at the Professed House of the French Province. It was to this house, incidentally, that Louis XIV, dismembered after his death on 1 September 1715, bequeathed his heart. Six Jesuits were called upon by Cardinal Rohan to stand watch over his body: and Fr Sabran noted a letter of the 8th from Fr Darell—"busye in making preparations to receive that night ye Kings heart". Another half-century and the Jesuits, English as well as French, had been expelled from the country by his successor.

It was to Paris too that the Rector had recourse in connection with the College theatre. "Acting sutes" were needed on various occasions. He enquired the price of cloth-of-gold, brocades and jewels, even "a gowne or manteau, or a Petticote or two, of any colour of silks etc for a present use here". And intermittently he wanted feathers[12]—quantities of them, fifty-one on one occasion, thirty-six on another, and of many colours, white, black, red, green, blue and "feuille morte", no doubt some shade of brown. The fifty-one feathers were wanted for "acting cloaths for Sintax"; and from the date it would seem that he had in view the "action" or drama of St Monocella on 7 May 1714, exhibited (he considered) "with great satisfaction". Fr Sabran was quite interested in St Monocella and begged the English Rector in Rome to obtain from the appropriate Sacred Congregation an Indulgence for the Saint on behalf of St Omers. Fr Richard Plowden made an attempt but, as he explained, the difficulty was that the name of St Monocella did not occur in the Roman Martyrology. One may wonder whether she "occurred" at all.

In addition to these stage requirements Fr Sabran bought his

---

[11] *Ibid.*, f. 121.
[12] "Would not this, Sir, and a forest of feathers ... with two Provincial roses on my razed shoes, get me a fellowship in a cry of players, Sir?"— *Hamlet*, III, 2.

prize books likewise from Paris. A list of books was sent to Fr Darell with the proviso that the cost must not exceed 125 livres (about £11). In the event the cost was 300 livres, but as Fr Darell explained soothingly, the books would be enough for two years. To Fr Coxon in London an order was sent for fishing rods and tackle: a natural need for boys when on holiday at Blandyke by the river Aa. But it is perhaps a little surprising to read of a request for a mastiff, "or dog of a large size". The request was on behalf of a boy named Fleetwood, but it does not appear whether the mastiff was to be a companion for the boy or a gift to the College as security against intruders. In any case, though Fr Coxon received more than one reminder, there is no mention of any dog's arrival.

Fr Sabran's last letter to his friend Fr Coxon (26 October 1715) describes, although very briefly, "in what condition I leave to morrow the house". He confines himself to the subject of finance. He is leaving in cash 3,500 florins—£300 or slightly more—over and above what he found on arrival. He is not including a debt of over £800 which he has for some while been urging the Provincial to pay. But his chief title to praise in this field is his restoration of seven out of eight free places, each of them the equivalent of the normal fee which still was £25. Whether by mismanagement or misadventure the capital sum that once had been accumulated for this purpose was no longer in existence until the Rector's unceasing care and energy provided another capital of about £3,060 invested in various Paris funds. It is interesting to note the frequent petitions he received for a free place or at least for a fraction of one. In exceptional cases he was willing to reduce the fee. It is clear that he was a kind and tactful Rector and, as it appears, a highly successful one. It need only be added that after another two years at St Omers as Director of the Sodality he was appointed Spiritual Father at the English College in Rome: and there it was that he ended his days in the January of 1732 at the venerable age of eighty.

The Jacobite Rising towards the close of 1715 had in its

aftermath the usual effect on St Omers, a diminution of pupils. Arrests and stringent measures of various kinds made Catholic life in England, already difficult, more difficult still. At the instance of the Provincial the Emperor and the Kings of Spain and Portugal were urged to intercede on behalf of the English Catholics. Communications between England and the continent were narrowly watched. The new Rector, Fr Francis Powell, and some of his successors must have felt the pinch. Although few details are available, one learns at least from scattered references that by 1723 the total of boys had dropped to 113. Four years later the number was down to 96: but there is a further reason for this, as we shall see in a moment.

Of Fr Powell's rectorate one hears little. He was kind, it seems, perhaps too facile and easy-going. His successor, Fr William Darell, the former Procurator at Paris, died after about six months of office. Fr John Turberville was soon appointed to take his place; but within two months of his installation he was released from his post on account of a sudden summons to England. For some years previously he had been chaplain at Lostock to the widow of Sir Charles Anderton, his first cousin. His sudden summons was no doubt in connection with the disastrous will of Lady Anderton, who had died during the previous August.[13] The choice of Fr James Gooden was apparently not a very happy one, for after a couple of years we find a Vice-Rector, probably Fr Coxon, taking temporary charge until the arrival from Rome and the installation of Fr Richard Plowden in May 1725. It was his second term as Rector of St Omers.

Four months later, about midnight on 23 September (O.S.) or 4 October (N.S.), Fr Plowden had to deal with another fire in the College, even more disastrous than that of 1684. What caused this second disaster is uncertain. Fr Turberville, now Provincial, gave it out that there was a "suspicion of malicious design in the affair". The Rector's brother Edmund (usually

[13] Cf. Rev. T. E. Gibson, *Lydiate Hall and its Associations* (1876), pp. 71 seqq, where some of Fr Turberville's letters are quoted.

known as "Gage" in England), the Procurator of the Province, seems to have been of the same mind.

'Tis a difficult matter to account for ye occasion. As it was a Thursday, which is a playday in ye afternoon, there were no studies after supper. At $6\frac{1}{2}$ when they go to supper, you know ye Prefect sees the candles put out, goes himselfe out last and locks the door. It can't be supposed any candle could then be left burning. But imagining that a snuff might have bin carelessly left in the socket, sure it would have shewn itself by 9 a clock when people were going to bed. But it must be observed that ye G^r Minister in making his Rounds was in ye study place at $9\frac{1}{2}$ and saw nothing amiss. Now it is hard to conceive how anything of a candle could be left at $6\frac{1}{2}$, remain till $9\frac{1}{2}$ without being discovered either inside or outside, and in about two hours after, break out into such a flame.[14]

Whatever may have been the cause, the result was calamitous, for the greater part of the College was gutted, ruined beyond repair. From Montbard's engraving of the College as restored after the fire of 1684, it is easy enough to gather the general lay-out of the buildings. The main part formed a handsome three-storied building surrounding a court or flower garden, with the main entrance and façade on the Rue St Bertin. This was called the "New Square". On the Walloon College or western side (the College faces north) are some lower buildings; the Church and the College Press on the Rue St Bertin, and behind these at intervals are two important buildings—the pantry and kitchen, with the College Infirmary above; and further back, beyond the kitchen garden, is the "Sodality" or Boys' Chapel. These lower buildings managed somehow to escape destruction. The other side of the College where the New Square bordered the Rue des Cordeliers (Rue Notre-

[14] S. Arch. Edmund Gage (veré Plowden) to "Mr Philips" (veré Richard Cotton, s.j.) "at Mr Stockdal(es) at the Hare and Hound in St Giles, Norwich", 9 October [O.S.] 1725. From a bundle of letters &c. (Galloway MSS) kindly presented to Stonyhurst in 1953 by Capt. Eyre-Huddleston of Sawston Hall, at the instance of his archivist, Mr T. F. Teversham.

Dame de Patience) was continued along that same side street in the form of a long and perhaps slightly narrower range of buildings containing the class-rooms with the school library at the far end, and above them the Study Place. Beyond this wing, along the modern Rue Gambetta, lay, quite separate from the class-room wing, the Boys' Infirmary (distinct from the College Infirmary), the Base Court (Playground?) and a medley of out-houses. These were untouched by the fire.

To quote again from the letter of Fr Edmund "Gage":

> The fire broke out at the further end of ye study place towards the schollars Infirmary: by that time people were got out of their beds, it had gained the space of two windows, and went on with that violence that in 8 minutes that whole range of building was in a flame: and what is more surprising, in half an hours time the fire had seized the 4 corners of the New Square. And in the space of 4 hours the study place, schooles and whole New Square were burnt down. The main walls of ye Square are standing; but to be sure, must be pulled down, at least to very near ye ground.

The fire might well have spread to the College Church, had it not been that at the nearest corner of the New Square was a room, once the First Prefect's abode, but now packed with "books in Albis"—a store-room, that is to say, for unbound books or unfolded sheets from the Printing Press. As Fr Richard Hyde, the College Procurator, explained, "they being very close corded up, the fire could not neer pearce 'em, and an engine continually playd from ye street on 'em". How the Boys' Chapel escaped is not very clear, except that it was much lower. As for the kitchen, its roof "joining with that of ye great dortory took fire and had been burnt had not a young Carpenter that serves our house cut it very dexterously whilst it was afire".[15]

Thus perished the class-rooms, the Study Place, the private rooms of the Fathers, and the boys' dormitories or "dorters"

[15] S. Arch., Anglia VII, No. 87. R. Hyde to T. Eberson (Rector, Liege), 11 Nov. [N.S.] 1725.

which occupied the top floor along two sides of the New Square: likewise the "great" theatre with the "little" theatre above it, the greater part of the College library and much else. Fr Hyde managed to save his account books and what cash there was in the house.

We had not above 180" [livres] in ye house; all our winter cloathing for Fathers and schollars was ready made and all lost; all ye schollars beding with most of the Fathers all burnt; all their gowns, books, musick instruments, in fine all lost: so that I count ye loss of moveables greater than that of the house.

The one consolation was that every one escaped unhurt. At first, says Fr Hyde, he managed to borrow some beds from the military barracks nearby, and about sixty were lodged "in a house we have in town", the rest in the boys' Infirmary. "But now they are all provided with new bedding from top to toe" and are lodged, twenty-seven in the boys' Infirmary, "some 60" in another building and twenty-three in a Canon's house in the vicinity. The total number therefore came to some 110. At the date of writing, 11 November, the normal routine of the College had been resumed. "We begin ye foundations for ye new schools to-morrow, and if God sends money I hope they may be finished by ye end of next May." This Procurator, like some of his more modern successors, was an optimist.

The Rector, Fr Plowden, had now the onerous and thankless task of begging for money, whilst to the capable Fr Hyde was given the charge of supervising the rebuilding of St Omers. The total cost of the new College is unknown, though some of the contributions are on record. Pope Benedict XIII gave 1,000 crowns, as also did the General and the Jesuit Province of Bohemia. The King of France gave a promise of a "liberal contribution" which one hopes he fulfilled; the King of Portugal came forward with 5,000 guilders. In February 1726, Fr Percy Plowden, the Rector's brother, is reported to have collected between £2,200 and £2,300 from friends in England. Poor as was the English Province at this period, Fr Turberville was able to scrape together £100 as his "Charity" to St Omers.[16] The College was evidently not without some generous friends and well-wishers.

Fr Hyde's optimism was certainly excessive: the rebuilding of St Omers in winter time during a period of only six months was a lost hope. The Provincial expected the wing being built over the ruins of the class-rooms and study place would be completed by the Michaelmas of 1726, but it is not clear whether his expectations were realized.

There remained the main part of the building, the New Square. By the May of 1727 at least the western side of the Square had been completed or nearly so. "To-day" [4 May], wrote the Procurator, "we dine for the first time in our new refectory, which is very handsome, being somewhat higher than it was, and paved with marble and other stones, and a new wainscot all round; the ceiling is also better than it was. We hope to have the Sodality ready for next Sunday, to resume our devotions there."[17] Ever since the fire, this chapel had had to serve as a refectory, for lack of other accommodation. As late as February 1728, Fr Tamburini agreed with Fr Hyde that it was better not to hurry but to finish what had been begun, leaving the Theatre to wait awhile. Three months later Fr Hyde himself became Rector: then after another fourteen years as Procurator he again was appointed Rector for a second term of office, in the course of which he died, early in 1744. The rebuilding and refurnishing of this new St Omers is thus to a large extent indebted to the zeal and competence of one who was not only an efficient Procurator and Rector but also without doubt a man of personal sanctity.

Montbard's engraving of Fr Warner's building after the first fire of 1684 shows, high up above the main entrance, the date 1689. Whether Fr Hyde's building also displayed a date is unknown; for no later engraving seems to exist prior to 1826 when yet another fire, of which little is known, may have

16 E. P. Arch. Thorpe's Notes and Fragments (section 2), f. 32.
17 Foley, IV, pp. 552-3, Cf. C.R.S., Vol. 30, p. 186.

S

altered to some extent the appearance of the former College.[18] We know however that Fr Warner included a "Clock Tower" in his building, although from the engraving a College bell is all there is to be seen. In 1728, we learn,[19] the steeple and clock of the church of St Denis close by had fallen down. In consequence the English Jesuits, "ayant augmenté le timbre de leur horloge", received a grant of 500 livres towards the cost, with the stipulation that the sound be loud enough to be heard over the whole town. Two years later the Rector, Fr Hyde, bought from the civic authorities a large bell which formerly had been at the Porte du Haut Pont. As a fire precaution he had already been directed to provide at the College a reservoir capable of holding "80 tons" of water: only on such a condition would he be allowed to use the surplus from the fountain near the church of St Denis.[20]

Perhaps a word may be allowed here, at the close of Fr Richard Plowden's rectorate, on the subject of this family. Richard was one of five brothers, four of whom became Jesuits. Francis, the eldest, was, it must be admitted, erratic. It was Richard who was the most prominent and the most hard-worked, for with intervals of a year or less he held successively the posts of Rector of Liege, of St Omers, of the English College, Rome, then Provincial (1716-1719), again Rector of Liege and once again of St Omers. Small wonder perhaps that he then retired to Watten and died in the following year. Edmund was twice a Rector, besides being for several years Procurator of the Province in very difficult times. Percy, the youngest of the four, was successively Rector at Rome, at Ghent and at St Omers (1739-1742). For those interested in "records", ten rectorates shared by three brothers would be hard to beat.

[18] A reproduction of this post-1826 front (in Gerard: *Stonyhurst College Centenary Record*, opp. p. 8) shows little difference in the façade except in the centre—the entrance and above it. Not much more remains at the present day than this side of the New Square facing the Rue St Bertin.
[19] Archives de Saint-Omer, Table des Déliberations des Magistrats, Reg. 00, f. 53.   [20] *Ibid.*, ff. 53, 63, 83.

Their only sister, Dorothy, deserves too a tribute of gratitude; and where else is she likely to have it if not here? Her second husband was Sir William Goring, of Burton Park, Sussex. He died "after seven years patience in great pain" early in 1724,[21] whereupon Lady Goring retired to Liège, spending the rest of her life in charitable works, in which the Canonesses of the Holy Sepulchre (now at New Hall) and the English Jesuit Seminary had a share. Her many gifts to the English Seminary —silver church plate of various kinds and undoubted beauty— have been gratefully inherited in due course by Stonyhurst College. The recipient of these gifts would have been her brother, Fr Edmund; for during part of that period he was Rector (1731-1734) and was allowed at her request to remain at Liege until her death in 1737. Many Masses were promised by the General for the soul of this "good benefactress of the Society".

The successor of Fr Hyde as Rector was Fr Thomas Eccleston (1731-1737), of whom it is recorded that having killed his opponent in a duel, he renounced his worldly prospects which were considerable and entered the Jesuit noviciate in Rome at the age of eighteen and died at the age of eighty-four. It is strong evidence of his success as Rector that he was an exception to the usual custom of changing Rectors every three years; he held his office for six. After every visitation of the house by the Provincial the report to the General, Fr Francis Retz, was invariably most laudatory. For the rest, as so often is the case, the surviving documents are silent.

A little more is known about the Rector who in September 1737 stepped into Fr Eccleston's shoes. Apparently they did not fit very well: by no means all are gifted with a special talent for government. Be that as it may, Fr Joseph Constable, elder brother of the well-known writer, was relieved of his office after two years, in view of his "continued bad health". The General showed little hesitation in agreeing with the Provincial's proposal, for he was convinced, rightly or wrongly,

[21] Thorpe (as above), f. 27.

that the discipline at St Omers was in a state of collapse or suspended animation.

What mainly caused him wonder and astonishment was a report from Fr Lawson, a former Provincial and now Master of Novices at Watten, that "equitation" was becoming customary amongst both masters and boys. Fr Retz was told that "nearly every day they go out riding over the country, and sometimes even spend the night away from home in neighbouring towns". Hence convivial evenings, late returns at night, and general loss of religious and scholarly discipline. He had heard too that there were some who had guns and went out on shooting expeditions. Asked for an explanation, Fr Constable excused himself on the ground that when in England the Fathers travelled on horseback; and therefore it would be well for future missioners to learn to ride. Horsemanship likewise was a useful means of physical exercise for the young. But the General was far from being convinced. The use of fire-arms must be forbidden absolutely: and as for riding, that too must be forbidden except in cases of necessity or extreme urgency. For the young there were several other more usual means of taking exercise.[22] Taking account of time and place, one can appreciate the anxiety of the General. St Omers was contravening the customs of other Jesuit Colleges in the country: and in any case it should not show signs of developing into a riding school at the expense of studies and discipline.

Very Rev. Father Retz was anxious about many things besides riding and duck shooting—or whatever was the quarry aimed at in this pleasant sport. He had fears that the English Jesuits might be becoming rather less addicted to plain living and high thinking than was good for them; and he wished to raise the standard. It was to the Rector of Liege that he wrote this same year (1738) on the subject of wigs and watches. Wigs of course were in common use during this eighteenth century; and the Jesuits amongst others, who obviously wore secular clothes when in England, would have been too easy a prey to

[22] Ep. Gen., III, ff. 311, 312ᵛ.

informers unless they completed their attire with the usual
wig. To that the General raised no objection. He had heard
however that some of the seminary students at Liege had
adopted the custom. And as the masters at St Omers were
recruited from Liege, St Omers too must have been in the
General's mind. (As early as 1714 Fr Sabran notes a request
from M. Van der Camere that his son be allowed to wear a
wig; but there may have been some special reason for that.)
There were wigs and wigs, of course. The Latin "ficti capil-
litii" gives us no inkling as to the fashion favoured at Liege.
Needless to say, Fr Retz disapproved of wigs, in particular of
the flowing, powdered wig of fashionable society. If a wig is
really needed, he writes, let it be such as will be scarcely
distinguishable from the original growth and will not pander to
vanity.[23] One may surmise that even in an age of wigs a class-
full of boys would offer but small opportunity for vanity to a
master so accoutred.

As an item of Jesuit social history it may be remarked that
watches (horologia "portatilia" or "rotata") were not yet in
common use in the first half of the eighteenth century. As in
the case of wigs, their possession was permitted to those sent
on the English mission; for apart from their obvious utility, a
watch was at this period inexpensive, and (as the General says)
in common use both amongst the nobility and amongst those
whom a contemporary writer refers to as the "mobility". In the
continental houses however Fr Retz forbade the growing
custom on the plea of poverty and of the custom of other
Jesuit Provinces.[24]

Ever since the advent of William of Orange in 1688, the
problems to be faced on both sides of the Channel had grown
and multiplied. England became more and more a dangerous
resort. We hear less at this period of Jesuits crossing over to
England for the sake of their health. Jacobite plots—the
"Fifteen" and the "Forty-Five" were only the more prominent
of them—kept the Government alert and suspicious. One

[23] *Ibid.*, III, ff. 312, 331.   [24] *Ibid.*, III, ff. 288ᵛ, 332.

reads of numerous arrests and imprisonments, usually followed by a period of liberation on bail. It grew more difficult for Provincials to cross in safety to England and no less dangerous to re-cross to the Continent. Official visitations of houses had therefore sometimes to be carried out by proxy. Letters to England were camouflaged. Fr Sabran, as has been seen, became Mr Whitmore; Fr Richard Plowden was addressed as Mr Riccardi, Fr Robert Beeston as Mr Robert Hill, Fr Powell, his Socius, as Mr Ashton, and so on. Even this did not prevent Provincials from being caught and imprisoned—Fr Thomas Parker, for instance, whilst acting as Vice-Provincial in 1708, or Fr Richard Plowden in 1719: in both cases a Jacobite plot, real or imagined, may well have been the occasion. It became usual therefore to appoint Vice-Provincials both in England and abroad. The Vice-Provincials functioned when the Provincial was on the other side of the Channel. Abroad it was, more often than not, the Rector of Liege to hold that temporary office and to make, as occasion offered, an official visitation of the houses.

If the standard of the English Province by and large had fallen somewhat from that of the preceding century, as the General was inclined to believe and as Fr Turberville when Provincial (1725-1731) would to some extent have corroborated,[25] then the remedy must begain at the source. A more thorough training of novices was called for, and a more careful selection of candidates. Since most candidates derived from St Omers, it was to this College that attention must primarily be directed. Yet here (as Fr Retz may have supposed) were masters and boys galloping about the country, shooting wild fowl or what-not, and living undisciplined lives. Doubtless it was not as bad as all that: yet, also without doubt, discipline and studies had suffered. Convivial evenings, for instance, have their after-effects: "a merry evening maketh a sad morning" and is not conducive to any intensive study of the classics.

[25] Cf. Thorpe (as above), f. 34ᵛ. Turberville to Sabran—December 1727.

In place of Fr Constable, Fr Percy Plowden, late Rector at Ghent, was sent to the rescue to St Omers: and next year Fr Charles Shireburn[26] was appointed Provincial (1740-1744). This was a happy choice, for from all accounts he proved to be one of the most capable Provincials of the "old" English Province. His many activities, his tact, his numerous proposals for the better ordering of the Province, all these were most warmly welcomed and encouraged by the General.

Fr Retz, however, had his own solution for one complaint emanating from St Omers College, namely that the Prefects were seldom adequate to their posts, being often such as were considered unsuitable for other employments; and that they were too frequently changed. A long-standing complaint, of course, taking us back to the days of Fr Warner and his struggles to obtain a more efficient and more permanent staff. Fr Retz suggested that no Prefect, if fit for his office, be moved until he had completed at least three years of office, nor appointed before his tertianship, lest he be negligent, knowing that he would soon be moved to Ghent. If a Prefect really must be moved, let it be the First Prefect, the Second and Third Prefects moving up a peg. And if by necessity a Prefect must be appointed before his tertianship, the solution would be to postpone the tertianship.[27] It will be noticed that the three Prefects are presumed to be priests, as indeed they had been for many a year. The masters on the other hand were at this period usually non-priests ("scholastics") with a priest occasionally amongst them.

Other plans too were concocted by the General and Fr Shireburn with the same object in view. Besides regulations governing the admission of St Omers boys to the Watten noviciate, the question of appointing a really good Spiritual

---

[26] Fr Shireburn was connected with the Shireburns of Stonyhurst, but the exact connection is uncertain. Sir Nicholas Shireburn's accounts show that he paid for his schooling at St Omers, from September 1697 "when he went over" to November 1702 when Sir Nicholas paid for his fifth year, adding two guineas as "a toaken at ye ending of his Rhetorick". (S. Arch., C. I. 10.)

[27] Ep. Gen., III, ff. 332, 334ᵛ.

Father was discussed. Eventually Fr "Levinus" [Lewin?] Browne, a former Master of Novices and now about seventy years old, was selected for the post; and there he remained, as we shall see, until his death in November 1764. One of his duties, it was suggested, might be the giving of an annual Retreat (the Spiritual Exercises of St Ignatius) to last three or four days "according to the capacity of the boys". This was no innovation at St Omers, although it may possibly have been a revival.

The tasks of Fr Shireburn were many and onerous. The Seminary at Liège had grown so poor owing to the non-payment of its yearly Bavarian pension that the course of philosophy had to be shortened to two years instead of three, whilst most of the theologians were gradually dispersed amongst other Provinces willing to accept them. There was too the troublesome and complicated issue concerning the inheritance that had come to Fr Gilbert Talbot, thirteenth Earl of Shrewsbury, involving a controversy with the Shrewsbury family and a final tactful compromise, by which the Pro-vincial managed to secure at least a "considerable sum".[28] With the General's strong approval the money so obtained was devoted, not as one might suppose to the alleviation of the Liege finances, but partly to the establishment of the American Jesuit mission so as to include Pennsylvania, and partly to the founding in 1742 of a Preparatory School for St Omers. Its comparatively brief history now claims our attention.[29]

In a choice of locality the proximity of the new school to the England Channel and its distance—not too near nor yet too far—from its parent College were matters to be carefully weighed. In the event it was Boulogne that was chosen, a town that seemed to satisfy both requirements. Sixteen years earlier,

[28] The facts are stated concisely by T. Hughes, s.j., *History of the Society of Jesus in North America*, Vol. II (Text), pp. 498-9. Neither Kirk (*Biographies of English Catholics, 1700-1800*) nor Foley (VII, 754-5) is accurate.
[29] For the following account, see P. Delattre, *Les Etablissements des Jésuites en France*, I, 823-824, with its references, especially A. Hamy, "Une expulsion de Jésuites en 1752", in *Bulletin Soc. Acad. Boulogne*, VII (1904-07), pp. 12-65.

in 1726, the founding of such a school at Boulogne had been seriously in the mind of the then Provincial, Fr Turberville, but the project had come to nought. The fire at St Omers a few months previously and the cost of rebuilding it must have over-ridden all lesser interests. Now in 1742 appeared a similar opportunity and it was quickly seized. Fr Retz sanctioned the undertaking on 30 June with considerable enthusiasm —"vehementer laudo et probo", he declared. A few weeks earlier a change of Rectors had been decided upon. Fr Percy Plowden, not quite so successful as had been hoped for—the number of boys had fallen to eighty-eight—gave place to Fr Richard Hyde, who now began his second term of office on 31 July, and had doubtless been consulted in the matter.

Some three kilometres from Boulogne a house was rented, known as the *Château de la Cocherie*, which had the advantage of a chapel attached to it. As Superior was appointed Fr William Blackiston, already established for some while in Boulogne as a missioner and by now a friend of the Bishop, Mgr d'Herville, who favoured the new school. Fr John Heatley was sent to assist him, together with two laybrothers, and the venture got under way almost at once, probably at the beginning of the normal school year on 1 October, feast of Saint-Remi. Boys "of all nations" were eligible from the ages of seven to twelve, to be taught the "three Rs", English, French, and the rudiments of Latin. The school seems seldom if ever to have numbered more than forty.

The *Château de la Cocherie* however was found to be inconvenient and rather difficult of access. So five years later, in July 1747, Fr Blackiston moved into the town, renting a house in the Rue des Pipots known as *La Double Croix*—it had been built as a brewery—the property of M. de Beaucorroy, an army officer away on military service.

But Boulogne proved to be something of a hornets' nest for these Jesuit "intruders". Though they remained there for another four or five years, they were decidedly unwelcome. The Oratorians who had for many years conducted a school in the town had at this period the reputation of being to some extent infected with Jansenism: they were certainly opposed to the Society of Jesus. Since many or most of the municipal officials and of the townsfolk had been educated at this school, it is not surprising that they commonly shared the views of their former masters—were in fact "tarred with the same brush".

The local clergy likewise looked askance at the newcomers and stood on their guard. A small incident was possibly symptomatic. A few days after the move into town one of the small boys, George Darell, fell seriously ill and was given the last sacraments. The curé of the parish complained that his rights had been disregarded. His appeal to the Bishop, M. d'Herville's successor, resulted in the immediate interdiction of the private chapel of the school. However, after Fr Blackiston had advanced good canonical reasons for what had been done, His Lordship reversed his decision and came in person to the chapel to give it his blessing.

When in 1751 M. de Beaucorroy, having now retired from the army, desired to take possession again of his old home, the Jesuits in default of a suitable alternative decided to build. They were well aware, of course, of the opposition this plan would arouse. So Mrs Panting and a friend came to the rescue. Full in the heart of Mrs Panting was her devotion to the Society, in which her son John was now a novice. It was arranged that this widow should purchase a plot of land in the lower part of the town "contre le bosquet des Capucins" in the Rue Charles Butor, and that she and her son should become naturalized French subjects. By this means she could legally hold possession of the property and at a later date leave it to her Jesuit son, or in other words to the Society. The purchase was made with the help of a friendly *échevin*, M. Bernard Cléry. It was a fairly substantial parcel of land, some 2,900 square yards, for which the contract was duly signed in March 1751.

But the Oratorians got wind of the affair: they had a keen sense of smell and were determined to expose this piece of "Jesuitry", as they would have called it. On such a site, they may have thought, not a Preparatory School but a large Jesuit College might eventually be established, a serious rival to their own vested interests. At any rate they complained to the Mayor, a former pupil of theirs, who took the matter up and addressed a lengthy *Mémoire* to the Council of State in Paris. M. Cléry, wrote the Mayor, had acquired the property in the name of Mrs Panting: but Mrs Panting was but a *prête-nom* of the English Jesuits. Several Paris lawyers were engaged at considerable expense, and an *arrêt* was at length obtained, dated 4 February 1752, ordering the Jesuits to quit Boulogne within three days, and forbidding them ever to establish a school in Boulogne, even though it should be in a rented house. So Fr Blackiston decamped, to set up his little school in a quarter of the Watten noviciate.

The remainder of the story has its humorous side. Mrs Panting was a valiant woman, a fighter. She was no *prête-nom* and was going to demonstrate the fact. The Jesuits might decamp but not she. The order of 4 February had nullified the acquisition of the property and authorized the Mayor to take possession, "moyennant le prix convenu entre les parties". There was her loophole. She continued in possession, stubbornly aware that it takes two to arrive at an agreed price. M. Coillot, the Mayor, must have been driven to despair. Before long a small house, a *maisonette*, made its appearance in the midst of the plot of land, with a garden to match. It is likely that at least until the expulsion of the Jesuits from St Omers in 1762, and possibly later, her house was used by the English Jesuits on their journeys between England and the Continent. But the property remained in the hands of Mrs Panting. A *prête-nom*, indeed! When in 1772 she finally disposed of the property, she *sold* it.

And what of the St Omers College Press these days? As we have seen,[30] its more flourishing period dates from the earlier part of the seventeenth century; and it ceased to function, to all

[30] See Chapter 6. For what follows we are mainly indebted, as before, to the articles of Fr C. A. Newdigate there noted.

appearance, upon the outbreak of the Civil War in England. An attempt was made in 1672 to start work again: but the wars in the Netherlands, the capture of St Omer in 1677, the Oates Plot and its aftermath, and then the destruction of the College by fire in 1684—these and perhaps other misadventures delayed further printing until 1691, by which time the College was again in regular working order.

The last sixty years or so of the Press show a decline in its importance and, as far as is known, in the number of books printed. Some forty volumes have so far been identified, and others may well come to light in course of time. During the brief years of James II's reign there was of course no hindrance to the printing and publishing of books in England. The King's printer for instance, Henry Hill, produced many such books at his printing house in Blackfriars until in 1688 a mob destroyed everything there of value, and Henry Hill escaped abroad, to settle down in Saint-Omer. It is not recorded whether or not he had anything to do with the re-starting of the Press a few years later.

It is noteworthy that in this final period of the St Omers Press books of devotion and lives of Saints (usually translations) had to a great extent superseded works of controversy. *The Life of Lady Warner*, published anonymously in 1691—a second enlarged edition appeared the following year—is perhaps the best known of these devotional works. Lady Warner and her husband Sir John, after their conversion in 1664 to the Catholic faith, agreed to separate and enter the religious state, as in fact they did in the following year. Lady Warner became a Poor Clare at Gravelines, taking the name Sister Clare of Jesus. Sir John Warner, partly perhaps to avoid confusion with the older Fr John Warner whom we have already met, chose to enter Watten under the *alias* of John Clare, by which name he is commonly known. This devout Life is usually ascribed to Fr Edward Scarisbrick; but there is some evidence at least which may suggest that Fr John Clare, then Provincial, was the actual author.

The controversial works, although fewer, are better known. It is only necessary to mention a revised edition of *Policy and Religion*, written by Fr Thomas Fitzherbert before his entry into the Society and now re-issued in four volumes. Another popular book in its day was Thomas Ward's *England's Reformation*, frequently reprinted, the first edition of which (1710), despite its imprint, is a product of St Omers Press. Fr William Darell too was responsible for two or three works of controversy, about one of which, *The Case Review'd* (1715), there is much correspondence summarized in the Letter-book of Father Sabran.

It was still unsafe—for both publisher or reader—to declare the place of origin or the printer of such volumes. The imprint is thus seldom of any assistance: if the printer or publisher is mentioned at all, the place of origin is generally fictitious. Hence such false scents laid as "Cullen" (Cologne), "Hambourg" or, more often than not, "London". This of course was no innovation. Some decades before St Omers was heard of, was not the first edition of Campion's *Decem Rationes* (which has no imprint) written as from Cosmopolis?

Some ten or more books printed nominally in London between 1691 and 1703 include in their imprints the name of the printer, Thomas Hales: and Thomas Hales beyond doubt was a Jesuit laybrother connected with the St Omers Press. Two or three other names occur which have not been identified, until from 1726 onwards one meets here and there the imprint, "St Omers. Printed by N. J. Le Fevre". Brother Nicolas Joseph Le Fevre saw the work of the printing press gradually diminish until with a few final flickers—a playbill or a Latin Ode for some minor occasion—the flame sank down and died away. A catalogue of 1758 describes him as "librorum compactor", presumably the binder of books that still remained in stock in unbound quires or unfolded sheets. But by 1761, the year before the expulsion from the College, he has severed that connection: "fuit Typographus, nunc Janitor". After thirty years and more of specialized work, doorkeeping must have appeared a poor substitute. "Ichabod", he may have muttered to himself, "the glory is departed."

Yet in truth the Press, with very much to its credit in past years, had by now achieved its purpose and become superfluous. Catholic publishers had already established themselves in England—Thomas Meighan from almost the beginning of the century, and others too, such as James Marmaduke in St Martins Lane. From about 1760 J. P. Coghlan's imprint is frequent on Catholic title-pages. There was no further need for a continental semi-secret printing press.

We are now at the eve of grave events, so far as St Omers College is concerned, and must look round awhile. It is France that is our immediate interest, for the same wave of anti-Jesuitism that overwhelmed the Society in France flooded likewise the Jesuit houses in Artois, subject since 1677 to the French monarchy. The two Colleges in Saint-Omer were thus included, the one because it was French, the other because it was Jesuit. At Liège and Ghent the Jesuit houses, being in no wise subject to France, remained intact. The Watten noviciate had its own particular settlement.

What precipitated the storm? Opposition to the doctrinal authority and stringent morality of the Catholic Church, and therefore to the Jesuits, described according to taste as the Pope's bodyguard or as his henchmen, his lacqueys, was but one though probably the most basic of the many reasons which every worth-while history of the Society discusses at some length. The immediate occasions of the contemporary expulsions from Catholic countries and States sprang of course from the particular circumstances of time and place. In Portugal and its overseas dominions it was the ravening ambition of Carvalho, later Marquis of Pombal, that led to the judicial murder of his enemies and to the appalling cruelty inflicted on his Jesuit victims. In France as in Portugal Jesuit influence was great, some would say excessive. The Confessors of the French Kings, for instance, had been Jesuits almost continuously for nearly two centuries: and not all of them—Père Le Tellier is often cited as an instance[31]—were equally remarkable for their prudence in office. The fate, however, of the Jesuits in France was cunningly contrived by means of what may be called a Court intrigue.

It was the abbé Chauvelin who got most of the credit for the result. Medals, we are told, were struck in his honour, stamps were issued, portraits of the champion were painted and engraved.

"Que maudit soit ton sort, Société perverse!
Un boiteux t'a fondée, un bossu te renverse."

Certainly the little abbé was a hunchback, and, it appears, extravagantly ugly—"d'une laideur effroyable"; but for that he was not responsible. Eloquent, astute and usually out of pocket, he played his part well and earned the gratitude of his master. For when all is said and done, he was but the willing instrument of a greater brain than his and of a larger vengeance. True, he had spent, some years previously, a period of imprisonment at Mont Saint-Michel for having flouted the King's authority and for that he held the Jesuits to blame and not himself. But what was that, or what was he, compared with Madame de Pompadour and her wounded vanity?

In her struggle to retain her ascendancy over the King and even to remain at Court, it was ever the Jesuits who thwarted her plans. Père de Sacy (and the Paris Jesuits whom in his unwisdom he had openly consulted in support of the obvious) had refused to accept her plan of "repentance" which expressly excluded an essential condition, the reparation of a public scandal—her withdrawal from Court. A year later, in January 1757, after Damien's attempted assassination of the King, Madame actually received her marching orders from Louis XV, whose spirit was temporarily willing to act aright, although his flesh was singularly weak. In a few days however his good resolution was forgotten and "la coquine du Roi", as the mob had called her, remained. But it was again a Jesuit, the King's confessor, who had nearly ruined her.

[31] Cf. l'abbé Georgel, *Mémoires* (Paris, 1817), I, pp. 47-49.

When the Duc de Choiseul rose to power by favour of Madame, he it was who was entrusted with the task of executing the vengeance of his benefactress. A fitting instrument he was: genial, witty, cynical, without morals and without mercy, he held his high position only by the favour, the continued favour of a woman as merciless and relentless as himself. The plan of campaign was carefully prepared, with the secret aid of certain members of the Paris Parlement, of whom the Jansenist Chauvelin, the abbé Terray and M. Laverdy were the most notable. As is well known, this plan was betrayed in all its details to the local Jesuit Provincial. A *Mémoire* was drawn up which the friendly Dauphin presented to the King; and the career of the Duc de Choiseul, if not that of Madame de Pompadour, seemed to be in the balance. That storm was weathered by the Minister. But henceforth a double vengeance pursued the Jesuits, nor was it sated until the Society of Jesus was banished, not from France alone but from Spain and all the Bourbon lands, until finally its total suppression was in 1773 decreed by the Franciscan friar, now Vicar of Christ, Pope Clement XIV.

Of course the matter was not so simple as all that. The Society had many friends in France but also numerous and influential enemies—Jansenists, Gallicans, infidel "Philosophers", free-masons and the like, all of them more than willing to see their opponents banished from the country. The story would take far too long to tell in any detail. At all events the Paris Parlement, scarcely in need of the oratory of the abbé Chauvelin, cooperated enthusiastically with Madame and the Duke.

A golden opportunity presented itself with the failure of the banking house of Lioncy Frères (and others), owing to the immense debt incurred by the hapless Père La Valette, Superior of the French Jesuit mission in Martinique. Not for himself but for the sake of his mission he had engaged in commerce in a very large way, borrowing heavily to finance his schemes. But luck, if one should call it luck, was against him. A whole fleet of ships, carrying to France the products of his sugar and coffee plantations, was lost in a storm; another fleet was captured by English privateers. Grown desperate, he flouted Canon Law and the Jesuit Constitutions by buying goods to sell later at a higher price. He was fighting recklessly against odds.

When after four fruitless attempts a Jesuit "Visitor" managed at last to reach Martinique and institute an enquiry, it was too late. The creditors of Lioncy demanded that their money losses be made good by the French Jesuits, and in 1760 a lower court decided in their favour. The debt, according to some, amounted to four and a half million livres, although La Valette declared it should have been at the highest not more than two and a half millions. Père Georgel (as he was until the suppression) states the amount claimed to have been 1,502,266 livres, with costs.[32] Whatever it was, it was an immense and frightening sum.

An appeal lay either to a Royal Commission established by Louis XIV for such cases as this, or to the Grand Chamber of the Paris Parlement. Without consultation with the three other Provincials in France, the Provincial of the Paris Province unwisely chose to appeal to the latter. In May 1761, after confirming the sentence of the lower court, the Grand Chamber demanded that a copy of the Jesuit Institute be submitted for inspection. The fat was now in the very middle of the fire.

On examination the Institute was blithely announced to be offensive to both God and man. Its decrees and rules were declared intolerable. The works of twenty-four Jesuit writers —St Robert Bellarmine included—were ordered to be burnt by the public hangman. Needless to add, these proceedings of the Paris Parlement had the full support and active encouragement of the Duc de Choiseul. So, step by step, notwithstanding the efforts of Clement XIII, the intermittent suggestions of compromise made by the weak, well-meaning King and the support for the Jesuits voiced at a convocation of the French Bishops, the predetermined end was reached.

[32] *Ibid.*, I, p. 57.

T

A heavy bombardment of anti-Jesuit pamphlets, brochures, *comptes rendus*, flying sheets preceded and accompanied the final *arrêt* of 6 August 1762 forbidding the existence of the Society in France. The series of accusations in justification of the decree are quite ludicrous, although for the hapless victims it was no laughing matter. Jesuit doctrines are declared, for instance, to favour the heresies of Arius, Nestorius, Luther, Calvin and most others—Jansenism of course being excluded. They encourage murder, parricide, suicide, sacrilege, idolatry and such other "moral turpitudes" as the Parlement could think of at the time. The Fathers were forbidden to obey the rules of the Society, to wear its habit, to live in common, to correspond with one another. Their property was sequestred: churches, colleges, libraries were despoiled. If they took an oath to defend the Gallican Articles they might live in France as private individuals on an allowance, if they were professed of four vows, of one franc a day. Though with little practical effect, Louis XV delayed for some while before giving way to the insistence of the Paris Parlement. The other local Parlements sooner or later followed the lead of Paris, some enthusiastically, some with reluctance and by a very small majority of votes. Five Parlements, Artois and Flanders amongst them, refused to condemn the Society. All opposition however faded out when in November 1764 a final decree was reluctantly signed by the King, destroying the Society in every part of his dominions. Six weeks later, on 7 January 1765, the Constitutions and Privileges of the Society were graciously and significantly confirmed anew by Pope Clement XIII.

II

EXPULSION FROM ST OMERS

THE *arrêt* of the Paris Parlement of 6 August 1762
extended only to those Jesuit houses that were within its
jurisdiction; but, as has been said, most of the other
provincial Parlements followed the lead of Paris, some enthusiastically, others with reluctance. Five Parlements refused,
Artois among them: whilst Douay declared openly for the
Jesuits and fought its case energetically in Paris, although
ultimately without success.

This *arrêt* was not the first of its kind. Just twelve months
earlier it would have been issued, had not Louis XV, that royal
Micawber, ordered a year's postponement, hoping, no doubt,
that something would turn up in the interval to avert what he
sincerely considered would be a disaster. The Paris Parlement
however had no intention of remaining inactive for so long.
The expulsion of the Society from France served also as
another step in the political struggle against royal authority
which reached its culmination in the dreadful excesses of the
French Revolution. The full force of the *arrêt* was indeed
delayed, but meanwhile much was done piecemeal to circum-
vent the King's moratorium.

Thus by an *arrêt* of Parlement all Jesuit Colleges within its
jurisdiction were ordered to be closed not later than 1 April
1762. The Province of Artois considered itself to be free of
Paris in such matters. It was governed according to its own laws
by a local Council seated at Arras. Nevertheless the Paris
Parlement was obviously claiming jurisdiction, for on 21
March Saint-Omer, like the other towns of Artois, was
placarded with copies of the Paris *arrêt*. The Magistrates showed
themselves timid and inclined to yield; not so the townspeople,
who soon tore down or tore up every copy. A courier from
Arras arrived next morning forbidding any regard to be paid

to this or any other Parisian decree. So developed a trial of
strength between the authorities of Paris and Arras. Each new
arrêt from one side was promptly cancelled by a contradictory
arrêt from the other. The quarrel was ultimately submitted
to the decision of the King's Council and decided in favour of
Paris.

In any case the Council of Arras had already considerably
weakened its position by issuing its own *arrêt*, ordering the
closure of all Jesuit schools in Artois by 19 April. By that
date in the Walloon College at Saint-Omer, as at Aire and
other towns, the Magistrates had introduced with some
solemnity a number of secular priests as masters to take the
place of the Jesuits. Copies of St Omers title deeds were taken
by the Procurator, Fr John Darell, and deposited with the
Council, in accordance with its orders.[1] Whilst at Arras this
very competent man—he had been Rector of St Omers from
1752 to 1759—was able to obtain an *arrét* from the assembled
Chambers allowing St Omers to continue to keep open the
school. It was a welcome concession, for which a previous
letter of the Bishop of Saint-Omer to the President of the
Council was partly responsible.

Meanwhile at the College fear and hope alternated with
each successive blast from Paris and counter-blast from Arras.
In March was made a public novena to St Francis Xavier, and
many acts of devotion were vowed by members of the community. Activity was not confined to prayer. Memorials were
drawn up and dispatched to the King of France, to the Dauphin,
to the King of Spain, to the Jacobite King in Rome, to any one,
indeed, whose influence might be of avail—even to the Duc de
Choiseul, of whose deep-seated hatred of the Society the
English Jesuits were not as yet fully aware. Fr John Darell was
the active agent in such matters, energetically supported by the

---

[1] The originals had been sent to the Chancellor at Paris in November 1761
(Hoskins, *Expulsion of the Jesuits from St Omers*, p. 28). Hodgson's statement
(*Dispassionate Narrative*, p. 15) that the Jesuits refused to produce them is
untrue.

Minister, Fr Thomas Lawson (Jun.), and by others. The Rector, Fr Scarisbrick, described as "indolent and quiet", looked on benignly and presently betook himself for a Retreat or a rest to a convent of nuns. A quaint procedure, no doubt, in such a crisis: but perhaps he acted wisely, since he left the situation in very capable hands.

Then in July Paris played the high hand. A party of men, some of them armed, was sent into Artois. On 6 July they forcibly seized the Walloon College at Arras. Thence to Bethune and Aire where they did the same. On the 9th they reached Saint-Omer and St Omers. Guards were set that morning at both gates, and the community was assembled and subjected to the reading of a long decree of the Paris Parlement. The unwelcome visitors then proceeded to the seizure of the household goods, of which they made an exhaustive inventory—it filled 174 folio pages of close writing —beginning, we are told, at the cellars (no doubt they had their reasons) and ending many days later in the attics.

The only interest of the *arrêt* on which they had been thus forcibly fed was the information that St Omers and the other Colleges in Artois were being seized under a warrant differing from that used in the case of the other Colleges in France. The new idea was to seize St Omers, not in the name of the Pro-curator General of the Parlement of Paris, but in the name of the creditors of Lioncy Frères, under a warrant issued from the Chancellor's office.[2] As the Jesuits discovered later, this change was a trick, a device to overcome the resistance of the Council of Arras. Disobedience to the *arrêt* of 6 August which was soon to appear was a matter of high treason. In a civil case however, such as prosecution for debt, and only in a civil case, was an appeal to Paris legal.

This was the first example, I believe [wrote one of the Jesuits] that a man, a House, a Royal College had been seized for debt without ever having been summoned to pay, and without having been informed what the debt was, how it was contracted, to whom it was owing, and how much of it to be paid fell to our share.[3]

The new warrant provided for a while a flicker of hope; even a "naked house" could in time be refurnished, for movable goods could be seized but not the house or lands, according to the letter of the law. Fr Lawson, the Minister, acting now as Vice-Rector, went off on 13 July to Paris to engage what help and influence he could find: it was not much. And meanwhile there arrived at St Omers another set of men, under Monsieur Roze, the chief Commissioner appointed for the seizure of the Colleges in Artois: their immediate concern was to take exact account of the books in the College Library. The first gang of men, on completing their inventory of goods, proceeded to the country house at "Blandyke" for a similar purpose.

At Paris during his month's visit Fr Lawson was able at least to pick up some bits of information.[4] A *Mémoire*, he learnt, had already been drawn up and presented to the Parlement, praying that the College of St Omers, "the ancient possessors being now deprived of the same and incapable of possessing it any longer", should be handed over to the English Clergy for the good of the English Mission. Fr Lawson may well have pricked up his ears at this news, and then indignantly laid his ears well back, if we may so express it, asking himself who had been meddling in this affair. Since the English Jesuits had not as yet been deprived of their College, or at least were not without hope of retaining it, it was obvious that the *Mémoire* had been drawn up by some one who was in the secret of the designs of Parlement. A certain Dr Joseph Holden, ex-Superior of St Gregory's, Paris (a house of higher studies for the English secular clergy), a man at whom his fellow priests were apt to look askance, was known to be openly bragging that it was he rather than some rivals who had been chosen as the future

---

[3] E. P. Arch. (1), f. 142.
[4] S. Arch., Reeve. *Plain and Succinct Narration*, &c. pp. 37 seqq.

President of St Omers. His friendship with the little Counsellor of Parlement, the abbé Chauvelin, who was espousing his cause, provided a possible, even a probable clue to the provenance of the *Mémoire*.

It is grievously unfortunate that the imprudence or worse of the unpopular Dr Holden and a few others in Paris should have given rise to the subsequent groundless suspicion that the English Clergy as such were at work to dispossess the Jesuits of their College in favour of themselves. Though they took no action in support of their countrymen—they were not, as a body, notable lovers of the Society—it is clear that they took no positive action against them. Yet the course of events coupled with an apparently silent acquiescence in the transfer of St Omers into their hands (at least two of the Vicars Apostolic were notable exceptions) aroused in some quarters the mistaken judgment that the English Clergy were in sympathy with the mischief-making of Dr Holden and his friends. Once again, as in the case of the Jesuits themselves, it was the common error of blaming the whole body for the indiscreet actions of a few.

Fr Lawson was still in Paris when the fatal blow was delivered. On the night of 6 August, after a sitting of sixteen hours, the Parlement passed unanimously in full session the famous decree or *arrêt* suppressing the Society of Jesus within its jurisdiction. Most of the provincial Parlements following suit, some 3,500 Jesuits found themselves homeless. Again Louis XV suspended the operation of the decree, on this occasion for a period of eight months: but it seems to have been no more than a paper suspension, with the victory on the side of his political opponents. To this *arrêt*, in so far as it affected St Omers College, we shall presently return.

Early in this same month of August a whispered rumour reached the ears of Fr Lawson that a decree was in preparation forbidding the boys to leave the College. The prospect of such an outrageous decree (it was actually issued two months later) shocked him considerably, as well it might. Writing on Friday,

13 August, to his Rector, now apparently at Bruges, he says—

> I set off this morning for St Omer and shall be there on Sunday. I took this resolution in consequence of a long conference with the Spanish ambassador. Nothing, I believe, is to be hoped for, unless in the Council. . . We must get the schollars away. No doubt of it. All our friends here tell me so. No hopes unless of a miracle. . . .[5]

Presumably he had previously written much the same to St Omers. There, certainly, the hopes they had nourished of saving their College were dying or already dead. The Parlement's device of a warrant for the payment of creditors had been, they now realized, but a legal trick to enforce their authority. The situation was about as depressing as a coffin lid.

On Saturday, 7 August, it was decided that unless better news arrived during the week-end, they would begin to evacuate the College on Monday. No fresh news reached them and they set to work. The boys were told of the projected plan and of course were delighted at the prospect of adventure. That morning Fr Darell set off for Bruges, accompanied by one of the older boys, a Poet—John Lawson, the heir of Brough Hall and nephew of the Minister. Their purpose was to blaze the trail for the rest and to complete such arrangements as might have been made for them at Bruges. About one o'clock (dinner was probably at 11 a.m. as in the early days) "when few people were stirring in the street", a party of twenty-four boys with some Masters went off into the country for a class walk. That was a common enough sight for the townsfolk: and it was hoped that the few they might meet would fail to notice that the boys' pockets were bulging with such personal property as they could stuff into them. Nobody seems to have observed that these classes never returned. This first contingent was followed next morning by a second, of twenty-eight boys; whilst on the following Monday, 16 August, thirty-three younger boys with three members of the Community took

[5] E. P. Arch. (1), f. 113.

similar evasive action. The same amount of provisions continued to be ordered for the kitchen and elsewhere, and nobody outside the College appeared any the wiser. Rhetoric and Poetry remained for the present at the College. Being older boys and thoroughly in sympathy with the Fathers, they could be relied upon to take care of themselves in case any violence should be attempted in order to keep them at St Omers against their will. Their presence served to hide the fact that most of the boys had decamped; and they were also, it appears, "of great service in helping to get out of the house what effects had been saved from the common shipwrack".

This last remark requires perhaps some explanation. In the French houses, after an inventory had been taken, the Jesuits were forced to take an oath as to its correctness. Not so at St Omers and elsewhere in Artois: and the whole proceeding of the Parlement being held eminently unjust—Pope Clement XIII strongly supported that view—they had no scruples in discreetly appropriating, when feasible, their own property. But there was no question, as far as one can gather, of falsifying the inventory. They merely anticipated here and there the inventory-makers during their slow progress from cellars to attics. To quote a contemporary letter:

What they could seize they did, and we saved what we could. But it was impossible to save much. . . . We saved some Acting Suits, Silver Cups, the Tabernacle and a great deal of the Silver in the Sodality: some books also of the Library. We burnt most of the papers in the Archivium; saved some and left the room quite empty.[6]

"It was impossible to save much." When several months later complaint was made to Propaganda that the Jesuits had more or

---

[6] *Ibid.*, f. 114, in a letter without date (? September 1762) and without signature. The tabernacle, "a beautiful and splendid tabernacle of four faces, and a door composed of rock chrystal", which had been captured in a Spanish prize, was presented to the Boys' Chapel by the Hon. Peregrine Widdrington, an Old Boy of St Omers, the second husband of the Duchess of Norfolk (Mary Shireburn).

less denuded the College of necessary furniture, the accusation took no account of the fact that after the final departure of the Jesuits, and even earlier, there was ample opportunity for servants, officials, guards and others to help themselves or turn a dishonest penny whilst helping their friends. That to some unascertained extent such looting of "movables" did take place there can be no reasonable doubt.

The fateful *arrêt* of 6 August was not served at St Omers until 23 August. We shall not stop to speculate on the reason for the delay. On that Monday morning (most events seem to have happened on a Monday) Fr Lawson, now back from Paris, received official communication from the local *bailliage* on behalf of the Paris Parlement, ordering the Jesuits to quit within eight days and to discard their religious dress. Later in the day some of these "bailiffs" arrived with the parish priest of the district to take possession of the sacred vessels and plate belonging to the church and the chapel of the house. Three days later these officers came again to acquaint the Community with yet another *arrêt* of 13 August, whereby, as Mr Jenison, now at Bruges, informed his elder brother,

> they permit each Jesuit to carry of[f] half a dozen shirts, 12 handkerchiefs, his bedding etc. and whatsoever belongs to him *en propre*: the Reason assigned is, because it appears sufficiently from lists already received that there is more than enough to satisfy all Creditors.[7]

There is evidence here of the inextricable mixture of the two different warrants, the warrant of expulsion and that for recovery of a debt. At all events these effects were licitly and validly abstracted and packed off by Brother Blyde on two barges for conveyance by canal to Bruges.

The College was due to be vacated by 1 September. But a sum of money had been allowed each Jesuit for travelling expenses; and as the money had not arrived, they were told to wait for it. (Arrangements for the future government of the

---

[7] Jas. Jenison, s.j., to Fr John Jenison, s.j., 23 August 1762 (*Ibid.*, ff. 120–121).

College were not yet completed.) Actually they waited another seven weeks.

If the Jesuits were allowed to take away their personal effects, the boys had a better title still to appropriate theirs. Hitherto they had taken only what they had crammed into their pockets: and officially they were still at St Omers, since the departure of nearly ninety boys was as yet a secret. A petition was accordingly drawn up—accommodatingly enough by one of the Parlement's officials in the College—and signed before a notary on behalf of the parents by one of them. This was Mr Gastaldi, sometimes referred to as Count Gastaldi, a former ambassador at the Court of St James, now resident at Saint-Omer so as to be near his two boys at school. A friend living in Paris, Lady Webb, wife of Sir Thomas Webb of Odstock, Wilts, kindly consented to present the petition. This was favourably received. The favour, it was admitted, was no more than had been granted to other Jesuit Colleges in France. An *arrêt* was drawn up on 7 September and within a day or two the sealing and other formalities had been completed.[8]

Then there was a lull: the *arrêt* was not delivered. Having waiting a week or so, Lady Webb by advice of her lawyer sought and obtained an interview with the *Président des Vacations*. The interview is described by her in a letter of 18 September, and again on 16 October. A stormy interview, one gathers. "J'ai dit tout ce qu'on pouvoit dire", she says—a statement full of possibilities. The petition, she was told, had been discovered, fortunately in time, to be a Jesuit trick: information had been received that Mr Gastaldi was but a "prête-nom pour les Jésuites", with no authority to speak for English parents. "And who told you that story? The Abbé Holden, I suppose", said Lady Webb, adding an impromptu character sketch of that rather unpleasing priest.

"Ce n'est pas lui", m'ont ils dit, "c'est l'Anglois le plus respectable qu'il y ait en France. L'autre à la verité nous a été

8 S. Arch., Reeve, pp. 68-9.

presenté; mais c'étoit un piège que les Jésuites nous tendoient, nous donnant un mauvais sujet." Ensuite ils m'ont dit qu'ils avoient donné le Collège à Mr Talbot.[9]

The idea of Dr Holden having been suggested by the Jesuits themselves to replace them at St Omers is delicious; but at the moment it did not so appear to Lady Webb, nor did the other items of information she received. Both sides finally lost their tempers and she was hustled out of the building.

The Rev. and Hon. Thomas Talbot, who, as Lady Webb now learnt, was chosen to be the first President of St Omers—the *arrêt* was likewise dated 7 September—was the brother of the recently consecrated Coadjutor to Bishop Challoner. He was in England and had not been consulted in the matter, but it was hoped he would accept the post. The wording of this *arrêt* did not satisfy the Abbé Plowden, a priest under some vague suspicion of Gallican sympathies, now living in Paris as a sort of free-lance. From a letter of his,[10] evidently addressed to his cousin, Dr Charles Howard, Superior of St Gregory's, Paris, one learns that he had recently presented a *Mémoire* to the Parlement, which however had omitted to make all the "alterations" he had suggested. The College, he complains, is not entrusted to the English Clergy as a body, Mr Talbot being the only person mentioned. "There is no order to deliver to him the possessions and revenue attached to the College. However, this is naturally included in the nomination of a person named to administer a College." One wonders what other alterations in the *arrêt* this busy Abbé wanted. He ends his letter with the hope that the Court of Vienna will refuse to permit the establishment of a new Jesuit College "at Bruges or Brussells".

It turned out that Mr Talbot was as reluctant to accept this

---

[9] Lady Webb to Fr T. Lawson, Paris, 16 October 1762 (*Ibid.*, pp. 135-139).
[10] Abbé Plowden (Paris) to Dr Charles Howard, 10 September 1762 (Westm. Arch. (1), 2nd pt, No. 4). Abbé Francis Plowden was of the family of Plowden of Plowden Hall, as were the four Jesuit Plowdens mentioned in the preceding chapter. But there is some doubt as to his rightful perch on the family tree. Hodgson, whenever quoting from the Abbé's letters, strangely omits to name the writer (e.g. pp. 31, 41, &c.).

delicate responsibility as in later life he was to be made a Bishop. The President of Douay, Dr Green, and the new Vice-President, Mr William Wilkinson, when applied to for assistance in the matter, showed themselves almost equally reluctant to meddle in the affair. Dr Green, indeed, in a previous letter[11] to Fr Corbie, the Provincial, had expressed his determination "to do nothing in this affair without your consent & the approbation of our Lawful Superiors". This friendly letter, alas, met with no response till more than a month had elapsed, when a reply was received but, it seems, a totally inadequate one. Fr Corbie's feeble excuse was that he had been "in a smart feaver" when he got the letter. He thereby caused much offence and was criticized by Clergy and Jesuit alike.

When at first consulted, both Bishop Challoner and Bishop Hornyold expressed their distinct disapproval of any cooperation with the unjust proceedings of the Parlement of Paris. And even apart from such cooperation, Challoner was of opinion that the proposed acceptance of St Omers by the English Clergy would do more harm than good to their College at Douay and hence to the English Mission. In any case "Hilton" or "Mr Abraham" or in other words Rome should certainly be first consulted. Rome *was* consulted and in consequence both Bishops modified their earlier views and acquiesced. Dr Green, whose sincerity is manifest, had seen for himself the need for Propaganda's approval of the "take-over" and wrote to the Clergy agent in Rome for that purpose. In due course he learnt that, although no answer would be given in writing, lest Propaganda should be taken as condoning in any way the violent acts of the Paris Parlement, nevertheless acceptance of the College by the English Clergy would meet with the cautious approval of the Cardinal Secretary of Propaganda.[12] Incidentally it may be added, but without

[11] Dr Green to Fr Corbie, 12 August 1762. (S. Arch., Reeve, pp. 146-7.)
[12] Dr Stonor to Dr Green, 11 January 1763. (S. Arch., B. V. 4, pp. 251-2). This volume contains (pp. 167-278) summaries of letters of 1762-1763 concerning St Omers. It is possibly an earlier and less orderly version of what Hodgson frequently refers to as the "Douay Collection".

prejudice to the present reply, that Cardinal Marefoschi, the said Secretary, and the Jesuits held widely differing views on *la question Jésuitique*.

Mr Talbot—to cut a long story shorter—finally consented to take over the direction of St Omers but was unable to leave England till November. The Seven Years War was nearing its end but had not quite reached it. Meanwhile, as a result of considerable pressure from M. Roussel de la Tour who was directing operations from Paris, Mr Henry Tichborne Blount, a member of the Mapledurham family and head of the recently established preparatory school at Esquerchin, reluctantly consented to act for Mr Talbot until the latter should arrive. He was urged to take possession of St Omers as quickly as he could, and accordingly in company with Dr Green (under similar pressure from Paris), arrived at Saint-Omer on 6 October. Only then was it realized that not a single boy remained in the College. The newcomers, we are told, "questioned servants, barbers &c to know if any were lodged in town". Mr Blount even went to look for them at Blandyke, but obviously to no purpose. What had happened?

After the three batches of boys had been evacuated from St Omers, there remained behind, as will be recalled, only the two top classes, Rhetoric and Poetry. On 15 September a letter from Paris reached the College addressed to the "Supérieur du Collège du Clergy Anglois à St Omer". Inadvertently Fr Lawson opened and read it, only to discover it had been wrongly addressed, its purpose being to acquaint the Superior with the definite appointment of Mr Talbot (Dr Green was well aware of the fact) and to desire either Dr Green or Mr Blount to take immediate action. The letter was re-addressed to Dr Green with suitable explanations and apologies.[13] But the information thus learnt by accident—there can be no doubt of Fr Lawson's honest mistake—convinced him that it was

[13] M. Joly de Fleury (*Procureur Général*, Paris) to "le Superieur du Collège du Clergy Anglois à St Omer" (no date given); Fr Lawson to Dr Green, 16 September 1762. (S. Arch., B. V. 4, pp. 205-6.)

high time for the rest of the boys to decamp. No time was lost. Six Rhetoricians had already chosen, in spite of present troubles, to enter the Jesuit noviciate at Watten on the customary day, 7 September. Four other Rhetoricians were presently to become novices elsewhere. (Did the whole of Rhetoric turn Jesuit this year?) Meanwhile these four, together with the Poets, now eight in number, for John Lawson had previously left for Bruges, set off that same afternoon of 15 September with Fr Emmott, the First Prefect, and Mr Reeve, Master of Poetry, reaching Bruges on the evening of the 17th.

That was three weeks before the arrival at Saint-Omer of Dr Green and Mr Blount. They expected to find the appropriate *arrêt* awaiting them, but they were disappointed. So they retired to Dunkirk, to return a week later, the *arrêt* having now arrived.

> The Jesuits have received their money and waite only for my entering in order to their departure [wrote Mr Blount on 18 October]. I believe six or seven are still in ye house. I have visited F. Lawson in a friendly manner and he shewed me the whole house; wherein a good deal of furniture remains, but I believe much more is transported. He tells me there is abundance of wine in ye cellars. Today he and ye Procurator of Watten are expected to dine with us at Madame Ricouart, who entertains us indeed with great civility & familiarity.[14]

Fresh legal difficulties made by the local *bailliage* still delayed the formal installation of Mr Blount and five Masters from Douay—but no pupils—until 29 October, ten days after the Jesuits' final departure.

The delayed *arrêt*, dated 5 October, had arrived at Saint-Omer on the 12th. By this decree[15] Mr Tichborne Blount is authorized to take possession of the College and to nominate

14 Mr H. Tichborne Blount to Mr W. Wilkinson, 18 October, copied in a letter of Mr W. Wilkinson (Douay) to Mr Eyre, 20 October 1762 (Westm. Arch. (2), p. 785).
15 Copy in E. P. Arch. (1), f. 131-2.

Professors; the *"ci-devant soi-disans Jésuites"* are to receive the money allowed to them and then quit the College, and they may not carry away with them any article of the College property. There is here presumably some distinction made between College and personal property, for two months previously permission was given to take what broadly speaking might be considered as a Jesuit's own. Finally no pupil may be removed by the Jesuits, nor may the new Masters allow any to leave until their parents shall signify their will in this matter on some date subsequent to 5 October. This last injunction Mr Blount can have found no reason to disobey.

An extract from a letter written at St Omers on 16 October may be of some interest. It is quoted by Mr Jenison in a letter of the 21st.[16]

> Early this morning we were warned by a friend that something serious would happen to us as a result of orders received yesterday from Paris. At 9 [a.m.] the Magistrates of the Bailliage came. The affair was ye Box of ye Relics of our Martyrs in ye musicians Choir. Mons. le Roy read privately to us ye secret Instructions he had received from ye Parlement. These ordered him to go immediately to the English Jesuits where he would find in the jubé [loft] of ye Church near ye Organ the Bones of ye traitors Henry Garnet and Edward Oldcorne under the title of "Reliquiae SS nondum *vindicatorum*". They proceeded to ye shutting up of the Box by two thick Chains and 6 scellés. After it was nailed up Aston [S.J.] desired it might be open'd that he might make a Catalogue of what was there. We were pleased to find the only 2 Jesuits, viz. Thomas Garnet and Peter Wright and 9 secular Priests. Thus ye glorious MM, after having been chain'd in England for their faith are now so here for their Profession. I suppose you know the Inscription of the Armoire in question—"Reliquiae SS nondum approbatae et monumenta virorum piae memoriae".

On the 17th M. Roze, the head Commissioner in Artois, paid the Jesuits the sums of money for which they had been

16 *Ibid.*, f. 135.

waiting since 1 September. The money was distributed to the
Fathers and scholastics according to whether they were over
or under thirty-three years of age. Seven of the Fathers received
425 livres (a livre being at this time equivalent to 1s. 6d.), five
younger Jesuits received 300 and three Brothers 225 livres.
Those absent were recommended to make their applications
for payment at Arras.

That same day M. Roze was invited by the Vice-Rector to
join the now diminished Community at dinner. M. Roze had
from the beginning been on friendly terms with the Fathers,
and his sympathies were clearly with them rather than with M.
Roussel. As the dinner proceeded he grew confidential. It was
almost his last meeting with them and he chose this occasion
to tell his hosts "several curious anecdotes", as the records
phrase it, which served to confirm suspicions that had now
been growing for some months. To quote from a letter written
the next day to Bruges—

> [He] shew'd us several Letters whereby both ye Court and
> Parlement seemed to be sensible of our Case. It appears
> evident that ye Intercession of Spain and Italy operated so
> effectually that we shoud certainly have been preserved had
> not our Clergy used both money and sollicitations to change
> ye disposition of ye Parlement. Roze had orders to sell ye
> effects of all ye Colleges of Artois besides [i.e. except] ours;
> to give Pensions to all besides us &c &c and several other
> things too long to pen down; and he himself says there is no
> doubt but we shoud still be here, had it not been for private
> enemies.[17]

These letters of instruction from Paris, probably from M.
Roussel, would be of interest did they still exist. The conclusions
drawn from them were of course M. Roze's own, and it must
be admitted his opinion had weight. At all events he convinced
his hearers that their suspicions were justified.

It must be recorded that Jesuit documents cite three other

[17] From St Omers, 18 October, quoted in a letter of (Mr) Jas. Jenison to
Fr John Jenison, 21 October 1762 (*Ibid.*, f. 136).

U

opinions in corroboration of this conversation with M. Roze. Two of them were those of two Counsellors of the Parlement, expressed during the crisis. Their views are not given in detail, but they were evidently the same as the conclusions of M. Roze. Finally there was a remark made by M. Petit de Coquil, the *Procureur du Roi* or King's Attorney at Saint-Omer. When Mr Blount expressed his embarrassment at finding no scholars in the College he had come to take possession of, M. Petit was reported to have replied, "If you had not been so anxious to acquire the College you would have avoided this embarrassment".[18] As applied to Mr Blount in person the reply was certainly unjust; but it was of course interpreted in a wider context.

One is glad to record the various expressions of sympathy—from Dr Green, Mr Wilkinson, Mr Blount and others—which must surely have consoled, to some extent at least, these Jesuits in their distress. Poor souls, they were surely in need of some comfort. Most of them had known the College from their boyhood days; they were pround of its history, its past glories, its traditions and achievements; it was their home, their Alma Mater. Now they were to be driven out by a foreign Parlement, unjustly, ruthlessly, relentlessly. They had many friends in Saint-Omer and elsewhere: but their enemies in France were voluble and loud-voiced. Now they were told—and they believed it—that but for some of their own countrymen all this misery would have been avoided. Small wonder that in their weaker moods they felt bitter and resentful.

To cap it all, a French translation of Dodd's two works, the *History of Douay College* and the *Secret Policy*, written some fifty years ago against the English Jesuits in general and against St Omers in particular, was now published, supposedly in England if one is to judge by its London imprint.[19] These

---

[18] "Si vous n'avoiez pas tant sollicité pour avoir le Collège, vous ne seriez pas dans cet embarras" (S. Arch., Reeve, p. 150).

[19] According to Gillow (*Bibliographical Dictionary of the English Catholics*, V. 550) the two works were really published at Douay by J. F. Willerval in one volume.

"libelles infernales", as Fr Darell described them, were spread about, care being taken that Saint-Omer should not be lacking in copies. All the old calumnies were revived, going as far back as Fr Persons' supposed embezzlement of monies meant for the secular English mission but misappropriated for the foundation of St Omers. One has only to read Hodgson's *Dispassionate Narrative* or a letter of M. Roussel de la Tour (to be referred to presently) to see that Dodd's wild statements were taken as sober history. Who was responsible for this translation and for its by no means fortuitous publication at such a time seems to be unknown. Certainly not Dodd himself, who was dead these twenty years. It could have been a Frenchman, but of course the Jesuits put it down to the English Clergy.

A word should be added concerning the terms of that last sentence. "The Jesuits" accused "the English Clergy", and in turn "the English Clergy" accused "the Jesuits" of accusing them. The pot was calling the kettle black. But which was the pot and which the kettle? Were they not both of them pots and somehow both kettles? It may be that both parties were guilty of the common fallacy of ascribing to the whole body the particular misdeeds or indiscretions of a few. If so, the Jesuits should have been more cautious, since throughout its long history the Society has constantly been the victim of such faulty logic. But it is no less likely that both "clergyman" and "Jesuit", if pressed to be precise, would have agreed at once that he was accusing, not the body as such, but individuals of the body, perhaps few, perhaps many, but certainly an indeterminate "some".

The various actors during this quarrelsome period being now as dead as Queen Anne, one may ask as a matter of historical curiosity whether any of the accused "English Clergy" can be identified. Undoubtedly they can. No one has ever denied that Dr Holden in Paris was implicated in the affair, even a month or two before the *arrêt* of 6 August was issued. His friend the Jesuit-hater, the Abbé Chauvelin, had told him he was the Parlement's choice for the Presidency of St Omers. He bragged about it openly and everywhere, "at the English Nunns, Fossé St Victor, at the Scotch College & wherever he went".[20] But whether Dr Holden, a rather disastrous ex-President of St Gregory's, working in collaboration with the little hunchback, originated the policy of including St Omers in the general ruin in order to become once more a President—that certainly is unproved and is probably incapable of proof.

Nor is it likely ever to be known to what extent were involved in this affair the Abbé Plowden and his cousin Dr Charles Howard, successor of Dr Holden as head of St Gregory's. That they were both busy and eager in support of M. Roussel's arrangements for the disposal of St Omers is quite clear. Over two dozen letters to and from these Paris priests survive,[21] all of them concerned with the same subject, and addressed to or received from such correspondents as Mr Wilkinson, Dr Green, Mr Blount, M. Roussel and others. The great majority of these letters are dated 1762, from 9 August onwards.

The first known letter of 9 August will bear quotation, if the reader will be patient. It is a letter "from Mr fr[ancis] Plowden to Dr Charles Howard then at Douay". The original being apparently lost, one must be content with the faulty summary:

> Informs of the Dissolution of the Society by the Arret of Parlement of the 6th. . . . Tells [of] his conference with Mr Clement de Feillette counselor of Parlement and one of ye principal Commissaries, who has taken measures to inform the first President of the Approbation of himself etc [and?] Commissaries regarding the Destination of St Omers Eng. Coll. and to carry the project into Execution. . . .[22]

The implications of this are disputable: but, to say the least, the

---

[20] Fr Lawson to M. Roussel, Bruges, 26 October 1762 (S. Arch., B. V. 4, p. 245).
[21] Westm. Arch. (1 & 2); S. Arch., B. V. 4, passim.
[22] S. Arch., B. V. 4, p. 201.

Abbé Plowden was certainly deep in the counsels of the Parlement. A month later, as already noted, when Lady Webb's petition on behalf of the St Omers boys' personal property had failed, this Abbé tells of a *Mémoire* he had previously presented to the Parlement suggesting "alterations" in one or other or both of the *arrêts* issued on 7 September.

Of Dr Howard less can be said, although he and Plowden were obviously thick as thieves, and the Doctor was as keen to "carry the project into execution" as was the Abbé. It may be true that both of them were no more than enthusiastic cooperators with M. Roussel in the details of a plan for which they were in no way responsible. Nevertheless their actions rather naturally aroused suspicion. The Abbé's activities are less easily discounted. It is apposite to recall a remark of Mr Tichborne Blount in a letter to Mr Alban Butler. Lamenting that he too, like Dr Green and others, had been censured ungenerously by "many of the Padri", he explained that "letters informed me that I was represented in ye most odious light . . . in short such would they have my conduct to be, that they thought no one but a H**den or a P***den could be capable of the like".[23] The conjunction of these two names, Holden and Plowden, is by no means flattering to the latter.

And what of the accusers of the English Clergy? Dr Green, Mr Wilkinson, Mr Blount, Mr Talbot all complained of the attacks made upon them, and one cannot doubt that they must have had some reason for their complaints. All the evidence goes to show that they were innocent of any intriguing to oust the Jesuits from their College. The English Catholics, however, were divided in their sympathies. Parents of the exiled boys, for instance, one may suppose to have been particularly exasperated that their sons' personal effects had been seized, in order, so they understood, to pay the debts of some foreign missionary in Martinique. Why on earth hadn't the Jesuits at St Omers done something to stop this robbery?

[23] Mr Tichborne Blount (Esquerchin) to Mr Alban Butler, 21 January 1763. (Westm. Arch. (1), No. 14).

They *had*, so the local Jesuits would have explained, perhaps with bitterness; but a "respectable English Abbé" in Paris had maliciously frustrated their efforts. Laymen—not to mention laywomen—and Jesuits too would no doubt have abused this English Abbé and all his tribe. Many a wild accusation was hurled about, irrespective of the evidence. The "jarrs" in the English mission, which Bishop Hornyold foresaw might result, lasted at the least until in 1773 the whole Society of Jesus came temporarily to an end, and the greater disaster overshadowed the lesser.

But these would have been spoken words, of which no direct record remains. The war of words was not, of course, confined to one side only. Of individual Jesuits, Fr Corbie is said by Mr Blount, a man of temperate views, to have complained publicly that Dr Green could ever have allowed himself to accept of St Omers. If the facts were as reported to Mr Blount, then Fr Corbie was certainly to blame. A few letters that survive, written privately from one Jesuit to another, repeat the familiar tale told them by M. Roze, that but for the "English Clergy" the College would not have been seized. There may have been others who blamed the Clergy in public: but when it comes to actual names, it is always Fr Lawson who has to bear the brunt. He is reviled as the arch-calumniator. Why that was we shall see in a moment. Amongst his fellow Jesuits he was known as a most courteous gentleman and exemplary priest—the last man, one would suppose, to have wished to wound the feelings of any one. Since he was acting as Rector at the time of the expulsion, an explanation seems to be needed.

The President of Douay, Dr Green, worried and wearied with reports of slanders and calumnies against him, wrote finally to M. Roussel on 30 November begging that he will "use what means he judges proper to defend him . . . knowing that far from seeking he has always dreaded the charge of that College".[24] A very reasonable and just request. M, Roussel

[24] S. Arch., B. V. 4, p. 224.

chose to comply by means of what was in effect a public letter addressed to the *bailliage* of Saint-Omer, who he asserted—and this at least was true—were of the Jesuits' way of thinking. For his text he used a private letter sent to him six weeks before from Bruges on 26 October.[25]

What had this "ci-devant Recteur, nommé Lawson" said? He informed M. Roussel that the Jesuits had quitted St Omers in obedience to the orders of the Parlement. He asked for the issue of the *arrêt* of 7 September which Lady Webb had failed to secure, and for "the liberty of disposing of the ground of our houses in Town and Country". To soften his heart he dwelt at some length on the hardship of being turned out of St Omers for no justifiable reason and, as he had on all hands been assured, in consequence of "the sollicitations and intrigues of the English Clergy", as the Douay summary has it.

M. Roussel first quotes Fr Lawson, "that they are assured that the Parlement had a mind to save them and would have done so, had not some members[26] of the English Clergy by their sollicitations and intrigues prevented it"; and "What connection can be shown between us and a missionary in Martinique?" On the contrary, he comments: it was not the bankruptcy of Lavalette nor the intervention of any English priest that induced the Parlement to include St Omers in the common disgrace. It was not just the French Jesuits but the whole Society that was in question. "C'est la Société, son Institut, son régime et sa morale, qu'il a trouvé également contraire aux loix humaines et aux loix divines." Did he, could he have believed that nonsense? And had he forgotten that St Omers was seized on a warrant for debts claimed by the creditors of Lioncy Frères and on no other warrant?

The remainder of the letter elaborates his views on the

---

[25] Fr Lawson to M. Roussel, Bruges, 26 October 1762 (S. Arch., B. V. 4, pp. 243-245). Roussel's letter in full is in S. Arch., Reeve, pp. 106-112, and summarized in B. V. 4, pp. 229-233. The date is given as 9 December (Reeve) or 12 December 1762.

[26] "quelques Messieurs du Clergé Anglois", writes Roussel; but the summary in the Douay version (B. V. 4) has simply "the English Clergy".

wicked Society and on the English Province, with excursions into the latter's past history as conceived by Dodd in his "*Secret Policy*" (the French translation had obviously been well thumbed). The College, he informs the *bailliage*, was founded in 1593 with the aid of money meant for Douay but diverted by Fr Persons to St Omers. What more appropriate than to return it to the English Clergy? The College was re-built by the generosity of English Catholics desiring a suitable education for their sons; and that the English Clergy are being asked to provide. And so on. M. Roussel skips over the fact that these monies were given, not, as Fr Darell noted, to the English mission in general but to the Jesuit English mission in particular; and that the "suitable education" desired was still obtainable at Bruges. As a sane defence of the Paris Parlement and its decisions this letter of M. Roussel appears utterly worthless. It is thus a pity that so much reliance by so many was placed on so tendentious a document. Dr Green or one of his colleagues could have produced a far better and more credible apologia.

To complete the documentation one other item should be given, mentioned more than once in Jesuit records and best quoted from a letter to Fr John Jenison at Wardour Castle from his younger brother now settling down at Bruges.

"We hear in a letter from Fr Booth [Rector of the English College, Rome] that King James had just received an answer from Choiseul in the name of King Louis, saying

> that it was never his intention to involve ye English Jesuits in the fate of his own subjects; that he might make himself easy, as our Property woud not be hurt and all ye rents and funds destined for ye good of ye Mission most certainly be secured for us. This news he had from Père Forestier. . . ."[27]

This, as will be noticed, is clearly not first-hand evidence: but that is not the point of the quotation. Whether good evidence or not, Fr Booth's information was accepted as yet another reason for suspicions of interference with the destiny of St

[27] 28 September 1762 (E. P. Arch. (1), f. 128).

Omers. Of this at least we may be sure, that if the Duc de Choiseul by order of the King wrote anything like what is reported, he must have derived considerable amusement from his composition. He understood his King far better than did the Jesuits.

Let it not be supposed that what has here been written has any controversial purpose. The one and only end has been to present—we believe for the first time—the view, as far as one can gather it, which rightly or wrongly these Jesuits of two centuries ago adopted. There are of course other points of view. One such was that published in 1768 by Ralph Hodgson, written, he says, for his own amusement, but far too passionately to deserve the title of *Dispassionate Narrative*. A manuscript account was written by Fr Joseph Reeve some years earlier, but too close to the events in which he had a part to be considered as at all dispassionate. More recently, in two chapters of Dr Burton's *Life and Times of Bishop Challoner* may be found a very sympathetic account, serving as a background to the Bishop's concern in these events. Yet, like Ralph Hodgson and even Fr Reeve, he lacked some of the documents that have here been used. There was thus room, even a need in a history of St Omers, for a fresh account of these troubled months from the view-point of the Community of that College. The reader, if sufficiently interested, can weight impartially (as far as impartiality is ever possible) the pros and cons of what long ago aroused such acrid controversy but is now, one hopes, no more than a subject of historical research. As matter for internecine controversy it is surely dead and cold beneath a heavy gravestone. There may it long rest in peace and quiet.

We return to St Omers where we left M. Roze at dinner on 17 October, telling "several curious anecdotes" to his Jesuit guests. On the following day Fr Lawson dined, as has been mentioned, with Mr Tichborne Blount at his lodging in the town. The next day M. Roze, on orders from Paris, was due to carry out the formal expulsion of the few Jesuits who still remained in the College. Three of these, however, had to be left behind on account of old age or infirmity—Fr Levinus Brown, a former provincial, now an old man of ninety-one, Fr John Hawker, aged seventy-five, and a laybrother, Adrian Stevens, still in his early sixties but too ill to move. Brother Thomas Padbury was left to look after them. The Abbé Plowden, one is not surprised to learn, considered they had been left behind as spies on the secular clergy. There are conflicting statements as to their treatment, but there is no need to discuss the subject. All three, as it happened, died within nine months of each other, the oldest, Fr Brown, being the last to depart, on 7 November 1764.

On Tuesday, 19 October (1762), so as not to embarrass either M. Roze or themselves, Fr Lawson and his fellow Jesuits set out early for Bruges, at 6 o'clock in the morning. A cheerless, dismal parting it must have been. A formal protest had previously been drawn up, signed by Fr Lawson and three others and duly attested. One copy was deposited at the office of the *bailliage*, and another for Mr Blount, who had already agreed to receive it. The protest was of course against the proceedings of the Paris Parlement to the prejudice of their just rights, which they declared they would never cease to claim.

So ended the Jesuit connection with St Omers after 169 years of more or less peaceful occupation. The essential "collegium" and "convictus" of staff and students still functioned as before, though in another locality. As in past years continuity had not of course been broken, although twice the College, destroyed by fire, had needed to be re-built and re-furnished, so now the moral continuity persisted no less. What actually had to be left behind, in addition to the lands in Saint-Omer and at Blandyke, was a "modern" building not much more than thirty years old—a fine building it was, and, as the Procurator, Fr Darell, proudly boasted, the equal of any College in France. More intimate was the severance of all the ties of association and friendship formed in the course of long years of close contact. It is pleasant to hear that the townsfolk and town officials lamented the departure of the Jesuits; that even the officers from Paris charged with the duty of expelling these Jesuits performed their duty with evident reluctance. Nevertheless such comfort as that afforded would in no way have lessened the sense of grievance. The loss of the College buildings, its lands, its funds and investments was indeed grievous. That was an injustice which was felt by all the Colleges and houses in France. It had been characterized by Pope Clement XIII as a "most blasphemous attack of worldly powers on the sanctity of the Church and on learning". It was a blow, he held, that was aimed indirectly at Catholicism itself. At St Omers it was the suspected manner whereby this loss had come about that upset them even more than the material loss. Yet what still remained in their keeping was the better part of St Omers—its customs and traditions, the fame of its scholastic achievements, the memory of its martyrs and confessors, the continued patronage of so many friends in England and elsewhere.

There yet remain a few facts that need to be chronicled before this chapter closes. Ten days after the departure of the Jesuits the requisite formalities had been complied with and Mr Blount, acting for Mr Thomas Talbot, entered into possession of the College. The installation had been delayed because by the terms of the *arrêt* of 5 October the actual presence of the new masters was needed, and the authorities of Saint-Omer insisted on the letter of the law. The masters arrived from Douay on the 28th, five of them—Messrs George Beeston, Philip Maudsley, James Nicolas, Thomas Story and Mr Lonsdale,[28] the first two mentioned being already priests. Mr Wilkinson some four or five days earlier had replaced Dr Green who, suffering from a bad attack of gout in the stomach, had gone back to Douay. When next day, the 29th, formal possession of the College was taken, "the Lioncy two guards were dismissed".[29] A faint reminder, this, of the original warrant for debt. The debt indeed was being paid, but not to

[28] S. Arch., B. V. 4, p. 217.   [29] *Ibid.*, p. 218.

the creditors! However, the absence of any boys to be taught rendered the presence of five Masters superfluous; so on 2 November the two young priests were put in charge of an empty house whilst the rest returned to Douay. Early in this November the new President, Mr Talbot, managed to cross the Channel. After a hurried visit to St Omers he too returned to Douay where he remained till towards the end of February.

Quite a number of letters or summaries of letters survive from this period of Mr Talbot's three or four months' stay at Douay. There was much paper work to be done—regulations, College rules, arrangements of one kind and another, all of which needed the sanction of M. Roussel and his Parlement. One notes attempts being made (but not by Douay) to find historical justification after the manner of Dodd for the present occupation of St Omers. The Jesuits, wrote Dr Stonor, the clergy agent in Rome, did not own the College and its revenues; "they were only the administrators for the Education of the English Youth, therefore if they can no longer comply with that, the Nation ought by no means to be deprived of the benefit".[30] This is what the grammarians might call an hypothetical condition unfulfilled in the present. So too M. Roussel entreats Mr Talbot "to send him all the anecdotes regarding the foundation he can find, to enable him to give a clear account of it to Parlement".[31] As to the revenues of St Omers, a Paris official had so far discovered by the May of 1763 investments producing an income of 3,890 livres payable at Paris to the College, apart from other *rentes* payable in the province of Artois.[32]

A Memorial drawn up on behalf of Mr Talbot by Dr Stonor for presentation to the Pope appears to date from the January of 1763. It begs His Holiness to give his consent and approbation to the occupation of St Omers by the English Clergy. The Bishop of St Omers wrote a friendly letter on

[30] Dr Stonor to Dr Green, 25 January 1763 (*Ibid.*, p. 256).
[31] M. Roussel to Mr Talbot, 25 April 1763 (*Ibid.*, 265).
[32] M. Roussel to Mr Talbot, 19 May 1763 (*Ibid.*, p. 268).

12 February to Fr Darell[33] warning him of the fact and of the complaints that were included in the Memorial—complaints of gross slanders against the clergy and in particular against Mr Talbot, and of the removal from the College of much needed furniture and effects. On the main point Mr Talbot was evidently reassured, else he would have refused to take any further action. But the order of subsequent events is not very clear. Ralph Hodgson's account[34] is certainly mainly guess-work and misleading.

It seems however beyond doubt that another Memorial was sent to the Secretary of Propaganda, Cardinal Marefoschi, setting forth "the whole affair of St Omer" from the point of view of some person described as "Mr Roussel's friend".[35] Whether this friend was the Abbé Plowden or another is unknown. Nor is its date at all certain. But leaving guess-work aside, one is on sure ground in recording that by an order dated 5 April the Jesuits were formally cited to appear before the tribunal of Propaganda and there plead their title to St Omers.[36]

This summons placed the Jesuits in a very awkward position. They were by now established in Bruges by favour of Her Majesty Maria Theresa, but subject to certain conditions. They were forbidden to teach or to hold that Rome had any jurisdiction over the temporalities of secular Princes. To appear as defendants before Propaganda would thus be to run the risk, the very grave risk, of being expelled from the Austrian dominions. That would have wrecked all their hopes and plans. On the other hand the citation of Propaganda demanded respect, even though the Society's long experience provided no great hope of a favourable verdict. In this particular case a strong rumour had reached Bruges that Propaganda had already prejudged the issue and sanctioned the occupation of St Omers by the Clergy. Their reply to their Lordships in fact said as much, though in very guarded language. "God forbid

---

[33] S. Arch., Reeve, pp. 112-115.   [34] *Dispassionate Narrative*, pp. 110-130.
[35] *Ibid.*, p. 113.   [36] S. Arch., Reeve, p. 82.

that we should give credit to rumours of such a nature." After long and careful deliberation the decision was reached that they would not plead to the indictment but would justify their refusal with the aid of three Memorials, or perhaps one Memorial in three parts.[37]

In the first they presented their excuses for refusing to plead. Not only would their appearance before such a tribunal imply (they said) the admission of a doubt as to their title, but it would injure and alienate their English friends to whose generosity they owed so much and who were deeply involved in this matter. St Omers having been founded by one King and its possession confirmed by another, it would be an insult to regal authority to submit this absolute dominion to the cognizance of any other Court, not to mention a foreign tribunal. Furthermore the relations between the Courts of Rome and France, already strained, would perhaps reach the breaking point if Propaganda claimed any jurisdiction in temporal matters within the French King's dominions. The same reaction might be expected from the Court of Vienna. They begged therefore to be excused from provoking such evils.

Lest however their Lordships the Cardinals should think their refusal to plead argued lack of proof for their claim to St Omers, they proceeded in a second part to rebut the charge that the College was no more than a preparatory school, a *pépinière* for the ecclesiastical seminaries in Rome and Spain, of which the Jesuits had somehow, probably fraudulently, acquired the administration. To such charges the obvious answers were given. The complete freedom of choice of a way of life, the absolute donation of St Omers by Philip II, confirmed by Louis XIV in 1680, a prescriptive right of 169 years of uninterrupted and unchallenged occupation—all this and more will be clear to readers of the preceding chapters. The third part deals with the accusation that the Jesuits had stripped the College of even the usual necessities. The answer was again

[37] *Ibid.*, pp. 83-86, and at greater length in E. P. Arch. (1), ff. 214-228.

an easy one. Nothing contained in the long Inventory of 174
pages had been removed, unless in the Inventory was included
the personal effects of each Jesuit as allowed by the *arrêt* of
13 August. For the rest, whatever might be the true state of the
case, blame, not the Jesuits, but the looting of the College
which was wide-spread and notorious. The Memorial did not
add what Fr Darell, the Procurator, mentioned in his letter to
the Bishop of Saint-Omer, that no less than 30,000 livres had
to be spent at Bruges to supply the "necessities" which the
Jesuits were accused of having removed.

No doubt these Memorials were not composed in a day or a
week. When completed they were not at once dispatched to the
English College at Rome for presentation to Propaganda. In
view of the condition laid down by the Empress, it was judged
best to send first a copy to the Court of Brussels lest any misunderstanding should arise. Fr Elliot, Rector at Bruges since
the preceding October, must have felt relieved on receiving
from the Governor of the Netherlands a letter dated 17 June,
which gave added support to his refusal to plead before the
Roman tribunal. Its gently worded command will bear tran-
scription.

Charles Alexandre (&c &c)

Cher et bien aimé, comme il nous revient que les Jésuites de
la province Angloise dont le principal établissement est
transferé aujourd'hui dans les terres de la domination de
l'Imperatrice Reine se trouvent cités à Rome devant la
Congregation de Propagande à l'instance de quelques
membres du Clergé Seculier d'Angleterre possesseurs actuels
du Collège Anglois de St Omer; nous vous faisons la
presente, pour vous dire que toute evocation des sujets de sa
Majesté devant les Congregations ou tribunaux de Rome
étant interdite et reprouvée par les lois fondamentales des
Pays Bas, nous vous defendons d'entrer dans aucune espece
de contestation sur l'objet, dont il s'agit, devant la Congregation de Propagande; voulant au surplus que vous
informiez sans delai la Père Provincial de la Province

Angloise de notre presente disposition, pour qu'il s'y con-
forme pareillement à tout.

Cher et bien aimé, Dieu vous ait en sa sainte garde.

De Brussels le 17 Juin 1763

Charles de Lorraine,

Par Ordre de son Altesse Roiale.[38]

This prohibition of the Governor was evidently taken to
apply to the personal citation, not to the dispatch of a Memorial:
accordingly it was in due course presented to the Prefect of
Propaganda. Ralph Hodgson is here quite amusing with his
guesses and comments. He had read all or some of the first
part of the Memorial, which he characterizes as "rant", with
other opprobrious remarks. "It could never be of use to their
interest before the Congregation", and so on. But, says he, it is
very certain that the Jesuits did present a Memorial, "and it
is as certain it met with a very cool reception". This statement,
be it said gently, is misleading, as the following brief letter of
8 October from Count Cobenzl, the Imperial Resident at
Brussels, makes clear.[39] The letter, we are told, was written in
English in the Count's own hand.

Reverend Father,

As there is no doubt to be made of your being directly
acquainted with the favorable turn of your affairs at the
Propaganda, I think it superfluous to dwell on this head.
But if contrary to my expectation you were a stranger to
what happened there, I must previously inform you, that
the Chief of the Propaganda highly condemns the irregular
proceeding of the English Clergy, suggests to your Father
General not to appear before the Judge, and considers your
accusers as real Intruders. I am very glad of this happy event,
and am with all my heart,

R^d F^r,

Y^r most humble serv^t and friend

Cobenzl.

Brussels, 8 October 1763.

[38] E. P. Arch. (1), f. 228^v.   [39] S. Arch., Reeve, p. 87.

Whether this was the first intimation received by Fr Elliot of the result of the Memorial is not known. Coming from such a man as Cardinal Marefoschi, the views expressed, it must be admitted, are wholly surprising and quite inconsistent with his previous personal assurances as reported by Dr Stonor. Was the Cardinal perhaps out-voted by the members of the Congregation? One cannot say. And since Count Cobenzl's letter appears to be the only document that bears upon this matter we can but imitate Ralph Hodgson and "leave the candid reader to form what judgment he pleases".

V

12

THE SETTLEMENT AT BRUGES

WE may now go back some months to follow the College boys on their way from St Omers to Bruges, well beyond the reach of the aggressive Paris Parlement. The Spanish Netherlands had by now become the Austrian Netherlands. After the War of the Spanish Succession the Treaty of Utrecht (1713), or rather the subsequent "Treaty of the Barriers" two years later, had effected the change: and from 1748, after yet another war of Succession, the Empress Maria Theresa ruled securely in Vienna, her brother-in-law, Charles of Lorraine, representing her at Brussels as Governor of the Belgian provinces. As yet permission to settle permanently in Bruges had not been given, although, as we shall see, a provisional permission was obtained a week after the arrival of the first batch of boys.

It is of this first batch and its adventures in transit that Fr Joseph Reeve, who conducted it, has left us a manuscript account. Not yet ordained priest, he had just completed a year as master of Poetry, to become Rhetoric master at Bruges and then for a year or more Prefect of Studies. He was learned in the classics and had recently composed a Latin translation, much admired by his friends, of Addison's tragedy of *Cato*— the precursor of several works in Latin and in English published in the course of his long chaplaincy—over half a century —to the Clifford family at Ugbrook Park. His account in manuscript of the expulsion from St Omers, *A Plain and Succinct Narrative*,[1] is a very competent and useful work although written in a somewhat injured tone that would be tedious were it not for his quaintly lacrymose and rather pompous manner which unintentionally arouses here and

[1] S. Arch., A. III, 19.

there amusement rather than the sympathy that misfortune deserves.

The scene opens about noon during the after-dinner recreation of Monday, 9 August 1762. Some two dozen boys selected from the middle of the school were summoned to Mr Reeve's room for reason or reasons unknown to them. When they had assembled—some of them, no doubt, with consciences not quite at ease—they were informed of the projected plan and asked if they were willing to take part in it. All expressed "the most earnest readiness to go wherever the Jesuits should think fit to lead them": they were, in fact, most willing to miss afternoon schools and two hours of Night Studies and as much else as possible. No other boys as yet had any inkling of the plan. The secret had indeed been well kept, partly because it was suspected the local authorities would oppose the migration —for the College was both popular in town and financially profitable—and partly for fear that their movements might be under the observation of "spies" of the Parlement of Paris. The initiates were told each to procure a change of linen and stockings, with such "trinkets" as they might wish to carry with them, and then to reassemble in his room.

Thus they started on their journey, as if for a class walk into the country. The master of "Little Figures", Mr James Ewen, whose very pro-French attitude—he had been brought up in France—was not conducive to internal harmony, was detailed to accompany the party. About 1 o'clock they set off, one may suppose, two and two through the town in crocodile fashion, as was the foreign custom, until they presently reached the Dunkirk Canal. There a "pleasure-boat" was awaiting them and they were soon afloat, with the noviciate of Watten, some five or six miles ahead, as their destination. When about half-way there, they sighted in the distance the public Dunkirk barge making its slow course to Saint-Omer. So, lest undue curiosity should be aroused, "we immediately tacked and turned up a narrow creek which led to an island spot delightfully chequered with verdure, wood and rising ground. We there landed, and the thoughtless Innocents amused themselves with play until the Barge was passed out of sight."

Watten was reached in the early evening. They were kindly welcomed by the Rector and Novice-Master, Fr Robert Constable (brother of the former Rector of St Omers), who, forewarned, had had prepared for them "an hospitable repast", or in other words, a good feed in the refectory. "For he was a good religious man, and the Spirit of God was in him." Supper was followed by bed, in view of an early start next morning.

The rest of the journey was to be by land and by unfrequented roads. Two market waggons had been chartered, fitted out with mattresses laid along the floor and fastened to the sides. At the hour of 5 a.m. they waved good-bye to Fr Constable and began the day's journey prayerfully with the Litany of Our Lady. The journey lay eastwards. Nerves were doubtless taut until they crossed the frontier into the Austrian Netherlands on their way towards Ypres. Unexpectedly towards noon two other waggons were sighted which had left the vicinity of St Omers that same morning, 10 August, with a load of another twenty-eight boys in the charge of Fr Thomas Brent, the First Prefect, and of the master of Rudiments, Fr Edward Walsh. "The meeting", writes Fr Reeve, "was unexpected and affecting: a sympathy of joy mixed with grief heaved in the breasts of all."

Trouble arose at the frontier. Some officials, "commissioners of the King's duties", seized Mr Reeve's waggons and horses—the other party seems to have fared better—on the pretence that he had not made a due declaration. The "vulgar harpies" were bent on extortion and would not listen to reason. Much time was lost, but at length the officer in command was found and interviewed, a reasonable duty was paid and a permit was obtained to continue the journey without further molestation. Mr Ewen, incidentally, with his fluent French, was not available on this occasion. He refused to co-operate, and Mr

Reeve "had the mortification to see himself abandoned by his Colleague". Perhaps the reason was that Mr Ewen already felt his interest in Jesuit affairs to have grown faint. At all events it was not long before he decided to follow another way of life.

Once across the frontier and beyond the reach of the French the tension relaxed, the need of secrecy was removed. "Curiosity soon discovered to the villages we passed through who we were and for what cause we fled. The tear of compassion gushed from the eyes of those good villagers, who knew how to feel for oppressed innocence, and to pity even strangers in affliction." Thus they travelled to Poperinghe, preceded by Fr Brent and his party of thirty all told. At Poperinghe, a small unfortified town some six miles west of Ypres, was a Benedictine house under the jurisdiction of the great Abbey of Saint-Bertin at Saint-Omer. Fr Darell on his way to Bruges a day or two before, had called on the Superior or "Provost" and had made all suitable arrangements. The news of their coming had spread, for the streets, we are told, were lined with inhabitants who had come out to welcome the strangers to the Imperial territories.

The long day however was now drawing to a close, the delay at the frontier had upset the time-table, everybody was tired and hot and bothered. Mr Reeve conferred with the Provost, who tactfully agreed that Ypres might well keep for another day. His co-operation was most generous. Clearly the arrangement had been that Fr Brent's contingent should spend the night at Poperinghe, whilst Fr Reeve and company should out-span at Ypres. Now at short notice the Provost hospitably insisted on entertaining nearly double the number. The voracious appetites of over fifty boys after a long journey— to say nothing of the four Jesuits—would surely have emptied the Benedictine larder. That disaster was obviated by the Provost who bespoke a supper for some of them at the local inn. Thence, replete and sleepy, these boys returned to the Prévôté for the comfort of a good night's rest.

Fresh horses and waggons had been hired for the remaining journey, and early next morning they all set off again, intending to reach Bruges by night-fall. That would mean a journey of perhaps forty miles or so. Of Fr Brent and his party we hear no more: if they had adventures they are not recorded. Not that anything very exciting happened to the party led by Mr Reeve; but he and some of his boys managed at least to lose themselves.

The day was very hot and sultry, he tells us. The horses "grew faint" and when the way of the waggons lay through a long stretch of soft sand, the passengers had to get out and walk. Presently the waggon track took the form of a wide semi-circle; and it was pointed out that by striking across country they would save themselves much walking and could meet the waggons again at a village where the sandy road came to an end. "Several of us unadvisedly entered into the bye track which led us into the middle of a wood, and there divided into several paths that pointed different ways. We found ourselves in a labyrinth not knowing what direction to take and having no landmark to go by." In this not uncommon predicament good Mr Reeve betook himself to prayer. Meanwhile an enterprising boy, considering doubtless that God helps those who help themselves, selected a suitable tree and swarmed up. Heaven was benign to this combined effort, for from his high perch the boy "descried a distant steeple which we concluded to be the point of our destination". What is more, the conclusion turned out to be correct, even though the distance proved to be decidedly deceptive.

But Mr Reeve's troubles were not quite at an end. Spent with thirst and the heat of the day a young boy, after the manner of the waggon horses, "grew faint and ill".

No house was near, the country afforded nothing for his refreshment; no time was to be lost, lest we might chance to lose the waggons, which we supposed to be at some distance before us. We were under the necessity then of dragging him on, when we were revived at the sight of a miserable cottage. The hope of finding something for our refreshment made us knock earnestly at the door, but extreme poverty had nothing to offer but a cooling draught of water for our fainting youth. Some of our more vigorous wanderers had by this time reached the village where the waggons and our other travellers were stopped to bait. We joined them soon after with great satisfaction and after a short refreshment continued our journey with them towards Bruges.

The long, weary journey ended, or was expected to end, with their arrival at Bruges about 9 o'clock, but they were only to find the town gates already closed. These eventually were opened for them and the two waggons trundled in the darkness through the silent streets. It was 10 o'clock before they reached their appointed lodging. Half of them were by this time asleep, but roused themselves on hearing they had reached their new haven of rest. Here Mr Reeve is really at his indignant best and we can but listen:

By the glimmering light of a farthing candle they were conducted into a naked room, where not so much as a chair was provided to sit upon. In the middle stood a table made of rough boards and on each side a temporary bench which fell to the ground the moment they were sat upon. Three roasted legs of mutton were immediately set upon the table, but neither knife nor fork nor plate had been thought of. The Fleming who produced the meat had luckily brought his great knife along with him, else the mutton might have remained untouched. Slices of bread and meat were cut and given to the scholars, who with their fingers and teeth managed as well as they could. This ceremony was soon over: from thence they were shown into an adjoining room, where they found mattresses with straw placed in a double row upon the floor: here without sheet or blanket they were to take their repose pell-mell together: this after all their fatigues was the accommodation they met with on the evening of their arrival at Bruges the 11th of August, 1762.

With a new dawn came courage and a new hope. At all events they were now beyond the grasp of Paris. A tour of exploration, however, did not reassure them: it revealed a series of empty rooms, unfurnished, unequipped. The Rector, Fr Scarisbrick, who had been staying for some weeks at the Franciscan Convent of Prinsenhof in Bruges, had, it seems, secured the house only a few hours before their arrival. His belated activity coincided with the coming to Bruges of Fr Darell on the previous day. Both these Fathers came that morning to take up their residence at the Maison d'Argille, as the house was named—an old Spanish dwelling-house situated near the Cistercian monastery of Hemelsdael. It should be added that this house was not large enough to hold them all. On the night of arrival eleven boys and a master had been accommodated at an inn, the Hôtel de Commerce, where by comparison their lot was luxurious.

The days and weeks that followed were full of bustle. More boys were arriving: the last contingent of twelve reached Bruges about 18 September. These last were also under the care of Mr Reeve, who for some reason or other had returned to St Omers, possibly for such a purpose. They had travelled "by way of Watten, Bergue, Furness and Newport"—a route that suggests a journey by canal. Over a hundred persons had to be provided for and at short notice. Carpenters and other workmen were engaged; sheets and blankets were bought, beds were provided and all the other necessities of school life. Assistance in the task of furnishing the "naked rooms" came generously from the Flemish Austin Friars and from the two local English Convents, that of the Franciscans of Prinsenhof and the Augustinian Canonesses (Dames Anglaises) in the Rue des Carmes. Witness the Diary of these Canonesses:

> The English Jesuits being banished from France came into the Queen's dominions, being much invited by the magistrates of this town; they came a few at a time, their students also in different companies which was judged more safe. We helped them all we could by sending some beds, chairs, tables and what else we could pick up throughout the house, for their present convenience.

What is more, the account books of this Convent testify that 3,000 florins were lent on this occasion to help the Jesuits in their urgent need.[2] Fr Darell's letter to the Bishop of Saint-Omer has already been cited,[3] wherein he reckoned the cost of supplying the needs of this new establishment to have amounted to 30,000 livres in the course of some six months. Certainly these Jesuits were not destitute of many generous friends and benefactors.

As yet the settlement at Bruges was but provisional. The local magistrates of the town had warmly welcomed the English Jesuits on their arrival. To this friendly attitude they had been led in part by the influence of a certain Mr Porter, a magistrate of one of the tribunals and a kinsman and casual correspondent of one of the St Omers Fathers, Fr Nicholas Porter. His tactful approaches were no doubt in harmony with the business instincts of the authorities, by whom the prospect of a considerable annual revenue of English money would be given full weight. If the "tear of compassion" was also allowed to play its part, it must needs have been, as it were, a provisional tear, almost an illegal tear; for the coming of the foreigners was as yet unsanctioned by the Government of the Austrian Netherlands. The desired permission was however granted by a decree of the Court of Brussels, 19 August, but it was not more than provisional: it forbad any acquisition of property until Vienna should be pleased to issue Letters Patent.

The Jesuits were thus prevented as yet from buying a house, but they were not forbidden to hire one. Meanwhile they carried on as best they could. From the Maison d'Argille boys had had to be accommodated, some at the Hôtel de Commerce and others at another inn, the Fleur de Blé, referred to in one of Mr Jenison's letters as the "Cornibloom". The food was sent in, ready cooked, from the Hôtel de Commerce until on 17 August there arrived from St Omers the College cook.

[2] C. S. Durrant, *A Link between Flemish Mystics and English Martyrs* (London, 1925), p. 353.
[3] E. P. Arch. (1), ff. 184-189 (19 February 1763).

Some days later the Jesuits were granted the use of another house "belonging to the Archers", that is to say, the Arquebusiers de St Sébastien, an ancient guild with head-quarters in the Rue des Carmes, not far from the convent of the Dames Anglaises. Presently therefore the boys were removed from the inns and lodged either in the Maison d'Argille or that of the Archers.

They had soon come to the conclusion that if they were to establish a College at all in Bruges, they must acquire a house capable of accommodating the whole school, boys and masters combined. Intercession to Our Lady brought them a prompt answer. Within a week of the decree just mentioned Mr Jenison is informing his brother at Wardour that "we have at last obtained leave from Brusselles to hire in this town a large stately building in which we shall live till we can procure letter Patents from Vienna, but we cannot enter upon our new settlement till the beginning of next month".[4] This "stately building" was evidently the house sometimes referred to as "Le Gouvernement" or as the "House of the Seven Towers" (Het huis der Zeven Torens), near the centre of the town in the Rue Haute (Hoogstraet) or High Street. The acquisition of this large building, whereof "the apartments were airy and roomy and might easily be modelled into all the purposes of a College", was due to the verve—some might call it the nerve—of Fr Darell, the Procurator and former Rector. Knowing well how urgent was the matter and that the chance was not likely to be repeated, he urged his phlegmatic Rector to take immediate action. Failing in this forlorn hope, he took the matter into his own hands and, as Mr Reeve tells us,

> entered into contract with the proprietors of the Government House, presuming on the approbation he expected of his mediate Superiors. The thing was no sonner done but universally applauded. Every hand was immediately set to work, schools, dormitories, private chambers, study room,

[4] Mr James Jenison to Fr John Jenison, 27 August 1762 (E. P. Arch. (1), ff. 122-3).

refectory, chapel and domestic offices were fitted up with all
expedition and made ready to receive our whole number by
the beginning of September. Then as it assumed the form,
it also received the title of College. Here under the protection
of her Imperial Majesty the Jesuits of the English Province
continued the same plan of education as at St Omer . . . were
enabled to keep up the same number of students . . . till an
unexpected thunderbolt from the Vatican at Rome blasted
all their hopes at once, and put a period to their religious
existence as a Body.[5]

Mention of a chapel in this new College brings to mind an
incident that occurred a few weeks later. Application by the
Provincial, Fr Corbie, was made to the Bishop of Bruges, Mgr
de Caimo, for leave to erect a domestic chapel and to reserve
therein the Blessed Sacrament, to administer the Last Sacraments to scholars and domestic servants in need of them; and
for the scholars and domestics to fulfil, not only the Sunday
precept, but likewise the obligation of Easter Communion in
this same domestic chapel. To these last two requests the curé
of the parish, like the curé at Boulogne, raised considerable
objections. His Lordship, uncertain how to act, wrote to the
Bishop of Saint-Omer, asking if such privileges had really
been allowed to the Jesuits at St Omers. We have not the
reply: but there survives a letter written by Fr Corbie's friend,
Count Neny (an Irishman whose native name was Patrick
MacNeny or something near it), testifying that at St Omers
where he had studied for four or five years, the boys at all
events had had the benefit of all these concessions: as to the
servants he had no knowledge. For the leave to administer the
Last Sacraments the Bishop was moved by the plea that the
minister should deliver an exhortation to the dying, who
usually would be more responsive to language he could understand.[6] If the Bishop also granted exemption from the law
that then prevailed, obliging the faithful to make their Easter

[5] Reeve, p. 66.
[6] E. P. Arch. (2), ff. 5, 7, 8.

Communion in their own parish church, we have no record of the permission.

Formal application to the Court of Vienna was made on 11 September for leave to settle permanently in Bruges. A favourable reply was expected, backed up as it was by the local magistrates, but the issue was of course uncertain. Meanwhile the final evacuation of St Omers on 19 October brought the remainder of the Fathers to complete the Community at the House of the Seven Towers. By this date a more or less normal routine had been established. The various migrations in August and September had taken place during the vacation period and studies had not been very seriously interrupted. At all events the usual inauguration of the new school year ("Ascensio Scholarum") was on 20 September or thereabouts, the only departure from the traditional custom being the omission of a High Mass.[7] Within a week of the arrival of the last Fathers from St Omers Fr Nathaniel Elliot entered into office as Rector (1762–1766), his predecessor, the popular and dilatory Fr Scarisbrick, being appointed "Prefect of the Sodality"— that is to say, its Director. It was anticipated—at least by Mr Jenison—that the new Rector, unlike Fr Scarisbrick, would be a strict disciplinarian. That he was a successful Rector is suggested by his next appointment as Provincial—the second last Provincial of the Province before its suppression. At last, "on the feast of St John" (27 December), Fr George Mannock[8] arrived with good news. He had brought with him the Letters Patent from Vienna, dated 1 December, granting the desired permission.

There were, however, conditions attached—six of them and none of them quite welcome—the recommendations of the Privy Council. They were as follows:

[7] Mr James Jenison to Fr John Jenison, 28 September 1762 (E. P. Arch. (1), f. 128).
[8] In 1781, having survived three elder brothers and a nephew, he succeeded as the 9th and last Baronet. The Mannock family resided at Gifford's Hall, Suffolk, an old Jesuit chaplaincy (Foley, V, 546–552).

1. That they renounce all privileges inconsistent with the good of the State.

2. Never to teach that the Pope had any power over the independence of Her Majesty in temporal matters, but on the contrary to teach the opposite doctrine.

3. To teach nothing contrary to *la saine morale*.

4. The plan of education to be always subject to the control of the Government.

5. That the Great College (the House of Seven Towers) be staffed by not more than "twenty Caps and 15 black servants"; the Little College to be limited to "3 Caps and 3 black servants".

6. That all purchases of houses or land be notified within the next twelve months for the purpose of obtaining the necessary governmental sanctions. This condition to be accepted under pain of revocation of the Letters Patent and expulsion from Her Majesty's dominions without compensation.[9]

The "Caps" and more especially the "black servants" may perhaps have aroused speculation in a reader's mind. It is Mr Jenison who uses these terms which one may suppose had an intimate history familiar to his correspondent. But the black servants must not be taken, so to speak, at their face value. They were not negroes from Père Lavalette's coffee plantations. The Commissaire who wrote the report of the seizure of the Colleges in 1773 makes it clear that Mr Jenison's "black servants" were Jesuit laybrothers, in distinction perhaps from the servants of the house, whose dress would not have been the Jesuit habit or soutane. The "Caps" were the Jesuit members of the teaching staff.

The conditions, some of them not more than tactless, had of course to be accepted. Next month certain privileges or exemptions were sought and obtained from the local magistracy, largely, it would seem, in connection with the future import of building material. Later in the year Vienna conceded a two-years'

[9] Mr James Jenison to Fr John Jenison (E. P. Arch. (1), ff. 147-148); Rapport du Comité Jésuitique du 7 Decembre 1773 (E. P. Arch. (2), ff. 50 seqq.).

extension of the last condition. Finally in the summer of 1764 the Rector designated the houses and land he proposed to acquire and asked for the requisite permission to mortgage this property as sureties for the creditors. On the same occasion he petitioned for the annulment of all the conditions. The first three, he explained, were humiliating in that they presupposed the Jesuits to be suspect and their doctrine to be corrupt. The plan of education that had been submitted was for English youth, and only Englishmen could fully appreciate their needs. As to the last condition, they lacked as yet the money needed for building, for they depended on intermittent gifts of friends as well as on borrowing on the security of their property. Not only did he need permission to mortgage, but he also asked that he be guaranteed freedom to dispose of such property, in case circumstances should oblige the Jesuits to seek a fresh asylum.

The Privy Council was for rejecting outright the Jesuit *Mémoire*. The Empress however was not unobservant of the implied hint that the Jesuits, if driven too far, might be driven to go elsewhere. That would be to the disadvantage of Bruges, "cette grande ville depeuplée et languisante", where the inflow of English money would be so very welcome. In the end this sixth condition was in the main annulled, reasons being found for refusing to withdraw the other five.

It was in 1765, so one gathers, that some property was bought with the aid of a loan: but what with the daily expenses of the school and the interest to be paid on the loan, building operations were out of the question. Nevertheless the Privy Council took umbrage at the delay and at the close of 1766 the Fiscal of Flanders was ordered to inform the Jesuits that they must begin building in the following year and meanwhile make due preparation of material. It was represented however to the Governor, Charles of Lorraine, that this order was quite impossible of execution. There was no lack of will but considerable lack of money: the spoliation of St Omers had impoverished the Jesuits. But of their desire, their anxiety to build, the Governor need have no misgivings. The confined, ill-adapted house in which they lived huddled together, with the resulting inconvenience both for religious exercises and for studies and discipline should afford evidence enough of their determination to commence building as soon as they could possibly afford to. The reply satisfied the Governor and the orders to the *Conseiller fiscal* were suspended.[10]

Undoubtedly the intention was, as soon as feasible, to build from the foundations a new College on the site the Jesuits had acquired. This was a property west of the House of the Seven Towers or the "Great College" as it was already called. It was in fact on the west fringe of the town itself, where now is situated the railway station, once bordering the Marché du Vendredi or Friday Market. The extent of the property is not stated; the price, we are told, was £4,000 (some 48,000 florins), a quite considerable sum in those days. It was scheduled for building purposes, and there it remained. When the College was suppressed in 1773 it was still scheduled for building purposes. An obvious lack of funds for so large an undertaking, together with the doubtful, even threatening politico-religious situation made the Jesuits cautious. Early in 1767 the Society was expelled from Spain, and further Bourbon action could very reasonably be expected.

Building of some sort had nevertheless to be undertaken, both to relieve the congestion in the College and to avert fresh remonstrances on the part of the Brussels Government. It was decided therefore to acquire another property, no doubt smaller than that at the Friday Market, and to build there the Little College. With perhaps a redistribution of classes the pressure would be relieved and provision could be made for a further intake of boys. In January 1768 application was made for the necessary permissions, which were granted by a royal dispatch dated 11 April. The permissions asked for included a declaration that the loans to the Jesuits would not be confiscated in

10 E. P. Arch. (2), ff. 5, 7, 8.

any future crisis that might arise; and that the number of Jesuits allotted to this Little College be increased. Both these requests were granted, the number of Jesuits allowed in the Community being doubled, from six to twelve. At the date of the Suppression in 1773 the Jesuits were nine in number, including two laybrothers.

What was actually done was to buy a building on the Quai du Miroir, to the north-east of the town near the old Pont St Jean (Sint Jansbrug) no longer existing: nowadays, transformed into a girls' school, it is close to the more recent Pont du Roi or Koningsbrug. To this house the Jesuits planned to add a substantial wing. It was estimated that the contemplated mortgage would not be less than 70,000 florins of Brabant (over £5,800). The *Rapport du Comité Jésuitique* of 1773 which we have been mainly following tells us that at that date the wing had not quite been finished; it was already large enough to lodge 100 scholars, although at the time the actual number was 81.

Fr Charles Plowden, who was in 1773 Minister at the Great College, has this to say on the subject[11]

Fr William Aston was appointed Superior: one of the best and most shewey houses in Bruges was purchased, an additional new building was erected; and in a short time the little school was advanced to a degree of neatness and elegance, neither known at St Omer nor imitated at Liege, which obtained universal applause and soon filled the house with students. So great was the confidence of Superiors that Fr General Ricci once took the resolution of appointing Fr Aston Rector of both houses, in order to forward them both to the desired perfection: but this project was superseded, and Fr Thos. Stanley was named Rector, by whom no work of activity was likely to be undertaken; and his successor, Fr Thomas Angier, had not been three months in office when the final catastrophe arrived.

[11] C. Plowden, s.j., *Account of the Destruction of the English Colleges at Bruges*, p. 5. This MS. was written in 1807 from notes taken at the time whilst a prisoner (S. Arch., A. III. 21).

So much for the material progress of the settlement at Bruges. The English Jesuits were welcomed by the Courts of Vienna and Brussels, not so much for sympathy with their distress—French Jesuits were denied entrance into the country —as from expectation of financial benefit to an impoverished town. Of the attitude of the townsfolk, apart from those who traded with the Colleges, we know little or nothing, although there is a suggestion that the boys found the Flemish language and sometimes the manners of the local inhabitants uncouth and boorish. Moreover if we may trust—yet surely not without reservations—some lines of a drama composed in English at Liège by that accomplished scholar, Fr Thomas Barrow, and acted there in 1788, we should gather that, for some at least, Bruges had its drawbacks as a resort for schoolboys. The five characters of this play, be it noted here—it will again be quoted later—were all at school when in 1773 the Great College was suppressed, and were still alive: Hugh Clifford, William Anderton, Walter Tempest, Simon Scrope of Danby, and Thomas Bedingfeld. Hugh Clifford (by this date fifth Lord Clifford of Chudleigh), acted by his younger brother Thomas, is comparing the surroundings of Liège with those he knew at Bruges:

Clifford. View the neighbouring hills and woods:
Each step gives new delights, new scenes and prospects.
How much unlike to this our seat at Bruges,
Where wide extended plains, without a stream
Or fountain, tire the eye. No hill, no slope,
No eminence, to rest the wearied sight,
Unless perchance some long canal, or pool
All mantled o'er with nauseous film and weed,
Skirted with birch and alders, nests of vermin,
Varies the scene, while its unwholesome vapours
Infect the air and scatter sickness round.
Anderton. The landscape's ugly.
Clifford. Say, is it not the true one?
Anderton. Yet my delighted eye has travelled o'er

W

Those level plains and swamps, for there my heart
Enjoyed content and peace.[12]

For the eleven years spent at Bruges there is little information
to be gleaned. "A fragment of Latin verse that has chanced to
survive tells us that the old stables of the new dwelling [the
Great College?] were used for a Study Place, and that the
numerous rats made great ravages among the boys' books."[13]
Beyond doubt the traditions and customs of St Omers were
continued at the Great College as far as was practicable. To
replace the Villa house at Blandyke, another was acquired in
the vicinity, so Fr Gerard assures us, by name Momelbeke,
"situated at Coolkirke, and on the Liswecke Watergang".
Yet whereas "Blandyke" is still a household word amongst
Stonyhurst boys after three centuries and more, and "Chèvremont" (the Liege equivalent) continues to have Jesuit associations at least locally, the word "Momelbeke" means nothing
now; it has sunk beneath the surface, leaving no faintest ripple
to mark the spot.

It has already been noted in a previous chapter that the
scholar's uniform at the Great College was still black, and at
least not unlike the contemporary Jesuit habit: at all events it
was described by a Protestant visitor as the "Jesuit habit". The
difference between the two eludes us. As to numbers, that
same visitor learnt in 1766 that the total was 175, the Preparatory School or Little College being no doubt included.
According to a Commissaire's list of boys whose fees had not
been paid up to 10 October 1773 — and that would probably
include almost all of them — the full total amounted to some
230, of whom 107 were in the Little College. It says much for
the efficiency of Fr Aston that since its arrival from Watten
this Little College contained well over twice as many boys.

News from France kept trickling in to the exiled Jesuits,

---

[12] The play is summarized, with several quotations, by Fr John Gerard in
Memorials of Stonyhurst College (London, 1881), pp. 32-39.
[13] J. Gerard, *Stonyhurst and its Tercentenary* (Clitheroe, 1892), p. 14. The
Tercentenary was celebrated a year too early.

who naturally were eager to gather all the latest information: how, for instance, at Paris the famous *Instruction Pastorale*, refuting the charges against the Jesuits, had by order of the Parlement been burnt in public and its author the Archbishop, the devoted Christophe de Beaumont, cited to appear before its court. That indignity, as is well known, was too much even for Louis XV, who changed the order to one of exile at La Trappe. The oft-quoted Mr Jenison, sending his brother this rather belated news, tells[14] too of the confinement of four "Soidisants" (i.e. Jesuits) and ten other persons in the Bastille.

> Notwithstanding these proceedings the Bishop of St Claude has ordered the same [Pastoral] to be printed for his own Diocese: we have it also printed here. The Court of Brussels, it seems, is variously influenced: from the first appearing of this great performance it forbad all pamphlets relating to either side of the question; insomuch that the Flemish Rectors oblige their subjects under precept not to distribute any copy thereof, or to say they have seen it.

A far less important incident is reported in the same letter concerning some "acting-suits" which, it may be recalled, were among the few belongings that the Jesuits, whilst still at St Omers, had managed to secure ahead of the inventory-makers. Some of these suits, perhaps not all, would have been the personal property of individual boys. They had been taken to the Abbey of St Bertin for temporary keeping; and there they had remained for well over a year.

> The Acting-suits, for which we were so much in pain, are at last safe at Bridges: the manner of their recovery or rather extortion is something curious. Le Roi (the chief of the Bailliage) seeing all other means ineffectual, at last fore-warned in private the Chapter of St Bertin to return us our depositum; and in case of a refusal threatened them with a warm visit the next day, to seize the said depositum, and to accuse 'em at the same time for having presumed to

---

[14] 29 February 1764 (E. P. Arch. (3), No. 30), the English mildly modernized

receive it against express orders to the contrary. As this would have exposed 'em too much, they thought proper to acquiesce to the former.

M. Le Roi had less reason to side with the Paris Parlement than had M. Roze, an agent from Paris who nevertheless possessed an independent mind. The former seems to have been frankly pro-Jesuit, as were others of the *Bailliage* and local officials at Saint-Omer. But the attitude of the Chapter is certainly "something curious" and unexpected.

The circumstances attending the expulsion from the Watten noviciate, whither the Preparatory School had moved from Boulogne in 1752, need some investigation, so far as that is possible. There is a strange dearth of documents on the subject; and the little that has since been written is full of contradictions. Canon Mahieu[15] is certainly in error when he maintains that the noviciate and school were abandoned on 1 April 1763 and was then occupied by English secular priests from St Omers. A Jesuit Catalogue of April 1764 continues to record the "Convictus Wattensis" as in previous years, under Fr John Chamberlain as Superior (he would seem to have succeeded Fr Blackiston in 1757) with another priest and two laybrothers to help him. Nor did any of the English Clergy occupy Watten either then or later, although they would have dearly loved to do so. After the departure of the Jesuits a long and tiresome controversy arose between them and the Bishop of Saint-Omer who strongly urged his claim to regain possession of the property long ago handed over to the English Jesuits by Bishop Blaise. Both parties issued *Mémoire* after *Mémoire* in support of their respective claims until finally, as late as 1776, the Bishop was adjudicated to be the rightful owner.

"Under ye Protection of Doway Parliament Watten begins to enjoy herself again. The Scholar-Novices amount to Twenty-one: 5 of Fr Chamberlain's Scholars are in possession

---

[15] Canon Mahieu, "Les Biens des Jésuites du Collège de Watten" (*Bulletin de la Société des Antiquaires de la Morinie*, XVII, Juillet 1950, p. 373). A MS. copy of this article was very kindly sent by M. Frédéric Fabre.

of ye new building under ye care of Fr Henry Brent." So Fr George Bruning from Liege in November 1763,[16] seven or eight months after Canon Mahieu's supposed expulsion. The fact is that the Parlement of Douay claimed Watten as subject to its jurisdiction, and Douay was very decidedly in favour of the Jesuits. The various *arrêts* from Paris fell on deaf ears as they had done for a while in Artois. The President of that Parlement, M. d'Aubert, travelled to Paris in defence of his rights, and was able at least to hold his own for some years, until in November 1764 a royal edict made further resistance futile. That copious letter-writer, Mr James Jenison, tells how

> the Parliament of Douay forbad ye [French] Jesuits to let the Paris Commissaries make any Inventory of their Churches: accordingly that of the above-mentioned town was shut up and entrance refused. In consequence those Gentlemen applied to four different Blacksmiths to force the doors, but they unanimously made answer that they would not do any such thing unless the Bishop wou'd head 'em and give the first knock.[17]

When after the royal edict the Parlement of Douay had to give way, it nevertheless softened the blow. In contrast to the ruthless conditions imposed by Paris, the Jesuits were allowed to remain as secular priests in the Colleges where they had previously lived; nor did they need to subscribe to the calumnies of the notorious *Extraits des Assertions* which vilified the doctrine and morals of the Society. An *Arrêt* from Douay of 17 March 1765 ordered the closure of Jesuit Colleges and houses on the following 1 April: it was then that the household at Watten reluctantly abandoned its ancient home to seek security and peace elsewhere. The noviciate, it is known, found a refuge at the House of Tertians in Ghent; and there it remained until 1773 when the house was suppressed in accord-

---

[16] G. Bruning to J. Thorpe, 19 November 1763 (E. P. Arch. (3), f. 28).
[17] Mr James Jenison to Fr John Jenison, 17 September 1762 (E. P. Arch. (1), ff. 124-5).

ance with the terms of Clement XIV's Brief. At that time there
were thirteen novices, four of whom, possessing secular
clothes, were sent away at once. The other nine were youths
from St Omers, "n'étant pourvu que des habits de Jésuites que,
sortant des études du ci-devant Collège de St Omer, ils ont
apportés en entrant au Noviciat dans cette maison". The
"ci-devant Collège" referred to, one may take it, can only
mean the Great College at Bruges. So secular clothes were
hastily made for these nine before they left, with £10 for each
novice according to what the Rector declared was the usual
custom.[18]

As to the Preparatory School, it was assuredly at Bruges by
1766, occupying the hired house—whether the house in the
Rue des Carmes or the Hôtel d'Argille or another one cannot
say—which the Protestant visitor previously mentioned in this
chapter referred to as the Little College. What is more, there
survives a claim for an annual pension of 300 livres (for non-
professed Jesuits), to date from 1 April 1765, made by Fr
Thomas Daniel West, the well-known historian of Furness.
He declares that since the preceding July he has been "praefé
de l'école à Watten".[19] It seems therefore that the school
migrated at the same time as did the novices, namely on 1 April
1765. Nor is there any good reason for supposing that its
immediate objective was other than Bruges.

Ralph Hodgson, writing from St Omers just five months
after the dissolution of Watten, informs his correspondent that

Father Molien, under the assumed titles of Mon⁵ l'Abbé and
M. Principal de Watten, has opened a school there, and
publicly applies for pensioners by Affiches one of which I
will endeavour to procure you. Methinks it is somewhat odd
—yet the grand Vicar has taken away his faculties. His
Assistant, F. Panton [Fr Panting?] is at present Confessor at

[18] 1ᵉʳ Procès Verbal (Ghent), 22 September 1773 (E. P. Arch. (2), ff. 16
seqq.).
[19] The document is preserved at the Catholic Presbytery in Hornby,
Lancashire.

Gravelines and has faculties for one month only; so that the Vicar seems disposed to keep them under.[20]

Since the Bishop of Saint-Omer and the occupants of St Omers were already in dispute over the possession of Watten, the withdrawal of faculties—if the information be correct—is perhaps not quite so odd as Hodgson thought it to be.

Fr Molien was a native of Calais who had entered Watten as a novice in 1721. At the time of the suppression of the Society he was at Ghent: the Procès Verbal sent to Prince Starhemberg on that occasion explains that Fr Molien had formerly been at Ghent, but had left it for Watten in 1765. "Expelled there, he went to Liège and came here this year." It seems therefore that a new "College" or school at Watten, established by an *arrêt* from Douay of 19 May 1765,[21] was staffed by "M. l'Abbé Molien" as Superior, with Fr (or l'Abbé) Panting as his assistant: and that at some time or other they were "expelled" from that house. Beyond that meagre information the documents are silent as the grave. Watten was a bone of contention between the Parlements of Douay and of Paris, and it is quite likely that Paris eventually got the bone. By 1768 at all events we find Fr Chamberlain catalogued as in charge, not of a "Schola", but of a *Domus* Wattensis", his subjects being Fr Charles Byerley, who for many years had been more or less insane, and Fr William Howard, over eighty years of age and described as "infirm". Both of them died there, Fr Byerley as late as 1796.

20 R. Hodgson to [Dr Charles Howard], 1 September 1765 (West. Arch., C. 16, pp. 795-798).
21 Canon Mahieu, *art. cit.*, p. 373.

13

SUPPRESSION OF THE BRUGES COLLEGES

JUST eleven years after that memorable trek from St Omers to Bruges during the August of 1762 there was published in August 1773 the Brief of Clement XIV, *Dominus ac Redemptor*, suppressing the Society of Jesus throughout the world. It was not unexpected: the hot issue of suppression had had its influence in the election to the Papacy of Cardinal Ganganelli, the former Fra Lorenzo of the Order of St Francis Conventual. For four years he had managed to postpone the fateful issue, whilst the demands, one might almost say the peremptory orders, of the Bourbon royalties had grown ever more and more insistent. Portugal, France and Spain were in full agreement on at least this one subject: yet it is of some interest to note that the reasons proclaimed in Portugal and France for expelling the Jesuits from their dominions and from the world at large quite blatantly contradicted one another. Pombal had invented crimes for his purpose, accusing the members of the Society of having degenerated from "the holiness of their pious Institute". In France however it was the Institute that contravened the laws of God and man, whereas the individual members, once freed from their unholy fetters, could be treated as normal subjects.[1] Charles III of Spain, an imperious and obstinate King, was cajoled into believing that the Jesuit General—the pious Father Ricci, of all men!—was plotting his overthrow[2] and that the Spanish Jesuits were fomenting riots against his despotic government.

Clement XIV had his own reluctant way of satisfying the Bourbon demands. The final blow that now seemed to him

[1] Cf. L'abbé Georgel, *Mémoires pour servir a l'Histoire des Evénements . . . depuis 1760 jusqu'en 1806-1810* (Paris, 1817), I, p. 114.
[2] Ibid., p. 95.

necessary if a rupture of diplomatic relations, followed perhaps by a schism, was to be avoided, must be carefully made way for by previous piecemeal confiscations of Jesuit property, closure of Jesuit Colleges and noviciates in the Papal States, and so forth. Thus the Roman Seminary, early in 1772, was taken out of the hands of the Jesuits, after an official visitation made by two "professed enemies of the Jesuits", Cardinal Marefoschi (whom we have met before) and Henry, Cardinal York. It was to the Cardinal York likewise that a brief was issued that same year, transferring the Jesuit property in Frascati to his episcopal Seminary in the town. In his Lordship's letter-box, it is said, some cynical resident placed a copy of the scriptural passage relating to Naboth's vineyard, with a request that the Cardinal would expound the text in his next discourse in the Cathedral.[3]

All such partial measures nevertheless served but to exasperate the Bourbons and their ambassadors in Rome, not least Monino, ambassador of Spain, who brutally badgered the unfortunate Pope in a manner surely foreign to normal diplomatic usage. The French ambassador, Cardinal de Bernis, was equally determined but far more polite, with something approaching to sympathy or pity for the Pope's repeated endeavours to procrastinate. "He has gazed for too long into the ditch he has to jump", wrote the Cardinal: and "He is wasting time *sniffing* his medicine".[4]

Although France and Portugal were at one with Charles III, whose livid hatred and fear of Jesuits surpassed even that of the other activists in the affair, the Pope would not jump the ditch or swallow his medicine until he had the assent of Austria, the most important of the Catholic Powers. Maria Theresa was not at all ill-disposed towards the Society. Indeed, as she informed Charles III, she had a high esteem of them and of the good work they were doing in her dominions. Nevertheless,

[3] S. Arch., A. III. 14, No. 17. Cf. Pastor, XXXVIII (English translation), 245-6.
[4] M. Cheke, *Cardinal de Bernis* (London, 1948), p. 243.

when pressed for a definite statement, she finally allowed herself to be persuaded. If the Pope wished to suppress the Order, no doubt he knew what was best for the Church and she would raise no obstacles. But she insisted that there be no interference with her right to dispose of the Jesuits and their properties. Her desire of a marriage for her daughter, Marie Antoinette, with the Dauphin of France, and therefore the maintenance of good relations with Louis XV, had its due influence on her decision. As Pastor expresses it, for the sake of her daughter's marriage she sacrificed the Jesuits, removing thus the only obstacle to their downfall.[5]

The long delayed Brief, dated 21 July, was published on 16 August 1773 and at once put into execution at the Gesù and the other Jesuit houses in Rome. Contrary to custom this Brief was not published *urbi et orbi*, but separately in each house of the Society. At Liège the ritual of suppression was carried out on 9 September, whilst in the Austrian Netherlands it was settled by Prince Starhemberg, to whom the details had been entrusted, that "zero hour" should be 7 a.m. on Monday, 20 September. Maria Theresa had expressed her will that neither now nor in the future were the former Jesuits to be treated with any discourtesy. She herself appears to have regretted her previous complaisance and continued to show them marks of her favour.[6] At Brussels, however, amongst the Ministers and Government officials many were hostile to the Society. The "courtesy" displayed in their dealings with the English Jesuits may be judged from what is now to be related.

For the account of the suppression at Bruges we have two authorities to guide us: the *Procès Verbaux* or official reports sent up from time to time to the Brussels headquarters, and a manuscript account "collected and copied in 1807 from memoirs written in 1773 and 1774 by an Eyewitness of the whole transaction". The eyewitness was Fr Charles Plowden, nephew of the four Jesuit Plowdens mentioned in a previous

[5] Pastor, *op. cit.*, pp. 261-262. Cf. Georgel, *op. cit.*, pp. 137-38.
[6] Pastor, *op. cit.*, p. 344.

chapter, who in October 1772, a young priest of thirty, had taken up his first appointment as Minister at the Great College. He soon learnt that the calls upon a Minister's time were frequent and exacting. "My room is like a public house, open to all comers", he told his brother Robert. In later life he found himself immersed in ever more exacting duties, as Master of Novices in the restored English Province, as Rector of Stony-hurst and as Provincial. In that last responsible office he died— very literally worked himself to death in his efforts to counter the opposition of those who still objected to the presence of Jesuits in England. His virile narrative of what happened to himself and others at Bruges differs considerably in style and manner from Fr Reeve's account of the migration thither. As always, he is precise and outspoken, leaving the reader in no doubt as to his opinion of the various officials with whom he came in contact.[7]

When news reached Bruges of the execution of the Papal Brief in Rome—and bad news travels fast—the new Rector, Fr Angier, took the only course that seemed to offer hope of favourable treatment for his two schools. He wrote to the President of the Privy Council at Brussels, Count Neny, an "old boy" of St Omers, whose influence in government circles was extensive. The Count's father, an Irishman, poor and talented, had been educated by Jesuits at Louvain and had risen to be a lawyer of some eminence. His son, following the same profession, had attained even greater distinction: but he had imbibed the prevalent anti-clericalism, and turned out to be as shifty as a flea. His reply to the letter was so vague and elusive that the Rector and Fr Aston, Superior of the Little College, decided to interview Count Neny in person. It was to no purpose; their arguments passed him by. His main interest, they felt, was to pump them as to how they had managed eleven years previously to remove their scholars and some of their effects without the knowledge of the Paris Parlement.

[7] What follows, unless otherwise noted, is from Fr Plowden's narrative of events.

He seemed to be planning that such an enterprise should not be repeated.

The two Jesuits, baffled, returned to Bruges with the knowledge that Count Neny's civil offer of assistance was utterly worthless. Already, so they learnt later, a Committee had been set up under the direction of the Count, with his son, a noted disciple of Voltaire, as Chairman of the Board, to arrange for the seizure of the various houses of English and Belgian Jesuits in the Austrian Netherlands. The friendly Count Cobenzl was now dead, and from his successor as First Minister, Prince Starhemberg, no mitigation or compassion was to be expected. The Jesuits could but wait for what should happen.

It happened as arranged, at 7 o'clock on Monday morning, 20 September. At that early hour the two Colleges were invested by armed soldiers who mounted guard on all gates and entrances. A group of civilian officials entered, headed, in the case of the Great College, by a member of the Council of Flanders, Van Volden by name, who caused the community to be assembled and read to them the long and dreary Brief of Suppression. They were warned that they were prisoners of the State, they were charged not to leave the house nor to correspond by word or letter with any one outside the house. In addition they were relieved of all authority over the boys. The intention had been to place armed guards in the Study Place during this lengthy procedure. It was with great difficulty that the Rector was able to persuade Van Volden that by so doing he would be surely asking for trouble. We may presume therefore that the boys were left to their own devices for the time being. The Rector was allowed to address the boys and exacted a promise that they would not create a disturbance. It was clear, however, that they resented the treatment meted out to their masters and wholeheartedly sympathized with them in their distress.

During these earlier proceedings there arrived the Bishop of Bruges with his secretary, he being responsible for executing the Brief, although by a precise order of the Court of Vienna the ecclesiastical was placed entirely subordinate to the civil power, which brooked no interference with its temporal authority over persons and properties.[8] The "rough secretary read out a revocation of spiritual faculties, and forbade every priest in the house to administer Sacraments". The Community, composed of twenty-one members—seven priests, seven non-priests and seven laybrothers—had of course to discard their Jesuit dress and clothe themselves as did the local clergy. The Bishop then formally inducted a Flemish priest as Superior of the house and put him in possession of the Rector's room. He explained—it was sufficiently obvious—that this new Superior could not conduct the business of the College without masters. The ceremonial, he added, was merely an official compliance with the terms of the Brief; the administration of the College would very shortly be restored to the Fathers; and he knew for certain that the Government had many special favours in store for them. We shall return to the Bishop in a moment.

As has been said, the Commissaire in charge of operations was Mynheer Van Volden—a mild, tolerant gentleman, no enemy of the Jesuits, but timid and diffident. He disliked the duties entrusted to him but disliked still more the prospect of dismissal from office. His second-in-command, Louis Maroulx, was an insufferable young puppy, "fresh from school, forward, overbearing, restless, pert and insolent. It was his first step to public notice; he assumed to himself the whole importance of the commission, which indeed devolved to him by the indifference or disgust of his principal, and he omitted nothing in the discharge of it which would recommend his services to those above him." Fr Plowden then turns to the Little College where the position was reversed. The Commissaire in charge, Massez, was "a low-bred, violent and rude lawyer, from whom no compassion could be expected". But his subordinate, Mynheer Zoetaert, once a boy at St Omers, was sympathetic,

[8] Pastor, op. cit., p. 344.

and was able at times to make up for the rudeness of his principal. The minor officials were mainly automatons, carrying out the orders given them.

The succession of orders was much the same in both Colleges —indeed in all the Jesuit Colleges of the Austrian Netherlands. There were interrogations of each member of the Community with minute inquiry into the life-history of each, inventories of every object in the house, frequent oaths administered so as to secure a complete and entire declaration of all property belonging to the College or to individuals. All letters directed to the College were intercepted and read: every movement within the house was subject to suspicion. The papal suppression was itself hard enough to endure: this quite uncalled-for churlishness and inhumanity was nearly intolerable. "Fiscal avarice" is Fr Plowden's explanation: the authorities were after the famous "riches" of the Jesuits and were increasingly annoyed at finding none. He gives a sample of their methods:

> At an unexpected moment Maroulx appeared at the house, attended by a rout of smiths, joiners and carpenters: he confined all the prisoners under guard in a separate room, while the workmen, armed with poles and iron tools, proceeded to beat up the quarters in order to draw imaginary treasures into light from supposed lurking holes and dark recesses. . . . They searched, they probed, during a whole morning, every wall, floor, ceiling, beam, desk and table: they even pulled up the board on which the taylors worked, and at length they retired in the vexation of disappointment, leaving the prisoners to contemplate the odious scene in silent amazement and despair.

Before very long Van Volden, "calling in a slight sickness to his assistance", left most of the work to his assistant, Maroulx. This increase of authority went to the head of the "obnoxious youth". One day on coming out of the room where he transacted business, he encountered in the gallery a certain Higher Line boy (as we may call him), Hugh Clifford, the heir to the Barony of Chudleigh, and ordered him to go and call

the Rector; he had "immediate need of him". According to Fr
Plowden "the young nobleman answered that he was not a
servant to be sent upon his messages, etc." What the "etc."
stands for one cannot say: it is likely that Fr Plowden was not
told. But one feels that further words and stronger were used
on that occasion. At all events the sequel was a plan among
Clifford's friends "of muffling and beating" the obnoxious
Maroulx on the next provocation. The design, however,
would only have provoked reprisals against the whole College.
In any case it was discovered by the Rector—or more probably
by the First Prefect—and the boys were reminded of their
promise not to create a disturbance. Their resentment
smouldered but for the present did not burst into flame.

We return to the Bishop, Mgr de Caimo—an honest,
upright prelate, "lordly and imperious in his dealings, inacces-
sible to advice, eager, even impetuous, in the pursuit of
whatever he undertook". Trained at Louvain in the pervading
anti-Jesuit atmosphere, he was nevertheless aware that if the
two Colleges were to continue to function, for the good of
Catholicism in England and the financial profit of Bruges, it
would be necessary at least for a time to retain the service of
the ex-Jesuits. Prince Starhemberg had assured him that the
Empress wished to preserve these two Colleges, and had
instructed him to draw up regulations in conjunction with the
two Commissaires, to appoint suitable masters, and so forth.
Delighted with the confidence thus seemingly reposed in him,
he assembled the Community, continued each master in his
former post, "talked wholesale of systems and regulations and
honorary salaries, with much good humour and reciprocal
satisfaction". He at once sent off a printed circular to the
parents for the purpose of allaying their alarm and annoyance
at the reported seizure of the Colleges. All was well, he said;
there is no cause for disquiet; the Colleges will continue as
before under the same masters to whom you have entrusted
your dear children. And in fact the usual routine of schools
and studies was resumed. The Community and boys were still

confined to the house: but the armed guards were removed from the gates, which were now guarded from the inside by a "crew of underlings" who were quartered upon the house. His Lordship was very happy.

In Brussels meanwhile the Government was maturing its own plans. From the point of view of Starhemberg and Count Neny the question of staff was the vital issue. If suitable masters could be supplied, the boys, they thought, would remain: otherwise their parents would recall them. For the moment let the Bishop retain them by what method he thought best; his arrangements could quite easily be cancelled later. The ex-Jesuits were out of the question: they could not be trusted. Yet Belgian secular priests, according to the Bishop, were not available, since so few had any knowledge of English. The choice therefore was practically limited to English clergy.

The Bishop had in mind a temporary mixture of English secular priests (if they could be procured) and ex-Jesuits, the latter to be gradually eliminated as the supply from England increased. He wrote to Bishop Challoner to this effect, but seemingly without success. The Ministers at Brussels, for their part, were scarcely interested in what the Bishop thought or did not think. He was of use to them for the time being, and that was all. In their view to run the two Colleges with an ex-Jesuit staff under an English secular priest as President would result in the establishment becoming a *pépinière*, a nursery of Jesuits "sous la direction d'un Superieur étranger". The consequence of forming a staff composed of seculars and ex-Jesuits would be either that they would quarrel or else that the wily "ci-devant soi-disans" Jesuits would seduce the seculars secretly to join their party. No, there must be no fusion of seculars and ex-Jesuits. Some one must then have suggested the idea of summoning the English Dominicans to fill the gap. The suggestion seemed hopeful. If they could be induced or forced to take the place of the "Soi-disans" (as they began to call themselves jokingly), the religious requirements of the parents might be satisfied, at least in essentials. For Count

Neny and company, whose religious aspirations seem to have been meagre, the continued attraction of English money to Bruges was all-important.

The English Dominicans at this period had two establishments on the Continent: a house of studies at Louvain, and a College and noviciate at Bornhem, this latter dating from 1658 or thereabouts. Bornhem is a Flemish village near the Schelde to the south of Antwerp, some forty or fifty miles westward from Bruges. The school, as originally founded by Cardinal Howard, had within a few years come to grief but commenced again in 1703 with greater success. At the period we speak of, the boys would have numbered about 100—much the same as at the Great College in Bruges.

Within a fortnight of the seizure of the Colleges, on 30 September, negotiations with Bornhem were begun. The Prior deputed his Sub-Prior and Procurator, Fr Austin Noel, to discuss the matter. Fr Noel proved amenable to the proposal of taking over the Little College and staffing it with competent masters. No doubt it might well prove useful as a Preparatory School for Bornhem. As to the Great College he was not enthusiastic. Bornhem, which had just been extending its buildings, would, he considered, accommodate the boys with less trouble and less expense. However, he agreed—he had little option—to staff it on a temporary basis. It was finally settled that the installation of the Dominicans should take place on the morning of 15 October. Fr Noel himself with two others would look after the Little College, whilst Fr Albert Underhill, a professor from Louvain, would become provisional Head of the Great College with four Dominicans and two or three of their Brothers to assist him. So all was well. The Bishop was informed, to his surprise and indignation, of the final plan, the reversal of all his hopes and schemes and promises. But he was ordered at his peril to keep the matter secret until the moment of execution arrived.

October 14, feast of St Donatian, the Patron of the diocese, was a public holiday in the town. That morning Maroulx got

x

to work. Assembling the Community again, he read to them for a full hour the final version of the Inventory. He then prorogued the meeting. At sunset, said he, he would return to receive the oaths of every individual that the items he had just read to them were exactly correct. That done, he would have the pleasure of setting them at large, since his instructions ended with the administration of the oaths. This was exhilarating news for prisoners who for nearly three weeks had been cooped up in confinement. Yet some anxiety still lingered in consequence of an improbable story secretly conveyed to them by a certain "Mr O'Donough", one of the town magistrates, the evening before. He had informed them that far from assenting to a petition of the Bruges magistrates in favour of the Jesuits, the Privy Council had resolved to replace them by "a colony of English Dominicans drafted from their convent at Borneham". After Maroulx's definite statement this story seemed more than ever improbable.

As night set in, the Fathers and Brothers assembled once again according to appointment, in the hall by the main entrance. A rumbling of many carriages presently caught their ears: it seemed to cease outside the gates.

They had not time to reconnoitre the situation when they beheld Maroulx bursting into the chamber, attended by a numerous retinue of civil officers and guards, all robed in their badges of distinction. He immediately assumed an air of authority, and called forth the Fathers Angier, Plowden and Carroll to follow him. In vain they sollicited the favour of being allowed to go, each to his own chamber, for a few moments; it was sternly refused. They were conducted through files of armed soldiers, who filled the vestibule, to the first coach, into which Maroulx entered with them; and without being informed of their destiny, they were driven in silence amidst surrounding guards, to the college of the Flemish Fathers, who had also been kept in strict durance from the first day of the seizure; and they were then consigned to other soldiers, whom they found stationed at the college gate.

The rest of the Community were made to follow, three in each carriage under the guard of an officer. And as the procession of carriages made its lumbering way to the Jesuit Flemish College near the Place Saint-Jean, windows flew open and a mob quickly gathered along the route and around the Great College.

It is needless to remark that the gathering of the crowd did not escape the notice of the boys, who were incredibly reported to have been at this time engaged in their studies, with no one to supervise them. It was no difficult matter for them to discover that the ex-Jesuits had been "evacuated" and that a troop of armed soldiers had occupied the house to maintain order until the arrival next morning of the Dominican Fathers. So that was the idea; a set of foreign gendarmes proposed to keep a college-full of English boys in order? With the forcible abduction of their friendly masters, their fellow country-men, there departed also, so they considered (if indeed they considered at all), the obligation of their promise to create no disturbance. And at once utter pandemonium broke loose.

There was a rush to the entrance gates, but the soldiers with their bayonets drove them back. The civilian officials called for order, but their voices were drowned by the shouts and yells of the boys. Further attempts were made to get out, and in the scrimmage a number succeeded in forcing their way through the guards. Others escaped over the walls, through the windows, by various uncovenanted ways of exit. These fortunate ones "ran up and down the streets in quest of their masters"—were they meditating a rescue?—"and nearly all of them were humanely taken in and accommodated by different families of the town, whose indignation at the violence of these proceedings was now inflamed to a high degree".

Many of the boys remained perforce in the College; and, as is the nature of such, they showed their anger and resentment by the first means that came to their hands. All over the house there was wreckage: "they broke everything they found, and tables, desks, chairs and windows were dashed to pieces on every side". With a clear conscience (as we may charitably hope) in the thought that the household property was now nobody's, a "res nullius" as the theologians might say, they rioted and smashed to their heart's content. How very satisfying they must have found it! The guards were aghast. They were vocal, no doubt, in a raw vernacular that would be more vivid than picturesque. Yet they could but stand helpless, exhausted, shattered, whilst the little world around and above them heaved and crashed.

Leaving for the present these boys to their revels, we may turn to the Little College, where since the execution of the Brief on 20 September similar proceedings had been carried out. One signal blessing had come to them. There had been chosen for the post of Superior the only English secular priest available, Mr Thomas Berington. He was the chaplain of the Austin Canonesses in the Rue des Carmes and a warm friend of the Jesuits, as was also the Mother Superior of that Convent, Mistress ("Mrs") Mary More, sister of Fr Thomas More, the last Provincial of the English Province. Many were the kind offices which both of these benefactors performed in alleviation of the hardships of their friends. Their memory deserves to be held in benediction.

In the evening of 14 October, whilst Maroulx and his minions were busy at the Great College, Massez had correspondingly repaired to the Little College with a proportionate number of assistants. But by this date his savage breast had been somewhat soothed under the benign influence of the ex-Superior, Fr Aston. Massez even condescended to ask Fr Aston's advice as to how to perform his present duty with least upset. It was agreed between them to leave the ex-Jesuits in charge that night. On the morrow at 8 o'clock he would return without military parade of any sort; whilst Fr Aston and his Community of nine would reciprocate by going quietly to their new place of confinement. The plan was foiled by Maroulx, as will appear.

As has been said, Maroulx conducted the Community of the

Great College to the Jesuit Flemish College, where for reasons unknown they were to be kept apart from their fellow prisoners, the Flemish Jesuits. At a later hour he reappeared, briskly divided the company into two more or less equal bands and ordered "eight or ten" of them (they were twenty-one in all) to leave Bruges early next morning and to quit the Austrian Netherlands as soon as possible. To these he distributed money —100 florins (about £8) to each priest and half that sum to the others. On his way out he met "one of the prisoners"—Fr Plowden himself, no doubt—"walking along, with a dejected countenance, in a contiguous darksome passage". With unexpected civility Maroulx condoled with him in his unhappiness and enquired if he could serve him in any way. He was clever enough to catch Fr Plowden off his guard. Yes, replied Fr Plowden; Maroulx, if he would, could serve him. Some manuscript volumes in a drawer of Fr Plowden's room, of historical but of no financial interest—could he have them? Why not? replied Maroulx: he should have them next morning. The volumes asked for, explains Fr Plowden in a note, comprised "several volumes of the College Register or Diary ... from the earliest times of S. Omers College to the present day", And in addition a valuable manuscript history of English Catholic affairs from 1558 to 1640, of "more than 1200 pages", the work of Fr "Sanford", the *alias* of Fr John Huddleston. Precious volumes, if they still exist in some forgotten corner of a library!

Whether the promise of Maroulx to Fr Plowden was sincere or not one cannot say, nor is it of importance. In any case he soon convinced himself that here was a key to the Jesuit "riches". The volumes were carefully conveyed to a place of safety, to be searched for hidden items of information: he had, he thought, outwitted the Jesuits. But that was not the end of the matter. Meeting Massez and learning of his humaner treatment of the Little College, he worked himself into a fury of zeal. Fr Aston, he reminded him sharply, would have now a whole night in which to hide or destroy documents of similar importance. If he did so, Massez must answer for it to the Privy Council.

That was enough to convince Massez that he had been duped by the wily Fr Aston. It was not long before carriages stood waiting at the entrance of the Little College and the dismal procedure was repeated here. Not a moment's delay was granted. The small Community of nine was bundled out of the house whilst some of the little boys, alarmed by the noise, came running down the stairs in fright. Armed soldiers occupied the house, whilst the ex-Jesuits were taken to join their confrères in the Flemish College.

In the days that followed Mr Berington, abundantly supported by Mistress More, did all they could for both boys and Community. Into the outbuildings of the Convent they gathered as many boys from both Colleges as they could manage to withdraw from the custody of the soldiers—or who were able to withdraw themselves. Some they even "ransomed" by paying the arrears of pension demanded by the Commissaires before they would allow any boy to depart. Some fifteen or twenty, if not more, must have been lodged at the Convent, though perhaps not all at the same time. To the community imprisoned in the Flemish College "many tokens of friendship, many temporary reliefs" were smuggled through the sentries. Mistress More insisted that the ex-Jesuits, as soon as they should be released, must look upon the Convent as their home as long as occasion should require. "Such services", writes Fr Plowden, "were beyond requital: the Fathers, in the midst of their afflictions, found themselves loaded with debts of gratitude which they knew not how to discharge."

We return to the riotous scene at the Great College in the evening of 14 October. There with considerable difficulty the boys were presently manoeuvred by the soldiers into their dormitories, in the hope that they would go to bed and fall to sleep. But there was to be little sleep that night. The boys had become "untractable", writes Fr Plowden; so much so that at length Maroulx could think of no better solution than to request the help of the Jesuit prisoners. The *Comité Jesuitique* glosses over this incident. Van Volden, it says, reported on the 15th that after the departure of the Jesuits, "les écoliers . . . avoient mené un bruit et un vacarme si abominable (ce sont ses termes) qu'il n'avoit pu les contenir qu'avec l'aide des magistrats, gardes et soldats de la ville". Such a "vacarme", it is added, reflects little credit on the discipline enforced by the previous authorities of the school. No doubt it was a humiliating moment for Van Volden and Maroulx when, upon the arrival about midnight of the deposed Rector and the First Prefect, Fr Richard Morgan, peace and tranquillity were instantly restored. At all events the situation could now be surely considered saved? But no, it was far from being saved. The two Fathers returned to their prison, and at once the boys returned to their rioting. How it ended we are not told. One would have presumed that sleep at last asserted its claims upon these weary youths, although we are assured of the contrary.

Next morning his Lordship the Bishop arrived and, having reprimanded the boys for their evil ways, he proceeded with extreme embarrassment (for all his plans and assurances had gone awry) to install the Dominicans, in accordance with the orders of Prince Starhemberg. Naturally he was much mortified by this enforced commission: his circular letter, for instance, to the parents in England would now be regarded as sheer bluff on his part. But what could he do? What actually he did was to lay the blame on the ex-Jesuits. Having inducted the Dominicans he repaired at once to the Flemish College, assembled the prisoners and upbraided them severely for their misconduct. What this misconduct amounted to he did not, could not say: but they *must* have done something very evil to provoke the Government to change all his cherished plans. It did not occur to him that there had been no change of plan as far as the ex-Jesuits were concerned; that he had all along been used as a tool, and that now they needed the tool no longer. "This sickening interview", writes Fr Plowden, "was the last concern that the prisoners had with the stately prelate,

Monseigneur de Caimo, Lord Bishop of Bruges."

Of that memorable wild night of disorder the account that we have is graphic enough, but of course written from the "Olympian" point of view. What did the boys themselves think of it, at least in retrospect? It would be interesting to read some of the many letters that must have reached their parents during that September and October. At least one such letter survives,[9] written by Simon "Scroope" (Scrope) of Danby, a boy of about fourteen and apparently in Grammar. A few sentences may be given here: the date is 25 September, five days after the seizure of the Great College.

> . . . Perhaps you have not heard of our hard condition. The Society of Jesus is destroyed, and the Bull was read to all the religious on the 20th of this month. . . . A Clergyman of the town is put over us and the Fathers, but does not give us any trouble. The Fathers are not only obliged to change their habits, but are also forbid to stir out till further orders. . . . That hinders us from going out ever, for the Fathers will not let us go out unless one of them accompanies us: however, we have a good deal of play. . . . The Court desires to preserve the College, but the Fathers are resolved not to stay unless with the conditions they desire. I desire that I may remain if they do. If they depart, I hope that you will take me away, and not send me to another College before I see you. I will inform you when this affair is over.

Master Simon, it will be noticed, writes rather stiffly, in a style which doubtless he thought right and proper for his father to read with approval.

Fifteen years later, when Fr Thomas Barrow wrote his "elegant drama" recalling the first days of the Liege "Academy", the story of the *vacarme abominable* was in danger of becoming an honoured legend. But Fr Barrow knew well the facts—his last two years at school would have been at Bruges—and he was close enough to his boys to have caught something of their vicarious relish for those past achievements.

[9] J. Gerard, *Centenary Record* (1894), p. 15 note.

The *dramatis personae* of the play, as was mentioned in the previous chapter, were, all five of them, at the Great College in 1773 and evidently "in at the kill".

> *Scrope.* When on that night—our masters torn away
> By treachery unforeseen, ourselves hemmed in
> On every side, and every door and passage
> Guarded by sturdy sentinels with bayonets fixed,
> While we pursued in peace the muses' song,
> Our evening tasks—'twas like a city
> Taken by storm and given to spoil and plunder:
> And we poor wretches like abandoned slaves
> Sold to new lords.
> *Anderton.*   But we had British hearts
> And nobly scorned the yoke they would impose
> Against our freedom and our parents' orders:
> And God has crowned our labours with success.
> *Scrope.* Ha! lives then that free spirit in thy breast
> Which shone so glorious on that busy night
> And with thy Clifford led the wild uproar,
> Defying armies and uplifted weapons?
> I thought it spent and gone.
> *Anderton.*   It chills my soul
> To think what anguish rent my parents' breast
> To hear their son was made a prisoner,
> And guarded by a band of ruffian soldiers.
> *Scrope.* Nay, more: I saw two of my schoolfellows
> Led off like felons to the common jail.
> The cruel sight rekindled all my fury. . . .

On 15 October Fr Albert Underhill, O.P., took over the charge of the Great College: "a harmless youth", it appears, who from the beginning admitted his incapacity for the post and even put his frank avowal into writing in presence of the Commissaire. He deserved considerable sympathy, for his was an almost impossible task. The boys had evidently made up their minds that they were going to be taught by their former masters or by none; and in such circumstances to bring order and discipline to a cage-full of monkeys would have been a

simpler matter. For the events of the next few days the details
are scarce, although it is clear that schools or studies were out
of the question. For several days, we learn, the boys were
"dragooned by troops of armed men", and for help in emer-
gencies the authorities called in some of the "Mad Monks",
as Fr Plowden elsewhere calls them—Alexian Brothers, that is,
who looked after the local mad-house and the house of correction. "Several of the students were carried away under arms
to confinement; and one in particular" (two according to the
play?) "for having lifted his hand against a soldier, was dragged
through the streets to the public prison."

The *Procés-Verbaux* in the Brussels Archives include two
reports or letters of the Bishop, of 16 and 17 October. His
Lordship tells how on the 15th, having exhorted the boys and
installed the Dominicans, he returned that same evening,
delivered another exhortation to the recalcitrant students and
forbad them to leave their dormitories after the hour for
retiring to rest. Most of the boys had gone quietly to bed and
sleep—they needed it, no doubt at all!—although some half-
dozen older ones had paraded the "court" all night, refusing
to go to bed. Two of them he caught next morning and
punished by solitary confinement in empty school-rooms—
"car il n'est nullement question de commencer l'enseignement,
il n'est pas meme possible de les rassembler tous ensemble".
In an hour or two, however, they were released on the petition
presumably of one or more of their friends, who promised
better behaviour. That evening trouble arose again from those
same two boys—one of them Charles de Vaux of Brussels, son
of a "lieutenant du Grand Veneur", the other an Irish boy,
George or Christopher Fagan (both brothers were in Rhetoric),
who had chanced to hit the man-cook over the head, and on
arrest had been found to be harbouring in his pockets a pistol
of some kind, a large knife and a pair of pincers. This fearsome
Apache, in fact both of them, the Burgomaster, summoned to
maintain order, had confined in the College Infirmary, a
building separate from the main College: and Fr Underhill

had been ordered to report the matter to their parents. Evidently the situation could still be described as somewhat effervescent.

The Report of the *Comité Jésuitique*, after quoting these two episcopal letters, proceeds rather dejectedly to finish off that unpleasant subject. After these "wise measures" of the Bishop (it continues), order and tranquillity were re-established in the Great College. "Yet every day one learnt of fresh excesses on the part of these young men, who so far exceeded the limits of what was lawful as to make a great stack of their books and set it on fire—an example which was followed by the children in the Little College, where the contagion was already beginning to develope." The standard of "order and tranquillity" must have appreciably declined since the departure of the Jesuits. In point of fact, within a week or two the chief Commissaires, Van Volden and Massez, were dismissed, the *Procureur Général* or Attorney General of the Council of Flanders, Causmaecker by name, was sent to Bruges in place of both, and the Great College was closed. Fr Underhill returned to Louvain and the other members of his Order were drafted into the Little College.

By this time, what with withdrawals of boys by their parents, the ransoming of others by Mistress More, and successive escapes by enterprising youths from the College, there remained but forty-three in the Great College at its closing. These were distributed temporarily, until their parents made up their minds or, it may be, till they paid their accounts, among other establishments—twelve to the Little College, others to Bornhem or to the Bruges houses of the Carmelites or the Flemish Dominicans, and seven "des plus méchants" to the Alexian Brothers, the "Mad Monks" already mentioned. The closure of the College seems to have taken place early in November or perhaps late in October.

The fate of the Little College was not so sudden. There Fr Austin Noel, O.P., had been installed as Superior, as had Fr Underhill, on 15 October: and with him had come at least two others, one of them Fr Robson, who became Prefect. Of the new Superior Fr Plowden's opinion was distinctly unfavourable. We read of his "numberless extravagances" and follies which soon "filled Bruges with indignation"; but he does not descend to particulars. He should be absolved from any "odium theologicum" or sense of rivalry in this matter. He justly recognizes that the Dominicans neither asked nor wanted to come to Bruges, but had to submit to the requisition of Government. Nor could they easily spare the men for this undertaking. "Every man whom they sent upon the hopeless expedition was a loss to their own house at Bornhem, Noel alone excepted." A letter of 10 May 1774,[10] written by one of Mistress More's nuns on her behalf to an ex-Jesuit friend in Liverpool, throws some homely light on Fr Noel's domestic economy.

> Some Dominicans were on ye spot to take Mr Aston's school, which accordingly they did, but the boys could by no means be content under their jurisdiction, and I do not wonder, for they were so eaten with vermin that they poor things were in open sores: such complaints from the Children, such discontent amongst their parents that Rev. Mother and Mr Berrington were sollicitated on all sides to take 'em away, which they did, to about the number of fivety, yet not without great difficulty and trouble. . . .

We have seen that the thrilling example of a bonfire of books caught the imagination of the "children" at the Little College, with the result that they too had their bonfire. But—to conclude the story of the Little College—a certain "order and tranquillity" must have been established, since the reign of the Dominicans there lasted for a year and a little more. The gross incapacity of Fr Noel to have the care of small boys—he was Count Neny's choice for the post—at last convinced the Brussels authorities that this College too must be closed. The Bruges magistrates petitioned more than once, it seems, that the ex-Jesuits should resume their former posts; it was rumoured, too,

[10] E. P. Arch., *Letters of Non-Jesuits, 1766-1857*, f. 11.

that the Empress was beginning to think that this would be the best solution. It may be, as Fr Plowden suggests, that Brussels, utterly averse to any such arrangement, welcomed a closure that would interpose a *fait accompli* to the wishes of Her Majesty. If the "ex-Js" were excluded, the only alternative to Fr Noel's continued incompetence was to close the College, for nobody was forthcoming to take his place. The date of closure is uncertain; but probably it was either in January 1775 or slightly earlier. The number of boys had already dwindled down to "about 16". Those under fourteen were sent to a small school at Wilhours, just west of Ath: the others joined the nine from the Great College who had gone to Bornhem. There, we are told, the Bruges contingent staged another insurrection, which required the aid of the local magistrates for its suppression. It may be added that both the Bruges Colleges were sold, to cover the expenses of the Government's discredited adventure.

We return to the ex-Jesuits, prisoners in the Flemish College, of whom some eight or ten had been set free a few hours after their arrival on 14 October. Others were released within a few days; and with the arrival of Causmaecker, the Attorney General—a verbose, tedious man, with something of the mind and heart of a ferret—the remainder were soon dismissed with definite orders to quit the Austrian Netherlands without delay. But there were three exceptions. The heads of the two Colleges, Fr Angier and Fr Aston, together with the Minister, Fr Plowden, were retained as "hostages" for the payment of boys' fees and the recovery of monies and papers which (so Causmaecker wildly asserted) had been secretly conveyed to England. These three Fathers after a week or two were taken "in the disgusting company of Maroulx" to the Flemish College in Ghent, and a fortnight later were moved, at the unearthly hour of 1 a.m., to the "Black Austins of that town" —in other words to the Convent of Augustinian Friars. General Plunkett, then Governor of Antwerp, whose two sons, Francis and John, had been at the Little College, offered to be responsible for these friends of his, but his offer was flatly refused. Here then they remained at Ghent under guard until the following May—"nearly nine months" of close confinement, says Fr Plowden, as well it may have seemed, although mathematically it was somewhat less.

They were treated with kindness by the Friars, three of whom were accustomed to join them at meals. "One", wrote Fr Plowden to his brother, "is the Procureur General's spy, another rather disagreeable, and ye third (ye prior) a most honest and amiable man."[11] From time to time Mynheer Causmaecker visited them, being desperately anxious to preserve the Little College for the benefit and profit of the people of Bruges and no doubt for his own reputation as an organizer. Aware of Fr Aston's exceptional talents, he even suggested to him that he should become a Dominican and take the place of Fr Noel. He must have forgotten that one does not enter fully a religious Order by merely donning the appropriate habit! It is clear, however, that Fr Aston would have dearly loved to return to the Little College in almost any capacity. Causmaecker for his part was prepared by this time to staff the school with ex-Jesuits, provided they would accept a Flemish secular priest as Superior. That idea was unacceptable to all three. Their constant answer was that in such circumstances English parents would not send their sons to Bruges: and they proved it by the replies from England to their letters of enquiry sent at Causmaecker's request or demand. Nor of course were they blind to the fact that he needed them only as stopgaps, to be removed whenever circumstances should warrant.

During all these months, with the help of Mistress More, another correspondence, but a secret one, was carried on with their friends. Finally when all hope of securing money from Fr Williams, the Procurator in London for the two Colleges, had vanished, the three Fathers were set free, with orders "to stay in ye country no longer than is necessary to remove out

[11] C. Plowden to R. Plowden, 6 February 1774.

of it", as Fr Plowden announced to his brother Robert. So at
dawn on 25 May they joyfully set off by coach for Liège, a
two days' journey. Mistress More in a letter of 3 June[12] tells
of the reception they met with:

> All three got to Liege before ye letter arrived which was to
> give notice of their coming. The students were half mad,
> they rung ye bells, shot off canons or whatever they cou'd
> get hold of. The Gentlemen used all endeavours to quiet
> them but to no purpose. To effect it they order'd ye bell
> ropes to be cut, but ye boys ran up to ye towers & along ye
> ridges of ye houses, & made what noise they cou'd upon ye
> bells. Mr Aston says, they had not been half an hour in
> Liege before ye whole Town was acquainted of their coming.

The Jesuit Seminary or "College" at Liège, after a chequered
and usually impoverished life of some 160 years, had been
suppressed a week or two earlier than had the houses in the
Austrian Netherlands. The Prince-Bishop of this small Princi-
pality, Mgr de Velbruck, had named 9 September as the date
for executing the Brief. The procedure was similar to that
carried out at Bruges—the reading of the Brief, the compiling
of an inventory, withdrawal of priestly faculties and so on.
M. Légipont, curé of the parish, was appointed Superior. But
there were no armed soldiers inside or outside of the house, nor
were the occupants—Fathers and students of theology and of
philosophy—forbidden to leave the house, provided that they
wore the dress of a secular priest. The official formalities were
observed without any rupture of the friendly relations existing
between the Prince-Bishop and the Seminary.

It may be of interest to quote here some lines of the day-by-
day log or diary kept by the "beadle", official representative of
the students of theology.[13] Vacation that summer of 1773 had
begun on 16 August, and in the course of it the theologians and

---

[12] E. P. Arch., *Letters to Non-Jesuits, 1766-1857*, f. 13, Mistress More to
Fr R. Johnson, (Bruges, 3 June 1774).

[13] S. Arch., B. I. 8. This Beadle's Log—it is the only one that has survived
—runs from 1 October 1767, to 12 December 1775. It is in Latin.

philosophers, some two dozen in number, had gone to the Villa house at Chèvremont on the 24th. On their way back on 3 September they met the Professors who were outward bound for Chèvremont.

On our way back the Professors met us and broke the news that the Pope's decree had at last arrived whereby was suppressed and abolished for ever the Society of Jesus, our very dear Mother. Reactions varied: but on one point all were agreed, that the matter must be left to God and His Providence as the basis of our trust. And if such a decree should actually take effect, then we could do nothing more pleasing to God than resign ourselves without reserve to His supreme Will. So, torn between hope and fear, we hurry with all possible speed to the College, where we learn to our utter sorrow that the report is perfectly true.

After the formal execution of the Brief the ex-Jesuits were free to stay or leave according to their will. The Prince-Bishop's representative, Baron van der Heyden à Blisia, the Grand Chancellor, had been handed at his demand the key of the main entrance; but before departing, his unpleasant duties completed, he handed back the key to the former Rector, Fr John Howard, telling him to carry on as before until further orders. This devout man, confessor for several years to the Sepulchrine nuns whose Convent was on the Avroy in the lower part of the town, was soon granted a renewal of his faculties as confessor, provided he did not live in the College. So he moved his belongings to his nunnery, where he appears to have resided off and on for several years, coming up daily to write letters and transact what business was necessary The Abbé Légipont continued as nominal Superior of those who remained at the Seminary, but he too did not reside there: he had his own parish to attend to. Nevertheless the regular order of studies, lectures, repetitions and the rest went on more or less as before: but reading between the lines of the beadle's log one is tempted to surmise that the pace was more leisurely than in earlier days. After such an upheaval of their lives as they had just experienced, that can scarcely be matter for surprise.

When the S.J.s were turned into Ex-Js—as one of Mistress More's nuns put it—two or three of the non-priests returned to civil life—notably an uncle of the famous naturalist, namely Christopher Waterton, a master at the Little College at Bruges, who in the course of years reared a thriving family in Demerara. Some half-dozen returned to their native land in America: four novices from Ghent arrived to begin philosophy, as well as six Rhetoricians from Bruges who in other circumstances would have probably gone to Watten. The beadle's log, which is of course more interested in the ex-Jesuits than in any others, informs us that to the close of 1773 a dozen of the Bruges Communities had trickled back to Liege at various dates, in nearly every case with a few boys in their company. By the end of the year the number of boys had mounted to twenty-seven. Just three years later the total reached 133 (or 144 if a class of "lay philosophers" be included), with a considerable percentage of former Bruges boys in the higher classes. There can be no doubt as to the continuity of the Bruges Colleges in the "Liege Academy" when the latter was established.

14
THE LIEGE ACADEMY

THE situation of the Liege Seminary had certainly been well chosen. It stands well above the town, to the north or slightly north-west of it, and its long garden climbs —or at least used to climb—still higher in four terraces towards the Citadel above. In the angle formed by the steep Rue des Anglais (formerly the Rue des Jésuites Anglois) and the Rue Montagne Ste Walburge the building in Jesuit days was entered from the former street: but it meant a climb up an outside stairway of some eighty or more steps before the entrance door was reached. Nowadays the entrance to this establishment, extensively altered and transformed into a large and up-to-date hospital, is from the more level Ste Walburge side, with the climb continued to the top of the Rue des Anglais.

It seems unnecessary to describe the original house in detail, even were that practicable. In point of fact, the only pictorial representation of the house and garden is a somewhat diagrammatic engraving by Remacle Leloup illustrating the notice of the "Collège des Jésuites" by Saumery in 1738.[1] There were changes that took place since that date, possibly even before the additions made for the accommodation of the school. It will suffice to note that there was a central block facing the Rue des Jésuites Anglois, with two wings added so as to form three sides of a square. From the court thus formed one climbed a series of steps to reach the first terrace: or alternatively, on a higher level, a bridge from each wing to the terrace saved the climb from below. In the centre of this large stretch of grass stood sun-dials, the work of the well-known Fr Francis Line who a century earlier had professed mathematics and Hebrew in the seminary. Another climb to the second

[1] *Les Délices du Pais de Liège* (Liège, 1738), I, pp. 219-222.

terrace, and again by a stairway of twenty steps one gained the
third terrace—both terraces, it would appear, devoted largely
to fruit trees and vegetables. Finally one mounted to the top-
most terrace, where the students could recover their breath,
play games or otherwise disport themselves. The older Fathers
doubtless kept to the lower terraces. Thus far Dejardin,[2]
Capitaine du Genie, basing himself primarily on Saumery. But
of the subsequent additions or modifications required to meet
the needs of an Academy of between 100 and 150 boys he,
like the rest of us, knows nothing.

The Villa House, usually known as Chèvremont, is of interest.
Actually it was at Heid du Loup on the slope of Chèvremont
in the *commune* of Vaux-sous-Chèvremont. There a house and
a farm stand facing one another on either side of a road. Near
the house is a well with the date 1652 and the monogram used
by the Society. On the lintel of the entrance door of the farm
is inscribed "1688". Lord Castlemain is credited with the gift
of the Villa or the farm or of both: but neither date is suitable,
the former being too early and the latter too late. At Liège is a
legal document[3] recording the purchase of a farm (also called a
villa) "neer Chivermont" on 6 April 1678 for the sum of 1,100
patacons, or 4,400 florins of Brabant. It is vouched for by Fr
Michael Kinsman, the Procurator at Liège. The significance of
the earlier and later dates must remain unsolved.

There is no mystery about the date "1688" above the
entrance to a small chapel at the top of the hill. The seminarians,
probably after the acquisition of the Villa, had devoutly
constructed a small shrine, using stones from the ruins of an
old castle nearby. In it they placed a statue of Our Lady,
carved in terracotta. Before long the countryfolk began to
visit the shrine to make their requests to the Mother of God,
often with happy results. As these pilgrimages increased,
authorization was obtained in 1686 from the reigning Prince-
Bishop to enclose the shrine in a small chapel. Hence the

---

[2] A. Dejardin, *Notice sur le Collège des Jésuites Anglais à Liège* (Liège, 1865).
[3] Liège, Archives de l'Etat—Jésuites Anglais, pp. 288, 318-9.

pentagonal chapel, completed two years later, and below the statue a legend which derived, it may be recalled, from the very early days of St Omers—

16 S. MARIA ORA PRO ANGLIA 88

Since 1688 there have been additions to the chapel and some alterations within. Pilgrims in their thousands and tens of thousands have flocked to the little chapel. At the close of the last century the Carmelites built, not far from the chapel, their magnificent Basilica, a landmark dominating the countryside.[4] The care of the Jesuit shrine is in good hands. It may be added that when they removed to their convent the four statues that had stood in their niches perhaps from the beginning—St Hubert, patron of Liège, St Ignatius, St Francis Xavier, and "Saint Eloi", patron of the *cloutiers*, the nailsmiths who were numerous in the locality—the Carmelite Fathers presented one of them, the statue of St Ignatius, to Stonyhurst, where it has been given a position worthy of its provenance.

The Academy was formally established in mid-December 1773. What the two dozen boys did with themselves previously goes unrecorded. They seem to have made free of the house, so that their elders felt constrained to omit certain customs they had hitherto followed. Under the date Wednesday, 15 December, the Liege log records—

> Today his Highness the Prince gave public notice in the Liège Gazette that he had established in our English College an Academy in which youths of all ages would be taught a full course of subjects. On the same occasion to our great delight he named the Rev. John Howard as Director of the Academy. That this announcement might be more widely known he took steps to have it published in all the Gazettes of Holland and Germany.[5]

So from henceforth or at any rate from the new term after

---

[4] For the shrine and its history see J. Demarteau, *Notre-Dame de Chèvremont* (Liège, 3 ed., 1913); J. Brassinne, *Les Jésuites Anglais de Liège et leur Orfèvrerie* (Liège, 1948); L. Willaert, s.j., "Chèvremont" (an article in the *Stonyhurst Magazine*, VIII, 387-392 (October 1902).

[5] S. Arch., B. I. 8.

Christmas the Academy got under way, with the same boys as at Bruges for the most part and under some of their former masters. As the news spread in England that at Liège the Prince-Bishop had re-established the school which the *Comité Jésuitique* had dissolved at Bruges, the number of boys rapidly increased. An extension to the existing buildings appears to have been quickly added; for as early as the close of the following March the Prince is recorded to have paid a visit to the Academy and inspected "the House and the new buildings".

The traditions of St Omers and subsequently, with minor modifications, of Bruges were doubtless perpetuated in the Liege Academy; and the customs and traditions of Stonyhurst in its earlier days were transported directly from Liege. It is therefore of interest for more than one reason to gather what one can from this Liege or Beadle's log. The "status" of the Community for 1774-5, giving the names and occupations of each member, is informative. In October 1774 the Community numbered forty-seven, including four students in the theology course and twelve in philosophy—a large number in view of the fact that the usual financial sources of supply were no longer available. There were the normal six classes, from Rhetoric to Figures, and also a lower class, possibly two of them; for Mr Marmaduke Stone, the solitary fourth-year theologian, was "Magister Parvulorum" as well, and Mr John Nihell was the second master of the same. Fr Richard Morgan —he who with his Rector had been summoned from prison to quell the riot at Bruges—was still First Prefect, and so remained for another two years or more. Fr Aston, the former Superior of the Little College at Bruges, was at this date "Principal" of the Academy under Fr John Howard. Deterred by conservative opposition, he did not remain long at that post. The love of school-mastering, however, never left him. When the Academy migrated to Lancashire, he remained at Liège and started a small school of his own, with small success. Three years later Fr Thomas Barrow, then in Liège, wrote that Fr Aston "has one boy, named Burke, who wishes to get to

England".[6] He seems to have lived by his writing until his death in 1800.

From other entries in this log one learns that, the Society being now suppressed, all distinctively Jesuit feasts and devotions could no longer be allowed. Thus for instance the novena in March in honour of St Francis Xavier had to be omitted, and in June the feast of the Sacred Heart. That however did not hinder the Community from their annual Retreat of eight days. Nor did it prevent the "Humanists", that is to say the schoolboys, from making their annual, presumably traditional, three days of "Recollection" at the beginning of the school year. Perhaps now, and certainly in later years at the Academy, this Retreat was for the three top classes only: the rest continued with their studies. In 1774 the Quarant'Ore or Forty Hours devotion, although not of specifically Jesuit origin, was omitted, perhaps as a precautionary measure, since the Society in the past had been active in the spread of the devotion. There can be no doubt that critical, hostile eyes were watching the Prince-Bishop's every move in this affair.

Comte de Velbruck had some good reasons for this favourable treatment of ex-Jesuits, which though not unique was unusual. Whatever else may be said of him—he was a friend and to some uncharted extent a follower of the free-thinking *Philosophes* and Encyclopedists, and almost certainly a freemason (but at a period previous to any papal condemnation of that society)—he deserves the gratitude of English Jesuits for this vital deed of kindness. Although a man seldom acts from one motive alone, yet gratitude should not diminish for lack of knowing which motive predominated. Certainly the Prince-Bishop suffered no financial loss by this transaction. The house and garden were left in the possession of those who had owned it. No *pension alimentaire* was distributed as had been done at St Omers and again at Bruges. On the contrary the establishment was required to support some eight or ten priests who for the most part were past the age of any useful employment.

[6] T. Barrow to C. Wright, Liège, 24 April 1797 (S. Arch., C. II, 4c, No. 26).

And he could now pride himself on a school of his own founding, its students wearing the maroon uniform of his Court—a school showing promise of bringing in a considerable amount of foreign money to the benefit of the thrifty Liégeois. As to the additional building that was needed, "le Prince y donna sa protection et ses armes, mais il ne donna pas un Ecu".[7]

Of those eight or ten priests just referred to, three were of the French Province, exiles from France. There was also a secular priest living in the house, Thomas Phillips, an honorary Canon of Tongres, who had left the Society before his ordination. After many years as a chaplain in England and with a contentious book to his credit, *The Life of Cardinal Pole* (1764), he returned to Liege some five years later, bringing with him what is now known as the "Stonyhurst Gospel", a seventh-century Gospel of St John which had been presented to him when chaplain to one of the Earls of Lichfield. This he presented in 1769 to the Liege Library or Archives. That it was an old and valuable manuscript, beautifully written, was clear enough. But of its priceless value as the oldest surviving example of decorated English leather binding and as intimately associated by tradition with the great St Cuthbert himself—this of course was unknown either to Mr Phillips or to anyone else at that period. Mr Phillips resided at the Academy at his own expense until his death in 1774. He is said to have been negotiating for his re-entrance into the Society until in the autumn of 1773 he learnt that there was no longer any Society to enter.

A Prospectus of the Academy survives, printed in 1774 at Liège, "de l'imprimerie de J. J. Tutot, imprimeur de l'Académie".[8] The fee, we learn, was at that time 18 guineas or louis d'or per annum; hitherto it had been £25, but £20 for those in the Little College at Bruges. For that price the

---

[7] Fr Barrow's Mémoire pour l'Academie Angloise presenté à la Prefecture du Departement de L'Ourte, 1802. (S. Arch., C. IV. 2, No. 37), cf. *ibid.*, C. II, 4c, No. 20.

[8] J. Brassinne, *op. cit.*, pp. 71-73.

Academy would provide board and lodging, fires, light and "linge de table et de lit". Parents were welcome to provide all else. Alternatively the Academy would do so: for another four guineas would include washing, books, paper and pens, as well as the costs of a hair-dresser (*perruquier*) and a dancing master. Add yet another ten guineas and nearly everything else would be provided—clothes, doctor's fees and medicines. But drawing, music and fencing still remain beyond the reach of 32 guineas: such items will be added to the account. The parent, it might seem, is being led gently up the garden path. Finally, says the Prospectus, riding will be taught by experienced riding-masters. Good Fr Retz, the General of forty years ago, would surely have disapproved of so frivolous a venture, as he did in the case of Fr Constable. But now of course there was a Jesuit General no more. Fr Laurence Ricci, the ex-General, prisoner in the Castle of Sant'Angelo, was slowly and patiently dying of ill-treatment.

The Academy clearly was intent on spreading its net widely, as witness the following paragraph—

> Boys are accepted from the age of six. They are taught to read, to write, and every part of literature and philosophy; English, French, German, Latin, Greek and Hebrew; sacred and profane history; geography, arithmetic, algebra, geometry, astronomy, experimental physics and mathematics.

This seems a generous supply of learning for 18, or even for 32 guineas. The Academy must have thought so too; for we find that in the course of ten years or less the annual fee had been raised from 32 guineas to £50.[9]

Besides the seven classes at the Academy, ranging from Rhetoric to Preparatory, there was in 1776-7, as has been remarked, a "class" or set of lay philosophers, eleven in number, bringing the total of students to 144. Four of these were foreigners. Of the remainder the majority had come across

[9] See the accounts charged to Richard Bedingfeld (later 5th Baronet) for 1783-4. (C.R.S., vol. 7, 211.)

from the Great College at Bruges. William Anderton, one of the characters in Fr Barrow's play of 1788—he was then master of Figures and probably watched himself being acted by Dominic Teighe—was no doubt destined for the priesthood. He was in fact ordained at Liège in 1780 and later on from about 1799[10] till his death in 1823 was a missionary at Hereford, having joined the Society of Jesus at its restoration. But that not all intended to become priests seems clear from the presence, for example, of Charles Clifford, brother of Hugh, who in due course succeeded Hugh as sixth Lord Clifford of Chudleigh. It may be recalled that in the previous century Rhetoricians and others used to attend the lectures of the philosophy course until in 1635 the General, Vitelleschi, saw reasons for forbidding the presence of externs at the Seminary lectures. He had heard that the attendance was then in the neighbourhood of forty. But at a later period the prohibition must have been relaxed, at the insistent demand of the municipal authorities. The philosophers are now attached to the Academy side of the house, probably with special privileges in view of their ages. It was not until the middle of the First World War that the similar custom ceased at Stonyhurst.

It may be remarked too that the list of 1776-7 shows that certain boys in the school had special "prefects" assigned to them from amongst the Community not otherwise provided for. Such exceptions had been allowed, if we mistake not, for special reasons at St Omers and possibly at Bruges. Thus in 1776 a Fr Schwartz, presumably a German ex-Jesuit, had the care of a boy in Figures, Prince Aloysius Hohenlohe. So too Fr George Maxwell, of the Kirkconnell family, ex-Rector of the Scots College at Dinant, was prefect of his two nephews; Fr Edward Wright was in charge of Thomas and James Arundell, both of them in Rudiments; and there were two other such

[10] Foley, VII, 12. But see E. P. Arch., Strickland Letters: Strickland to Stone, 11 December 1799.
[11] Foley, VII, pp. l-liii.

prefects.[11] But what precisely was the function of these prefects, appointed, one presumes, at the request and expense of
the family concerned, it is not easy to determine.

Mgr Velbruck may have felt that his establishment of an
Academy staffed by members of a disbanded Order needed for
completeness and safety the sanction of an authority higher
than his own. Evidently he waited until after the death of Pope
Clement XIV in the September of 1774 and the election of a
new Pope, Pius VI, who proved to be friendly towards the
suppressed Society. There was not much that Pius VI could do
in face of the Bourbon opposition. To attempt at present the
restoration of the Society would have been politically disastrous; but what little he could do he did. At the Prince-
Bishop's request he issued a Brief, *Catholici Praesules* (15
September 1778), whereby he gave his approval to all that the
Prince had done. He placed under his authority this part-
Seminary, part-School, which he styles "a new kind of establishment, an offshoot, as it were, of the original missionary
seminary". The Director was to be elected by the chief
members of the staff; and the Director in his turn must select
his officials from the members of the ex-Jesuit Community. In
both cases the reigning Prince-Bishop's approbation must be
obtained. So all was well and Mgr Velbruck's scruples, if he
had any, were set at rest.

Five years later in the October of 1783 died the "Director",
better known as the President of the Academy, Fr John
Howard. He had held a difficult post when, after having for
five years been Rector of a religious Community, he became
President of a house staffed by ex-Jesuits, that is to say by
secular priests, bound to him by no vows of obedience but
continuing at their often wearisome work of professing or
teaching for as long as the spirit moved them to do so. If one
may judge from some of the letters written privately by Fr
Charles Plowden to his brother, or from the comments made
by Fr Strickland when he arrived at the Academy, it would
appear that some irregularities had begun to creep in, that

masters and prefects were not always at their appointed posts, that in general there was need for stricter discipline. Yet on the whole it is to their credit that they carried on as loyally as they did, buoyed up by the firm hope of a resurrection, if not of the Society, at all events of themselves in heaven.

It was the opinion of Fr Charles Plowden—and Dr Oliver has echoed it—that Fr Howard spent more time at the Convent than was compatible with his duties as Director of the Academy. At the Convent on the Avroy he was looked upon as a saint; and without doubt he was a wise and most saintly director of souls. Although latterly he lived in the Academy, he had always a room in the outquarters of the Convent. It was there that he fell ill and died. "On the morning of his death he said to his attendants, 'Lift me up that I may once more see my angels go to Matins'." Two days later, in the presence of the Community and boys of the Academy, his angels buried him on the right side of their high altar. After the fashion of those times a lengthy tablet of some 150 words recorded his many virtues. He had been their spiritual director for twenty years: "Penetrated with Grief and Gratitude, his spiritual children erected this Monument to the Memory of the Best of Fathers."[12]

As confessor and spiritual director of the nuns Fr Howard was succeeded by Fr Francis Clifton—his real name was Fanning—hitherto the Prefect of Studies at the Academy. For the time being he also became Vice-President. But an entry in the contemporary Prefect of Studies' Diary at the beginning of 1784 places Fr William Strickland as "Director" and in his absence, as Vice-Director, Fr Thomas Ellerker, professor of theology. Though he may perhaps have paid a brief visit at that time to Liege, many months elapsed before Fr Strickland arrived to take actual charge of the school.

We must here turn for a moment to England at the suppression of the Society. It is well known that Fr Thomas More, the late Provincial, was appointed by the kindly Bishop

Challoner to be Vicar General of his former subjects. The fourteen "Districts" of the English Province, each with its local Superior, had been severally more or less endowed with funds; and, as the Vicars Apostolic informed the ex-Jesuits, such property and funds remained theirs, their use limited of course to their original purpose, the benefit of the English mission. There had been in addition a more general fund, administered by the Procurator of the Province. Fr More, a most self-effacing man, did little or nothing to solve the many problems that arose in consequence of the suppression until in 1776 he was at length persuaded to summon a Congress of representatives of each District, which met that April in London and agreed upon some at least of the matters, largely financial, that needed a solution.

What concerns us here however is a second similar Congress[13] summoned to meet at the Queens Head Tavern in Holborn in the July of 1784—four years after the Gordon Riots. Fr Strickland was again present, not, as previously, the representative or agent of Northumberland, but as representing Liege, both seminary and Academy. Liege was financially in dire distress; the Community, or some of it, was physically tired and jaded, mentally or morally dispirited. There was considerable need, if this establishment was to continue, for a strong and vigorous President who would bring with him fresh inspiration and restore a more fruitful sense of purpose.

The assembly decided that for the management of the central fund—"Office", it was called—One Administrator would be of more practical use than a Board of two. The choice however was difficult. Father More declined the offer and there were objections to others proposed. Fr Strickland suddenly rose and surprisingly offered his services. Was he thereby abandoning Liege and its Presidency to which he had legally been elected? Not at all: he was willing to act in both capacities, and was quickly voted Administrator, with £150

---

[13] A report of the two Congresses drawn up by Fr Jos. Reeve, the secretary at both meetings, is in E. P. Arch., Miscellaneous Documents, 1763-1829.

a year for expenses. Presently was discussed the subject of Liege, the only remaining continental house that shared the fortunes of the English ex-Jesuits. The Academy, admittedly the heir of the Bruges Colleges, and no less the Seminary side of the house were finally voted to be of use to the ex-J missions in England. The Academy must be encouraged and supported: a subscription must be raised for the founding of free places for the education of ecclesiastics. Although the sum subscribed is unknown, one may presume that one or more free places were in fact established at the Academy for this purpose.

Before the Congress ended it was resolved "that a coalition and connexion of direction on one hand and of dependence on the other be formed between the Mission and the Academy". On the strength of that it was decided that the office of President of the Academy and that of Director of the nuns were incompatible; and Fr Strickland was requested to draw up a code of rules for the internal government of the house and to place it on such a foundation as might best answer the purpose of its existence. There survives a manuscript code of rules, dated 1788; but it is evidently designed rather for the seminarians than for the young "convictors" of the Academy.

Fr Strickland was formally installed as President, so it would appear, at the beginning of the school year of 1784-5,[14] which was still 1 October as in former days. Three years later he changed it to 15 September, but without shortening the month's vacation. Heir to the Sizergh estates in Westmorland which he renounced in favour of his brother, he worked in England, mostly at Alnwick, where he was missioner from the June of 1770 until early in 1784. He it was who later took the leading part in securing the aggregation in 1803 of the English ex-Jesuits to the Society still existing in White Russia. Indeed, as the General, Fr Gruber, wrote to him from Russia,[15] he would have been appointed Provincial rather than Fr Marma-

---

[14] S. Arch., B. 1. 7, Prefect of Studies Journal, 1778-1805.
[15] E. P. Arch., Strickland Letters: Gruber to Strickland, 1 March 1803 (N.S.).

duke Stone, were it not that age, health and a certain reluctance on his part were against such a choice. A practical, common-sensical, determined sort of man he was, as his many letters demonstrate, always ready to translate his ideas into deeds, but humble enough to accept advice which he considered good advice. As Administrator of the general finances of the ex-Province and later as Procurator of the resuscitated Province almost until his death at the age of eight-eight, he has not always received the recognition due to his many and varied services.

Being Administrator as well as President of the Academy, Fr Strickland divided his time between Liege and London. Every year he spent some months in England: but he had the satisfaction of being able to leave the Academy during his absences in the capable hands of Fr Charles Wright, the Procurator of the Academy. Fr Wright was a priest some twenty years younger than the President, of a disposition and calibre not unlike that of Fr Strickland. But after five years one finds with some surprise that for the school year 1789-90 Fr Wright's place as substitute for the President had been taken by Fr Marmaduke Stone, now listed as Vice-President and previously as the second of four Prefects. A good choice it turned out to be, even though he lacked some of the qualities one might look for in a President. Fortunately for the Academy, Fr Wright continued there his successful work as Procurator —a post which he held at Liege and at Stonyhurst for nearly forty years.

Some of the Liege customs, many of them transported later to Stonyhurst, can be gathered from a Prefect of Studies' Journal (1778-1805), written mainly in English except for a year or two when Fr Barrow preferred to write in Latin. The annual Retreat of three days at the beginning of the school year, confined however to the "higher schools", has already been recorded. On the first day of term the class lists were read out, after which ceremony Mass of the Holy Ghost was sung, with the hymn *Veni Creator*. Periodically, shortly after the

several "Compositions" had taken place, names were again
read out—the names of the "Six First" in each class, who were
in due course rewarded by a day's outing at the Villa at
Chèvremont. Contrariwise, on the eve of the four vacations
during the year—"Vacancies" they were termed—the names
of those who had deserved a "Second Exam" were read in
public. No doubt a special programme of studies was arranged
for at least part of the ensuing vacation to enable such to make
up for wasted time and too great economy of labour. The
Journal recorded on 23 December 1790, "At night no scholar
was condemned to the 2nd Examen—for the first time". The
term "Second Exam" will not be unfamiliar to an older
generation of Stonyhurst men.

The Christmas "Vacancy" was short—from Christmas Eve
to the end of the year. But as 1 January was a High Mass day
and a holiday was usually granted on the day following, the
vacation lasted normally for ten days. At Easter there was a
fortnight's holiday, ending on Low Sunday; at Pentecost a
week. The "Great Vacancy' lasted a month; on the eve there
were "schools till 8½ [8.30 p.m.] after which were sung Our
Ladies Litanies and the Te Deum in Music". That all these
vacations be spent at the Academy or on occasion at Chèvremont was still the rule—to which exceptions were doubtless
made in special circumstances, as they had been made even in
the days of Fr Sabran. In addition there were the usual
"Carnival Days" at Shrovetide. A "Monthly Recreation" is
regularly noted in the Journal: but the "Blandyke or St
Joseph's Day" is an additional holiday in the summer months
from April to September. On the whole the boys seem well
treated in this respect, if we take account of the period in
which they lived.

There are several references in the Journal to "Academical
Exercises"—a comprehensive term which included both the
customary Academies of the top classes, designed to exhibit
turn by turn the classical attainments of these "schools", and
also the plays performed at the end of the school year or on

other particular occasions. Where the play is actually mentioned by name, it is no longer a Latin but an English play. Fr Barrow's "elegant drama" in 1788, already mentioned, was followed in August 1789 by "The Faithful Friends". Next year there was an "Exhibition"—the death of Nicaeus and Euryalus; on another occasion a "drama on the Siege of Gibraltar". But for the most part these plays are merely referred to as "Academical Exercises", staged at times in honour of some distinguished guest.

As one turns over the pages of this Journal the eye is caught here and there by some odd and often unrelated item which the Prefects of Studies thought fit to record. For instance, although after the suppression all distinctive Jesuit feasts and devotions were banned by Fr Howard, yet one finds that by 1783 the feast of St Ignatius was being kept publicly and solemnly with High Mass and Solemn Vespers. This can have been no flaunting of authority: the first fervour of the suppression was going the way of all flesh. For in 1791 the same solemn feast was graced by the presence of the Pope's Nuncio who "officiated Pontifically". Other feasts, such as those of the Sacred Heart and of St Aloysius, were similarly kept. Always a Latin sermon was pronounced, apparently in the afternoon, in honour of St Aloysius. The speaker is usually named, sometimes a lay philosopher, more commonly a Rhetorician.

This is a tradition that was continued at Stonyhurst, the more naturally in that St Aloysius is the patron saint of the College. At what date St Thomas of Canterbury retired in favour of St Aloysius is unknown. In the Beadle's log under date of 29 December 1773 is entered "Festum S. Thomae, Academiae Patroni". The customary panegyric of St Aloysius, as recorded yearly in the Prefect of Studies' Journal, offers no conclusive evidence, for St Thomas' feast occurs during the Christmas vacation and the Journal skips all the vacations until after the migration to Lancashire. There, during the school year 1802-3, a sermon was preached on *both* feasts—the "usual

sermon" on St Thomas' feast, preached by the master of
Figures (Mr Pugh) in the chapel, and on 21 June, "Festum
Angelici Aloysii Studiosae Juventuti Patroni", a panegyric
"as usual", delivered by Robert Newsham, a Rhetorician.
This again is not conclusive, though we seem to be getting
warm on the track. St Omers College was the proud possessor
of two patron saints, St Augustine of Canterbury being only
secondary to St Thomas. Has St Aloysius perhaps become the
secondary patron?

There is now a gap in the records until September 1817,
when the "Minister's Journal" commenced. About six months
later (on 5 April, to be exact) Fr Stone, the recent Rector of the
College, became Minister: for the first few years this Journal
is concerned largely but not exclusively with what the boys
were given to eat. There is henceforth no reference to a sermon
on the feast of St Thomas; on the contrary in 1817-18, "the
vacation being shortened, the day was kept as a common
recreation day". On 21 June a panegyric is not mentioned,
though we learn that there was roast beef and potatoes for
dinner, followed by a tart of some kind, gooseberry with
luck, otherwise probably rhubarb—simple fare, of course, but
let us hope ample. A year later we are rewarded. "There being
no Rhetoric this year, there was no panegyric in honour of the
Saint". One may surmise that St Thomas was quietly dropped
in favour of St Aloysius at some date between 1802 and 1818.

We have wandered far and at a tangent from Liege and the
Prefect of Studies' Journal. The name of Jean Pierre Blanchard
may be familiar to many, for he it was who in the company of
an American, Dr Jeffries, first crossed the English Channel
from Dover in a balloon. That was early in 1785. Nearly two
years later Blanchard must have been in Liège; for our Journal
records on 18 December 1786 that the boys were very considerably distracted from their studies by the sight of Blanchard's balloon ("aerostatica Blandchardi machina", in Fr
Barrow's best Latin) and its projected ascent, which however
did not come off. It may be that it was on the top of the hill

Z

above the Academy that the balloon was inflated and thus became visible from the windows of the school, to the delight of the wandering, observant eyes of youth. There is little that a boy will miss unless it be his lessons.

Le Vicomte Walsh (Joseph Alexis Walsh) wrote his memories of the Liege Academy from a distance of fifty years.[16] He has frequently been quoted as a reliable authority, but it must be admitted that imagination has at times played havoc with his memory. Distance has lent enchantment to his view. He entered the Academy in September 1792 at the age, he tells us, of eight—or more accurately at the age of nearly ten and a half[17]—to join a school of "over 400 pupils". One can check this wild statement with a dozen lists of boys at Liege, most of them contained in the above Prefect of Studies' Journal and ranging from 1776 to 1790. If the few lay philosophers be excluded, the number varied from a maximum of 133 to a minimum of 83: the usual total was between 100 and 110 or thereabouts. As for the lay philosophers, they were never more than twelve and generally far fewer.

Fr Strickland returned from one of his sojourns in England in the May of 1790. By the following September he evidently had resigned, for we find the Vice-President, Fr Stone, listed as President. Twenty-seven years of Presidency he had ahead of him before he was relieved of office. A man in his early forties, he had been since his ordination in 1775 a master of Elements and later a Prefect. As may be surmised, he could not lay claim—nor did he—to any great scholastic attainments nor to unusual administrative ability such as his predecessor possessed. But he had a big heart, embedded, so to speak, in a big body. He was pre-eminently a man of prayer, and his evenness of temper, his capacity as a peace-maker or peace-preserver, his outstanding sincerity and singleness of aim were

[16] *Souvenirs de Cinquante Ans*, I, pp. 78 seqq.
[17] He was born on 25 April 1782 (*ibid.*, p. 13), entered the Academy on 15 September 1792, and completed his school days at Stonyhurst, leaving on 6 January 1799.

more important qualities at this period of the school. He had
his faults of course, like other men. But if, as often happened,
he found it difficult to make a decision—and there were many
occasions to come that called for decisive action—his subordinate, Fr Wright, was always capable and ready to make up
his own mind and Fr Stone's as well. Fr Wright, a member of
the Kelvedon banking family, inherited his father's shrewd
business instincts. He possessed many of the virtues of a
successful gentleman farmer. Some of his colleagues at Liege
and later at Stonyhurst considered him a somewhat ruthless
Philistine: and quite certainly he was no aesthete. But he kept
the Academy on its financial feet, and managed to repeat the
miracle with even greater success at Stonyhurst.

Even before Fr Marmaduke Stone's first entry into office
thunder-clouds had burst over the city. The French Revolution,
it will be recalled, had followed the summoning of the States
General in the May of 1789; and in July the populace of Paris
had taken matters into their own hands and stormed the
Bastille. A month later, on 17 August, rioting broke out in
Liège. A section of the citizens, in sympathy with the prevalent
revolutionary ideas, captured the Citadel which almost overshadowed the Academy just below, and took over the government of the city. The summer residence at Seraing of the
Prince-Bishop was invaded and Mgr de Hoensbroeck was
brought to Liège and placed under house arrest in his episcopal
palace. Eventually he escaped to the abbey of St Maximin at
Trèves.[18]

For nearly a year and a half the city was in the hands of the
"Patriots". It does not appear that the Academy was seriously
affected, although a number of requisitions, small but vexatious,
was made. The Canonesses of the Holy Sepulchre (now at New
Hall) were less fortunate. For a few days down below on the

[18] This and what follows to the end of the next chapter is mainly derived
from Fr John Laurenson's MS. account (84 pp.) of the events preceding and
during the migration from Liege Academy to Stonhurst (S. Arch., A. III,
22). It was finished at Brough Hall, where he was chaplain, in 1828.

Avroy they had soldiers quartered in their Convent: and among other exactions that well-known gambit of a "patriotic gift", demanded of all ecclesiastical establishments and assessed at a quarter of the annual revenue derived from landed property, cost them 1,000 florins, the nominal equivalent of about £100. As the Academy (so we read) had "little or no landed property in the country", it suffered little or nothing.

At the Villa house at Chèvremont, however, there occurred a small but unpleasant incident. Such of the Community as could be spared had gone there for a rest during the short holidays at Whitsuntide. Early on Whitsunday morning, writes Fr John Laurenson, they were aroused by a "lawless, drunken herd of Cloutiers" or nailsmiths from the neighbouring village of Vaux, who demanded admittance and refreshment. Meeting with a double refusal they threatened to force an entrance. As the only available weapons of defence were "the kitchen utensils and a few empty bottles", the inmates had recourse to soft words and a few pieces of money passed through the shutter of the entrance door. The besiegers, though discontented, were unable to agree, it seems, to implement their brave words. At all events they contented themselves with firing off a gun or two and damaging some panels of the door before departing. It was not a pleasant beginning of a holiday.

On 12 January 1791, an Imperial force entered Liège from one side whilst the revolutionary Patriots discreetly retired at the other end of the city. A solemn Te Deum was sung in the Cathedral and there was general rejoicing. A month later returning from exile, His Highness the Prince made his solemn entrance, welcomed by the guns of the Citadel and innumerable church bells. On the following Sunday, noted the Prefect of Studies, "Most Splendid illuminations over the whole town for the Prince's return". There could have been few better views over the town than from the windows of the Academy. On 14 April "His Highness paid a Visit to the Academy and was complimented by the scholars after his return. He granted 3 Recreations." The first of these holidays was celebrated next day, the eve of the "Easter Vacancies", perhaps marred for a few in the evening when the names of the "Second Examiners" were read out.

For the best part of two years Liège remained secure and peaceful. But of course the news from France was alarming. Early in 1792 Austria and Prussia entered into an alliance against France, and in April France declared war on Austria. During that September news would have come of the "September Massacres", which has added 191 beatified martyrs to the Church's Roll of Honour, including 23 French ex-Jesuits. On 5 December began the trial of King Louis XVI; but by that time Liège was again preoccupied with its own troubles. French armies had invaded the Netherlands: the victory at Jemappes (6 November) left the country open to the revolutionary troops. Brussels was occupied by General Dumouriez on the 14th, and by the 26th he was at the village of Waroux, only a few miles west of Liège. On the following night the Austrians, defeated in battle, effected their retreat across the Meuse and Dumouriez entered Liège on the 28th. For some three months the city remained in French occupation until the first week of the following March.

On the evening of the French entry a detachment of soldiers was billeted on the College. The Procurator, Fr Wright, acting, no doubt, on behalf of the President, assigned to them the playrooms on the ground floor as their quarters. The officer in charge demanded better accommodation upstairs. "No, there are no beds unoccupied", was the reply. "Well, let them take a turn at sleeping on the floor", said the angry officer and made for the stairs, only to find Fr Wright stoutly defending the bottom step. The officer turned feebly away. "Bravo", said he, whether sincerely or in mockery one does not know. He did not fare badly by his acquiescence. Beds and bedding were somehow procured and a plentiful supply of provisions. Indeed such happy, noisy sounds proceeded presently from the playrooms that an old Scottish Father, Sir Alexander Strachan, who was ending his days at the Academy,

issued in alarm from his room upstairs, clad far too scantily for
the season, and caught his death of cold—not quite literally
since his illness continued for another twelve months. Next
day the billet was removed elsewhere.

In these troubled times Liège had been a popular rendezvous
for French émigré families, flying from the wrath of the Paris
mob; but with the threat of French occupation most of them
had sought refuge further east. The British however had
mostly remained, since as yet England and France were at
peace. Dumouriez was moderate and sympathetic (in another
four months he deserted to the Austrian side): his second-in-
command, General Dampierre, showed himself quite friendly
to the English residents. Very soon there called at the Academy
Philip Devaux, an "old boy" of the Academy—he had left in
1778—now aide-de-camp to Dumouriez. It was not an official
but a personal visit, and not a very welcome one at that. He
seemed civil and friendly, says Fr Laurenson, but showed
himself in conversation "so thorough-paced a revolutionist
that we did not venture to give him our confidence". This
same young man was dispatched some while later by
Dumouriez to Paris, to announce further gains by the French
army. Being a Count, he was promptly guillotined—a warning
which Dumouriez himself would no doubt have taken to
heart.

For three months Liège was a city of confusion. What
with the excesses of the army of occupation, fully supported
by the Patriots who of course had now returned, one could
but live from day to day in dread of what might happen. Most
of the churches were turned into stables or store-houses or
barracks. From the windows of the Academy could be seen
one day in the Convent garden of the Poor Clares near by a
body of sansculottes at shooting practice, the target being a
statue of our Lady strung up by the neck to a convenient tree.
Nor did matters improve when on 1 February (1793) France
declared war on England.

Ten days earlier Louis XVI had been executed. The news

reached the Academy whilst the boys were at football. One of the boys, son of Comte d'Argenteau, heard it from his parents who had called to see him. Returning to the playground almost in tears, he was soon surrounded by some of his French and Belgian friends to whom he broke the news. Sobs, groans and execrations filled the air, writes Vicomte Walsh. Their nerves were on edge and there was clear need for sympathy and kind words. Other boys had by now joined the crowd: and an English boy used the occasion to remark that this was not the first time that royal heads had been cut off, that the English too in times past had known the best way of punishing a tyrant. If his politics were unpopular, his manners were more so. The tactless ass was rescued by the Prefect, at least for the time being, from being mauled as he deserved. In the boys' Chapel next morning was celebrated a Requiem Mass and the famous preacher, Père Beauregard, at that time resident in the Academy, delivered a fine panegyric on the "royal martyr".[19]

Presently the troops under Prince Saxe-Coburg, now reinforced, attacked with success. On 5 March 1793 the French retired from Liège and the Imperialists marched in. By the end of July the French appeared to have lost all Belgium. Would they ever return? The odds seemed to be against such a calamity; but by the beginning of 1794 Fr Clifton, successor of Fr Howard as Director of the Sepulchrine nuns, was convinced that they would. Not only did he convince himself, but his oracular prophecies of woe, a subject of mirth for most of his colleagues, carried conviction to the nuns whom he directed.

By his advice—excellent advice, as it turned out—the Mother Superior arranged for a couple of large barges to be at her disposal when need should arise. A house in Maastricht was rented on a three-months' lease, renewable at will; and after much difficulty leave was obtained from the Prince-Bishop, Comte de Mean, to transfer to Maastricht their more valuable belongings, such as their foundation deeds, their

[19] Vicomte Walsh, *op. cit.*, I, 80-81.

Registers and their church plate. Mgr de Mean had stipulated that all this should be done secretly, lest the townspeople should take alarm; but of course their precautions became known and talked about. Such a clamour arose that the permission of the Prince was withdrawn. Still, by the end of January 1794 the nuns were to a great extent prepared for the worst. The same cannot be said of the authorities at the English Academy.

Early in May the French forces, now thoroughly reorganized, again entered Belgium. General Jourdan invested Charleroi and placed his army between the Allies and Liège. Liège was in peril and there was consternation in the city. The Prince-Bishop sent for Fr Stone, explained that the city could not be defended and authorized him to take what precautions he might judge best.

Common prudence demanded that some action should be taken, for England and France were now actively at war. It was decided to send home such boys as lived not far away. The rest were marched off in groups to a large house in Wijk (now a suburb of Maastricht) which Fr Wright had been able to rent for the purpose. After about a week, the news being more cheerful, they all returned hopefully to Liège. Not so the English nuns who also had migrated to Maastricht, to the house they had so providently rented in the previous January. Less optimistic than the Academy authorities, they applied for passports to enable them to travel through Holland: and five weeks later, on 8 July, they resumed their journey in coal-barges from Maastricht, to reach Rotterdam eventually on the 22nd.

It is unfortunate that the surviving Prefect of Studies' Journal breaks off abruptly at the end of April. We learn, however, from Fr Laurenson's account that the Academy did not just passively await whatever turn events might take. The Prefect of Studies, Fr Herman Kemper, a Westphalian by birth, travelled as far as Munich in search of some temporary retreat from the threatening storm. He returned without success. Fr Wright is described as wearing himself out in the business of settling accounts, not only for the Academy but also for various English families in town. The most valuable books of the Library were packed up and sent by water to Wijk; but the cases were so large and heavy, writes Fr Laurenson who was the Librarian, that it was only with great difficulty they could be moved at all. A quarrel at Wijk between the College servants and the licensed wharfingers who claimed the exclusive right of handling the goods was settled favourably for the Librarian after appeal to the local magistrates. We shall see presently that these cases had to be left behind when the final exodus took place.

"The political welkin", one reads, "became now daily more and more overcast and lowering." The decisive victory of Jourdan at Fleurus (26 June) settled the fate of the Netherlands. The inhuman decree of the previous 26th of May passed by the French Convention, that no quarter should henceforth be given to any English soldier, had indeed been indignantly rejected by the soldiers of General Jourdan;[20] but the news of it can have done nothing at Liège to brighten the "political welkin". Brussels was once again occupied on 12 July, and already the countryside was thick with fugitives. As has been noted, the English nuns had fled from Maastricht on the 8th. Jourdan was slowly advancing eastwards—actually he reached Liège on 27 July. Mgr de Mean, last of the Prince-Bishops of Liège, had already packed up (so to speak): his archives and valuables were gone, he himself was only waiting for the General, the Prince of Würtemberg, to give the word. It was high time for the Academy to quit.

[20] Stanhope, *Life of Pitt*, II, 234.

15

MIGRATION TO STONYHURST

ABOUT a fortnight before Liège was occupied by the French, the Academy prudently decided to take active emergency measures for its safety. Early on Monday, 14 July, the Procurator's only horse and cart began to convey luggage to the waterside below the Pont-des-Arches, where lay in readiness some barges purchased a few weeks earlier. It was admittedly a slow procedure, but no additional conveyance could be had for love or money. One gathers that other goods and chattels, in addition to the books already mentioned, had by this date been housed at Wijk: but much still remained at the Academy. This Monday morning was not a lucky morning for Fr Wright. One or two journeys to and fro, and horse and cart were commandeered by the army authorities who also were preparing to retreat. Here an "old boy" of the Academy, "young Mr O'Shee",[1] aide-de-camp to the Prince of Würtemberg, came to the rescue and kindly intervened. Twice again during that morning the cart was requisitioned but each time the aide-de-camp put matters right. Such interruptions, however, must have considerably curtailed the morning's work.

After an early dinner Community and boys went down to the Quai de la Batte where lay the barges already loaded. The season was unusually dry and the water unusually low: the barges had been so heavily laden that they were lying immovable in the mud. Here then was another hitch. Some of the baggage had to be taken out—enough to set the barges

---

[1] Probably John O'Shee (1786-1790), whose two other brothers were at the Academy. Most of the O'Shees were on the French side, including John's uncle, General Richard O'Shee of the Irish Brigade. Cf. Mr Richard Hayes' "Biographical Dictionary of Irishmen in France", in *Studies*, 1945, pp. 529 seqq. But Mr Hayes kindly informs me that John became a Colonel in the Austrian army.

afloat—and piled up on the quay. With the help of the town crier an improvised auction sale (for ready money) was held, the management of which was left in the hands of the College bailiff. The proceeds of the sale are said to have been quite considerable. One reads of no remonstrances: to any possible outcry of the kind the Procurator's customary answer would doubtless have been forthcoming—"Stuff and nonsense; we need the money"—and the President would have concurred.

So with buoyant barges if not with buoyant hearts they set sail down the Meuse and reached Maastricht in the evening. There the travellers distributed themselves, some going to the house at Wijk, the others to the house on the other side of the river, recently evacuated by the English nuns, but of which the lease had not yet expired. The nuns had kindly placed this house at the Academy's disposal. And there at Maastricht for some unexplained reason the party delayed for the space of nine days. If this stay was premeditated, as it seems to have been (although just possibly it was not), it is difficult to understand the need for the hurried auction of part of the College effects on the quayside at Liège.

Fr Charles Plowden took no part in this migration. As chaplain to Mr Weld of Lulworth he had accompanied him during the previous year to Lièege, and when Mr Weld had left Liège with three of his schoolboy sons at the close of May 1794 Fr Plowden returned with them to Lulworth. But it is only honest to note that in later years he was severely critical of the manner in which the Academy had been evacuated. In an undated note which has survived[2] he comments scathingly— he was always a plain speaker—on the way in which during some thirty or forty years the College at Liège with its once ornate, well-kept gardens had been neglected, its amenities destroyed. As for Fr Wright, he blames him, rightly or wrongly, for "having defaced the bowling green, turned St Joseph's [a building in the garden] into a stinking cow-shed, and reduced the rest of the garden to a waste . . .". He con-

[2] S. Arch., MS. A. II. 29, No. 17.

tinues: "I say nothing of his disposal of the library, the mathematical room, the church plate, and Fr Wright the Martyr's body, all which at a moderate expense and with some care might have been brought to Stonyhurst". The President, Fr Stone, one notices, is not mentioned in this outburst. As we know not what defence the Procurator would have made, we must leave the matter there. This at least seems plain that the English nuns under the leadership of their Director, "the Prophet Clifton" as he was now sometimes called, were more provident in their preparations than were the authorities of the English Academy.

As day followed day at their lodgings in Maastricht, evidence was piling up of the danger of delay. Successive bodies of the defeated Austrian army were passing eastwards through the city and supplying the latest news of the French advance. Still the travellers hesitated to resume their journey. They must have been waiting, Micawber-like, for something to turn up that would allow them to return to their beloved home as they had done a couple of months previously. At last on the morning of the tenth day, 23 July, only four days, as it chanced, before the French entry into Liège, definite information reached them that a more speedy retreat had been ordered and that in pursuance of that order a pontoon was that very day to be thrown across the river below the Bois-le-Duc gate. Obviously escape by water would become impossible once the pontoon was in position. Again therefore at the last possible moment there was a hurried scramble for safety. The story goes, possibly mythical, that Fr Stone, anxious to save what he could, hurriedly put into his pocket what was nearest to hand, which chanced to be a few pepper castors.

Contenting ourselves with what effects were necessary and indeed with what we found afterwards to be far less than necessary, and leaving all the rest at our house in Wijk, as we thought from the strength of the works in perfect security, we immediately ordered our boats to proceed to the north of the Bois-le-Duc gate, and after a hasty meal we all went on board. We had not long been there, when we were eye-witnesses of the closing of the pontoon bridge, which had threatened to cut off our retreat. Having thanked heaven for our escape, and nothing now occurring to detain us, we began our voyage about 2 o'clock, and made the best of our way down the Meuse. The fineness of the weather, the variety of successive objects on both sides of the river, and the novelty of our situation afforded us some relief and consolation in the distress of our departure.[3]

So the journey began. Nowhere are we told the number of those who were members of the party. During these last few years, if one may judge from an old Liege ledger book, the flow of boys from England had very understandably decreased, their places being supplied in part by others from Belgium or France. Many too had left during the last few dangerous months: and some, it may well be, did not join the party, preferring to make their own arrangements. We are not even told the number of barges that were needed. If we put the total of travellers at forty or fifty we are but making a venturesome guess.

The journey down the Meuse to Rotterdam occupied eight days. After a day or two the weather, hitherto mild and genial, became "chilly, bleak and unhealthful"—the after-effects of a violent storm. Though the barges were provided with awnings, they were rather of the nature of parasols than of *parapluies*. Provisions too were bleak and scanty: but they hoped to increase and improve their rations at the first available opportunity. When however at night-fall they reached the little village of Stevensweart and landed in search of food, they drew an utter blank: there was nothing the villagers were prepared to sell. Hence Fr Laurenson's disgruntled description of Stevensweart as "a wretched village in a wretched country where nothing could be purchased for love or money". He sounds retrospectively hungry and ill-treated!

Earlier that afternoon they had passed Maeseyck (birthplace

[3] Fr John Laurenson, pp. 53-54.

of the brothers Van Eyck) some twenty miles from Maastricht. Near this little town was situated a "palace" which had once belonged to the Prince-Bishop, Mgr de Velbruck. According to Fr Laurenson, he had offered it in 1773 to the suppressed Jesuits as an alternative to the Academy at Liège: according to Fr Stone it was the later Prince-Bishop, Comte de Mean, who generously offered it in 1794 "if we chose to retire thither". It is of course possible that both of these offers were made at these different dates.

It was at Maeseyck too that a former Liege Academy boy, Matthew Toole—he had left from Philosophy in 1783—overtook the barges. He had come to say good-bye and was riding a horse bought from Fr Wright—was this the horse (without the cart) already mentioned which was so persistently commandeered by the Austrian military? "This interesting young man" rode along the bank for a while, engaged in conversation with his old masters who had a high opinion of his merits. Then he disappears from view, probably in flight also from the oncoming French.

At Venlo which they reached the following evening, they found they had overtaken the Comte d'Agrain, father of yet another of their "old boys", Marc d'Agrain (1786-1788). The meeting was providential, for by this time one of the barges was leaking badly, and indeed soon became unserviceable. The Count very kindly offered to share his boat with them: he too was on the run. So until they got to Dordrecht (Dort) which is about a dozen miles from Rotterdam, the two parties travelled together. At Venlo there was better fortune than was found at Stevensweart: a store of provisions was bought, to supplement the meagre and monotonous fare they had brought with them from Maastricht. It did. We learn, not without due sympathy, that some of the provisions were wasted: the fresh stock included a quantity of meat which was far from fresh, though this fact seems to have passed unobserved by the cook or even by the consumers. The inevitable result was distressing; for to the "bleak and unhealthful" weather were now added bleak and quite unhealthful stomachs. "Many of us", writes Fr Laurenson discreetly, "were reduced to the same condition as that of our heroic ancestors before the battle of Agincourt, and from the same cause." Let us leave it at that.

By the evening of the 25th they were at Grave, a small town some few miles south-west of Nijmegen. Here

> we met with great difficulties, from not having had the precaution to procure passports through Holland. The magistrates at first were very resolute in opposing our further progress, but were at length prevailed on to allow us to proceed: so that luckily we purchased at a cheap rate the lesson of prudence, which we might and ought to have learned cost free from our good countrywomen the Nuns.

Not yet were they at the end of their troubles. The next evening, Saturday evening, they were at the island fortress of St Andries, near the junction of the Meuse and the Waal. Wind and weather, with the increasing roughness of the broadening river, made it now imperative to exchange their fresh-water barges for some more substantial craft. A contract therefore was made with a local Dutch Jew—the place was full of them —for the hire of a larger vessel to convey them the rest of their journey. Alas, Fr Wright was lacking in experience of Dutch Jews. Having signed the contract, he discovered on closer inspection that the vessel was quite inadequate, not to say unseaworthy. It wouldn't do at all and Fr Wright was for rescinding the contract. "Oh no", said the other, "a bargain is a bargain." He was quite ready, so he declared, to fulfil his part of the contract, even if it should result in the foundering of his vessel with the loss of all hands. The man was impervious to argument and the matter was urgent. Very reluctantly, we may be sure, Fr Wright paid the price, and then looked about for a better bargain.

A strongly built vessel was presently hired from another Dutchman: as was afterwards discovered, the price was about three times higher than the normal charge. At the moment the vessel was freighted with corn; and it was not until Tuesday

that the corn, which had begun to ferment, could be removed
and the vessel made ready. Meanwhile there was Sunday Mass
to be thought of. They were directed to a church a mile or so
away in the Bommler Waardt, a sort of island formed by the
Meuse and the Waal—the "Insula Batavorum" of Caesar's
Commentaries, so Fr Laurenson informs us. The Mass was very
short and the sermon very long, not a word of which they
could understand. But it was of course the Mass that mattered.

At last they got moving again on Tuesday afternoon. The
boat had been equipped and duly stocked with provisions, the
skipper was honest and friendly, the cabin boy alert and good-
natured. Nevertheless it was a cheerless and uncomfortable
journey. The owner had removed the fermenting corn but
not the smell—"a very distressing and unwholesome scent".
The Liège barges had been sold and the awnings with them:
there was now no shelter at all on deck from the rough weather.
The interior disturbances resulting from the Venlo diet had
not yet subsided; nor did the increasing swell of the waters
as they approached the sea do anything to alleviate their distress.
That evening they got as far as Bommel and the next evening
to Dordrecht, where they regretfully parted company with
Comte d'Agrain. It was thus on 31 July, feast of St Ignatius,
that they reached Rotterdam, but at an hour too late for any
of the priests to say Mass. Weary, forlorn and depressed by the
fatigues and hardships of the week's voyaging, they could now
most heartily thank God that this part of the long journey was
at an end.

The bright spot for them at Rotterdam was Gilles Legipont.
At the time of the suppression of the Society he had been a
young laybrother at Liege: he was now a fairly prosperous
merchant of Rotterdam. Everything he could do for the
travellers he did. Some of them he lodged in his own home,
and found other lodgings for the rest. He sought out a ship to
take them across the Channel and took charge of any goods
they chose to leave behind. Contrary winds kept them ashore,
sight-seeing, for a week. Down the coast at Hellevoetsluis,

which was the terminus of a packet boat, the English nuns
were held up for the same reason; and it was not until the
evening of Thursday, 7 August, that our travellers embarked
on the *John o' Yarmouth*, Captain Scott, bound for Hull.
During the next two or three days little headway was made.
On the Saturday they lay off Brielle, only sixteen miles from
Rotterdam: and some of the Fathers went ashore and walked
the six miles to Hellevoetsluis to visit their relatives and friends
among the nuns. On Sunday, it appears, some of them played
cards on deck, to the great scandal of the evangelical Captain
Scott. He blamed the Fathers

> at our not hindering some of the children from playing Beg
> o' my neighbour with an old pack of cards which they
> accidentally had with them. Shocked at this profanation of
> the Lord's day, one of the crew was heard to say that he
> should not be surprised if the ship were to go to the bottom,
> and the Captain took fervently to his bible, to ward off the
> thunderbolts of heaven.

However they were slowly progressing, though it was only on
Tuesday, 12 August, that they sighted the English coast,
reaching Harwich the following day.

Here there was a parting of the ways. "Many" masters and
boys—how many we are not told—disembarked, to visit their
homes before proceeding northwards. Of boys we learn of
only two by name—Thomas Gage (1793), heir to Sir Thomas
Gage of Hengrave Hall, and his brother Robert (1793) who
later assumed the name of Rookwood. A party of five or six
priests accompanied by "some scholars" set off for London, Fr
Laurenson himself travelling with them as far as Witham in
Essex on his way home. It is important to note that whereas
up to this point Fr Laurenson has been a first-hand witness of
events, the rest of his narrative is derived from the accounts of
others, reconstructed in tranquillity at Brough Hall after the
lapse of more than thirty years.

The *John o' Yarmouth*, having discharged these passengers and

AA

some cargo, proceeded with the remainder of the party up the coast to Yarmouth, where they were entertained by the Captain's wife, and so to Hull, the terminus of their sea voyage. We learn at last some names and figures. The passengers who now landed numbered twenty-one. There were three priests, Fr Kemper, now in charge of the party, Fr Semmes and Fr Ellerker, described by Dr Oliver as "one of the ablest professors of theology that the English Province ever produced". With them were four "Juniors"—ecclesiastical students not yet ordained—Rev. Walter Clifford, Charles Brooke, Thomas Collingridge and John Tate, a dozen boys, to be named later, and two servants, Honoré Hareng and Laurent Wilmot. These last two, servants at the Academy, had elected to follow the fortunes of the Academy in England rather than submit to French domination.

Let us leave them at Hull for the present, to return to Fr Stone and Fr Wright, who both were of the party which disembarked at Harwich and took the coach next day to London. There no doubt they would have visited, perhaps stayed with Fr Strickland, now living in Edgware Road and continuing his work as Administrator of the central funds of the ex-Province. Awaiting them in London they found an invitation to visit Lulworth Castle. On their way thither they were met at Winchester by Mr Weld's eldest son, Thomas, the future Cardinal, at present a young man recently come of age. Their visit to Lulworth cannot have lasted long, not more than a week at most. And there no doubt they discussed with Mr Weld, amongst other subjects, the final details of the lease of Stonyhurst.

Perhaps something should briefly be said here of this new establishment they were going to, although for most readers the information will probably be stale. Stonyhurst in 1794 was an unoccupied "Hall", standing above the Ribble valley on the lower slopes of Longridge Fell which rises above to the north. The building had been begun in an expensive style in 1592 by Sir Richard Shireburn on the site of an older house, and was not completed: a half-house, as Oliver Cromwell called it—"the finest half-house" he had ever seen. There had been minor additions in later years, for which Sir Nicholas Shireburn (1650-1717) in particular was responsible. But the solid columned entrance tower, designed to form the centre of the western front, still lacked a northern wing. Through a stately entrance, guarded by Sir Nicholas' wrought-iron gates, one entered an incomplete "quadrangle", whence could be reached by a wide balustraded stairway a large and imposing banqueting hall at the far side. The central tower and the Quadrangle had to wait well over two centuries before becoming either central or four-sided.

Sir Nicholas was the last to reside at the Hall. His only son died in his boyhood, and his daughter, heiress of Stonyhurst and extensive Lancashire estates, was married to the eighth Duke of Norfolk. Visits to Stonyhurst by Duke or Duchess were infrequent. A steward and the chaplain or parish priest had the house usually to themselves during most of the eighteenth century. On the death of the widowed, childless Duchess in 1754 the property passed to the Weld family in the person of Edward Weld of Lulworth, grandson of Sir Nicholas' sister Elizabeth. By 1794 the owner of Stonyhurst was Mr Thomas Weld, a younger son of Edward. Thomas Weld had been a pupil of the Jesuits at Bruges. Three of his sons had but a few months ago retired with their parents to Lulworth from the Academy, to continue presently their course at Stonyhurst. The Weld family, like many of the Shireburns, was friendly and generous in their contacts and dealings with the Jesuits. Here then was a house in Lancashire which might well go to rack and ruin unless it were again occupied and maintained. Kindness prompted Mr Weld to offer the house and surrounding demesne to his friends and former masters.

We come to the first of two traditional legends which must be dealt with. According to Fr Laurenson it was during the visit of Fr Stone and Fr Wright to Lulworth that Mr Weld "offered to make over to them, for a college, Stonyhurst

Hall". What is more surprising still, Fr Gerard[4] uncritically accepted this statement, though the evidence to the contrary was plain to see. The *John o' Yarmouth*, we have seen, having discharged some cargo at Harwich, sailed up the coast to Hull with its twenty-one passengers. Where was Fr Kemper's party making for? From Hull they made a bee-line across country for Stonyhurst Hall. Since an angelic message seemed out of count, Fr Gerard postulated a letter from Lulworth to Fr Kemper at Hull, telling him where to go. There is no mention elsewhere of any such letter, and the time-factor renders it almost impossible, even if Fr Stone had known where to address the letter. The question still remains unanswered: Why in the first instance had the party gone north to Hull instead of waiting at Harwich for further directions?

The answer should be obvious enough. The travellers knew their destination before ever they set out from Liège or Maastricht. A letter from Fr Joseph Reeve, chaplain at Ugbrook, to his brother at Liege, dated 2 January 1794, provides proof positive. He has received a letter from Fr Stone and comments: "The main point is gained by his consenting to the desirable plan. By Mr Weld's generous offer nothing more is yet gained than a house for a school." Again he wrote on 15 August giving his brother the news, derived from Fr Strickland, that Fr Stone was daily expected in London and "that the rest sailed for Hull in their way to Stonyhurst".[5] Mr Weld and his wife had been staying in Liège for many months before May 1794, when for safety's sake they left Maastricht with their chaplain for Bois-le-Duc. "This town", wrote the chaplain, Fr Plowden, on 27 May, "is already crowded with emigrants . . . from Liège. Not an English man or woman remains there: they would not be spared in an insurrection. Most of the Academy is here: the rest of the Nuns are expected to-morrow morning. This night I set out with Messrs Weld

[4] Gerard, *Centenary Record*, p. 87.
[5] S. Arch., MS. C. IV. 15, Nos. 24 and 25.

for Bois le Duc."[6] Mr Weld must have made his offer some time in the preceding year. When in the May of 1794 he prudently anticipated the French occupation and fled, he must have felt quite sure that before long the Academy would follow him to England.

At Lulworth it was arranged that the two visitors should travel to Stonyhurst escorted by the eldest son. There Thomas in his father's name would put them officially in possession of the old Hall. Thus they arrived on Wednesday, 27 August, to find that they were not quite the first. An hour or two earlier Fr Notley Young, a young Marylander who had been master of Poetry during the preceding year, had found his way to Stonyhurst from London. The resident steward, Mr John Sparrow, had been amused by his question on arrival—"Is this Mr Weld's chateau?" He was able to assure him that it was.

We return to Fr Kemper's party which was unloaded at Hull. Having said good-bye to Captain Scott, they engaged a barge to take them to Selby; a tedious voyage of some fifty-five miles as the river winds, although little more than thirty by road. Selby they reached on 24 August, to be soon surrounded by a jeering crowd.

> The slattern and neglected dress and haggard looks of our folks made them be, everywhere in their journey through Yorkshire, taken for frenchmen. On their arrival at Selby, it being a Sunday, they were soon surrounded by an immense crowd of lounging idlers: some of whom seemed to pity, but more to slight and insult them. Of the latter one was heard to exclaim with a curse, "The rascals deserve all they have got for killing their King".[7]

Naturally therefore they made their stay at Selby as short as possible. Their journey continued by canal through Leeds and up Airedale to Skipton. Here Fr Ellerker, a delicate man at best and now weary with travelling, together with Fr

---

[6] S. Arch. (unbound).
[7] Laurenson, p. 81.

Semmes, "took a chaise for Stonyhurst, whither they arrived on the 28th of August". The rest of the party set off in small parties on foot, presumably next morning, to trudge the twenty-five miles or so that separated them from their journey's end—all of them, no doubt, eager to be the first to reach it. They travelled so by Hobson's choice, since no stage-coach plied between Skipton and Clitheroe either then or later.

The last lap of some five miles from Clitheroe to the Hall is beset with obstacles—at least for the historian or chronicler. Twenty miles over rough road from Skipton to Clitheroe is a fair walk: but there is nothing to remark about that part of the journey. They all reached Clitheroe safe and tired. According to Fr Laurenson (who was not there) the "children" were "quite exhausted . . . resting themselves at every door where they could find a convenient seat, perfectly indifferent to the stare and surprise of the inhabitants, that surrounded them". That much, with salt to taste, can be swallowed.

He adds that Fr Stone met the party at Clitheroe. That too is possible, for the arrival of Frs Ellerker and Semmes on the previous day would have given him warning. "After procuring for them a refreshment, which they stood much in need of, he accompanied them to Stonyhurst." Did they drive or walk? The question is not of much importance in itself unless the answer compromises the claim of George Clifford to be the first boy to arrive at Stonyhurst. If "the children were quite exhausted"—not to mention Fr Kemper and the four "Juniors" —one might well expect Fr Stone to procure "chaises" for this journey: and if Clifford walked, surely the chaises would have overtaken him. However, the delay in any case would have been quite considerable. The "children" had first to be found and collected from their various doorsteps, and refreshments had to be ordered, provided and eaten—this last would have occupied the attention of a dozen and more hungry boys for as long as the provisions held out. If they then drove rather than walked, the little village of Clitheroe would have to be searched for the conveyances needed. Provided that Clifford did not rest too long on his doorstep and denied himself the luxury of a "refreshment"—unless perhaps a quick one—his claim to be the first of the party to enter Stonyhurst Hall cannot be gainsaid.

One hears of no such similar claim made when St Omers moved to Bruges or Bruges to Liege. But at Stonyhurst his memory is assured, if only by means of his bust prominently displayed. There were several Cliffords at Bruges and Liege, and probably earlier. George Lambert Clifford (1788-1795) was the youngest of six brothers, all of whom had been boys at the Academy. They were sons of the Hon. Thomas Clifford, of Tixall in Staffordshire, and grandsons of Hugh, third Lord Clifford of Chudleigh. From George, although he himself never left England, derives the New Zealand branch of the Clifford family. It was his proud boast that he had closed the door of the Liege Academy and opened the door of Stonyhurst.

This brings us to the second legend referred to above—a golden legend, but most probably merely gilt. The traditional story goes that George Clifford and Charles Brooke, one of the "Juniors", arrived at the top of the avenue (one version allows them to arrive in a gig) and raced the half-mile or more to the front entrance for the distinction of becoming the "first boy". Charles Brooke reached the door first and urgently rang the bell: meanwhile Clifford discovered an open window and climbed through it.

The evidence must be considered meagre. Mr Tomlinson, working that afternoon in a field near the Hall, used in his old age to tell a story somewhat similar; and about a century later two old men, his grandchildren, repeated it to Fr Gerard. Their grandfather had seen Clifford "and another" come along in a fly, and Clifford "jumped out, and in through a window".[8] Lord Arundell of Wardour also "perfectly remembered" being told forty or fifty years previously by Fr James Laurenson (Fr John's brother) how Clifford and he had arrived in a fly and then raced for the Hall. Fr Laurenson "always admitted

[8] Gerard, *ibid.*, p. 90.

that Mr Clifford won, as he got in by a ruse . . .".[9] The objection to this version is that James Laurenson, after three years at the Academy, did not return to Stonyhurst till March 1795, several months after George Clifford. It must have been Charles Brooke or nobody. It is not always realized that this supposed rival in the race was not at this date a schoolboy at all, but a Junior who though only two years older had just completed his second year of philosophy. There was really no need for a race at all.

The best evidence on the subject would be that of George Clifford himself: and in fact there exist two accounts that derive from him. The first is a short, plain account of his part in the migration to Stonyhurst, of which the relevant passage states that having reached Skipton by canal, "from thence I walked on foot through Clitheroe to Stonyhurst, which I reached on August 29th, 1794". So at all events he did not drive from Clitheroe with Mr Brooke or with anyone.

In 1890 the late Fr Reginald Gibb (O.S.1875-82), then in his first year of philosophy at St Mary's Hall, took the wise course of consulting Clifford's son, Fr William Clifford, a priest in his seventies, who was stationed in the same house. His memory of his father's oft-told tale allowed him to amplify the written account which he still possessed and treasured. Mr Gibb committed the commentary to paper, obtained from Fr Clifford his "unofficial imprimatur" and contributed his article to the *Stonyhurst Magazine*.[10] It is of course secondhand evidence, though from a sound source. It is in any case the best one is likely ever to get.

Clifford, according to his son's recollection, reached Clitheroe alone, clad of course in his Liege uniform, now much the worse for wear. By this time too the soles of his boots were almost separated from their uppers: so he sat down on a door-

[9] *Stonyhurst Magazine*, IV, 511.
[10] For the two accounts (the first derived from Foley, V, 981) see *ibid.*, IV, 482-83.

step to tie them securely to his feet. Incidentally the house attached to his doorstep happened to belong to Mr Sparrow, who was Mr Weld's steward or agent for his Lancashire estates. Having asked his way to Stonyhurst, he set off again alone and arrived alone, passing unrecognized, near the house, young Thomas Weld who was in conversation with Mr Sparrow. He made his way at once into the "Quadrangle" without any hindrance and up the flight of stone steps (now no longer there) to the door that opened into the old Banqueting Hall, now the boys' refectory. Here he had to force his way in, aided by an iron bar that lay handy. The old door fell inwards, giving him admittance to that spacious apartment and to the rest of the house. There is no mention of Fr Ellerker or other occupants. He finally reached the roof of the tower, whence he saw in the Deer Park what caught his fancy—some deer that then and for many later years adorned the landscape. So, being bored with his own company, he wandered in the park for an hour or more, forgetting his long walk from Skipton. By the time he had returned to the house, his companions or many of them had arrived.

For the sake of completeness we may add here the names of the twelve boys—known as the Twelve Apostles—who arrived at Stonyhurst on that summer afternoon of Friday, 29 August. They were as follows: George Clifford (Liege, 1788), Philip Walsh (1788), Benjamin Faucon (1789), Charles and Augustus Claybrooke (1791), John Reeve (1791), Augustin de la Potherie (1791), Louis Jeanson (1792), Jean Casseaux (1792), Charles Froeser (1792), Stephen Clothier (1793) and Thomas Lorimer (1793).

The story of the first Night Prayers is always worth repeating: it can be given in Fr Clifford's own words. George Clifford, appointed "Peter" of the Twelve, was kneeling at the back. "Observing his comrades, who knelt along the wall side, sideling to and fro, heavy with sleep, under pretence of arousing the one before him Clifford gave him such a push that falling on his companions in front they were prostrated like a pack of cards, to the disturbance of the Master or Prefect who was saying the prayers".

A few jottings may here be added by way of tidying up the ground just covered. Fr Wright of course was busy for many a month with much-needed repairs. The chapel (of which the present Bayley Room was a part) and the quarters occupied by the missioner and by the steward were probably in fair order, but the rest of the house not so. At this period the chapel served also as the public church for the Catholics of the district. The roof, one hears, needed patching in several places: and where lead was needed Fr Wright, true to his temperament, melted down, in spite of aesthetic opposition, some local statuary adorning the front and gardens. The customary "Ascensio Scholarum" was delayed until 21 October, which according to ancient custom was a full recreation day. There was again recreation the following morning, again according to custom; but at last they got to work, schools beginning that Thursday at 1.30 p.m. There have been schools more or less ever since.

Stonyhurst with some adjoining land had been handed over to Fr Stone on a 99-years' lease at a yearly rental of £30 for the first seven years and £60 for the rest. Three years later, in 1797, it was agreed to exchange the yearly rent for the free admission of one boy, and after seven years, of two boys, to be presented by Mr Weld and his heirs. When in 1803 by a verbal permission (*vivae vocis oraculo*) of Pope Pius VII the English Fathers were allowed to aggregate themselves to the Jesuit remnant still working in White Russia, it was decided quietly to open a noviciate. Kind as ever, Mr Weld offered Hodder Place, above the river Hodder, a house that had come again into his hands after the recent bankruptcy of the tenant. This with some land attached was rented for £25 a year. To this noviciate, replacing Watten, was added, after some additions to the building, a small preparatory school, a single class of some twenty or thirty small boys, to whom the religious atmosphere of a noviciate would have meant nothing at all.

The school opened on 1 January 1807. Is it perhaps the oldest Catholic preparatory school in England?

Finally, on 31 July 1809, Mr Weld signed a deed making over the Stonyhurst lease of about fifty-two acres, and that of Hodder (about forty-seven acres) as "a free gift to the body". Exactly a year later, whilst singing a favourite song in the boys' refectory in the presence of his sons, the Community and boys —they numbered 187 at this date—he collapsed, and died next morning. It was of course the feast of St Ignatius that they had been celebrating. The name of Mr Weld has ever since been held in grateful benediction.

It would be pleasant to be able to say that "they all lived happily ever after", but it would not be quite true. The presence of a Jesuit College in England did not find favour with most of the Vicars Apostolic nor with Propaganda. Neither the verbal restoration of 1803 nor the canonical restoration in 1814 removed the opposition. Stonyhurst remained for many years in danger of having to retire again to the Continent or alternatively of having to close, for lack of the support of ecclesiastical authority. Every obstacle, however, was removed by a rescript of Leo XII dated 1 January 1829, written by him on the back of a Memorial presented to him by Bishop Baines. Thereby he declared that Pius VII's Bull of 1814 had full spiritual and canonical force in England, and that Bishop Baines, if he thought fit, might let the Vicars Apostolic know it. All open opposition ceased thenceforth.[11]

Here we have reached the *terminus ad quem* of this inadequate story, ranging from the days of Queen Elizabeth I to the later years of George III—a long stretch of 201 years. It seems worthy of note that in August 1963 Stonyhurst will be as old as was St Omers when the Jesuits were forced to flit. Before the end of the century, if the world and Stonyhurst survive so long, there will be still further cause for congratulation. The Rector of that time will perhaps grant an "exeat" on 29 August 1995, so that boys living in England may fly home for lunch, if not for

[11] Cf. *ibid.*, XXXII (1955), pp. 138-144.

breakfast and dinner as well. "All must be back by 9 p.m."
But the future of the College is in God's hands: may He
prosper it.

APPENDIX

The following lists of Provincials of the English Province S.J. and Rectors of St Omers, etc., are derived mainly from Province Catalogues and the Generals' letters. It corrects here and there the corresponding lists given by Dr Oliver in his *Collections* (1838).

Provincials:

Richard Blount	1623 (Jan.)	-1635 (*c.* Aug.)
Henry More	1635	-1639 (*c.* Sept.)
Edward Knott	1639	-1646 (*c.* Aug.)
Henry Silisdon	1646	-1650 (*c.* Feb.)
Francis Foster	1650	-1653 (*c.* Jan.)
Edward Knott (*bis*)	1653	-1656 (died 11 Jan.)
Richard Barton	1656 (15 Apr.)	-1660
Edward Courtney	1660 (15 July)	-1664 (Jan.)
John Clark	1664 (14 Jan.)	-1667 (Nov.)
Joseph Simons	1667 (14 Nov.)	-1671 (died 24 July)
George Gray	1671 (22 May)	-1674
Richard Strange	1674 (7 Sept.)	-1677
Thomas Whitbread	1678 (14 Jan.)	-1679 (June)
John Warner	[Vice-Provincial 1679 (Jan.)]	
	1679 (26 Oct.)	-1683
John Keynes	1683 (1 July)	-1689
William Morgan	1689 (22 Aug.)	-1689 (died 28 Sept.)
John Clare	1689 (4 Dec.)	-1693
Anthony Lucas	1693 (Aug.)	-1693 (died 3 Oct.)
William Mumford	1694 (16 Feb.?)	-1697
Henry Humberston	1697 (19 Dec.)	-1701
James Blake	1701 (3 Apr.)	-1704
Peter Hamerton	1704 (*c.* Oct.)	-1708 (Jan.)
Louis Sabran (Visitor & V-Prov.)	1708	-1712
Thomas Parker	1712 (21 May)	-1716
Richard Plowden	1716 (6 July)	-1719
Thomas Edisford	1719 (30 Oct.)	-1720 (died 30 Aug.)
(Vice-Provincial: Thomas Parker)		
Robert Beeston	1721 (18 Feb.)	-1724
Thomas Lawson (sen.)	1724 (*c.* Mar.)	-1725
John Turberville	1725 (20 May)	-1731
Richard Richardson	1731 (Nov.?)	-1733
Levinus Browne	1733 (1 Oct.)	-1737
Henry Boult	1737 (20 July)	-1740
Charles Shireburn	1740 (23 Oct.)	-1744 (died 17 Jan. '45)
Henry Sheldon	1744 (18 Nov.)	-1751
Philip Carteret	1751 (3 Oct.)	-1756 (died 28 Mar.)
Henry Corbie	1756 (17 July)	-1762

James Dennet	1762 (18 Oct.)	–1766
Nathaniel Elliot	1766	–1769
Thomas More	1769 (19 July)	–1773

Rectors of St Omers:

William Flack (Superior)	1593	
Jean Foucart	1594 (Feb.)	–1601
Gilles Schondonch	1601 (22 July)	–1617 (died 28 Jan.)
Philippe Dennetiers (or Dentier)	1617	–1621
William Baldwin	1621 (end)	–1632 (died 28 Sept.)
Thomas Worsley	1632	–1636
Thomas Port	(Vice-Rector, 1636)	
	1637 (Jan.,Feb.?)–1646	
Edward Courtney	1646 (27 July)	–1649
Henry More	1649 (July)	–1652
Charles D'Arcy	1652 (5 Aug.)	–1656
Thomas Babthorpe	1656 (19 Feb.?)	–1656 (died 20 Oct.)

(Vice-Rectors: Thomas Port, to Dec.
John? Stephens, to Apr. '57)

Henry More (*bis*)	1657 (7 Apr.)	–1660
Richard Barton	1660 (15 Sept.)	–1669 (died 13 Feb.)
Thomas Carey	1669 (13 June)	–1672 (died 10 June)
Richard Ashby	1672 (29 Aug.)	–1678
Thomas Stapleton (Vice-Rector, 1678–9)		
	1679 (27 Mar.)	–1683
John Warner	1683 (31 July)	–1687

(Vice-Rector, Michael Constable)

Michael Constable	1688 (8 Apr.)	–1692 (Dec.?)
Edward Petre	1693 (29 Apr.)	–1697
William Walton	1697 (16 Dec.)	–1701
Henry Humberston	1701 (11 Dec.)	–1705
Edward Slaughter	1705 (28 Apr.)	–1709
Richard Plowden	1709 (16 Apr.)	–1712
Louis Sabran	1712 (12 June)	–1715
Francis Powell	1715 (27 Oct.)	–1720
William Darell	1720 (5 July)	–1721 (died 28 Feb.)
John Turberville	1721 (29 July)	–1721 (Sept.?)
James Gooden	1722 (14 Mar.)	–1724?
Richard Plowden (*bis*)	1725 (22 May)	–1728
Richard Hyde	1728 (12 May)	–1731
Thomas Eccleston	1731 (12 Aug.)	–1737
Joseph Constable	1737 (29 Sept.)	–1739
Percy Plowden	1739 (22 Oct.)	–1742
Richard Hyde (*bis*)	1742 (31 July)	–1744 (died 16 Feb.)

(Vice-Rector, John Gifford)

| Charles Wells | 1745 | –1748 |
| Nathaniel Elliot | 1748 (12 Oct.) | –1752 |

John Darell	1752 (17 Sept.)	-1759
Francis Scarisbrick	1759 (May)	-1762
Bruges:		
Nathaniel Elliot (*bis*)	1762 (26 Oct.)	-1766
Thomas Lawson (Jun.)	1766 (24 Feb.)	-1769
Thomas Stanley	1769 (21 Dec.)	-1772
Thomas Angier	1772 or 1773	-1773
Liege:		
John Howard	(1768)	-1783 (died 16 Oct.)
William Strickland	1784?	-1790
Marmaduke Stone	1790	-(1817)

INDEX

("Fr" or "Père" denotes Jesuit priest; "S.J.", Jesuit not a priest; "Mr", secular priest; "Rev.", secular cleric not a priest; "M.", martyr.)

Agrain, Comte d' (and son), 388, 390
Ailesbury, Lord, 229
Aix-la-Chapelle, Peace of, 181
Albert, Archduke, 35, 46-7, 51-2, 60, 104, 105, 113, 132, 147
Alexander VII, 146, 210, 221
Alford, Fr Michael, 146
Allen, Dr (later Cardinal), 1, 6, 7, 8, 13, 17
Aloysius Gonzaga, St, 15, 120, 374-5
Anderson ("Munson"), Fr (O.P.), 225
Anderton, Lady, of Lostock, 259
Anderton, (Fr) William, 327, 351, 367
Andrew, Archduke, 28
Angier, Fr Thomas (Sen.), 326, 337-8, 344, 349, 355
Angier, Fr Thomas (Jun.), 205
"Apostles, The Twelve", 399
Aquaviva, Claudius (General, S.J.), 11, 17, 39, 51, 55, 65, 69, 90, 98
Argenteau, Comte d', 381
Arnold, John, 207
Arrowsmith, Fr Edmund (M.), 160
Artois, Parlement of, 281-2
Arundel, Lady, 103
Arundell, Thomas and James, 367
Arundell of Wardour, 12th Lord, 397
Aston, Sir Arthur, 67
Aston, Fr William 326, 328, 337, 346-8, 355-7, 363-4
Aubert, Monsieur d', 331
Augustine of Canterbury, St, 375
Austin Canonesses, Bruges, see More, Mistress Mary
Austin, Friars, Ghent, 355
Aytona, Marquis d', 148

Babthorpe, Barbara, 147
Babthorpe, Fr Thomas, 147
Baines, Bishop, 401
Baines, William, 150
Baker, Fr John, 191
Baker, Sir Richard, 227
Baldwin, Fr William, 32-3, 39, 40, 58, 103-6, 117, 120-4, 132
Baltimore, 4th Lord, 250
Barberini, Cardinal, 149, 170
Banister, William (S.J.), 138
Barrett, Dr Edward, 6-9, 13, 17, 23
Barrow, Fr Thomas, 327, 350, 363, 372

Barrow, Fr William (al. Harcourt, Waring) (M.), 118, 190
Barton, Fr Richard, 173-4
Beaucorroy, M. de, 271-2
Beaugrand, Br Cornelius (S.J.), 191, 239
Beaumont, Christophe de (Archbishop of Paris), 329
Beauregard, Père Jean, 381
Bedingfeld, Thomas, 327
Bedloe, William, 209
Beeston, Mr George, 305
Beeston, Robert (S.J.), 228, 268
Belgian Provinces S.J., 51, 68-9, 72, 90, 157, 220
Bellarmine, Cardinal, 279
Bellet, François (printer), 140
Benedict XIII, 262
Benedict XIV, 146
Bentivoglio, Cardinal, 47, 129
Berington, Mr Thomas, 346
Bernis, Cardinal de, 335
Berry (al. Hutchinson), Rev. William, 184
Billing, Thomas, 195
Blacfan, Fr John, 66
Blackiston, Fr William, 271-3, 330
Blaise, Bishop, 47, 49, 50, 51, 57, 60, 86, 121, 141, 142
Blanchard, Jean Pierre, 375
Blandyke, 116-7, 145, 151, 173, 182, 245, 304
Blood, Colonel, 188
Blount, Mr Henry Tichborne, 292-3, 296, 298-300, 303-5
Blount, Fr Richard, 99, 101, 102-5, 107, 112-5, 138-9, 154-5
Blundell, Nicholas, 173
Blundell, William, 138, 173
Blyde, Br Joseph (S.J.), 288
Bobadilla, Fr Nicholas, 76
Bolron, Robert, 207
Bona Mors Confraternity, 209
Booth, Fr Charles, 302
Borghese, Cardinal, 39
Bornhem (College O.P.), 343, 353
Boulogne, see Preparatory School
Boscard, Charles (printer), 142
Bray, Fr Henry, 24, 31, 35-6
Brent, Fr Henry, 331
Brent, Fr Thomas, 314-6

"Brereley, John", 142
Brooke, Charles (later S.J.), 392, 397-8
Browne, Fr Levinus, 270, 304
Bruges Colleges ('Great' and 'Little'):
arrival of boys and staff, 317-8, 322;
temporary lodgings, 318-21; permission to reside, on conditions, 322-4;
purchase of land, 324; of Little College, 325-6; surrounding landscape,
327; the Villa house, 328; number of
boys, 237, 326, 328; uniform, 237,
328; school fees, 157, 365-6; suppression, 334 seqq.; Dominicans introduced, 342-3, 352
Bruning, Fr George, 331
Buckingham, Duke of (George Villiers),
188
Burghley, Lord, 4
Burnaby (al. Blunt), Richard, 195
Burton, Dr Edwin, 303
Busby, Fr William, 202
Butler, Mr Alban, 299
Byerley, Fr Charles, 333

Caetano, Cardinal, 13, 39
Caimo, Mgr de (Bishop of Bruges), 321,
338-9, 341-3, 349, 352-3
Calais, 35
Calderon, Don Rodrigo, 130
Caldwell, Fr John, see Fenwick
Calvert boys, and family, 250-1
Campion, Fr Edmund (M.), 1, 4, 140, 275
Canonesses of the Holy Sepulchre, 377,
381-3, 391
Caraffa, Fr Vincent (General S.J.), 146,
169, 210
Carlton, Mr John, 101
Carroll, Fr John, 344
Carvajal, Luisa de, 50, 52
Cary, Fr Thomas, 176, 179, 180
Castlemain, Earl of, 192, 203, 205, 230,
361
Causmaecker, Mynheer, 353, 355-6
Cellier, Mrs, 205
Chaize, Père de la, 216-7
Challoner, Bishop, 290-1, 342
Chamberlain, George (Bishop of Ypres),
101
Chamberlain, Fr John, 330, 333
Chambers, Mr ——, 5
Charles I of England, 107, 155, 159
Charles II of England, 172, 178, 184,
191, 194, 205, 213, 227
Charles of Lorraine, 309, 310, 312, 324
Charles III of Spain, 334-5
Chauvelin, abbé, 277, 285, 297
Chèvremont, 205, 358, 361-2, 373, 378
Choiseul, Duc de, 278-9, 282, 302-3

Christophe de France (Bishop of Saint-
Omer), 153
Clarcus, Pater, 136
Clare, Fr John (Sir John Warner), 274
Clarendon, Lord, 67
Clavius, Fr Christopher, 77
Clay, Fr Matthew (O.P.), 227
Clement XIII, 279, 280, 287, 305-6
Clement XIV, 278, 334-5, 368
Cléry, M. Bernard (échevin), 272-3
Cliffords of Tixall, 397
Clifford, Charles, 367
Clifford, George Lambert, 396-9
Clifford, Hugh (later 5th Baron of
Chudleigh), 327, 340-1
Clifford, Thomas, 327
Clifford, Walter (S.J.), 392
Clifford, Fr William, 398-9
Clifton, Fr Francis, 369, 381, 386
Clitheroe, 396, 398
Cobenzl, Count, 310-11, 338
Coghlan, J. P. (Publisher), 276
Coligny, Gaspard de, 151
Collingridge, (Mr) Thomas, 392
Congress of ex-Jesuits (1784), 370-2
Constable, Fr Joseph, 265-6
Constable, Fr Michael, 230-1
Constable, Fr Robert, 314
Conway (al. Parry), William, 185, 196,
198-9, 228
Conyers, Fr Thomas, 40
Cook, Br James (S.J.), 228
Corbie, Fr Henry, 291, 300, 321
Corbie, Fr Ralph (M.), 160-2
Corbie family, 162-3
Cordara, Fr Giulio-Cesare, 117
Coulster, Sir Joseph, 193n.
Courtney, Fr Edward, 147, 165-6, 180
Courtrai, 36, 44
Coverdale, Miles, 90
Cox, ——, 196, 204
Coxon, Fr Thomas, 251, 256, 258-9
Cresswell, Fr Joseph, 50-1, 56, 98-9, 102-3
Croix, Sieur de, 24, 34
Cromwell, Oliver, 167
Cueva, Cardinal de la (Marquis of Bed-
mar), 132, 148, 150
Cuthbert, St, 365

Dalmerius, Père Christian, 16, 24, 30
Dames Anglaises (Bruges), 318, 320
Dampierre, General, 380
Dangerfield, Thomas, 205
D'Arcy, Fr Charles, 147
Darell, George, 272
Darell, Fr John, 282, 286, 297, 302, 304,
307, 309, 315, 318-20
Darell, Fr William, 256, 258-9, 275

Deale the Apothecary, 251-2
Decurion, 29, 30, 80
Dennetiers (or Dentiers), Fr Philip, 98-9, 102, 104, 106
Devaux, see Vaux
Digby, ——, 188
"Dodd, Charles" (Mr Hugh Tootell), 237, 252-4, 296, 302, 306
Dordrecht (Dort), 390
Douay, English College, 1, 2, 4, 5, 7, 8, 13-4, 17, 19, 21, 23, 73, 222, 252-4
Douay, Jesuit College (Anchin), 7, 8, 90
Douay, Parlement of, 281, 330-1, 333
Ducket, Mr John (M.), 162
Dumouriez, General, 379, 380
Dupont (Pontanus), Père, 72

Eccleston, Fr Thomas (Sen.), 204
Eccleston, Fr Thomas (Jun.), 265
Edmondes, Sir Thomas, 51
Elizabeth I, Queen, 1, 45
Ellerker, Fr Thomas, 369, 392, 395, 399
Elliot, Fr Nathaniel, 311, 322
Encratides (Encratia), St, 176
English Vice-Province S.J., 99, 103, 113
Ernest, Archduke, 27
Esquerchin, 292
Eu, School at, 4-8
Evans, Fr Philip (M.), 206-7
Ewen, James (S.J.), 313-4

Fagan, George (or Christopher), 352
Farnese, Cardinal, 39
Fenwick Fr John (M.), 189
Fernando, Don, see Infant, Cardinal
Fisher, Fr John, 144
Fitzherbert, Robert, 245
Fitzherbert, Fr Thomas, 275
Flack, Fr William, 9, 12, 15-26, 30, 33, 33, 35-8, 56-7, 85, 105, 120-1
"Flamstead," 138, 245
Fleron, Père François de, 91
Floyd, Fr John, 100, 165
Forestier, Père Mathurin le, 302
Fortunatus, St, 204
Foster, Fr Francis, 118, 163
Foucart, Père Jean, 22-4, 30, 36-8, 42
French Province S.J. expelled, 276-85, 305
Frias, Duke of, 128
Fuentes, Comte de, 15, 18

Gage, Sir Henry, 66-7
Gage, Fr Philip, 225
Gage (Rookwood), Robert, 391
Gage, Thomas (O.P.), 160-1
Gage, Thomas (of Hengrave Hall), 391
Garnet, Fr Henry, 53, 294

Garnet, Fr Thomas (M.), 53, 95, 142, 294
Gascoigne, Sir Thomas, 205, 207
Gasquet, Cardinal, 222
Gastaldi, Count(?), 289
Gaven (Gawen), Fr John (M.), 190, 198-9, 208, 234
Gee, John, 144
Georgel, abbé, 279
Gerard, Fr John (d. 1637), 52, 58, 66, 115, 121
Gerard, Fr John (d. 1912), 394
Gerard, William, 186
Ghent, House of Tertians, 103, 151, 163, 167, 229, 276, 331-2
Gibb, Fr Reginald, 398
Giffard, Charles, 199
Giffard, Daniel (veré Coulster), 193
Gonzales, Fr Thyrsus (General S.J.), 224, 232, 235-7, 241
Gooden, Fr James, 259
Gordianus, St, 204
Goring, Lady (Dorothy Plowden), 265
Goring, Sir William, 265
Gottifredo, Fr Alessandro (General S.J.), 169, 170
Gray, Fr George, 172
Green, Dr William, 291-3, 296, 298-300, 302, 305
Grove, John (M.), 189
Gruber, Fr Gabriel (General S.J.), 371
Guise, Henri, Duc de, 5

Haggerston (al. Howard), Henry, 195 228
Hales, Br Thomas (S.J.), 275
Hall, Henry, 193
Hall, Dr Richard, 39
Hanmer, Fr John, 251-2
Harcourt, Fr William (M.), see Barrow
Harwich, 391, 394
Hareng, Honoré, 392
Hawker, Fr John, 304
Hay, Malcolm, 208
Heatley, Fr John, 272
Heigham, John, 142
Hellevoetsluis, 391
Henrietta, Duchess of Orleans, 182
Henrietta Maria, Queen, 155, 159, 163
Herennius, Père Jean, 65, 66, 99
Herst (or Hayhurst), Richard (M.), 160
Herville, Mgr d' (Bishop of Boulogne), 271-2
Hewitt, Br Richard (S.J.), 213
Hildesley (al. Mallet), 21
Hill, Henry (Printer), 274
Hodder Place, 400-1
Hodgson, Ralph, 297, 303, 307, 310-11, 332

Hoensbroeck, Mgr de (Prince-Bishop), 377
Hohenlohe, Prince Aloysius, 367
Holden, Dr Joseph, 284-5, 289, 297-8
Holland, Fr Thomas (M.), 160-2
Holt, Fr William, 6, 16, 18, 19, 31, 37, 39
Holtby, Fr Richard, 56
Hornyold, Bishop John, 291, 300
Hoskins, Fr Anthony, 55
Howard, Dr Charles, 290, 298-9
Howard, Henry, see Haggerston
Howard, Hon. Henry, 255
Howard, Fr John (veré Holme), 358, 362-3, 368-9, 374
Howard, Cardinal, 222, 343
Howard, Hon. Philip, 255
Howard, Fr William, 333
Huddleston, Mr John (later O.S.B.), 172
Hull, 392, 394
Humberston, Fr Henry, 242
Humieres, Marechal d', 182
Hunter, Fr Thomas, 253-5
Hyde, Ann, Duchess of York, 178
Hyde, Fr Richard, 261-4, 271

Ibarra, Diego de, 25
Ignatius of Loyola, St, 76, 362, 374
Infant, Cardinal, 148
Innocent X, 146
Internuncio (Brussels), 216-7
Ireland, Fr William (M.), 189, 191-2, 227
Irish Regiment, 240
Isabella, Infanta, 42, 52, 105-6, 113, 132, 147-8

Jackson, Fr Ambrose, 251
Jackson, ——, 199
James I of England, 45, 52, 142
James II, 178, 213, 218, 224-6, 230, 243-4, 274
James III (Chevalier St George), 231, 302
Janion, Fr William 213
Jefferies, Thomas, 32
Jeffreys, Sir George (Chief Justice), 225, 227-8
Jeffries, Dr, 375
Jenison, James (S.J.), quoted, 288, 294, 302, Chap. 11 passim, 319, 320, 322-3
Jenkins, Mr Secretary, 225
Jodici, Fr Anthony, 231
Jourdan, General, 382-3
Justiniani (veré Ayroli), Fr John Baptist, 256

Kemper, Fr Herman, 382, 392, 394-6
Keynes, Fr George, 57
Keynes, Fr John, 210, 212, 226, 229
Kinsman, Fr Michael, 361

Knott, Fr Edward, 115, 123-4, 155-6, 163
Knowles, Simon, 31

Langhorne, Richard, (M.), 203, 205, 229, 234; his sons, 203
Langworth, Fr Basil, 178
Laurenson, Fr James, 397-8
Laurenson, John, 378, 383, 391, 393, 396
La Valette, Père Antoine, 278-9, 301
Laverdy, Monsieur, 278
Lawson, John, 286, 293
Lawson, Fr Thomas (Sen.), 256, 266
Lawson, Fr Thomas (Jun.), 283-6, 288, 292-3, 300-1, 303-4
Lee, Fr Roger, 58, 60-2, 85
Le Fevre, Br Nicholas (S.J.), 275-6
Légipont, l'abbé, 357-8
Légipont, Gilles, 390
Leloup, Remacle, 360
Leo X, 134
Leo XII, 401
Le Roi, Monsieur, 329, 330
L'Estrange, Sir Roger, 189, 227
Le Tellier, Père Michel, 276
Liege Academy: continuity with Bruges, 359, 363; house and gardens, 360; formally established, 362-3; number of boys, 359, 376; school fees, 365-6; celebration of Jesuit Feasts, 364, 374; lay philosophers, 359, 366-7; special Prefects, 367; Catholici Praesules of Pius VI, 368; Presidency of Fr Howard, 362-3, 368-9; of Fr Strickland, 369-72; of Fr Stone, 376 (see also s.v. Stone); during revolutionary period, 377 seqq.; departure, 384-7
Liege Seminary (College S.J.), 52, 56, 77-8, 99, 107, 121-2, 187, 193, 205, 211, 240, 266, 270, 276, 336, 357-8
Liège Episcopal Seminary, 249
Line, Fr Francis, 36
Lioncy Frères, 278-9, 283, 301, 305
Lloyd, Mr John (M.), 206-7
Longueville, Duc de, 35
Lonsdale, Rev. John, 305
Lords in the Tower, 191, 199
Louis XIV, 166, 181-4, 201, 217, 240, 243, 257, 279, 308
Louis XV, 262, 277, 279, 280-1, 285, 302, 329, 336
Louis XVI, 379-81
Louvain, house of studies O.P., 343
Louvain, noviciate S.J., etc., 52-3, 99, 122
Lucas, Fr Anthony, 229, 236
Lydcott, ——, 205n.

Maastricht, 381-7
"Mad Monks", The, 352-3

Maeseyck, 387-8
Mahieu, Canon, 330
Manare, Père Oliver, 16-7, 30-1, 33, 36-7, 46, 65
Mannock, Fr George, 322
Mansfield, Comte de, 15, 18
Mansfield, Chief Justice, 242
Marefoschi, Cardinal, 292, 307, 310-11, 335
Maria Teresa, Infanta (dau. of Philip IV), 181
Maria Theresa, Empress, 307, 312, 321, 335-6, 355
Marmaduke, James (Publisher), 276
Maroulx, Louis, 339, 340, 343-9, 355
Martina, St, 176
Mary of Modena, Queen, 230, 256
Massez, ——, 339, 346-8, 353
Mathew, Sir Tobie, 44, 143-4
Mathews, Edmund (al. Poins, Poyntz), 174-7
Mathews, George, 176
Maudsley, Mr Philip, 305
Maxwell, Fr George, 367
Maybury, Lawrence, 207
Mazarin, Cardinal, 163, 166
Mean, Comte de (Prince-Bishop), 381-3, 388
Meighan, Thomas (Publisher), 276
Meuse, journey to Rotterdam, 387-90
Mico, Fr Edward, 188, 190, 206
Molien, Fr John Baptist, 332-3
Monck, General and wife, 172
Monino (Spanish ambassador in Rome), 335
Monterey, Comte de, 181
Monmouth, Duke of, 188-9
Monocella, St, 257
Montmorency, Père Florent de, 170
Morales, M. de, 122
More, Fr Henry, 42, 66, 74, 95, 106, 139, 147, 154, 156, 166, 171
More, Mistress Mary, 346, 348, 353-4, 356-7
More, Fr Thomas, 346, 369, 370
Morgan, Fr Richard, 349, 363
Morgan, Fr William, 193, 200
Morley, George (Bishop of Winchester), 224
Mumford, Fr William, 239
Munster, Peace of, 166

Neny, Count, 321, 337-8, 342-3, 354
Newdigate, Fr Charles, 145
Newport, Fr Maurice, 136
Newsham, Robert, 375
Newton, Francis, 161
Nickel, Fr Goswin (General S.J.), 171

Nicolas, Rev. James, 305
Nihell, John (S.J.), 363
Nijmegen, Peace of, 182-3
Noel, Fr Austin (O.P.), 343, 353-5
Norfolk, Duchess of (Mary Shireburn), 255, 393
Norfolk, 8th Duke of, 255
Noyelle, Fr Charles de (General S.J.), 210-12, 215, 217-8, 224, 230

Oates, Titus, 184-200, 203-6, 208-9, 214, 224-9, 239
Oath at English College, Rome, 121-4, 240
Oldcorne, Fr Edward (M.), 294
Oliva, Fr John Paul (General S.J.), 173, 179, 210, 246
Oliver, Dr George, 147, 369, 392
Oranus (d'Heur), Père Jean, 26, 38
Oratorians in Boulogne, 272
Orleans, Louis Philippe, Duc d', 182, 183
O'Shee, John(?), 384
Owen, Fr Thomas, 68, 99
Oxford, Earl of (Robert Harley), 250

Padbury, Br Thomas (S.J.), 304
Palmer, Henry, 199
Palmer, ——, 199
Panting, Mrs, 272-3
Panting, Fr John, 332-3
Paris Parlement, 278-91, 299, 301-2, 304, 313
Parker, Fr Thomas, 246, 250, 254, 268
Parry, William, see Conway
Paston, Dr Edward, 253-4
Paul V, 51
Penal Laws against Catholics, 1-2, 10-11, 73, 108, 141, 178, 241-2
Pennsylvania, 270
Percy, Fr John, see Fisher
Percy, Dr William, 13
Persecution in England, 1-4, 10, 159, 160, 164, 200, 241, 243, 259, 268
Persons, George, 19-22, 106
Persons, ——, 106
Persons, Fr Robert, 1, 4, 6, 8, 11-7, 25-8, 33, 37, 43, 50, 52, 68, 140-1, 297, 302
Petit, Roger, 245
Petit de Coquil, 296
Petre, Fr Edward, 191, 193, 208, 212, 224, 230-3, 235, 239, 240
Philip II of Spain, 12, 15, 17-8, 23, 25, 27, 43, 96, 104, 147, 184, 308
Philip III, 28, 51
Philip IV, 148, 156, 167, 181
Phillips, Mr Thomas, 365
Piccolomini, Fr Francis (General S.J.), 146

Pickering, Br Thomas (O.S.B.) (M.), 189
Pius VI, 368, 400
Plessington, Fr John (M.), 206
Plowden family, 264-5
Plowden, Fr Charles, 204, 326, 336-7,
    339-41, 344, 347-8, 355-6, 368-9, 385,
    394
Plowden, Fr Edmund (al. Gage), 259-61
Plowden, abbé Francis, 290, 298-9, 304,
    307
Plowden, Fr Percy, 262, 269, 271
Plowden, Fr Richard, 257, 259, 262, 268
Plunkett, General, 355; his sons, 355
Pollock, John, 194, 196-9, 206, 208
Pombal, Marquis of, 334
Pompadour, Madame de, 277-8
Port, Fr Thomas, 146-7, 151, 155, 164-5
Porter, George, 239
Porter, Fr Nicholas, 319
Porter, Monsieur, 319
Poulton (al. Palmer), Henry (S.J.), 159
Powell, Fr Francis, 259, 268
Poyntz, Mr Austin, 252-4
Preparatory School S.J.: at Boulogne
    (1740), 270-3, 330; at Watten (1752),
    273; expulsion, 330-2
Primarius, 36
Prinsenhof, Franciscan Convent, 318
Propaganda Fide, Congregation de, 287,
    291, 307-11
Pyrenees, Treaty of the, 167, 181

Ratio Studiorum, 69-72, 77, 81, 133-4, 139
Reeve, Fr Joseph, 293, 303, 312, 337, 394
Relics and reliquaries, 121-3, 176
Retz, Fr Francis (General S.J.), 265-9,
    271, 366
Rheims, 3, 5-7
Ricci, Fr Laurence (General S.J.), 326,
    334
Robson, Fr (O.P.), 354
Rohan, Cardinal de, 257
Rome, English College, 13, 37, 84, 108,
    151, 171, 221, 240-1; see also s.v. Oath.
Rookwood, Ambrose, 20, 29
Rookwoods, 19, 20
Rotterdam, 382, 387, 390-1
Roussel de la Tour, Monsieur, 292, 295,
    297-8, 300-2, 306-7
Roze, Monsieur, 284, 294-5, 300, 303-4,
    330
Ruga, Fr Bartholomew, 231
Rye House Plot, 189

Sabran, Fr Louis, 231, 249-54, 267, 275,
    373
Sacy, Père Jean de, 277
St Andries (fortress), 389

St Germain-en-Laye, 230-1, 243-4, 256
Saint-Omer, town council and bailliage,
    13, 16-8, 25, 46-7, 104-6, 149, 264,
    288, 293-4, 301-2, 304-5, 330
Saint-Omer, Walloon College S.J., 8, 20,
    22, 25, 35-6, 62-4, 66, 73, 91, 153, 246,
    282
St Omers English College S.J.: mistaken
    origin, 5, 7-9; why founded, 11-15,
    220; foundation, 15-22; final settle-
    ment in Rue St Bertin, 33-4; national-
    ity of Rector, 23, 27-8, 104-6; number
    of boys, 19-21, 32, 38, 41, 54, 107, 149,
    156-7, 164-5, 179, 201, 211, 213, 237,
    243, 256, 259; prefects, 38, 212, 269;
    'seminary' or 'college'?, 38, 45, 219-21;
    Constitutions of 1600, 40-1, 86, 220;
    Church, 46-8, 83, 87; printing press,
    48-9, 85, 140-5, 273-6; financial
    troubles, 55, 107, 123, 156, 164, 173,
    178-9, 183, 233, 239; music and
    theatre, 56, 78, 125-40, 157, 214-5,
    257; separated from Walloon College,
    62; proficiency in studies and 'dis-
    putations', 63, 75, 180, 215 and passim;
    curriculum, 76-92; Custom Book,
    79-89, 96, 217; voyage of 12 students
    to Seville, 108-12; under siege, 151,
    182; school fee, 12, 156-7, 165; games
    and sports, 175, 246-8; subject to
    France, 183; witnesses against Oates,
    192 seqq., 227-8; fire of 1684, 215-8;
    fire of 1725, 259-63; College uniform,
    233-7; free places, 258; wigs and
    watches, 266-7; seizure by Paris
    Parlement, 281 seqq; migration to
    Bruges, 286-7, 293, 313-7, 322; cited
    to plead before Propaganda, 307 seqq.
Sanders, Fr Francis, 231
Sanford, Fr (=Fr John Huddleston), 347
Scarisbrick, Fr Edward, 274
Scarisbrick, Fr Francis, 283, 286, 318,
    320, 322
Schondonch, Fr Giles, 43-7, 49-51, 54-5,
    57, 59, 61, 64-6, 71, 74, 76, 78-9, 84-6,
    92-8, 118, 120, 125, 127-9, 141, 156,
    169, 180, 214, 217
Scroggs, Chief Justice, 190-1, 194-8,
    203-5
Scrope, Simon, 327, 350-1
Selby (Yorkshire), 395
Semmes, Fr Joseph, 392, 396
Sergeant, Dr John, 208-9, 224
Shaftesbury, Lord, 188-9, 195
Shireburn family, 254, 392-3
Shireburn, Fr Charles, 269, 270
Shireburn, Mary, see Norfolk, Duchess of
Silisdon, Fr Henry, 61, 66, 114-5

Simons, Fr Joseph, 136-8, 173, 178
Skipton (Yorkshire), 395
Slaughter, Fr Edward, 245
Smith, Clement (S.J.), 228
Smith, Fr Nicholas, 19, 20, 22, 31
Smith, Br Thomas (S.J.), 257
Smith, William (schoolmaster), 227
Smithers, Fr William, 218
Society of Jesus, 279, 301 *and passim*
Sodality, B.V.M., 79, 81, 87, 90-4, 117-20, 175, 179
Spanish pension, 15, 25, 27-8
Spanish Seminaries, 4, 15, 108-9, 112, 150, 156, 169, 185
Sparrow, John, 395, 399
Spinola, Ambrogio, 132, 148
Stafford, Viscount (M.), 184
Stafford, Fr Robert, 152
Stanley, Fr Thomas, 326
Stanton Fr (? *veré* Shackleton, William), 66
Stapleton, Fr Thomas, 186, 200, 209, 210, 212, 223, 229, 230
Stapylton, ——, 199
Starhemburg, Prince, 336, 338, 341-2
Stephens, Fr Henry, 249
Stephens, Fr John, 147
Stevens, Br Adrian (S.J.), 304
Stevensweart, 387
Stone, Fr Marmaduke, 363, 372, 375-6, 382, 386, 392, 394, 396, 400
Stonor, Dr Christopher, 306, 311
Stonyhurst, 43, 63, 77, 87, 92, 175-6, 180, 205, 210, 238, 367, 386, 392 seqq.
Story, Rev. Thomas, 305
Strachan, Fr (Sir) Alexander, 379
Strange, Fr Richard, 184-6
Strickland, abbé, 255
Strickland, Fr William, 368-72, 376, 392, 394
Stuart, Henry, Cardinal York, 335
Suffolk, 2nd Earl of, 150
Sunderland, Earl of (Robert Spencer), 226, 232
Swinburn, Fr John, 232
Syndicus, *see* Decurion

Tableaux Vivants, 131
Talbot, Fr Gilbert, 270
Talbot, Fr Peter, 172
Talbot, Mr Thomas (later Bishop), 290, 292, 299, 305-7
Tamburini, Fr Michael Angelo (General S.J.), 245, 263
Tate, Mr John, 392
Teighe, Dominic, 367
Tempest, Walter, 327
Terray, abbé, 278

Thomas of Canterbury, St, 48, 127, 374-5
Thomas of Hereford, St, 180
Thornton, Henry, 185
Thunder, Fr Henry, 81, 83-5, 89, 91, 120, 152, 161
Thurston, Fr Herbert, 247-8
Thwing, Mr Thomas (M.), 207
Tomlinson, ——, 397
Tonge, Ezrael, 187-8
Toole, Matthew, 388
Towneley, Christopher, 193, 199, 200
Turberville, Anthony, 195
Turberville, Christopher (of Sker), 206
Turberville, Fr John, 259, 262-3, 268, 271
Turner, Fr Anthony (M.), 190
Turner, Fr John, 169
'Twelve Apostles' (names), 399

Underhill, Fr Albert (O.P.), 343, 351-3
Uniforms, 233-9

Valladolid Seminary, 21, 40-1, 53, 150, 161, 185, 203
Van der Heyden, Baron, 358
Van Volden, Mynheer, 338-40, 349, 353
Vaux, Charles de, 352
Vaux, Philippe de, 380
Velbruck, Mgr (Prince-Bishop), 238, 357, 362, 364, 368, 388
Venlo, 388, 390
Vernois, Jean de (Bishop of Saint-Omer), 27-8, 34, 50
Vice-Province, English S.J., 99, 103, 113
Vienna, Court of, 319, 320, 322-5, 327, 339
Visconti, Fr Herman, 235-6
Vitelleschi, Fr Mutius (General S.J.), 51, 55, 61, 98-9, 102, 106, 120-1, 123, 153-5, 163-4, 367

Wadsworth, James, 75-6, 81, 83-4, 86-8, 109, 111, 160-1, 233
Wakeman, Sir George, 205
Waller, Sir William, 199, 200, 208
Walker, William, 227
Walpole, Fr Henry (M.), 17-8, 26
Walsh, Fr Edward, 314
Walsh, Vicomte (Joseph Alexis), 376, 381
Walton, Fr William, 240
Ward, Mary, 56-61
Ward, Thomas, 275
Warner, Fr John, 182, 188, 191, 193, 200-2, 205, 208-19, 221-6, 229-31, 250, 264, 269
Warner, Sir John and Lady, 274
Waterton, Christopher, 359

Watten Noviciate, 49-52, 88, 121-3, 151-2, 158, 163, 167, 170, 177, 182, 192-3, 205, 269, 293, 314, 330-3, 359
Webb, Lady, 289, 290, 301
Weld, Edward, 393
Weld, Rebeccah (Mrs Oates), 229
Weld, Thomas (Sen.), 385, 393-5, 400-1
Weld, Thomas (Jun.), 392, 395, 399
Weldon, Fr Bennet (O.S.B.), 243
West, Fr Thomas, 332
Westphalia, Treaty of, 166, 181
Whitbread (al. Harcourt), Fr Thomas (M.), 185-8, 190-1, 206, 211-2
White, Fr Andrew, 21, 53
White, Mr Robert, 162
Whitgrave, Thomas, 172
Whitmore, see Sabran
Widdrington, Hon. Peregrine, 287n.
Wijk, see Maastricht
Wilhours (school), 355
Wilkinson, Mr William, 291, 296, 298-9, 305
William of Orange (William III), 183, 229, 239, 267
Williams, Fr John, 356

Wilmot, Laurent, 392
Wilson, Mr John, 95, 100-1, 116, 141-2, 145
Wintour, Sir George, 101
Witham, Dr Robert, 253
Worsley, Fr Thomas, 123, 146, 154, 156
Worthington brothers, 2, 19, 20
Worthington, Fr John, 3, 154
Worthington, Dr Thomas, 2, 13-4, 20
Wright, Fr Charles, 372, 377, 379, 382-3, 385, 388-9, 392, 400
Wright, Fr Edward, 367
Wright, Mr John, 39
Wright, Fr Peter (M.), 67, 294, 386
Wright, ——, of Kelvedon, 251
Würtemberg, Prince, 383-4
Wythens, Justice, 229

York, Duke of, see James II
Young, Fr Notley, 395
Ypres, Bishop of, see Chamberlain, George

Zoetaert, Mynheer, 339
Zueda, Countess of, 42

DATE DUE

MAY	1 '91		